SACRED SHELTER

SACRED SHELTER
THIRTEEN JOURNEYS OF HOMELESSNESS AND HEALING

EDITED BY
SUSAN CELIA GREENFIELD

Empire State Editions
An imprint of Fordham University Press
New York 2019

Visit us online:
www.empirestateeditions.com
www.fordhampress.com

Library of Congress Cataloging-in-Publication Data available online at https://
catalog.loc.gov.

Printed in the United States of America

21 20 19 5 4 3 2 1

First edition

*To all those still suffering the indignities of homelessness,
in honor of your right to the sacred shelter of a home*

Contents

Editor's Note

Any royalties for this book will be divided evenly among Catholic Charities of the Archdiocese of New York, the Interfaith Assembly on Homelessness and Housing, and Life Experience and Faith Sharing Associates.

The views and opinions expressed by each contributor are his or her own and are not intended to reflect the views or opinions of any organization the contributor may mention or with which he or she may be affiliated.

For a Readers' Guide to *Sacred Shelter*, visit https://fordham.bepress .com/soc/3/.

Background

Sacred *Shelter* focuses on graduates of the life skills empowerment program for homeless and formerly homeless individuals. The program was founded in 1989 by the Catholic Charities of the Archdiocese of New York (hereafter referred to as New York Catholic Charities), in collaboration with the Interfaith Assembly on Homelessness and Housing (hereafter referred to as IAHH). George Horton is the director of the Department of Social and Community Development for New York Catholic Charities. Marc Greenberg is the executive director of the Interfaith Assembly on Homelessness and Housing. Both men were involved in the program's founding.

Over the years, this program has been replicated by a number of different congregations and organizations. These replicate programs all have their own names, but for clarity's sake, all are referred to as either "the program" or "the life skills empowerment program" in this book.

In 2010, the leadership of New York Catholic Charities and the IAHH joined forces with Fordham University's Bertram M. Beck Institute on Religion and Poverty. Since then, the Beck Institute has been conducting an evidence-based study of the life skills empowerment program to gain a broader understanding of program participants and to generate capacity in response to needs of participants and congregations who provide programs. From 2010 to 2012, two pilot demonstrations funded by the New York Community Trust supported further program replication of the life skills empowerment program. Since 2013, the Beck Institute has been supported by several major foundations and the Fordham University

Graduate School of Social Service to further expand replication built on evidence of efficacy and sustainability. In 2013, Beck developed an educational collaborative of the leadership and staff from existing and newly developed programs (including all the programs described in this book) to further understand, support, and refine program adaptations in different congregational and community settings. (To learn more about the Beck study, see notes 12 and 13 of the Introduction.)

Glossary and Names of Replicate Programs Represented in *Sacred Shelter*

All Angels' Church   Provides many services for homeless people, including a community ministries program; several of this book's contributors refer to it. It is located on the Upper West Side of Manhattan. All Angels' hosted the Panim el Panim life skills empowerment program (see below) for six semesters.

Coming Home   Life skills empowerment program for formerly incarcerated individuals, established at the Reformed Church of Bronxville in partnership with the IAHH and replicated at Riverside Church in Manhattan.

EOP, Education Outreach Program   The original and longest-running life skills empowerment program, sponsored by New York Catholic Charities and established in partnership with the IAHH.

IAHH,   Interfaith Assembly on Homelessness and Housing

LEFSA, Life Experience and Faith Sharing Associates   A New York City–based ministry program that tends to people in shelters and on the streets. It was founded in 1986 by the late Sister Dorothy Gallant, SC, and the late Sister Teresa Skehan, RSM. LEFSA is not the name of a life skills empowerment program, but it is affiliated with the program, and many of this book's contributors have participated in it.

Life Skills Empowerment Program   The umbrella name this book uses to describe all individually named programs.

Living Well   Life skills empowerment program for survivors of domestic violence, established by the IAHH in partnership with Connect: Safe Families, Peaceful Communities.

L–STEP, Life Skills Training and Empowerment Program   Life skills empowerment program founded at St. Francis Xavier Church in Lower Manhattan; the program is now run by Xavier Mission.

New York Catholic Charities   Abbreviated name for the Catholic Charities of the Archdiocese of New York.

Panim el Panim, from the Hebrew, meaning "Face to Face"   Life skills empowerment program founded at Ansche Chesed Synagogue and now run by the IAHH in collaboration with a variety of New York City congregations.

SACRED SHELTER

Introduction

Susan Celia Greenfield

In *Sacred Shelter: Thirteen Journeys of Homelessness and Healing*, thirteen remarkable people tell their life stories. All of them were once homeless in New York City. All were involved in a life skills empowerment program for homeless and formerly homeless people, founded in 1989 by New York Catholic Charities and the Interfaith Assembly on Homelessness and Housing (IAHH). One of the authors was present at the initial vigil that led to the life skills program's founding. The twelve other contributors graduated from a life skills empowerment program between 1993 and 2013. Interspersed among their life stories are short reflections by some of the programs' directors and facilitators, clerics and congregants, mentors and volunteers.

The first and longest-serving life skills empowerment program was—and continues to be—sponsored by New York Catholic Charities and run by George Horton, who cofounded the program, and Alison Hughes-Kelsick. This program is called the Education Outreach Program (EOP)—"education" to signify the goal of bringing out what is sacred and empowering in each person, and "outreach" to mark the hope that graduates will become emissaries to others in need and will help raise awareness about the lives of homeless people. Since its founding, the EOP has inspired a variety of replicate programs, and today there are several different versions of the program across the New York metropolitan area. Each of these programs has its own independent name (located in the Glossary), but for clarity's sake, all are referred to in this book as either "the program" or "the life skills empowerment program."

The purpose of *Sacred Shelter*'s design is twofold. The book gives pride of place to the program graduates who were once homeless and marginalized, recording and honoring each of their histories from childhood to adulthood. In their life stories (organized chronologically based on graduation dates), the memoirists describe being children who loved their families, played with friends, went to school, grew up, got jobs, fell in love, and had children of their own. At some point—and often more than once—each of them was traumatized or had a crisis. Though rarely in any kind of linear fashion, this contributed to their becoming homeless, which is itself a trauma and crisis. Eventually all the contributors in this book found healing and rebuilt their lives. Their stories refer to mental illness, substance use, sexual abuse, and domestic violence. Though no demographic group is immune to such suffering, the majority of this book's contributors are people of color (eight are African American) who were born poor.

This Introduction will touch briefly on the socioeconomic implications of their experiences, but *Sacred Shelter*'s overriding objective is much simpler and more personal—it aims to give its formerly homeless contributors an opportunity to narrate their autobiographies in their own terms and to celebrate their whole sense of their lives. Homelessness is obviously an important issue in *Sacred Shelter,* and the book bears witness to the resilience and faith involved in overcoming it. Nevertheless, the lives the contributors recount are much larger than their former homelessness. They include periods of joy as well as torment, and often (though not always) the narratives reflect the contributor's deep belief in the restorative love of God.

Sacred Shelter also aims to capture something of the workings and the collective spirit of the life skills empowerment program. This Introduction, as well as the two concluding entries, includes details about the program's origins and history. Throughout the book, some of the professionals and volunteers who have run or participated in the program reflect on their experiences. Their words are interspersed with the life stories to reflect the kind of larger community the program helps create. In the life skills empowerment program, the boundaries that typically separate homeless people from the housed can be challenged and traversed. For individuals in the program, becoming part of a life skills empowerment community can be healing and transformative. This is true not just for the homeless or formerly homeless people who attend the program, but also for those who participate in other ways. It has certainly been true for me.

Modern Homelessness and New York City Homeless Community Activism

Although *Sacred Shelter* offers neither a history of homelessness nor an analysis of its structural roots, some basic details can help contextualize the stories.[1] Most of the formerly homeless contributors were children or young adults during the mid-1970s. This is the period that witnessed what experts commonly refer to as the "rise of modern homelessness," whose causes and effects continue to today. For the first time since the Great Depression, the number of unhoused people around America began skyrocketing. The source and persistence of the phenomenon can be simply summarized: the availability of affordable housing decreased at the same time that poverty levels rose.[2] The loss of affordable housing resulted in part from neoliberal federal policies that promoted private real estate development and gentrification while sharply reducing the US Department of Housing and Urban Development (HUD) budget and restricting funding for public housing, housing assistance, and low-income housing development. One of the most-cited consequences of these changes included the disappearance of more than one million single room occupancy units (SROs), which had housed some of the most vulnerable urban Americans. In New York State, where thousands of patients were being deinstitutionalized and discharged from psychiatric hospitals, the lack of SROs drove many mentally ill people to sleep on New York City streets.[3]

Meanwhile, throughout America, poverty was escalating due to a variety of factors, including the loss of manufacturing jobs, the growth of a poorer-paying service industry, a rise in inflation, a reduction in income growth and real wages, and the systematic weakening of labor bargaining power. Social welfare programs and public assistance were cut.[4] Poor people were—and continue to be—far more prone to homelessness than other populations, and at least since the 1970s, people of color, especially African Americans, are often at the greatest risk. In this way, the rise of modern homelessness intersects with America's long-entrenched history of income inequality and systemic racism.[5]

By the early 1980s, New York City homelessness had reached epic proportions. Thousands of people were living on the streets, the population in homeless shelters had doubled, and over the course of the decade there was a dramatic increase in the number of homeless families.[6] New York Catholic Charities, which had been serving New Yorkers in need since 1917, turned its attention to the problem, as did a number of newly developed nonprofit advocacy and service organizations. Among these was the IAHH, cofounded and directed by Marc Greenberg in the mid-1980s. An umbrella organization for a variety of religious groups concerned about homelessness, including New York Catholic Charities, the IAHH's mission was to "address the growing [problem] on moral and spiritual grounds."[7] Beginning in June 1986, the group started hosting overnight vigils in City Hall Park at the onset of the city council's annual budget hearings. The goal was to influence council members to increase the allocation of funds for homeless services and permanent housing.

The commencement of the vigil, on June 1, 1988, was not auspicious. Hundreds of people, including many homeless ones, had gathered to parade to City Hall Park for a night of singing, praying, rallying, and perhaps even sleeping. The plan was for Mayor Ed Koch and the city council members to see them first thing upon arriving at work the next morning. The problem was that it began to rain—a lot! By the time the procession had reached the park, the rain had become so torrential that most of the people who could go home did so. Marc Greenberg was among the handful of soggy individuals who remained to spend the night. In his entry at the end of this volume, he recalls having used "the park benches (which in those days were not bolted in place) to construct rain shelters and made fires in metal garbage cans to keep warm against the unusually cold night wind. By the time the sun rose and the rain finally stopped, twelve of us remained—half of us were homeless." Though Mayor Koch arrived at city hall without taking any apparent notice of the park's wrung-out guests, a few of the council's most sympathetic members invited the group inside for coffee. There, according to John Jiler's *Sleeping with the Mayor*, council member Ruth Messinger gave the group an unexpected challenge: why not continue sleeping in the park for all of June? "I'm talking about staying here," she told her astonished audience. "The budget hearings go on for a month, not a day."[8]

In the end, the homeless members of the group not only accepted Messinger's challenge, they extended and elaborated on it, establishing a community of people who stayed in City Hall Park until Christmas. Within days of the initial vigil, more homeless people arrived at the park, transforming the area into a small village. The thirty-five or so individuals who eventually took up residence there developed their own system of governance and resource assistance and hoped to pressure the city into giving them a condemned building to fix up and inhabit. Mayor Koch was furious and embarrassed but ultimately powerless to make the homeless

No. 9   Summer, 1989

LIGHTS
on Christian-Jewish Relations

The bi-monthly newsletter of the Office on Christian–Jewish Relations of the National Council of the Churches of Christ in the U.S.A. (Commission on Regional and Local Ecumenism).

ACTING ON HOMELESSNESS: INTERFAITH GROUPS RESPOND

A vigil in front of New York's City Hall called for housing justice. Held on June 1, 1989, the vigil was co-sponsored by the Interfaith Assembly on Homelessness (which provided this photo).

by Susan MacDonald Roddey

Christians and Jews have joined together in several major cities to respond to the homeless. These interfaith groups are educating their religious bodies on the subject, mobilizing support from their communities against insensitive legislation and policies, helping provide and operate shelters, and focusing on the long-range issues of providing adequate housing.

Joining Together to Reclaim Hotels in LA

In Los Angeles, Leo Baeck Temple and All Saints Episcopal Church, which have had a fifteen year relationship of cooperation, formed the Church and Temple Housing Corporation. With the help of generous grants and the Las Familias del Pueblo social service agency, they transformed a run-down, "skid-row" hotel into the Genesis Hotel, which offers thirty low-income rental rooms.

Newsletter cover picture of the first-year anniversary of the Homeward Bound Community Services vigil, summer 1989 people leave the park. The group called itself Homeward Bound Community Services. The media, which relished the protest and its humiliating impact on Mayor Koch, called it "Kochville," mocking the mayor by associating him with the dreadful Hooverville shantytowns of the Great Depression.

The homeless leaders of Homeward Bound Community Services were Larry Locke, a man who called himself Duke York (both now deceased), and Nelson Prime, who tells his life story in this book. Nelson describes the empowerment, solidarity, and hope Homeward Bound Community Services members experienced at that time.

> How wonderful that homeless brothers and sisters were banding together to make our voices heard. We wanted to actuate our own niche into society. We wanted to be part of the solution instead of the perpetuation of the problem. . . . We knew we needed our own voice to speak to the public. Other advocacy organizations were trying to represent the homeless without letting us represent ourselves.

For the homeless people in the park, the ability to represent themselves—in terms of public appearances, resource development, and political demands—was a basic and hard-won right. For a remarkable 200 days, members of Homeward Bound Community Services maintained a round-the-clock presence outside city hall. Some of the leaders began sharing their life stories in public forums, leaving audiences transfixed. As a result of the extensive media coverage of the group's activities, Homeward Bound Community Services played a central role in educating the public about the general crisis of homelessness and about the personal experience of being homeless. In this way, the group is part of a rich history of homeless activists campaigning on their own behalf and organizing grassroots movements.[9]

In terms of policy, Homeward Bound Community Services had less impact; it had no effect on the New York City budget (which was a fait accompli before the hearings even began), and the members' demand for an abandoned building to repair and inhabit was unsuccessful.[10] As winter approached and the weather grew harsh, the number of park residents diminished. By Christmas, the small collection of remaining devotees (including Nelson Prime) were sleeping in the basement of St. Augustine's Church (near Henry Street), which had offered them shelter. By the first day of the new year, Homeward Bound Community Services' park vigil was over.

The Life Skills Empowerment Program and Life Stories

Even after Homeward Bound Community Services disbanded, the group's influence persisted—especially for Marc Greenberg and George Horton. During the budget hearings, George had told the gatherers, "We are here to pray and be together to witness that every person needs a decent place to live."[11] Like Marc, George was energized by the park residents and especially by their personal stories. "We were absolutely inspired by the people in the park," he told me in conversation. "They had enormous gifts. The only question was, 'How can we help them affect public policy?'"

To answer that question, George and Marc joined with Joan Minieri and Sister Ann Murray from New York Catholic Charities and Sister Agnes O'Grady from the Sisters of Mercy to begin planning the curriculum that eventually became the first life skills empowerment program. The original planning committee did not include any of the remaining homeless Homeward Bound Community Service members then staying at St. Augustine's (though homeless and formerly homeless people have since taken on many leadership roles in the program). Nevertheless, as George explained, every aspect of their discussion "was inspired by what we had seen in the people in the park. Our goal was to create a structure wherein what they were doing could be lived and developed."

Over time, the life skills empowerment program developed a three-part curriculum that remains in use today. Participants attend workshops about healthy living and social justice, are given individual mentors to work with on personal goals, and are asked to produce a version of their life stories to share with other program participants and, in some circumstances, with a broader audience. Like a semester-long college course, a typical program meets twice a week for twelve to fourteen weeks. To join, homeless and formerly homeless individuals must have at least three months' sobriety, be prepared to attend every session, and be willing to narrate and share their life stories. Each attendee signs a contract to certify his or her commitment to these goals. Participants also get a small stipend, a portion of which goes toward carfare. At each session meeting, dinner is served, which is key for the participants, most of whom are on fixed budgets and some of whom still live on the street. Each meeting begins with an inspirational or spiritual reading on which the participants are invited to comment. Often they do so by referring to God. Though the program is not affiliated with a particular religion, many of the participants (as well as the volunteers and coordinators) are people of faith. Their deep belief is a guiding force in many meetings.

In *Sacred Shelter*, the life story portion of the life skills empowerment curriculum is obviously influential and has essentially been integrated into the book's design. For many program participants, telling their life story is especially transformative. As Sophia Worrell reminisces in her contribution to this book, "It *was* difficult to share my story, but it was necessary because I wanted to get my past out in the open and get rid of it. I was determined to clean out my house. I was tired of my secret life—it was too much to carry." Storytelling led Cindy (pseudonym), another contributor, to a new sense of herself. "It was like, 'Wow! Did I really go through all this in the past seven years?' . . . I felt encouraged to know that I had all that strength. It gave me confidence that I could do anything I want to do."[12]

As noted earlier, the original and longest-running life skills empowerment program is the EOP at New York Catholic Charities, directed by George Horton and Alison Hughes-Kelsick (whom the participants fondly refer to as "Ms. K."—her name appears in many stories). Since 1989, the New York Catholic Charities program has graduated more than fifty classes, and nearly half of the contributors in this book attended it. Since then, a variety of different faith communities and other organizations have, in collaboration with New York Catholic Charities, the IAHH, or both, developed additional versions of the life skills empowerment program. In 2010, New York Catholic Charities and the IAHH began collaborating with Fordham University's Bertram M. Beck Institute on Religion and Poverty, which, under the direction of Professor Anita Lightburn, initiated an evidence-based study of the life skills empowerment program, designed a service manual about it, and helped generate new versions of the program.[13] Today, the New York metropolitan area features several programs, some of which service specific populations, such as people returning from incarceration, homeless veterans, or women who are homeless as a result of domestic violence. More than one thousand people have graduated from them.

Countless other people have also been involved in making these programs possible. Roughly twenty Catholic, Protestant, and Jewish communities provide funds, space, food, and volunteers. Congregants serve as mentors for individual participants, make and share meals with the classes, or run specific workshops based on their individual expertise. Some institutions, like St. Francis Xavier Church, the Reformed Church of Bronxville, and Riverside Church in Manhattan, have followed New York Catholic Charities in sponsoring their own individual programs. Other versions of the program rely on a group of congregations for support. In either case, the life skills empowerment program builds a collaborative community wherever it is run.

That collaboration is captured in the program's festive graduation ceremonies. There, family members and mentors, program directors and volunteers, clerics and laypeople gather to celebrate the participants. The event usually begins with a prayer and shared meal followed by a ceremony that the graduates themselves conduct. In addition to spiritual readings, speeches, and the usual list of thanks, there are always one or two graduates who tell their life stories. Invariably, this is one of the ceremony's highlights. The communal spirit is another. People of different races, classes, and religions sit down and get to know each other. They eat and pray together.

Sacred Shelter seeks to represent this sense of community in print. That is why the book juxtaposes the graduates' life stories with short reflections by a variety of people who have—in one way or another—supported the life skills empowerment program. Several of these reflections are by professionals affiliated with the program; in addition to George Horton and Marc Greenberg, clerics, social workers, and facilitators describe their experiences. Other reflections are by mentor volunteers—lay people who simply wanted to be of service to the homeless population. All of these contributors were asked to reflect on their personal experience of the life skills empowerment program. They were reminded that, like the book's graduates, they should discuss their own lives.

The sociologists Jason Wasserman and Jeffrey Clair have argued that an "us-them dichotomy" often "emerges in discourse to separate those who are homeless from those who are not."[14] The very structure of *Sacred Shelter* is designed to challenge this dichotomy. By interweaving the graduates' stories with reflections by other workshop contributors, this book seeks to show that there should be no "us" or "them" when it comes to homelessness. The whole community is affected when some individuals are homeless, and *Sacred Shelter* is based on the idea that everyone must strive to rectify this injustice.

My own experience with the life skills empowerment program began in the fall of 2009 when my rabbi, Jeremy Kalmanofsky (who has a reflection in this volume), asked for volunteers to serve as mentors in a program our synagogue, Congregation Ansche Chesed, was sponsoring in collaboration with the IAHH. At the time, I was having something of a midlife crisis and struggling with depression, a frighteningly familiar feeling in my life. When the rabbi called for mentors, I jumped at the opportunity, in part because I hoped to gain relief from my own mental health challenges by getting my mind off myself.

As it turned out, my mentee, Rodney Allen (whose life story appears in this book), became my mentor in many ways. In addition to being well on his way to recovering from homelessness, Rodney had joined a compassionate church community and renewed his religious faith. Though I did not share Rodney's Christian belief or his idea of God, I was awed by his spiritual transformation and heartened just by hearing about it.

Indeed, there was only one concrete thing for which Rodney wanted my guidance. As the program neared its end, he had yet to write his life story. "We have to get working on this," he told me as soon as I arrived at the mentor session one evening. As a literature professor and fiction writer, I was instantly excited. Writing and teaching writing is what I do for a living. At last, I had specific skills that could be of use to Rodney.

Rodney proposed that we get together at the church where he both worked and worshipped. Over the course of a few weeks, we met in the church's dusty reception room, which had a big old leather couch and a broken grandfather clock. I brought my laptop and typed as Rodney told his story. Throughout, we drew on the list of questions the program had provided: What would you like to share about your family? What was it like growing up? What factors led to your becoming homeless? What is something you learned during your experience with homelessness? What are your hopes for the future?

As with all program participants, the story of Rodney's journey back home was both personal and pragmatic. It was literally about having to find a place to live. But as I listened, I began to recognize what I am sure the program designers had long understood—that anyone who has ever felt lonely or lost might identify with and be inspired by Rodney's story, even those with no direct experience of homelessness. That was certainly the effect his words had on me. And that is the multifaceted power of the program's life story curriculum: In authoring their stories, participants gain *authority* over their history of homelessness and the narrative power to transcend their past. In offering their stories to demographically diverse audiences (like those at the graduation ceremonies), the tellers both connect with other homeless people and teach those who are housed what being homeless feels like. The shared inspiration that often results can be a potent source of advocacy.

After working with Rodney, I was hooked on the storytelling feature of the program. That spring, I met with graduates from earlier classes and arranged for seven of them to be interviewed at StoryCorps, a national

Sacred Shelter advisory board members (*left to right*): Marc Greenberg, Michelle Riddle, Susan Greenfield, Dennis Barton, George Horton, James Addison

nonprofit organization that records oral histories.[15] In the fall of 2010, Marc Greenberg asked me to be the "story-writing facilitator" for a program the IAHH was helping sponsor. From 2010 to 2014, I ran writing workshops and helped individual participants develop their life stories.

The Making of *Sacred Shelter*

In August 2013, George Horton told me that he had always hoped someone would publish a book of the graduates' life stories. As it so happened, I had an upcoming sabbatical and was in need of a new writing project. "I'll do it!" I told George without a moment's hesitation. I was practically overflowing with excitement. George was more measured. As a program founder who had facilitated individual groups for a quarter of a century, he would agree to nothing without a very careful consideration of details. Above all, George was adamant that any book about the program would have to involve graduates in the planning.

Thanks to him, we convened an advisory board for this book. In addition to George and me, the board included Marc Greenberg of the IAHH and three program graduates—James Arthur Addison, Dennis Barton, and Michelle Riddle (whose stories appear in *Sacred Shelter*). Throughout 2013 and 2014, the advisory board met many times in my apartment in Manhattan. There, we discussed our hopes and goals for the book, decided on a title, and considered the methods for selecting the contributors as well as documenting the graduates' life stories.

This last point deserves special consideration. As I have already noted, participants in the program are asked to produce a version of their life stories. The advisory board could have chosen to anthologize these versions of the graduates' stories.[16] Instead we decided that I would conduct more extensive personal interviews, which would then be transcribed for me to edit. The board reached this decision in part because the stories written as part of the life skills empowerment curriculum are short (limited to ten minutes of spoken narration) and often unavailable. Some participants tell their histories without writing them down, and many graduates, including all three on the advisory board, no longer have a written copy of their original stories. The advisory board also wanted to give graduates the fullest opportunity to tell their stories in detail, and an oral interview was seen as best suited to this goal. Finally, because the board wanted these narratives to reach the broadest possible reading audience, I carefully edited the interviews and sought to render them in accessible prose (discussed in more detail below).

The board also developed specific procedures for choosing which graduates I should interview. We settled on two primary objectives. The first one was simple: we wanted to identify a roughly even number of men and women whose graduation dates spanned the nearly quarter-century history of the program. The second objective was more involved. We wanted to feature graduates who had achieved some form of lasting recovery and whose own experience of homelessness had led them to commit their lives to helping other people in need. We wanted to feature people whose personal transformations had, in one way or another, led them to become leaders in their communities and sometimes in the program itself. And we wanted to feature graduates who would inspire the book's readers, including those who are or have been homeless, those who might identify with the graduates in other ways, and those (both homeless and housed) who could be prompted to action or service.

Everyone on the advisory board got to nominate a couple of graduates who met these objectives, and one cold day in February 2014, we sat around my dining room table and decided whom to contact. Though there has since been a little juggling, most of *Sacred Shelter*'s thirteen life story contributors were determined at that meeting. Careful and thought-

ful as it was, our method, like any selection process, was necessarily re-
strictive. For one thing, there are countless graduates who exemplify this
book's inspirational ideals but are not included due to space constraints.
All but one of the graduates whose names appear in the Contents had a
close relationship with someone on the advisory board.

For another thing, we ended up excluding graduates who had suffered significant setbacks in housing, mental health, or drug or alcohol
use, though of course such setbacks occur. Another selection committee
might have chosen differently. But because *Sacred Shelter* was designed to
inspire readers and ideally to motivate them to work for social justice and
change, success stories were prioritized. Moreover, people who have experienced homelessness have too few opportunities to describe their own
complicated and often tragic histories in a way that foregrounds their resilience, hope, and faith. *Sacred Shelter* gives graduates this opportunity and
asks readers to heed them with care.

At no point did the board attempt to offer a demographically accurate
representation of either graduates or homeless New Yorkers. There is no
substantial demographic history of the program participants since, until
recently, their backgrounds were not recorded.[17] And there are significant
differences between the storytellers' demographic breakdown and that of
currently homeless people in New York City. A large percentage of the
latter, for instance, includes young parents (especially mothers) with children, but twelve of the thirteen formerly homeless participants in *Sacred
Shelter* are over the age of fifty. Though the Coalition for the Homeless
reports that 31 percent of homeless New Yorkers are of Hispanic or Latin
American origin—and many with that background have graduated from
a life skills empowerment program—there is only one storyteller in this
book with a Latino parent. The high proportion of African Americans
and low number of whites in *Sacred Shelter is* similar to that of New York
City's homeless population, but that is coincidental and has nothing to do
with the advisory board's selection process.[18]

I conducted the first interview for *Sacred Shelter* in June 2014 and the
final one a little more than a year later. The vast majority of the interviews
occurred over two sessions, some in my apartment, some in a friend's office at Fordham University's Lincoln Center campus, some in the conference room at New York Catholic Charities, and some in All Angels'
Church; one interview (with Nelson Prime, who is now living in Texas)
was conducted via Skype sessions. The shortest interview was about
two hours, the longest more than ten hours, and most averaged between
four and eight hours. My work was approved by Fordham University's

Institutional Review Board, each subject signed a consent form, and all were given a $100 stipend for participation.

Throughout the interview process, I was guided by the storytelling outline provided by the program. I asked participants to discuss their childhood and experience growing up; to explain how they became homeless, what homelessness was like, and how they had recovered from it; and to describe their current situation and future plans. My technique was not that of a professional oral historian, whose "first requirement," writes Alessandro Portelli, is to "give priority to what [the informant] wishes to tell, rather than what the researcher wants to hear."[19] While I certainly encouraged participants to say anything they wanted, I was also very "newsy," as Dennis Barton often describes me. I peppered the participants with questions, urging them to elaborate on events and to be as vivid as possible. I wanted to know everything about their lives, to be able to visualize them as clearly as if I were watching a home movie.

The memories the interviewees recounted were sometimes horrible and heartbreaking; the majority of people cried more than once. But all who discussed their pain did so willingly. Though many had already described some of these traumas in public forums, they seemed to welcome the chance to offer more details for this book. As Sophia Worrell puts it above, they may have "wanted to get [their] past out in the open and get rid of it"; or, as contributor Deborah Canty says of her dual experience of sexual abuse and homelessness: "Maybe my words [will set other survivors] free to tell their stories. What they thought was their shame was not their burden to hold onto."

Still, however beneficial it may be, an interview is, by definition, a complicated and often unequal process. As the oral historian Michael Frisch puts it, "No matter how controlled the schedule of questions, the information is produced in a dialogue between individuals, each with a social position and identity."[20] The point warrants special attention in *Sacred Shelter*. I am a white literature professor who has been privileged all my life. The majority of the program graduates in *Sacred Shelter* are people of color who were born poor and lacked educational and socioeconomic resources. My conversations with the storytellers were no doubt shaped by these kinds of differences. I asked all of them to talk about race and racism, for instance, but I suspect some—if not all—of their answers would have varied if I were not white, just as my mode of questioning was surely shaped by my own racial position and unconscious prejudices. Comparable problems could be raised about our religious and class differences or about how our gender similarities or differences affected the individual interactions. These factors (and a host of others) have undoubtedly and indelibly imprinted the interviews. But I cannot begin to decipher or disentangle such effects. All I can do is appeal to the inherent duality of any interview process, which is always, as Portelli explains, "the result of a relationship, of a shared project in which both the interviewer and the interviewee are involved together, if not necessarily in harmony. . . . The final result . . . is the product of both the narrator and the researcher."[21]

The interviews themselves were further altered in my editing process. After each one was completed, it was transcribed by Samuel Robson, a professional oral historian. In addition, the transcript was rearranged in a separate document and put in rough chronological order.[22] In the process, the kinds of things a speaker may have referred to at different times throughout the interview—a childhood event, the loss of a parent, the experiences at a shelter, and the like—were consolidated and juxtaposed. Several of the graduates also had earlier interviews on which to draw, many of them archived with StoryCorps.[23] When available, these materials were transcribed and integrated into the chronologies as well. It was from these chronologies—most of which ran from one hundred to two hundred pages—that I edited and shaped the life stories that appear in *Sacred Shelter*. That these stories differ significantly from the original interviews is indisputable. After they were transcribed and chronologized, the texts were drastically cut and rearranged. I removed the record of my questions;[24] standardized the speakers' grammar and tense (except for descriptions of dialogue); changed the names of most family members and friends to protect their privacy; and freely added new sentences when I thought clarity required it.

As I edited, I was acutely aware that, while I wanted this book to be read by current and formerly homeless people, I also wanted it to appeal to and educate readers who have never been homeless. In both cases, I wanted the stories to inspire advocacy and action. In a context like this, Michael Frisch explains, the audience becomes "a far more explicit dimension of consideration" than it might be in other circumstances, and "the integrity of a transcript is [sometimes] best protected . . . by an aggressive . . . [and] substantial manipulation of the text."[25] I had good intentions in following such logic within *Sacred Shelter*. But that does not erase the implications of my interference.[26] The life stories you will read are not literal reproductions; they are significantly mediated versions of the speakers' meaning and intent.

Given such a context, how should the stories' validity be judged? Frisch suggests considering the mindfulness of the editor, who "must respect the original [transcript] enough to come to know it deeply, and this knowledge must be the benchmark for measuring the validity of any digest, excerpt or editing."[27] I find comfort in this perspective, for this much I know is true: In working on *Sacred Shelter,* I had deep respect for the transcripts of the interviews, because I deeply respected everyone I interviewed. I came to know their stories intimately, and I came to love both the tellers and the tales. Throughout the editorial undertaking, I tried to listen for and be guided by each storyteller's unique voice. Whenever possible, I preserved their exact words in the transcript, and I always aspired to convey the essential spirit of what they said. I wanted nothing more than to honor each narrator; to do justice to his or her use of language; and to give you, the reader, some sense of the poetry, beauty, and brilliance of what I heard. Each storyteller has also reviewed, revised, and sanctioned the edited manuscript. Every life story in *Sacred Shelter* has received the full approval of the person interviewed and his or her legal permission to publish it.

The Life Stories in Historical Context

For the most part, the stories you will read focus on individual experiences, not on systemic problems. The life skills empowerment program acknowledges the systemic roots of homelessness. Both of the founding organizations, New York Catholic Charities and the IAHH, are committed to social justice, and the IAHH in particular devotes much of its time and resources to political advocacy. But aside from a few workshops on social justice or public policy, the life skills empowerment curriculum generally does not dwell on the institutional sources of homelessness nor on the macrocosmic changes needed to address the problem in earnest. The program's aim above all is to help individuals examine their past and to improve their lives by becoming part of a supportive and often spiritual community.

The stories told in *Sacred Shelter* reflect this individualist orientation. James Addison, Dennis Barton, and Nelson Prime discuss the systemic roots of their experiences, but most of the stories dwell on personal experiences, not political problems; individual choices, not socioeconomic and historical forces. *Sacred Shelter* honors and respects the contributors' individual sense of their lives. It celebrates and supports the "active process of creation of meanings" that people everywhere undertake in remembering their past.[28] Nevertheless, the broader socioeconomic and historical contexts that affected the contributors' lives are clearly reflected in their stories, even if that is not the narratives' central focus.

For instance, all the formerly homeless African Americans in *Sacred Shelter* descend from the Great Migration. They or their parents were born in the Jim Crow South and joined the mass exodus of six million black people who, between 1915 and 1970, moved to northern cities like New York to seek a better life. But even if the North offered an improvement—and several contributors in this book suggest it did—racism was inescapable. Job and housing discrimination was rampant. As Isabel Wilkerson explains in her epic study of the Great Migration, the kinds of "apprenticeships and factory jobs" held by second and third-generation European immigrants "were closed off to black migrants," as was trade union membership. They were also "sealed off in overcrowded colonies," where they paid the "highest rents for the most dilapidated housing owned by absentee landlords."[29] The ghettos spawned by this segregation were the product of government-sponsored discrimination, as Richard Rothstein highlights: "Scores of racially explicit laws, regulations, and government practices combined to create a nationwide system of urban ghettos, surrounded by white suburbs."[30] The Public Works Administration explicitly segregated African Americans in public housing projects; cities developed zoning regulations to keep black families out of white neighborhoods; redlining prevented investment in African American communities; and black people were prohibited from buying government-subsidized suburban homes.[31] New York City was no exception. "For all of New York's rhetorical commitment to equality and racial justice," Joshua Freeman explains, "patterns of occupational discrimination, school segregation, and ghettoization endured and deepened."[32]

In *Sacred Shelter*, all the African American contributors as well as one of the white women came of age in New York City in the 1960s and 1970s. By then, even the low-level manufacturing jobs some of their parents had secured were increasingly unavailable.[33] By the mid-1970s, New York City had a fiscal crisis that almost led to a default. The city's poorest neighborhoods, like the South Bronx, were devastated by a variety of factors, including crime, violence, looting, drug addiction and drug dealing, and white flight. Cheaply produced and poorly maintained public housing buildings were deteriorating. Privately owned buildings were being neglected and abandoned by their landlords. Arsonists set fire to them, as did the landlords themselves, with the goal of collecting insurance money.[34]

Many of the contributors in this book know this story all too well. As Dennis Barton puts it, "Lots of people talk about white flight and the fall of the South Bronx. Well, I *lived* through that as a teenager. I watched the South Bronx disintegrate from a vibrant community where you could walk down the streets and hear different languages to where it looked just like those pictures of bombed-out Germany." Michelle Riddle describes how she and her siblings used to play in the burned-out store next to their tenement, until "pretty soon our own building caught on fire, and the Red Cross put us in the Brooklyn Arms Shelter." As a young child, Heidi Nissen lived in a condemned tenement on the Lower East Side. "There was no heat, and I guess the electricity had been cut off. On Christmas morning, [Mom] was in bed, and we all cuddled up with her under the blankets. There were no presents. There was nothing." In early adulthood, Nelson Prime found himself in a similar situation: "The superintendent of my building ran to Puerto Rico with all the rent money. They condemned the building, and everybody started moving out. . . . I was stuck there with no job. They turned off everything—the lights, the hot water. . . . [One day] I came back [and] my apartment had been ransacked, all my stuff was gone. I had nothing."

By the mid-1960s, heroin addiction began reaching epidemic proportions in the inner city.[35] Nelson remembers growing up with "people shooting heroin on the landing right above us." "The ghettoes were full of cheap heroin," recalls James Addison; by age fifteen, he (as well as most of his teenage friends) was already addicted to the drug. Heroin was so cheap, Dennis says, that "every kid with lunch money had enough to buy a bag of heroin." The Nixon administration responded to the heroin crisis with antidrug policies that were ultimately folded into the "war on crime" and explicitly designed to criminalize and incarcerate African Americans.[36] "As African Americans began filling cells in the 1970s," explains Ta-Nehisi Coates, "rehabilitation was largely abandoned in favor of retribution."[37]

Then things got worse. By the mid-1980s, after Ronald Reagan declared a War on Drugs, and at a time when urban poverty and unemployment were at an "all-time high," crack arrived in New York City. "No one," Michelle Alexander emphasizes in *The New Jim Crow*, "should ever attempt to minimize the harm caused by crack cocaine and the related violence."[38] Indeed, the contributors in *Sacred Shelter* who fell prey to the drug testify to its incomparable powers of devastation. They describe crack as "the most insidious thing that ever happened to me"; as taking "away what little self-respect and dignity I had left"; and as "my worst enemy, my rock bottom." And yet, instead of prioritizing prevention, treatment, and education programs that might have limited the drug's harm, Congress passed the 1986 Anti-Drug Abuse Act that, as Alexander notes, established "far more severe punishment for distribution of crack—associated with blacks—than powder cocaine, associated with whites." According to Harvard sociologist Devah Pager, between 1983 and 1997, the number of whites incarcerated for drug offenses "increased sevenfold"; the number of African Americans "increased more than twenty-six-fold. . . . By 2001, there were more than twice as many African Americans as whites in state prison for drug offenses."[39]

It is important to realize that African Americans and other people of color do *not* use or sell drugs at higher rates than whites.[40] Rather, drug laws and anti-crime policies have had a discriminatory effect. One need only consider America's current heroin epidemic, which (unlike the earlier heroin epidemic) disproportionately affects white people, to get a sense of this inequity. Today, heroin addiction is being met with calls for compassion and rehabilitation instead of crime and punishment. "White heroin addicts get overdose treatment, rehabilitation, and reincorporation," writes Cardozo Law School Professor Ekow N. Yankah. "Had this compassion existed for African Americans caught up in addiction," UCLA and Columbia University Professor Kimberlé Williams Crenshaw notes, "the devastating impact of mass incarceration upon entire communities would never have happened."[41]

Several African American contributors to *Sacred Shelter* were addicted to heroin or crack, or both, and were incarcerated for drug-related offenses. None of the book's other contributors, including those with substance abuse problems or who committed crimes, ever went to jail or prison. Given the extremity of racial bias in the criminal justice system, it is hardly surprising that incarceration patterns in *Sacred Shelter* reflect those of American society. The stories also refer to crime within the black community (what the media dubs "black on black crime"). But as Ta-Nehisi Coates explained in a radio interview, "Most people who live around each other commit crimes against each other. If you take a community and you over the course of generations deprive that community as a matter of public policy and private practice of wealth, it is not shocking that crime in that community would be higher."[42]

But the problem of internal community violence is hardly the only story worth telling. What deserves just as much—if not more—attention, as Dennis Barton suggests in his story, is the spirit of generosity and care that characterizes even the most devastated African American communities.

> People talk about blacks killing blacks, but nobody talks about how when you don't have a pair of shoes to go to your mama's funeral, somebody goes and gets you a pair of shoes. They don't talk about how when you don't have anything to eat, somebody will go in their cabinet and get you something to eat. When you need a bath, somebody will invite you in their house and give you a bath. Nobody talks about that.

In *Sacred Shelter*, the African American contributors *do* talk about this; they talk about it all the time, but they do so without fanfare, as if the obligation to be communally conscious and giving is so obvious and instinctual that it hardly deserves mentioning. Their stories' details are sometimes so violent and dramatic that it is easy to neglect the more subtle references to kindness, love, and a communal sense of responsibility. But these references also pervade the book, as when Edna Humphrey says, "I love doing things to help people. My grandmother brought me up that way"; or when Black (pseudonym) remembers how a church lady at the after-school program he attended would sometimes buy his family "one-hundred dollars' worth of food because she knew my father was struggling"; or when Michelle Riddle describes how, even in the thick of a voracious addiction, she gave money she could have used for drugs to the mother of a crying boy, because "that child [was] hungry."

Systemic gender oppression in the form of domestic violence (also known as intimate partner violence) also underlies many of the stories told in *Sacred Shelter*. Of the seven women interviewed for this book, five survived domestic violence and two of these five became homeless as a direct result of it (in all cases the perpetrator of the violence was male). The storytellers' experiences are representative of homeless women nationwide. In New York City, nearly a third of families with children (predominantly female-headed families) entered the shelter system in 2016 because of domestic violence, making it the top reason for family homelessness, ahead of eviction and overcrowding.[43] And even when intimate partner violence is not the immediate cause for homelessness, homeless women are commonly domestic violence survivors.[44]

Sexual and physical abuse during childhood has also been correlated with adult homelessness. Five of the seven women describe being sexually abused by their stepfathers or their mothers' boyfriends. Two of these women as well as two of the male storytellers were also battered by male family members. In addition, these men as well as four of the women grew up in households where their mothers, sisters, or brothers were sexually abused or beaten, or both. The mother of one of the male storytellers was murdered by his stepfather; the brother of one of the female storytellers was killed by her uncle; and another female storyteller saw her mother's boyfriend rape and beat her sister so badly she died.[45]

Not all the life stories in *Sacred Shelter* reflect or refer to the kinds of systemic problems, tragedies, and disadvantages I've discussed above. One contributor, Akira, grew up in an upper-middle-class family in Japan and was, for many years, an extremely successful international businessman; he supervised multimillion-dollar transactions, traveled around the world, and rented a big apartment in a high-rise building near the United Nations. Another contributor, Lisa Sperber, was raised in an affluent New York suburb by ambitious parents who generously supported her many artistic and musical talents. But no demographic group is immune to homelessness, and both Akira and Lisa ended up living on the streets of New York City. There, it is worth noting, they did have some modest advantages. As Lisa explains, "because [I was white], I was able to walk into a lot of big hotels, make believe I worked there, and take a shower. . . . If you were black and you tried that . . . , you'd be stopped." Similarly, Akira, who knew how to act like a businessman, remembers walking "like a guest into Barclay's, or the Hilton, or the Waldorf Astoria. The bathrooms had huge, spacious stalls with their own sink inside. . . . I would get in there and very carefully clean my whole body—wash my hair too with shampoo. Then I would clean the floor as if nothing had happened and come out." None of the African American people in this book who lived on the street describe comparable experiences.

Regardless of their racial and socioeconomic status, however, all the life story contributors in *Sacred Shelter* had a history of trauma or crisis that contributed to their homelessness and was exacerbated by it. With honesty and tremendous courage, they try to make sense of the circumstances and suffering that led them to live on the streets and in shelters. They recall the slow, painful, but also enlightening process of turning their lives around and becoming housed. There is no common denominator here—no collective cure that can be synthesized and offered up as a singular remedy for recovering from the trauma of homelessness. Rather, what the contributors offer are inspiring, bleak, and mundane details and events that, over time and in retrospect, seem to have enabled positive change. Some contributors suggest that they first had to hit a kind of rock bottom. This happened to Akira when he was caught stealing a winter coat, to Dennis Barton when he found himself the oldest man in a holding cell, and to Deborah Canty when she awoke from a blackout with no idea where she was. For James Addison, change came when he learned he was going to be a grandfather. Cindy had change forced on her when ACS (the Administration for Children's Services) said they would take her children away if she didn't enter a domestic violence shelter. For Edna Humphrey and Heidi Nissen, the decision to enter the shelter system was more prosaic. They did it because it was their only chance of eventually acquiring affordable housing.

If there is any common source of change in the stories, it is that the contributors' lives altered when they either sought out or were finally willing to receive help from other people who connected them to a larger institution or organization. For Rodney Allen, the idea of accepting help had seemed disgraceful. When family members offered to house him after he was evicted, Rodney chose the streets, "because I didn't want to burden myself on anybody." It wasn't until a fellow homeless man basically forced him to attend a church service and community meal that Rodney's life began to improve. Other storytellers, like Sophia Worrell—who spontaneously rushed into a hospital and told a receptionist about being battered—sought help when they reached a breaking point. For Michelle Riddle, help emerged in unexpected places. It was not until she was put in prison that she successfully completed a rehabilitation program and found God. "I always say I was rescued, not arrested," Michelle told me.

More often, the incarcerations recounted in *Sacred Shelter* were dangerous, degrading, and dehumanizing. "It was crazy in there," Dennis reports. "People fighting over the television, people fighting over commissary.... [They] gave me my number: Barton, 80A★★★★. For the rest of my incarceration, that's what I was known by." Black describes being forced into a sudden and excruciating process of withdrawal at Rikers Island, where his request for methadone was callously denied. These and comparable experiences point to a problem reflected in many of the stories: institutions and organizations can be punitive to homeless people—even, ironically, those institutions specifically designed to help them. As several of the stories emphasize and as is generally well known, homeless shelters (especially the big intake centers) are often dangerous and drug-ridden. "It wasn't a good place to hang out," Edna says of the first shelter where she went; "there were too many drugs and people fighting." As soon as Heidi Nissen arrived at her first homeless shelter, she witnessed the arrest of a bloody woman who had stabbed someone. "Turns out [that] was nor-

mal," Heidi points out. "The cops were there two or three times a week."
Residents were not the only problem. Heidi's first caseworker used crack
and sold it to shelter residents. At Fort Washington Men's Shelter, where
James Addison stayed, "they were selling drugs right there, and the security guards were loan sharks."

From security checks to living conditions to sleeping arrangements, contributors describe these shelters as inhumane. As Sophia explains, "They
would search your bag, your clothes, and your person. The beat-downs
were constant, and it was like being in prison." Lisa Sperber's first shelter was "horrendous. It wasn't clean, and the food was horrible. All the
women were in one room.... The beds were lined up in a row, literally."
The human misery, Deborah Canty emphasizes, was pervasive. At the first
shelter where she stayed, "I saw the elderly. I saw young kids. I thought,
'Where is your family at?'" At her second shelter, "a couple of ladies
died.... How sad to die and [have] nobody there to claim you."

Some contributors also recall positive shelter experiences. Cindy describes the domestic violence shelter where she first stayed as "one of the
most beautiful places I have ever seen. It was so clean—the people were
so loving." From his shelter bedroom window, Dennis had a beautiful East
River view "that people are killing for right now." Edna found her third
shelter very helpful: "They were nice there and had different programs. I
took a computer class.... I also saw a medical doctor ... and started getting therapy." Indeed, even when they hated their shelters, many of the
storytellers received medical and social services there and were able, as
Black puts it, to use the shelter system as a "stepping-stone" toward finding permanent housing.

Community, Help, and Faith

In the end, what most helped the people in this book recover from homelessness were the institutions and organizations that provided three basic
forms of assistance: they championed homeless people's right to individual power, dignity, and equality; they connected homeless people with
a supportive and responsive community; and they encouraged their members or clients to find deeper meaning in life, often (although not always)
by developing or intensifying their personal relationship with God. As
I've already indicated and will discuss in more detail in a moment, these
are some of the central goals of the life skills empowerment program. But
several contributors learned about the program only after becoming part
of another organization with these values.

Two of these organizations deserve special recognition. The first is Life Experience and Faith Sharing Associates (LEFSA), which sends team leaders to run faith-based community gatherings for homeless people on the streets and in shelters. The names of the nuns who founded the program in 1986—the late Sister Dorothy Gallant, SC, and the late Sister Teresa Skehan, RSM—appear in several of the life stories. So do references to LEFSA's emphasis on equality, community, and God. When James Addison attended his first LEFSA meeting in a city shelter, he liked it immediately, because "the meeting felt equal. Sister Dorothy and Sister Teresa didn't call themselves leaders. This was *our* group." LEFSA also provided a sense of community within the shelter. At the women's shelter where Deborah stayed, "the residents [always] called you the "b" word," but in the safe space of the shelter's LEFSA group, "everyone said, 'God loves you and we love you too.'" The idea of God is naturally central to the LEFSA mission. As the late Sister Dorothy put it, "In LEFSA's ministry . . . I have seen 'God make a way out of no way' in people's lives."[46]

The name All Angels' Church also appears in several stories. Located on the Upper West Side of Manhattan, All Angels' runs a Community Ministries Program dedicated "to empower[ing] and equip[ping] people struggling with homelessness, addiction and mental health challenges to be dependent on God, independent in self-care and inter-dependent with the community."[47] In addition to providing showers, medical services, a shelter, and community meals, All Angels' welcomes homeless people to its Sunday services and runs Bible study classes and leadership-training programs for them. Rodney describes the amazing communal impact of attending his first church service at All Angels' and seeing "some of the homeless people who sat on the benches at the park [there]. . . . After that, these same people, when we went back to the park, had something to talk about." As soon as Lisa Sperber attended a service at All Angels', "I felt like I was home. . . . I just felt the love and acceptance in the room." For Akira, the heterogeneity of the worshippers coupled with their singular devotion to God was transformative. "There were all kinds of people— homeless people, young people, old people, bankers, lawyers, architects. . . . [I began to be] influenced by the congregation's strong faith." Ultimately, Rodney, Lisa, and Akira became wellness leaders and helped run the church's Bible study class and leadership-training program for homeless people.

LEFSA and All Angels' Church regularly recommend people to the life skills empowerment program, as well as a variety of other organizations and institutions, for supplemental support. In theory, the program's support is more practical and communal than religious and theistic, though that can vary based on individual programs. In the programs for which I've volunteered, participants are given reflective readings and encouraged to find transcendent meaning in their lives, but there is no formal discussion of religion or God, though individuals often refer to God on their own. On the other hand, George Horton (who runs New York Catholic Charities' life skills empowerment program), sees it as a religious program that embodies religious principles. As he explains in his reflection, the participants' stories "are faith stories. The presence of God or a higher power in their lives, although not always explicit, is almost universally acknowledged. . . . At bottom (often the turning point in their lives is when they 'hit bottom'), they truly and deeply believe they have been saved." Indeed, the vast majority of this book's contributors are committed Christians who speak movingly about God's central role in their lives. Black speaks for many when he says, "I tell you, on this journey, God is powerful—so powerful. I don't see how a person can live without God."

Nevertheless, in this book, the contributors dwell especially on the program's secular benefits. They praise its life skills workshops and goal-setting curriculum, discuss the challenge and relief of writing their life stories, and speak powerfully about the communal bonds forged by common experiences. For Heidi Nissen, that identification was a source of strength: "I gained confidence talking to participants who had been through some of the same things as me." Cindy had a similar experience in her group for domestic violence survivors: "Being around the other ladies who went through some type of abuse really, really helped me. . . . Now I had many friends."

A number of participants also became friendly with their mentors, despite their apparent lack of shared experiences. Though some mentors were once homeless (several of the life story contributors in this book became mentors after graduation), many had more privileged lives. Akira's mentor was a successful businessman; Dennis Barton's mentor had a fundraising job at New York Catholic Charities; Rodney Allen's mentor was me, an English professor at Fordham University. When people's socioeconomic differences are so wide, it can be hard to foster a sense of equality. And yet, a sense of equality is exactly what several of the life story contributors describe. For instance, the day Dennis visited his mentor's office, his mentor told him to "go over there and sit in my chair." The invitation had a profound effect on Dennis. He was used to shelter guards, welfare agents, and parole officers looking "at you like you were piece of crap"; now his mentor was "telling me to sit in *his* chair behind *his* desk. It was a sign of respect. My mentor made me feel like a person." Deborah Canty was moved when her mentor, "a white woman . . . [who] was kind of obese," shared some of her own painful past: "People would make fun of her and put her down and degrade her. . . . My mentor's story made me more aware of what I said to people. It made me be more mind-ful." Of course, stories like these don't change the reality and injustice of socioeconomic inequality. But mentors and mentees can offer each other the respite and grace of reinforcing their shared humanity.

Socioeconomic difference is not the only obstacle to equality in the mentor–mentee relationship. Since the mentor's official role is to help his or her mentee set and achieve personal goals, the very nature of the relationship seems hierarchical: one person gives and the other receives, one person is in need and the other is needed. In this sense, the "needy" homeless person seems dependent; the needed mentor has the power to "help" him or her; and for all its good intentions, the life skills empow-erment program runs the risk of replicating the kind of "us/them" di-chotomy that the organization came into existence to challenge. There is no easy escape from this imbalance, and I'm sure the evidence of its en-trenchment pervades *Sacred Shelter*.

At the same time, mentors are often the recipients of their mentees' generosity. For one thing, the very act of accepting help is a kind of gener-osity in that it gives the "helper" the chance to feel good about himself or herself. That was my personal experience when I worked with Rodney. At a time when I was struggling with depression, Rodney's happiness in my presence and his willingness to accept my help made me feel better about myself and my life. On the surface, I was volunteering to assist him. In fact, Rodney's willingness to receive my assistance was doing me a world of good. A 2016 *New York Times* op-ed co-written by (the unlikely combination of) the Dalai Lama and the American Enterprise Institute's Arthur C. Brooks helps explain the kind of phenomenon I experienced.

> Virtually all the world's major religions teach that our diligent work in the service of others is our highest nature and thus lies at the center of a happy life. Scientific surveys and studies confirm the shared tenets of our faiths. Americans who prioritize doing good for others are almost twice as likely to say they are very happy about their lives.[48]

The reflections in *Sacred Shelter* are designed to highlight the mutuality of these benefits, not only for the voluntary mentors but also for the professionals involved in supporting the life skills empowerment program as directors, facilitators, or clerics. "What has the program meant to you personally?" the advisory board asked the contributors to the book. Some, like Alistair Drummond, pastor of the West End Presbyterian Church, which has housed and supported several programs and provided office space for the IAHH, answered this question in clerical and communal terms: "I gain spiritual encouragement by being of service. I exercise leadership in an area of ministry about which I myself am still learning. And I feel fulfilled when I can see the positive effect of my collaboration with other congregants and other program leaders." Other reflection contributors credit the program or individual participants with literally changing their lives. Dr. Dawn Ravella, for instance, who runs the Reformed Church of Bronxville's program for formerly incarcerated individuals, describes how, after a program participant "was accepted into a PhD program . . . [I] told him I'd always wanted to earn a doctorate degree. He looked me right in the eye and told me that I could do it and should do it." As a result of this encouragement, Dawn eventually earned a doctor of ministry degree at the New York Theological Seminary. For Stephanie Reid, a mentor in the Riverside Church's Coming Home program, a single circle session transformed the unrelenting guilt she had long felt about not writing to her brother when he was incarcerated. "That evening in the circle session, I had an emotional release. One of the formerly incarcerated participants said he saw a change in me after that experience. I had a more humble attitude." The reflections suggest that the best kind of help is always a form of humility and a means by which both giving and receiving are an act of service.

The life story contributors know both of these positions well. They received help when they were homeless, and now the vast majority of them work or volunteer to serve others who are homeless. They are mentors and facilitators in the program; they devote time to the IAHH, New York Catholic Charities, and other service organizations; they volunteer in shelters, food pantries, and soup kitchens. Most are also active in their religious communities, running leadership-training classes, serving on church boards, and attending retreats. Two of the graduates were ordained as ministers, and one is the deacon of his church. In short, the formerly homeless people in this book have transformed their suffering into a source of generosity. They tend not to applaud themselves for this work. Instead, their stories simply and matter-of-factly suggest how their own homelessness and trauma have inspired a form of compassion and identification that makes them uniquely qualified to help others in need. As

Heidi Nissen explains, "I can say, 'You know what? I did this. You can too.'" Or, as Michelle Riddle puts it, "I know what it is like to be hurt in life, so I have a lot of compassion for people."

Compassion was on my mind in the summer of 2016 when I was editing the life stories for this book. In July, the famous writer, activist, and Holocaust survivor Elie Wiesel died. Countless tributes to him poured out across the media. One on the radio, by Rabbi Ariel Burger, reminded me especially of the values I'd heard repeatedly in the interviews. "I think one of Elie Wiesel's messages was—and one of the things he modeled and demonstrated was—to take our own particular suffering and make it an engine ... and a motivation for a universal kind of caring."[49] That is what the formerly homeless people in *Sacred Shelter* have done. That is what many of the people who help run or volunteer for the program aspire to do. "Compassion," the Buddhist teacher Pema Chödrön says, "is not ... as often we think of it ... something about helping others or looking down on others who are unfortunate. Compassion is actually a relationship between equals."[50] At its best, the life skills empowerment program fosters this kind of compassion. It is my hope that *Sacred Shelter* reflects something of this ideal.

At the same time, *Sacred Shelter* is neither idealistic nor utopian. Compassion alone is grossly inadequate to address the injustice and suffering of homelessness. Today, the situation remains dire throughout America, and in New York City, homelessness is at record levels. The most recent statistics from the Coalition for the Homeless report that more than 63,000 people are being housed every night in New York City shelters. This does not count the thousands of people who sleep on the city streets, are about to be evicted from their homes, or are "housing insecure."[51] Except for a few passages in this Introduction, *Sacred Shelter* says virtually nothing about the socioeconomic conditions and inequities that cause homelessness. It offers no recommendation for how to alleviate the systemic forces that perpetuate it. That is best left to other books. What *Sacred Shelter* does offer is one particular program's history of healing and hope. In documenting the recovery of thirteen formerly homeless individuals—and suggesting how many other people have benefited from their lives—this book celebrates the transformative power of community building and support. That is something special, something worth striving for.

Life Story
Nelson Prime

Nelson Prime was born on August 3, 1960, in Harlem, New York. In 1988, he was part of Homeward Bound Community Services, the collective of homeless people who led a 200-day vigil in City Hall Park. In addition to the story of his life, Nelson gives a first-hand account of this remarkable event, which ultimately led to the foundation of the Education Outreach Program (EOP), the original life skills empowerment program.

I don't take tragedy and death too well. I have seen people's brains blown out. I've seen people get gutted. I've seen people get raped. Speaking of deaths, I'm the only one still around that had anything to do with the leadership of Homeward Bound Community Services. Everyone else is dead. It's a sad thing, how drugs and alcohol can waste your life away. I'm glad that I was never too caught up in it.

I was born in 1960, and I grew up in a very strict household with good family values. Things were pleasant until I was five years old. My father was very intelligent, and my grandfather was street smart. My mother was extremely street smart. I was a very smart, bright kid. I didn't talk much, but when I did I expressed myself the best way I could, and they would all call me intelligent. I remember one day I asked my family to stop calling me "Junior." I guess I said it with the utmost respect. Afterward my grandfather was always raving about how smart I was and all this, that, and the other.

Around the time I was six, my parents broke up due to my father's alcoholism and his violent outbursts with my mother. I would say to him,

"Why don't you stop—please, please stop!" And I would take the brunt of his anger. I was punished and not fed and stuff like that to let me know my place. I didn't know that my father was an alcoholic. I just knew that I loved him. I just loved the ground he walked on.

I was still kind of happy then. Even though my parents were separated, we would go see our father at his apartment, and my mother would still send him food through us. She loved him, but she could not live with him. At that time, I had two siblings who were really close to me—my sister, who was one year older than me, and my brother, who was two years younger than me. My father instructed us to protect my sister, and I was honored to be given that mission by my father because I really respected him even though he was an alcoholic.

My mother, sister, brother, and I moved to 137th Street between Fifth Avenue and Lennox—the slums of Harlem. We were the new kids on the block and would often get teased. I guess the other kids wanted to test us. We had to fight all the time. Like I said, my father gave us charge to protect my sister, and that's exactly what I did.

We were poor, very poor, and lived in a run-down tenement. We made the best of it—we would clean all the time, but there were still holes in the walls. There were killings in the building, a whole bunch of stuff. They had people shooting heroin on the landing right above us. My mother tried to get along with the addicts, to tell you the truth. She told us, "As long as they have their drugs they're all right. But when they don't, watch out." I never forgot that, because it's true. There were rapes going on all around the area, in my building, too. Once this woman was screaming at the top of her lungs, and I rushed in and tried to help her. She was completely stark naked with whip marks on her body, and her lip was bloody. That was a horrible sight to see as a child—I was approaching eight years old. I told my sister to go into our apartment and my brother to go with her, and I brought the woman a blanket. Then I went to Harlem Hospital, because we lived right across the street, and they came over there and got the woman.

Through all this, I was a good guy. I was an avid reader, and I did my schoolwork. At church they would ask me to do things all the time because I guess I was well spoken. I didn't really like all the attention, but I started doing a lot of church announcements and I narrated a play. I just knew how to pronounce words the right way and articulate and project. I guess it was a natural talent that I had.

In 1968, my sister, brother, and I went to visit our father with a plate of food, because our mother said he hadn't been eating. When we got there, we found him dead. He was already three days dead and bloated. Smelled like alcohol and dead skin. Never forgot that smell. I smell it even now, talking to you. We stayed there crying, weeping the whole time, until my mother came to pick us up, and one of our family members who had a car drove us home.

I kind of snapped then. My father was a big support to me, and I lost it, to tell you the truth. I had to actually see a psychiatrist after that. I started to wet the bed and a whole bunch of stuff. The bed-wetting lasted all the way until I turned twelve.

But I still did well in school. I spent a lot of time doing homework and self-study. I would read beyond the assignment so I could get a grasp of where the lessons were going. I did little plays, won the spelling bee, got all these awards and honors for doing essays and different types of things. Even the assistant principal thought I was very intelligent because I used to ask questions all the time and research things. They took me to the Countee Cullen Library in Harlem, where I started reading all sorts of things, the Bible included. That's the first time I read poetry. I was also good at a lot of sports. It's just that I was short and would never get picked. My brother got his track trophies and basketball trophies and swimming trophies. Me, I was like a scholar or a scribe. All these things I did as a child, and I was living as a child and getting back to mental health after my father's death.

That's when my mother started going out with somebody named Le-roy. This guy was six foot six, 278 pounds, with about 20-inch biceps, no stomach, and cut from the head down. He was a Vietnam veteran and a bouncer and number runner at the time. My mother introduced him, saying, "He's going to be your stepfather from now on." I was very sus-picious because by then I was really the man of the house. He looked into my eyes and said, "I can tell you're going to be a problem," and he laughed, "Ha, ha, ha." From then on, he always told me that I was noth-ing—that I was not going to be anything in life.

One time my brother and I snuck into an R-rated movie, and we got in trouble. My mother got the belt out and was about to give us a whip-ping, but Leroy said, "No, let me do this." So my mother left the apart-ment and he proceeded into the room, and the beating lasted for about an hour. I was really scarred. My mother didn't know what happened until she came back. Apparently, she comforted me or whatever, and I said, "You've really got to get rid of him." I didn't know that she feared him.

By the time I was twelve, I was often in the hospital, because he didn't just beat me with a belt. There were iron pipes involved, hoses, extension cords; there were alcohol baths afterward and salt—all that stuff. Then there was being shut in the closet for a day while the blood dried. If you remember, I told you that we had holes throughout our apartment. Well, there was a big one in the closet. I had a rat visit me often, let's put it that way. When I went to the hospital, my mom taught me to lie about what happened. She was crying, pleading, and begging, because she feared what he might do if I told the truth.

When I was fourteen, I actually stole his knife, because he had already stabbed my mother months before. He caught me and I was beat to an inch of my life, but I had to go to school the next day. I couldn't keep telling them I fell down the steps. I finally took my brother, went to my English teacher, and told him what was going on. A guidance counselor came, and we were whisked away to St. Vincent's Home for Boys in Brooklyn.

After about three months at the home, I pretended my mother had gotten rid of Leroy and that she wanted me to come back. I lied because I wanted to be near my mother and to protect my sister. My younger brother stayed at St. Vincent's, and that was one less sibling I had to worry about.

Three months later, Leroy shot my mother in the chest but didn't kill her. I took the cartridge out of the gun and threw the clip out the window so he couldn't shoot her anymore. Then I grabbed a knife in the kitchen and just started whaling away wherever I could to get him off her. Yes,

Nelson (age fifteen) with his siblings and stepfather in Harlem, 1975

he was a big man, and he was combat trained, and he was delusional. But I fought that guy until the police came up the stairs, and he went up to the roof and got away.

After that, my mother let him back in the house. I was really upset and disgusted. "This man is going to wind up killing you and us," I told my mother. I guess I was being selfish at the time, or I wasn't thinking clearly, because if I really wanted him gone I would have done something about it.

Right before I turned sixteen, they split up. Finally, my mother got rid of him, and I was so happy. Then one day, we were upstairs, playing Monopoly of all things, and we heard sirens outside. I looked down out the window, and I was in shock. I saw my mother lying there in the middle of the street, her blood going down the gutter. I started to rush downstairs, but one of my older cousins met me halfway and grabbed me and wouldn't let me go outside. I think I bit his leg, and I went all the way downstairs, out into the street. It was around July 4, 1976, the year of the bicentennial. All around were celebrations, gunshots and firecrackers, but all that ceased on our block with the death of my mother.

And I completely lost it. I guess another personality came out of me at that time. I was on a search and destroy mission for him. They said Leroy had escaped into the East River. Knowing he was an expert swimmer and combat trained, I was sure he could survive. So when all my other family members left our apartment, I refused to leave. I set up booby traps in our house like in the movie *Home Alone.* I wanted him to come home. I wanted to mutilate him. But it was not to be. Three days later, they dragged the East River and found Leroy's body. I felt cheated out of my revenge. It kind of drove me crazy, and they put me in a straightjacket in the psych ward of Harlem Hospital.

They let me out for my mother's funeral, but I was in handcuffs. I cried over my mother's casket in handcuffs. Insanely crying. I let out all the years of hurt. I guess they thought I was even more crazy.

After the hospital, I quit high school and got two jobs. One was a messenger job, and the other was getting paid to be in plays. The first play was a lead role with the Grass Roots Players on 125th Street. In the second, I was an understudy in a play at Columbia University. I felt great when I was acting. I felt I could be a character other than me. The acting helped my self-esteem, because I finally found something people said I was good at and that I enjoyed doing. I could have auditioned for more plays, but I was too torn up inside to focus on that. I felt very depressed and guilty about not being able to save my mother's life. I started spiraling into depression. My brother had moved to a children's home in Staten Island called St. Joseph's, and I made a decision to leave Harlem and go to St. Joseph's. I graduated high school from there.

After that, I joined the service. Basic training was a culture shock. Because I grew up in Harlem, people automatically assumed I was a city slicker. That was one strike against me. The second strike came from being short. I was only five foot two when I entered the service, and people thought they could bully and pick on me. Now I'm five foot nine, but I was a late bloomer. Still, I did well in Basic. I was used to running through backyards in Harlem. Obstacle courses were nothing to me. I would do things to the letter—exactly how they were described. I have a good memory when it comes to things I'm interested in, and I was very interested in becoming a good soldier. I got high marks in everything. For Advanced Individual Training, I went to Fort Huachuca, Arizona, where I got my Military Occupational Specialty in surveillance equipment. It was intense training, with classes in algebra and physics.

After Advanced Individual Training, I went straight to Korea. This was 1978 and it was peacetime, but I still saw people killed. They put me in the DMZ, the demilitarized zone, which is the line that separates North and South Korea. I had to monitor the border. They put a lot of responsibility on privates, and I took that very seriously. In the DMZ, people did ambush and reconnaissance patrols. We had to monitor them too, to make sure nobody was infiltrating the line. My job was talking to command and telling them where things were. Clashes happened and people were killed under the rug, so to speak. During that time, I think I saw six people die. But I was a veteran to seeing death, you know what I mean? So I didn't take it to heart, because I was numb after my childhood trauma.

Remember I talked about those two strikes against me? Well, the third strike was my skin color. Everybody else in my platoon was white, and I was constantly getting threatened. They said they would throw me off the mountain. I was getting death notes and all kinds of stuff. I showed them to my commanding officer, who was the only other black person, and he said, "I can't do anything without proof." Eventually I had to leave the military under honorable conditions. I opted out of the four-year commitment and did three. That was my stint in the service.

When I came home, the unemployment office referred me to a job as a janitor, and I lived with my great-grandmother for about six months. Then I found out my mother had an insurance policy, and since she had a violent death, they gave it double indemnity. I got something like $20,000—a lot of money at the time. I got my own apartment and gave my great-grandmother some money because she helped me out. When I moved out, she told me something really strange. I'll never forget this because her daughter is still living, and she told me the same exact thing. They said that they were scared of me. It seemed, looking from the outside in, that I was unstable. I didn't have fits or anything, but I did have an anger issue if I was pushed to a certain point. I tended to take things out on family and people I was close to, more so than with anybody else. Years later, when I delved into my own history and character, I realized that yes, I had a problem with suppressed anger out of guilt for the things that happened in my childhood.

I quit the janitor job and went to Flatbush in Brooklyn, and I guess I spent a lot of the $20,000 partying with friends. There were times that I would wake up to reality and say, "Well, I got to do this and that if I'm going to hold on to the little bit of money that I have." I think I had only a couple of thousand dollars left. So I got myself into a Spanish-speaking rehab program called Resurrection House, all the way in the Bronx. I stayed there for a whole year. I met a girl named R—— at McDonald's, and we moved in together. My cousin got me a job in a women's clothing store called the Emotional Outlet. The owner was Jewish and had a psychology degree. He set the place up so that women would feel comfortable and be able to shop. I worked as a stock clerk and did security.

Seven years later, a succession of bad things happened. R—— and I had a baby who died of crib death. In February 1988, the owner of the Emotional Outlet died. His family came to take over the business, but everyone was fighting for a piece of the money, so the business went downhill and they decided to get rid of it. Once that happened, it was hard for me to pay the rent with my savings. In April, the superintendent of my building ran to Puerto Rico with all the rent money. They condemned the building, and everybody started moving out. R——— went back with her parents. I was stuck there with no job. They turned off everything—the lights, the hot water. Finally, I visited my sister in Brooklyn for a couple of days and got a reprieve. When I came back, my apartment had been ransacked, all my stuff was gone. I had nothing.

I didn't know what to do. Like I told you, I had an anger problem. I was absolutely enraged. I just felt like God had abandoned me. I almost felt like Job—I lost my job, my building was condemned, my child died. I was totally upset, really distraught. And that's when I became homeless, in April 1988.

I went to a new veterans' shelter in Flushing, Queens. There I met this guy named Larry Locke. Larry was running for a seat on the council at the VA shelter, and he asked for my vote. I didn't know him from Adam, but I said, "Yeah, you'll get my vote." I had never paid too much attention to politics. My mother did, and I would always help her write letters because I was that kind of kid.

I didn't see Larry again until June 1988, when I learned about the vigil for the homeless outside city hall. The vigil was supposed to last only one night, but the homeless had decided to stay there and band together in City Hall Park. I didn't go at first, because I was a suspicious person and I didn't feel like giving back to anybody. I just felt helpless and sorry for myself, like poor me.

But around the third day of the vigil, I went, and there was Larry Locke. He introduced me to Marc Greenberg from the Interfaith Assembly on Homelessness and Housing, who presented me with information about the whole system of homelessness and the bad policies in place. I began realizing that I was actually mad, but I didn't know how to deal with it. Maybe this vigil would be a lynchpin, maybe this would be something that could change minds. How wonderful that homeless brothers and sisters were banding together to make our voices heard. We wanted to actuate our own niche into society. We wanted to be part of the solution instead of the perpetuation of the problem.

There were around twenty-seven people staying faithfully in the park. Since it was a vigil based on responsibility, we had to form some type of government in order to best represent ourselves. We voted in a president and vice president, a secretary, treasurer, and other committee members. Larry Locke was the president, and a guy named Duke York was the vice president. At first, I stayed on the outside looking in. I wanted to observe Larry first because I was cautious, put it that way. But I also wanted to be of help. So I would work around the campsite, making sure whatever food and donations we got were accounted for, because people were giving us sleeping bags and things like that.

It wasn't until Larry asked me to give my opinion about a press conference that was coming up that I got involved. Because I had always been put down, I hesitated and procrastinated about stepping into leadership. Still, I gave my assessment of the plight of the homeless and where we could impact things. And I did it in such a succinct way that Larry, Duke, and the others thought I would be good at representing them at the press conference. To make a long story short, I got put onto the ad hoc committee.

On June 5, 1988, we held a press conference on the steps of city hall. I was the last person to go up to the podium, and I spoke straight from the hip, straight from the heart. I told them, "We are staying, the homeless are staying. We may be an eyesore, but as long as we're an eyesore people can be reminded that there are homeless in the city. You have family members who are homeless. You have siblings that are homeless, and you may not even know it. Anybody can be homeless. We've come to make sure that you see us out here. We're not going anywhere. We have held forth today." The newspapers and the radio talk shows just ate it up. We had an article on the front page of the *Daily News*, and John Jiler's article in the *Village Voice* included some of the things that I said.

About a week later, we decided to name ourselves Homeward Bound Community Services. I was officially voted in as the new secretary. The first thing I did was take charge of the Journey Book, which had newspaper articles and other writings about the vigil. It was almost like our bible.

But to really step up as secretary, I had to learn the ropes, and Marc Greenberg helped me with that. He took me to his office and taught me about organizing and about the paperwork involved. I learned to take proper minutes for the Homeward Bound meetings and to write letters, like I used to do for my mother. I wrote to different foundations and organizations to try to fund Homeward Bound Community Services as an independent entity, and I started working on how we could fit in with the other homeless organizations. Then the Food and Hunger Hotline offered us the use of their office. I was given the keys, and I could have even stayed there at night if I wanted to. Now that we had access to phones, it was a whole new ballgame. The Food and Hunger Hotline was right smack-dab in the middle of Wall Street. We nicknamed it "Yuppieville." Meanwhile, the media called the homeless people in the park "Kochville."

We knew we needed our own voice to speak to the public. Other advocacy organizations were trying to represent the homeless without letting us represent ourselves. We did not want them—and I need to say this—to get the grants without sharing the road. Some of them were getting funding for the homeless but not serving the homeless directly. I had a long talk with Marc Greenberg about this, and I got a lot of questions answered. He talked to me like somebody at his level, like a friend. The IAHH wasn't reaping any benefits from Homeward Bound Community Services like some of the other organizations. Marc had a one-man show going on at the time. He was really working hard for us, and I was kind of blown away.

I handled most of the second press conference by myself. I went up there and I brought out our agenda about how we wanted to be able to represent ourselves and how important it was. People were getting the wrong idea, I said. The first thing they say of the homeless is they're mentally ill or on drugs. But I was none of that at that time, even though I had gone through some horrible stuff. I had to go through all that on camera in order for them to get it right.

Still, reality used to hit us in the face because we had problems in the park. There were a lot of jealous people, and all the arguments came out at night—not in the daytime when the cameras were rolling. Hecklers came into the meetings. You had your drinkers and your smokers and other stuff I'm going to leave out. At night, we had to fend for ourselves. But we policed that area pretty well. We kept the drugs, the alcohol, and the violence out. Duke York was the main guy who did this. Duke had a lot of heart. He was the heart and soul of that park. Another guy we called Kung Fu Joe also held things down in the park. Joe was the real intimidator. You did not want to get past Joe. I felt safer because he was there.

Most days I wore a dress shirt and dress pants. At night I slept on a cardboard box on a bench. I had my notebook, the Journey Book, and we would hold our ad hoc meetings at night. It was the summer time, and the weather was nice mostly, and we just stayed in the park and went about our daily lives. We had a lot of support in the community from business owners that gave us food and all types of items that we needed to survive out in the streets. We even got a few tents. When our clothes got dirty, we'd wash them in the city hall fountain.

After the media hype, a lot of people wanted to be part of this big thing called Homeward Bound. We were like a jewel in the city where people could come and ask for opinions about homelessness and have intelligent conversations. When Jesse Jackson came to city hall for a voter registration drive, he came over to us. He started this "I Am Somebody" speech, and he and I were holding hands on the park bench. Reporters were out there, and the cameras were rolling and flashing away. I thought we were being exploited, but I said that was all right if it would give us a little publicity.

It wasn't until we got all this attention that Ed Koch really got out his punching bag. Since coming to the park, we were an eyesore to him. He would get out of his limousine every morning, look me dead in the face, and sneer. I was humored by it every morning. One day I was at the other side of the park, washing my clothes at the fountain, when Ed Koch came out of city hall with a bustle full of media people and the cameras rolling. Somebody ran top speed over to tell me, because Koch was picking on the people who were inebriated. "Why aren't you working?" Koch was saying to them. "I can offer you a job."

So I came over there and asked him in a very loud voice, "Can that job pay the rent?" Suddenly the cameras came over to me. "Can that minimum wage job you just offered pay the rent?" Rent was high because they were doing a lot of gentrification, and all the players involved from banking institutions wanted a piece of the pie. Ed Koch started fumbling over his words. "Well, if you would just work. . . ." And that was the very thing we were trying to prevent—people looking down on us. So while the cameras were rolling, I had to explain to Koch how the system worked. "The problem is that you're not in touch with homelessness from the homeless perspective. If you allow us to meet with you, we can discuss this matter and maybe we can shed some new light on the situation so that you don't have to come out here with all these TV cameras trying to exploit the homeless."

I said that on camera. The reporters and the camera crew were smiling and snickering in the background. Ed Koch stood dumbfounded.

The next day, the phones at the Food and Hunger Hotline were ringing off the hook. I had to hire a secretary to start screening my calls.

Between doing all the stuff in the daytime and trying to survive at night, I got a little overwhelmed. There was so much responsibility. I started needing more rest. Marc allowed me to stay at his home by myself for nights at a time. Like I said, Marc really took me under his wing and put a lot of trust in me. To this day, that has helped me realize that other people see more things in me than I see in myself. I believe every homeless person needs that kind of support. If everybody did something like Marc did, the world would be a better place. John Jiler from the *Village Voice* was another one. He actually took me on vacation to a bungalow on Fire Island for a whole weekend. I had one of the best times of my life.

But most of the time I stayed in the park. By the time fall came, fewer people were around. Things were fading as far as the press was concerned.

Homeward Bound started dying out from the inside. When November hit, it started getting really cold, and some nights were unbearable. Only a handful of us were still staying in the park. I could have gone somewhere, but I thought, "No, I'm not going to abandon them." I stayed with a few people huddled around just to represent that we were still down there. In December, after talking to Larry Locke, I made an announcement: "We're going to disband this park thing. It's getting too cold, and I don't want us to be responsible for anybody dying out here." That was the last hurrah for Homeward Bound Community Services.

But other things were happening. Canon Lloyd S. Casson, the vicar of Trinity Church, wanted to know what he could do for the homeless. I started a self-help group for homeless people to build leadership. Marc wrote a grant for Trinity Church to hire homeless people to run the group, and I was placed in charge of that. We also met someone at St. Augustine's Church who wanted us to help run his homeless shelter, because the people in the church didn't have a clue about that.

My hat really goes off to Marc, because he decided to start a Speakers Bureau of homeless people who would go out and give our testimony, our life story, to different groups. It was a chance for us to represent ourselves, after seeing how well we did in our press conferences and TV interviews. Larry and I picked people to tell their stories, and Marc matched them with volunteers and organizations that wanted to do something for the homeless.

Around this time, a nun named Teresa Skehan became my mentor. Marc had introduced me to her down in City Hall Park. She was really funny, and she was the first one to make me feel comfortable with my sense of humor. In a mentorship relationship, trust has to be built. Confidence has to be built. It's a nurturing that happens over a period of time. That's what I had with Teresa Skehan. I felt honored to know a person like her had my back. I told her in the beginning, "I want you to help me to help myself." At that time, I wanted an apartment I could afford based on my income from the Trinity grant. Sister Teresa and I had a dialogue with the Partnership for the Homeless, and they helped me get an apartment in the Bronx at 625 Jefferson Street. I also took a lot of pointers from her. I used to take on more than I could handle and get overwhelmed. I still have problems with that today, believe it or not. Sister Teresa brought me down to earth so that I could be realistic in my approach to self-help by practicing what I preach.

When my apartment was ransacked and I was in the veterans' shelter, I almost gave up. Now, after Homeward Bound, I felt good about myself.

My self-esteem came back and I could say, "This is who I am, and I am proud of who I am." No more of my stepfather's voice in the back of my head telling me that I'm nothing. Instead of damaging myself, I started to do something about homelessness, not only on a personal level, but also on a political level. I said, "I'm going to use whatever talents and gifts God has given me to get my life straight. I'm going to make a difference now. I want to be able to grow, and the best way I can do that is by helping myself to help others. I can see my path clearly now. This is what I was destined to do."

After Trinity Church, I worked at a place called Part of the Solution (POTS) in the Bronx that helped the homeless directly. I would dispense carfare, cook, and encourage the homeless. This put me in a pretty good position to help motivate more people. So did the spiritual breakthrough I had after going to Way Out Ministries Christian Church with my sister. I got saved and baptized, and I affirmed my faith in Lord Jesus for myself. When I was vindicated, I finally understood a lot of the things I was reading in the Bible. Around this time, I married a woman that I had met at the shelter at St. Augustine's Church. We had three children. There was little Nelson, and Sarah and Michael, my two twins. I had a nice life.

Even so, in 1993, I left my family in New York City and went to Atlanta, Georgia, to live with my cousin and work as a waiter in the Renaissance Hotel. That's when I started drinking. One night I got drunk, and two friends took me home. They went inside and my cousin—she pulled out a gun and was ready to shoot them. "Something has to be done," she said. I said, "Well, I'll leave."

I was scared of my alcohol problems because of my father, so I decided to go to a rehabilitation program at the Veterans Administration. At the same time, I became an activist and started helping homeless veterans. I represented homeless vets at government offices and explained how to best provide services. I also went to Beulah Heights Bible College and became a minister in the Church of God in Christ. Then I was able to give the Word of God and minister to the homeless. I opened doors to the church, worked in the church shelter, and talked to people who were broken down, finding ways to encourage them.

But again the rug was pulled out from underneath me. Remember I told you about my wife and children? Well, one night I got a phone call about a fire in the Bronx. I flew back to New York City. It was a mess—debris, ash, and fire. I'll never forget that smell either, like when my father died. I had to bury my wife and children. I was completely broken up all over. I had a lot of suicidal tendencies. I just couldn't go on living. Maybe the devil or whoever was trying to attack me. I don't know. At that time, I didn't care. As much as I'm glossing over this, that's really as much as I can talk about it right now.

I had no income, nothing to live on, and instead of living in somebody's program, I filed for Social Security. I lived with my sister in Poughkeepsie for a while, and then I got my own place. In 2007, I decided to get intensive therapy for the traumas I've been through—you can call it PTSD. I went to the VA and started their Comprehensive Work Therapy program. I saw a psychologist and a psychiatrist—one provided me something for my thoughts, and the other one provided medicine. The therapy was very helpful. I still go to a lot of groups within the VA, like one for mindfulness.

In 2010, I left New York City and went to Shreveport, Louisiana, for a job and a woman. But things didn't work out, and I was stuck there by myself. I continued doing the homeless ministry thing and lived with my pastor to share the bills. When he died, I came over here to Fort Worth and became homeless again. That was January 2014. I chose Fort Worth because of its homelessness programs, including a veterans' program. There's a community of homeless people in Fort Worth. On any given day, I'm going to say there are at least four thousand homeless in and out of shelters. I stayed in the veterans' part of the Presbyterian Night Shelter. While there, I told the residents, "We are our own best resources; we know more about what we need and how to get what we need than any social worker could. If we get that information together and do something constructive, maybe people will take us a little more seriously." I got a couple of resident councils together and started taking the kind of professional minutes I learned from my days with Homeward Bound. When I presented them to people, they were amazed, like, "This guy does minutes?"

Now I have a job with an organization called Feed by Grace that specifically hires homeless people to do gardening and community work. We grow vegetables and sell them to the community. We grow anything— zucchini, okra, collard greens, Swiss chard, and carrots. On Saturdays, there can be anywhere from two hundred to fifteen hundred homeless people in Unity Park, Fort Worth's park for the homeless, getting fed, playing basketball, doing something to get off the streets. I basically run that. I organize the service providers and run the food line where people can line up to eat. You may have four or five stands of different food, anything from chicken fried steak to all kinds of pasta dishes and other stuff.

My mission in life is to eventually be a lobbyist. That comes from my doing a lot of community partnerships and working with and for politicians. I also want to continue ministering for God to people who have no hope, telling them part of my story and how I came out of each and every challenge. "I cannot do this stuff by myself," I tell them. "It's going to take more than your will to get you off drugs, off alcohol, out of that mental depression, that state of mind that keeps you stuck in the homeless handout cycle. You have to speak up about the problems that you're going through and be brave enough to share with another. We have to consider where we can grow, little by little, so that our minds can be healthy enough to do the things necessary to climb out of that pit of homelessness." It's a spiritual well-being that needs to be established.

I want to leave you with a poem I wrote called "Choose the Solution."

The solution for your problems comes through your actions that
   follow
Live a lifestyle that's worthwhile, because we're not promised a
   tomorrow
We're born gifted to be uplifted, to build, to grow and to learn
How not to be shifted then sifted and lifted out to get burned

It's when we stop pulling ourselves down like crabs in a basket
That those ungrateful smiles turned to frowns as they look in our
   casket
If denying our history creates that mystery—what will we choose
   to believe?
Let our solutions be the evolution for what you and others can
   achieve

Solutions are not only found when we're down and in trouble
It's a place to pin up our hopes that bursts those still living in their
   bubbles
It is time we gave back and not be self-deceivers
By joining righteous causes, created and empowered by receptive
   believers

Finally, don't let problems be your jail, sentenced by that jury
   called doubt
Let go and God will pay your bail if you let him be your lawyer
   throughout
If you still think you've done a crime make sure you're not on
   your own prosecution
But defenders who redefine "doing time" with keys to set them
   free called solutions

Life Story
James Arthur Addison

James Addison was born on June 4, 1954, in Aiken, South Carolina. He graduated in 1993 from the Education Outreach Program (EOP), the original life skills empowerment program, run by New York Catholic Charities.

I am the great-great-grandson of Grandma Manley, who was born a slave in South Carolina. From what I know, she had a son whose name was Henry Addison, who was my great-grandfather. My great-grandfather had three sons, and one them was Arthur Addison, who was my grandfather. He had nine children, and one of his sons, James Arthur Addison, was my father. So I am five generations removed from slavery.

My dad and my mother picked cotton for a living. They were sharecroppers. Neither one of them finished high school. I remember my mother out in the field, and I remember running around, mimicking her picking the cotton. The house that we lived in wasn't like a regular house; it was more like a shack with a tin roof: bathroom outside, a stove where you had to put the wood in, that kind of a thing.

My parents had three boys. The oldest is Raymond Addison, and the youngest is Robert Addison. I was named James Arthur after my father. One day, in order to do better for his family, my dad went up to New York City. It was the Great Migration, and my dad was a part of that. He got a job at a company called Remco, parking all the trucks and cars in a garage. He knew everybody. They called him Jimbo or Jimmy. He worked there forty years until retiring in 1995. My dad was a good man.

When I was four years old, my dad sent for his wife and three boys, and we were off to Washington Heights in New York City. In the late 1950s and early '60s, the neighborhood was mixed. You had Jewish people there, you had black people there, you had Hispanic people there. It was wonderful. I loved the energy. We made scooters from milk crates and two-by-four boards. We made our basketball courts with baskets and some boards and nails. We would be there all day, playing basketball or riding our bikes or our scooters. The girls would be doing the double Dutch. There was an Italian family who lived on the second floor, and the two

James around age seven (circa 1961)

brothers flew birds. They had pigeon coops up on the roofs with lots of birds. You had homer pigeons, you had triplets, you had tumblers. It was so much fun. We would be up on the roof for hours.

Back then, people hung out on the roofs at dusk. My mother would be up there. She was very loud and always had a lot of fun. People loved her because she was the life of the party. My mother was tall, about six foot one or six foot two, and she could dance! They called her Long Tall Sally. That's what I remember a lot about her. Just how much she liked to laugh and have fun.

After a few years, my mother and my dad separated. I was nine or ten, and I took that pretty hard. I can still remember asking my mother, "Why ain't Dad home?" And she would say, "Well he's not." Nobody said anything to us about what happened. You didn't talk to kids back then.

Years later, I needed some answers. So I went to my father and said, "Dad, why did you and Mommy break up? That had a real effect on me when you broke up."

"You know," he said, "there was some cheating going on. I wasn't no saint either. I had to leave because I didn't want to do nothing that I would regret. But I want you to know that it was the hardest thing for me to leave my three boys. But I had to, son, because if I didn't I would've been in jail. I knew it was going to hurt you guys, but I had to." That was his explanation. I never did get my mother's explanation.

After the separation, I found out we were moving to the South Bronx. At the time, I had a fifth-grade teacher I loved, named Miss Thompson. She asked, "Arthur, you ever been to the library?" I said no. So Miss Thompson would send me to the library, and I was so amazed at all these different books, and I would read and come back and tell her what I read. She got me to thinking, and the books stretched my imagination. When I told Miss Thompson I was moving to the South Bronx, I saw a tear in her eye because she must have seen me crying. She just grabbed me and hugged me.

When my parents broke up, a stepfather came in. Actually he wasn't too much older than us, twelve years maybe. That's it. I can remember Mom trying to say, "This is your new daddy. You have to call him 'Daddy.'" And my older brother said to me, "Don't you dare call him 'Daddy.' He's not your father." So I never called him "Daddy." My sister was born in 1968. Two years later, my mother had another boy.

If we would do something wrong, my stepfather gave us the worst beatings that you ever could imagine. It was merciless how he used to beat us. It was like he was never going to stop. My mother would be saying, "That's enough, that's enough." I can remember her having a black eye one time. I had a lot of resentment toward my mother for letting this man beat us like that. Years later, of course, I realized that she was a victim also. My stepfather beat my older brother Raymond once, and that straightened Raymond out. Actually, Raymond thrived after that; he went to school, came home, got a part-time job, had a nice girlfriend. Later, Raymond received a basketball scholarship and went to college.

Me, I rebelled. I just totally rebelled. I said, "This man is not going to put his hands on me." A lot of times I reverted to the streets and hung out with my friends. There was a bunch of us young guys—me, Emanuel, and Jerry, who we called Sweet because when he shot the basketball, one of the guys said, "It looks so sweet." There was also Puna, and there was Larry, who we called Panda Bear. My nickname was Motor because an old-timer named Blue said, "You're always on the go—you're like a motor."

That was the time of the civil rights movement. On the street, some of the older people had a recorder, and we would listen to Malcolm X. In one of the albums, *The Ballot or the Bullet*, he said things like, "It's liberty or it's death—it's freedom for everybody or it's freedom for nobody." We loved Malcolm X. He just touched something deep inside of us. Here was a black man who was standing up to the powers that be.

Malcolm made so much sense to me; even at that young age, I already had all this rebellion in me. He made me think of my parents, who had to pick cotton for a living, and why my father had to come up to New York City. I remembered the shacks down in South Carolina. Some of my people didn't move out of those houses until the late 1970s. It was humiliating to my father and grandfather to be called a "boy." When you walked down the street, you had to keep your head down; you couldn't look a white woman in the eye. Growing up in the Bronx, you heard the same kinds of things about police: "Don't say nothing out of the way. Don't reach in your pocket 'cause you'll get killed." And today I have to tell my sons the same thing. Being a black man growing up, you have to take certain precautions that other races don't.

One day in junior high school, I asked the teacher, "Why don't you teach us black history here?" The teacher didn't say anything. So I asked again. I said, "Excuse me, why aren't you teaching us black history in this class?" And the other kids said, "Yeah, why aren't you teaching us black history?"

That night, the teacher called my mother, and said I was starting trouble in the school. She told my stepfather, and he beat me so hard with an extension cord that I had welts all over. All I wanted was to do something good and get black history for my school, but then I went home and nobody listened to what I had to say. It was just: "Why are you causing trouble in school? Don't you know you're not supposed to cause trouble in school?" So I got the hell beat out of me. That took a lot of spirit out of me.

And it made me go into the streets more. I was an angry young man, running away from home, getting involved with people I thought cared about me. As a lot of kids still do today, I was looking for love in all the wrong places.

Drugs flooded our neighborhoods in the 1960s. By the eighth or ninth grade, I was already into marijuana with my boys. The ghettos were full of cheap heroin, and soon a lot of us were addicted. A super who lived in the building next to mine was a heroin addict, and he would let us hang out down in his basement. I often slept there overnight. There would be quite a few of us guys down there, and some girls were there too. One of them, Lois, became my girlfriend. By age fifteen, we were heroin addicts.

I stopped going to school after tenth grade. Most nights, I slept in the super's basement. My mom was still living with my stepfather, but he worked a lot and messed around with a lot of other women. He was even messing around with a woman right up the street. When I was sixteen, my mom said to me, "Why don't you come home?" I said, "I'm not coming home unless you tell this man not to put his hands on me again. That's the only way I'm coming home." And she did it. She told my stepfather that. And I came back home.

But at that point, I was too far gone. I was already an addict, already involved with gangs, already robbing. There was a bunch of us young addicts burglarizing people's houses in the neighborhood. A friend and I even robbed my mother's next-door neighbor.

Somebody saw me and told my mother, and my father—my real father—came and he said, "You need some help, son. You've got to get some help. Or you're going to die out here." My father was really a special person in a lot of ways—not saying that my mother wasn't, because she was very special, and I know she loved us deeply. But she was a victim of alcoholism and of abuse, too. But if I needed my father, I could touch him. He made sure that he would talk to me. "Arthur," he would say, "You've got to stop doing what you're doing. I love you. You've got to stop."

When I was sixteen, my father talked me into going into a three-year Rockefeller Drug Program. They shipped me upstate to Matteawan State Hospital. One part of Matteawan was a state prison for the criminally insane, and the other part was a drug program. It was like jail in a way, because you were locked up. But it wasn't like Rikers Island, which is a different beast.

Before I went away, I met a lady named Diane, and we had a child together named Tara. Diane was just the most beautiful woman, really sweet. My mom liked her a lot. The first time I ever saw my baby girl was when Diane and my mother brought her up to Matteawan. I had never experienced anything like seeing my little girl. She was so beautiful. I was just so proud because my mother was there, and I could see my mother smiling. It was an incredible visit. It made me say all the right things. "I'm going to do the right thing when I come home. I'm going to do this for my baby girl."

And when I came home, I tried to do the right thing, but I went back into the same neighborhood. All my same friends were waiting. Lois was waiting. My boys were waiting. It didn't take long for me to get back into the same situations. I really didn't have a chance, you know. I was still rebellious, still an addict. We did whatever it took to buy drugs—stealing, robbing the school, robbing somebody's house, it did not matter. We did it. The people in our neighborhood were scared of us. That's how bad it was.

A lot of people trying to help would say, "Just give up the drugs." If it was that easy, I would have stopped years ago. But you're caught up in it. Your thinking is gone. And as bad as you want to stop using, you can't. It is like that scripture in Romans where Paul says, "I do not understand my own actions. For I do not do what I want, but I do the very thing I hate."[1] The people around you have so much influence. Now that I am in recovery, I understand that. It takes a lot of patience and work for people to stop. I saw my daughter here and there, but the deeper I fell into drugs, the more her mother stayed away. She was a responsible mother—she always took care of my daughter.

There were all these gangs in the South Bronx. You had the Seven Crowns, you had the Javelins, you had the Savage Skulls, you had the Black Spades. I wasn't totally in a gang, but I was connected to one of them. The president was my old friend from elementary school and junior high school. Most of the gang members were Puerto Ricans, but my friend would let me go down in the clubhouse and he would say, "This is my black brother." My friend sold a lot of drugs, and he would give me packages to sell. Many years later, he became strung out on drugs himself. Heroin does not care who you are, and it does not discriminate.

I wasn't paying rent anywhere. Nothing was in my name, period. I went from place to place. Sometimes I would stay with my girlfriend. Sometimes I would live at home with my mother. But my mother had pressures. She had her children who she worried about and an unfaithful man who slept around.

When I was eighteen, my mother started having nervous breakdowns. She would see things or hear voices. One time she just ran into the street, and she was so strong it took a whole lot of men to hold her down. I'd say in a two- or three-year period of time, she had six or seven breakdowns. She would be all right for a while, and then she'd have another one and have to be hospitalized. That was hard. I had a lot of guilt, because I would hear things from the neighbors like, "Man, them kids are driving their mother crazy." I felt so helpless during that time.

Whenever something happened to my mother, I would make sure I went to the hospital to see her. One day, my mother said, "Arthur, they're saying that my kids are driving me crazy. But it's not my kids that are driving me crazy. It's him"—meaning my stepfather—"that's driving me crazy." She told me that, and I never forgot it. It helped me out so much. I think my mother wanted to free me. I never told her I felt guilty about her breakdowns, but I think mothers know how their children feel.

She was a good mom. I remember that when I was younger, if she asked me to clean something or wash the clothes and I didn't do a good job or left things half done, she would sit me down and say, "Arthur, I don't care what you do, but whatever you do, Arthur, you have to do a good job. This is going to take you far in life. No matter what the work is. If you're going to be a janitor, be the best janitor." The qualities she taught me stayed with me after my recovery. Whatever you do, be good at it.

Eventually my stepfather and my mother separated, and he married someone else. My mother lost her apartment. For a while, she was homeless. She moved back to Washington Heights and stayed with a friend, and then she started living with my stepfather's brother in a basement. That wasn't such a good situation. I was so into drugs that I wasn't able to help her. My older brother Raymond helped her out a lot. Finally, around 1976, my mother got her own place in Washington Heights. My younger sister and brother lived with her.

I stayed in the Bronx and began living with my friend Sweet and his girlfriend Penny. Sweet had a few girlfriends. Sweet was a handsome man, and the girls really liked him. He was sweet in a lot of ways! One night after coming back from a party, Sweet and Penny had a big argument, and she stabbed him. When I came back from taking Sweet to the hospital, Penny's mother met me. "I have bad news for you, Arthur," she said. "I just got a call, and I'm sorry to tell you this, but your mother died tonight." My heart dropped. I could not believe what I was hearing.

Right away I went to Washington Heights. Sweet came with me even though he'd just been stabbed and was all stitched up. When we arrived at my mother's house, the police were around, and so was my family. I started asking, "Where's my mother?" Nobody would say. I went upstairs. My mother wasn't there. "Where is my mother? Where is she at?" Finally, they said, "She's in the backyard."

"How did she get into the backyard?"

"She jumped out the window."

I looked out the window, and I saw my mother in a pile of garbage. I said to the cops, "Why don't you go get her? Why is she sitting in a pile of garbage?"

They said we had to wait for the medical examiner before we could go to her, but I refused to wait. My older brother, Raymond, said, "Arthur, Arthur, please." But I wouldn't stop. I had to go outside and see my mother. I had to make sure. Finally, the police said, "Let him go, let him go," because they saw I was getting ready to flip out.

When I found my way to the backyard, my mother was just lying there. I grabbed her by her head. All I could see was blood. The skin was scraped off her face. I don't know how long I was back there. I was just holding her and crying and rocking my mother. She was forty-one years old.

I wasn't right for a long time after that. I was filled with guilt, and I was even angrier than before. I kept thinking about my little sister, Angie. She was there, and she had watched it happen. And I couldn't get the image of my mother out of my head.

For a lot of years, the only way I could stop seeing her was when I was high. Heroin and other drugs were like my painkillers, so I plunged more into them and spent a lot of time out on the street. My twenties and thirties are a blur to me.

I know I was in and out of trouble. I went to Rikers Island a few times for some petty burglaries. After I came home, I lived from place to place. I met Betty S—— in 1978. We were both on drugs, and she wound up getting pregnant. We had a son named Gary S——. I saw him on and off until he was three years old, and then I didn't see him for a long time because of my addiction.

By the 1980s, I had gotten into crack, and it was worse than heroin. The pull of crack made men and women do things that degraded them. Crack took away what little self-respect and dignity I had left. I would walk around for days with the same clothes on. I did not want to be around family looking like I did. My friends didn't want me around. I was at such a low point in my life that I said to myself, "I'm just going to go down to Thirty-Fourth Street and die with the rest of the bums."

Back then, you could take your cardboard box down to the bottom level of Penn Station early in the morning, from about two o'clock on. You'd see a lot of homeless people down there. We would sleep there, or we would find us a corner somewhere. And early, at about five or six o'clock, the police would come through and make you disperse because the businesses were starting to open.

At some point, I wound up leaving Penn Station. In the spring and summer, I slept in the parks quite a bit. There's a park on West Twenty-Ninth Street called Cardboard City, and at night it was nothing but cardboard in there. That was where a lot of homeless people slept. In the winter, they made little houses that were insulated with plastic, and believe it or not, those things were warm.

When it got cold, I stayed in the shelter system. In the late 1980s and early '90s, the shelter was insanity. That's the only way I can describe it, because you had all kinds of men lumped in there together. You had men with mental illness, you had men with drug problems, you had elderly men who were getting robbed. I stayed in Franklin Men's Shelter, which had about nine hundred men, and in Fort Washington Men's Shelter, which had a thousand. There were drugs everywhere. You didn't have to leave the shelter to get them. They were selling drugs right there, and the security guards were loan sharks. Fort Washington Men's Shelter was probably the worst in the city. They called it the House of Pain. Some men died of overdoses in the bathroom. There were a few stabbings. And they had one thousand men sleeping on the same drill floor—with no walls! Yes, one thousand men. And let me tell you, it was crazy. The agency had no control over the place. I was in and out of shelters for five or so years.

Throughout this period, my dad would often come looking for me. Always did. After he remarried, my father brought his wife with him. I loved his wife. We're still close today. "Your father accepted me and my kids," she once told me. "And even though y'all was grown, he loved y'all so much, I had to accept his kids. And that's what I did." My father dragged her all around with him when he went into the shelters to see if I was there. Or he would ask some people in the neighborhoods where I used to hang out, "Have you seen Arthur?" He dragged his wife into the prisons where my younger brother was serving time. He would look for his sons. That was the character of my father. He never made me feel like I wasn't his son. It's probably why later I looked so hard for my own son.

Sometimes I would let my father find me, and sometimes I wouldn't, because I was in such bad shape I didn't want him to see me. When I let him find me, he would take me over to his house in New Jersey for the weekend, and I would go down into the basement for two days. I was so tired I would come up just to eat and then go back down and sleep. That's how tired I was.

I have to say this. One day, when my father picked me up to take me to his house, he said, "You know, Arthur, I'm proud of you."

I got angry. "Dad, what do you mean you're proud of me? Look at me—I'm a drug addict. I'm dirty. What do you mean you're proud of me? What do you have to be proud of?"

My father said, "Son, I'm proud that you're my son. I'm not always proud of the things you do, but I'm proud that you're my son." God. I never forgot that.

Things really started to change for me one day when I went to see my father at his job to get some money to get high. I went with a scheme. But my father said, "Arthur, I have something to tell you. You're going to be a grandfather."

That knocked me off my feet. He was talking about Tara, my oldest daughter. I thought, "Oh, my God!"

I don't know, but it just did something to me. I took the money from my father for drugs, but I was changed a little bit. I wanted to get my life together. At that point, I was saying to myself, "I'm going to be a grandfather. I'm thirty-nine years old, I'm about to be a grandfather, I don't know where my son is, I don't know who my daughter is. Something has to give. I'm about to be a grandfather. It's time for a change."

This time, when I went back to Fort Washington Men's Shelter, I did something different. There were two nuns, Sister Dorothy and Sister Teresa, who came to the shelter every Tuesday evening. Sister Teresa was very short, with gray hair. We thought she was crazy at first. Here was this little white lady in a shelter with a thousand men. We would look and say, "What's wrong with her?" Both she and Sister Dorothy would try to get us to go into these groups called Life Experience and Faith Sharing Associates (LEFSA) where we could talk about our experiences. Usually I would avoid the sisters when they came.

But that Tuesday, when Sister Teresa said, "Would you like to join us for our Life Experience and Faith Sharing meeting?" I said, "Yes, I'm going to join." When she asked for my name, I said it was James. I changed my name that day. I didn't want to be Arthur anymore.

Right away I liked LEFSA. The meeting felt equal. Sister Dorothy and Sister Teresa didn't call themselves leaders. This was *our* group. Everybody who wanted to could share. I found it fascinating that people in the shelter I never heard talk before—people who I thought couldn't even talk—were sharing in this group. I liked it that everybody was heard— that made us feel like we were important. If Sister Dorothy and Sister Teresa had preached at us, it would have turned me off. We were there because we needed help. We needed companionship. I met Ernesto and Jesse in that group, and we've become lifelong friends.

From my early years, I've always felt a closeness to God. Even during my times of homelessness, even during the times of the abuse, I would talk to God, and pray, and ask God to help me, to help my mother, to help us. When I look back today, I believe that I was led to LEFSA. I believe that a force much greater than myself led me there. Pretty soon I started working part-time for LEFSA, and by 1995 I was working there full-time. Twenty-one years later, I'm still here. Now I'm the Operations Manager.

From the start, Sister Teresa took a special interest in me. I think our souls clicked. One day she said, "There's a life skills empowerment program, and I would like to recommend you for it—you and your friend Ernesto. It would be perfect for you, James. It's a three-month program where you can grow and set some goals for your life." I was ready to get my life together ever since that epiphany when I heard I was going to be a grandfather. There was only one problem. I only had one month clean, and you had to have three months clean of drugs to be in the program.

But George Horton from the program said, "James, I'll tell you what. We'll give you a chance. We're going to let you in, but you're going to have to go to an outpatient drug program. If you do that outpatient drug program, we'll let you stay here."

So my friend Ernesto and I said, "Let's just do it." Now all of a sudden, we were getting this wide range of different supports. I had LEFSA, I had an outpatient drug program, I had Narcotics Anonymous, and I had the life skills empowerment program, which was a fabulous program for me. Imagine you have an old car, and it has a hard time cranking up, so you have to give it a boost. Then all of a sudden it cranks up. That's what the program did for me. It got me going again.

I met people in the life skills empowerment program that I'm still friends with today. And I got to share my story in the group in a way that I never did before. I could feel myself being put back together a little bit. I could feel the bones coming together and the sinews coming together. The program was really a liberating experience for me. All this darkness that I had inside me became light. And that's where God is—in the light.

My mentor Jerry and I went over my goals, which were to stay clean, get an apartment, and find my son. The outpatient program and Narcotics Anonymous meetings helped me stay clean. Sister Teresa helped me get an apartment through supportive housing. It was unbelievable when I moved into an SRO studio in 1994, because I had never had anything in my name. Now I had my own keys, my own bathroom, a nice bed, and a TV. Jerry gave me a briefcase and a radio. "The only thing I don't like about the SRO," I told him, "is that you have to sign in at the door."

"Well, James," Jerry said, "that's fine. It's like a doorman. I have a door-man." He made me feel good, like, "Hey, I have to go through the same thing." I could not have accomplished these goals in a focused way without the help of the life skills empowerment program.

My final goal was to find my son. I had already seen my daughter, Tara. After my grandson was born, I went to Harlem Hospital and thanked God for his life, because his life had had such a profound effect on my life. I blessed my grandson, and I told Tara, "I know I wasn't there for you, daughter, but I'm here to ask you to forgive me." Tara said, "You weren't there for me, but you can be there for your grandkids." Yeah, my daughter taught me forgiveness. She really taught me that.

But I still couldn't find my son. One day, in 1996, Sister Teresa visited me, and I introduced her to a neighbor whose last name I didn't know. My neighbor said, "I'm Dorothy S——" I stared at her. "I have a son whose name is Gary S——." Dorothy said, "That's my nephew!"

It turned out my son was living in the Bronx with his aunt. His mother had died of a drug overdose. Then he moved in with his grandmother, and she died. Then he moved in with an aunt. Dorothy gave me the phone number.

I was so nervous that I was shaking, because now God was about to give me what I'd been looking for all these years. I was about to accomplish this goal. But would my son accept me? Would he reject me? Would I be able to handle it? Later, when I was alone, I prayed. Then I dialed the phone number and talked to my son's aunt.

The next day, I went to the Bronx, where my son lived. My son's aunt came to the door of the apartment building and told me, "Your son just got out of jail. He got into trouble for robbing somebody. Look, if you're going be in his life, you have to be in his life. Don't come in if you're just going to—"

I interrupted her. "I'm ready. I'm ready to meet my son. I need to see my son. I have three years clean, and I have a steady job."

"Let's go, then," she said. "Your son needs you." We went upstairs, she opened her apartment door, and there was my sixteen-year-old son. "Gary," said my son's aunt, "I want you to meet your father." My son jumped up and looked at me. "Where you been, man? Where you been?"

We went for a walk, and I decided to trust in the truth. I told him everything. "It's not that I didn't love you, but I didn't love myself," I said. "I was caught up in drugs. I'm sorry that I wasn't there for you. I'm sorry that when your mother died I wasn't there. I'm sorry that when your grandmother died I wasn't there. I'm sorry that I wasn't there to teach you about life and how to be a man. I'm sorry, but if you give me a chance, I'll make up as much as I can to you."

After that day, I had to build up my son's trust. I made sure to call him every now and then just to say hi. I didn't barge in and try to be daddy to him, but I did try to make friends with him and let him know that I was there for him. Over time, I got him involved with LEFSA, and we went on a couple of retreats together. We developed a relationship. One thing I want to stress is the importance of fathers being in their sons' lives. My son never went back to jail again.

One day, not long after I found my son, I came home from church and was thinking about my son and my daughter, my apartment and my job, and I started crying. I couldn't stop. I've never cried like that before. I just cried and cried. But it wasn't a sad crying. It was a kind of cleansing. I thought about what was happening in my life and all that I had been through and how God showed up for me. I felt safe. I felt that my life was meaningful, like I had purpose.

I have so many friends who aren't here: Sweet, Panda Bear, Vance, Lenro, Ronald—I could go on and on. Sweet contracted AIDS in the 1980s. We watched him deteriorate into bones. Ronald died of AIDS, too. Vance died of a drug overdose, Panda Bear the same thing. I had two more friends who died in jail, friends I knew from when I was a little boy. That's how life was then.

I shared some of their same needles. I was in just as many fights. I could have been killed. "Why me?" I would say to myself. "God, I know you loved them just as much as you love me. Why am I still here and they're not?" I thought about that for years, and it bothered me so much.

Then one day, I was reading John, chapter 21, right around the time of the crucifixion. Peter sees the man who betrayed Jesus and asks Jesus, "Lord, what about this man?" Jesus says, "What is that to you? You follow me!"[2] I started thinking the same thing about my friends. I could hear God saying to me, "Don't worry about them. That's my business. You just follow me." And I accepted that. It's not for me to understand everything. God says, "You just follow me." So that's what I'm doing.

Three years into my recovery, I started seeing this nice young lady named Phyllis, who also graduated from the life skills empowerment program and from Reality House, the drug treatment program I attended. Phyllis had three kids: Java was four, Ebony was sixteen, and Ladue was eighteen or nineteen. In 1999, when Phyllis and I moved in together, her sons became my sons, and her daughter became my daughter—not legally, but they're my kids. Life was good until Phyllis had some health issues.

She wound up passing in 2004. It was devastating to all of us. We came together in our grief and held on to one another for support.

Karen, one of my old girlfriends from the 1980s, had lost her husband a year before. When she heard that Phyllis had died, she came to support me, and after the funeral, Karen and I stayed in contact. She helped me with my grief because she had just gone through it herself. We wound up seeing each other and got back together. Eventually we fell in love and were married on October 20, 2007.

One of my children with Phyllis didn't take this well and refused to come to the wedding. So that was hard. We had to work through all that, but we did. Sometimes we give up too easily on each other.

We're a happy family now. All my kids call each other brothers and sisters.

I have twelve grandkids, and they all know and visit each other. My granddaughter Derrika works with me at LEFSA. After Derrika's first day, the team member she was working with told me, "James, she was fantastic, and she was looking just like you." I remember once when Derrika was a little girl, she had a balloon in her hand, and all of a sudden, she let it go. I said "Derrika, why did you let the balloon go?" And she said, "Because I wanted to give God a gift." Blew my head, this little girl. From that point on, I knew that God had a special purpose in her life.

LEFSA goes into the shelters and the streets. We recommend people to outreach programs like the life skills empowerment program, and we facilitate groups and create a safe space where people feel comfortable. When people talk about their issues—could be loneliness, hopelessness, or despair—we say, "How can your faith help? What is God saying about your situation?" We don't condemn people or make them feel bad. LEFSA is Christian based, but everyone is welcome. We have had Jewish people and Muslims in our group. There was once a Muslim who told me, "You know, we don't believe in Jesus as God." I knew he was looking for a debate or argument. So I said, "You're Muslim. I'm Christian. I'm not trying to change your mind or your faith, and you're not going to change mine. But don't you think we have to learn to live together on this earth and help each other? Jesus is the way for me. That doesn't have to be the way for you." He was okay after that.

In the late 1980s, I met a man named Chapman Payne in a homeless program we both attended, but I didn't see him again for a long time. When we connected again, he was Reverend Chapman. A few years ago, he said to me, "James, I've known you for a lot of years. You're already a minister. I've been to some of your events. The people reverence you. They love you. You really need to think about becoming a minister, because in reality that's what you are. You just don't have the papers. You need that certificate, because that's what's going to open more doors for you where you can do greater work for God."

I thought about what Reverend Chapman said for a year. I remembered my mother's words: "Whatever you do, son, you do a good job at it." My wife and I prayed on it. And God spoke to me, and I saw his hand in my life. I knew that God had something more for me to do.

I was ordained on June 29, 2013. That day was amazing. My family came from all over. My kids, my friends, the Sisters of Charity, and the LEFSA team were all there. Reverend Chapman put a shawl over my head and anointed it with oil, and then he laid hands on me and prayed for me. Some of my family and friends came down and laid their hands on me and prayed. God took me out of a pit and put me on the pulpit.

When I was homeless, a few people in my own family said, "He'll never make it. He won't. He'll never be anything." People who had no idea what I'd been through judged me. I believe my struggles have helped me to help others, and I know that being able to talk to different people and to hear their experiences has helped me.

For example, back when I was in the shelter, everybody made fun of one man who would talk to himself. People treated him bad. But I would ask him, "Hey, how're you doing?" I'd give him some clean socks. After I moved out of the shelter and came back to visit with LEFSA, he was still there, sitting by himself in the corner. I went over and asked him how he was.

He looked clear at me and talked for the first time. "You are always nice. You have always been nice to me." He told me he was from a Central American country—I think it was Panama. Something happened there, he said. "I watched my family get killed. My wife got killed right in front of me. My kids got killed. I've never been the same since. I've lost it." When I saw the tears come out of his eyes, the tears came out of my eyes. I didn't know what to say to this man, but my presence, my caring, my solidarity with him in that moment taught me something.

You never know what people have gone through in their life to bring them down. That stays with me. I don't know what people have been through. But I'm glad God put me in a position where people trust me and can tell me their pain. It's important that I treat people with dignity and respect. That's holiness for me. How can we say we love each other if we don't know each other's pain?

I cannot walk past any person, especially a homeless person who may be laid out on the street, without acknowledging him or her as a child of

God. I can't do it. I try to love every person I come in contact with, because love was so freely given to me. I know there are a lot of people like me that are still out there. People are grieving. They've lost their homes, they've lost their families, they've lost their children, they've lost their dignity, they've lost some of their self-respect. I want them to know that it doesn't matter how far you've gone—God can bring you back. And most of the time, God works through people, through a loving and healing community.

Reflection
Rabbi Jeremy Kalmanofsky

Jeremy Kalmanofsky is the rabbi at Ansche Chesed Synagogue in Manhattan. In 2008, he collaborated with the Interfaith Assembly on Homelessness and Housing to help found the Panim el Panim life skills empowerment program, which he and his congregation continue to help support. In his reflection, Rabbi Kalmanofsky describes why he chose the name "Panim el Panim" for the program.

Americans use several metaphors to portray our diverse society. Perhaps we are a "melting pot," which boils away immigrants' differences and makes them Americans. Perhaps we are a "patchwork quilt," as Jesse Jackson used to say, sewing citizens together while leaving each piece distinct. We may be a "gorgeous mosaic," as former New York mayor David Dinkins said, a vast work of art composed of tiny pieces of beautiful stones laid side by side. Each of those metaphors conveys something powerful but also leaves me unsatisfied.

The life skills empowerment program that our synagogue community at Ansche Chesed is involved with uses a different vocabulary. Called *Panim el Panim*, which means "face to face" in Hebrew, our program points toward a social fabric of encounter and recognition between strangers who overcome vast differences to face each other. The work of its participants, mentors, and leaders regularly makes me reflect on our enormous society, on what isolates us, and on what can connect us as Americans and as New Yorkers.

I first learned about the life skills empowerment program in 2003, when I attended the Interfaith Assembly on Homelessness and Housing's annual meeting at St. Paul's Chapel, beside the World Trade Center wreckage. That night I heard Dennis Barton and others tell stories of their own personal wreckage and rebuilding. They told some of the very stories you're reading in this book and others like them. They talked about the great suffering and misfortune that brought them to homelessness, how they found the words to convey their experiences, and how they found the strength to make new life choices.

A couple of years later, Marc Greenberg suggested we sponsor a version of the life skills empowerment program at Ansche Chesed. For that first year, we hosted the group in our synagogue, but our facility was ill-suited for the project. Since then, *Panim el Panim* has taken place at other locations, but our community has remained involved, with synagogue members serving as mentors, teaching some of the sessions, and feeding the participants. Especially in the earliest years, we regularly contributed a meaningful portion of the program's budget.

When we began developing the program and adapting elements, Marc urged me to select a name that would fit the first such program to be held in a synagogue. I turned to the Bible story of the reunion between Jacob and Esau (Genesis 32–33), twin brothers alienated by their different dispositions and experiences, and especially by the theft, trickery, and threats of violence they perpetrate on each other.

On the night before their meeting, Jacob fears his physically more powerful brother will kill him. He spends the night all alone on a river bank, where he is forced to wrestle a mysterious figure, part angel, perhaps part human. Very likely, the figure represents Jacob himself as he wrestles with his own self-doubt, regret, guilt, and fear. When Jacob fights this being to a draw, the angel gives Jacob the new name Israel and blesses him, saying, "You have striven with beings divine and human, and have prevailed." Jacob proclaims the site a holy place, "For I have seen a divine being face to face [*panim el panim*], yet my life has been preserved."

The next morning, Jacob limps toward his brother, but instead of warring, they tearfully embrace. "To see your face," Jacob tells Esau, "is like seeing the face of God."[1]

By drawing on the Bible's figure of a "face to face" encounter with God as well as with another person, I wanted to express that our life skills empowerment classes would be about developing relationships between people who might have very different experiences of life, who might be alienated from each other, who might even fear each other, yet who recognize that the path of their own growth requires them to look each other in the eye.

Over the course of several years of observing the classes, talking with those serving as mentors, and especially attending the graduations from the program, I have learned how crucial it is that the participants come to tell their personal stories. For the speakers to bring such painful stories to the surface is an act of real emotional and spiritual bravery.

Even very conventionally successful people have pieces of their past they won't admit to themselves or others. How much more profound is it for people deeply scarred by life to give words to the abuse they have suffered and the pain they have caused others? It leaves you speechless when someone stands before a room and testifies with deep honesty to drug addictions that led them to abandon children, to mental illnesses that drove them out of stable families, or to grinding poverty from which they never had much of a chance to escape. I recall a woman who described that she had a "happy childhood. Until I was six. Then my mother died." It makes you ask yourself: How long did my childhood last?

The name of our program reflects that the participants not only develop the strength to reveal their own *panim*, their own private face, but that when they do so, they will meet another face in response. Not only do they tell their own stories, but another person will listen, will care, will respond. Our common English word *responsibility* calls to mind every person's capacity, upon seeing suffering, to *respond*.

That's one reason I encourage people in our synagogue community to serve as mentors and attend the speakers' nights and have invited some of the graduates to speak at our synagogue. It helps our members cultivate their own ability to respond to another face.

Yes, we all must do acts of service for the poor. One of Judaism's central obligations is to give *tzedakah,* or charity. But in truth, you can give money, food, or clothing anonymously. In fact, Jewish tradition praises anonymous giving, as it safeguards the dignity of the recipient.

But if you give anonymously, you never have a *panim el panim* encounter. You don't hear another person's story and cannot respond to it from your own life experiences, across wide gaps in our backgrounds. How incalculably far is the distance between someone who grew up as drug addict in the South Bronx and one who grew up in Jewish day schools in Westchester? Yet across that distance, we still may face each other. In this gorgeous mosaic of a city, in certain ways it is not sufficient that we be tiles laid side by side. We have to touch.

Not every encounter goes perfectly. Our mentors have complained to me that some participants are too mentally ill or too early in their journey forward to really benefit from the program. But other times, mentors and participants develop ongoing and true friendships that last beyond the formal sessions.

As a side point, I don't mind that the life skills empowerment program exposes members of my Jewish community to the generosity and good works of Christian communities, such as New York Catholic Charities and All Angels' Church. Through centuries of being a persecuted minority, we have grown very good at taking care of our own people, building a strong ethic of group loyalty and responsibility within the walls of Jewish community and affirming, in the Talmud's words, that "every Jew is responsible for each other." We are less practiced at taking care of those very different from ourselves. I am glad that in the program we work alongside Christian communities, sharing love and care to many lost folks, including immigrants without strong communal connections, regardless of their faith and ethnicity. We Jews can learn a lot from Catholic Charities.

Often people can scarcely imagine the lives that others live. Those of us who live in greater comfort and security may have only the dimmest awareness of the experiences of poverty, addiction, illness, debt, and bad luck that drive people into homelessness and the humiliation and degradation of living there. We also have very limited awareness of the vast spiritual resources of homeless people who shift directions on their path and, with the help of programs like the life skills empowerment program, become more productive and stable. They even come to serve others making that same arduous journey.

By turning "face to face," those who volunteer and contribute to the program grow more aware of what Martin Luther King Jr. wrote from a Birmingham Jail: "We are caught in an inescapable network of mutuality, tied in a single garment of destiny."

Life Story
Black (Pseudonym)

Black was born in the summer of 1953 in Harlem, New York. He graduated from the Life-Skills Training and Empowerment Program (L-STEP), the life skills empowerment program at St. Francis Xavier Church, in the late 1990s.

Let's just call me Black. That was one of my names when I was on the street. They called me Black, they called me Slim, they called me Flaco. I didn't care what they called me as long as they gave me some drugs. My parents didn't raise me to end up like that. They were kind hearted and very loving. When we were supposed to get a beating, we got a beating, and I don't remember getting hugs. But my parents went out and worked hard for us. I remember my mother saying, "If you can't say nothing nice about nobody, don't say nothing."

My parents met in Charleston, South Carolina. They came to New York City to make a better life for us. I guess everybody heard that New York City is paved with gold, and if you can't make it here you can't make it anywhere. A lot of people from down South came too. My parents wanted a better education for their kids. In South Carolina, my father had to walk three miles to school. He never got past the sixth grade. In New York, my father worked for Con Edison for thirty-five years. He went out and brought home the bacon. My mother stayed home and cooked the food. They did the best they could with what they had. We ate every day. We never starved. We never had to sleep in the streets. After they raised us, my parents planned to go back to the South and retire. They built a house down there and everything. I miss my parents. I haven't talked about them in so long.

Park Avenue Market in East Harlem, 1960s
News Voice International. Photo courtesy of the New York Public Library Digital
Collection, Schomburg Center for Research in Black Culture, Photographs and
Prints Division

There were ten of us kids. I was number seven, the second boy, so I was known as the baby brother. We had a big house in Harlem—they called it a railroad apartment, because the rooms lined up like train cars. My sisters had one bedroom, and my brother and I had the other. Sometimes I slept with my sisters, and I remember wetting their bed. Oh my God, they'd have a fit. A lot of times we didn't have heat, so we would move this kerosene heater from room to room. You could also beat the heater like a drum, and then my sisters danced. My brother and I didn't have any toy guns, so we would use the hammer from the kitchen. Bang! Or my mom would give us money and we'd run and go get candy. Yeah—the good old days. We argued and fought like sisters and brothers do. But my older sister, man, if anybody in the neighborhood messed with me, she would fight them—my brother, too.

On Easter Sunday, we all got fly—we got new suits, new dresses, new everything—and the whole family went to church. We also went to an after-school program at the church, and sometimes a lady there would buy us one-hundred dollars' worth of food because she knew my father was struggling. Even though he had a good job, there were ten of us, and he could always use the help. Every year around the Fourth of July, we'd pack up the station wagon and drive down to Charleston, South Carolina, for vacation for two weeks. We stayed in the house my parents were building for their later years.

When I was eleven, we moved out of that cold place in Harlem and up to the Bronx, where a lot more white people lived. My father's cousin was a super in the Hunts Point area, and he got us an apartment on the fifth floor. I remember walking up and down those stairs sometimes ten, twenty times a day because my mother would send me to the store. If you brought back the wrong thing, you were going back to the store to get the right one.

I started sixth grade at P.S. 48. That's when everyone let me know I was black. I was real dark skinned, and they called me Black Sambo, Black this, and Black that. Kids can be so cruel. They probably didn't know what they were doing, but they did it anyway. You see, in Harlem, most people were black. So I didn't get discouraged down there like I did in the Bronx. I remember one of the counselors at the after-school program trying to lift my self-esteem. "You're black. So what? They're trying to make you feel bad. Don't worry about it." That helped me a lot, but still, light skin was in fashion back then. I'll tell you, at one time I wanted to be white. Yes, I did.

Junior high school was even worse, because the light-skinned black people thought they were white. But I made a friend who was light skinned with red hair. They used to call him Red. I started hanging out with him, so I was accepted now. At that time, I was a people pleaser. Whatever you would do, or you wanted me to do, I probably would do.

Right before I started high school, the reefer came in. Sometimes my little gang got together and smoked. Since there was always like ten of us on one joint, I never really felt anything. One summer night, my cousin from the old block in Harlem came up to the Bronx. "Do you smoke reefer?" he asked me. "Yeah," I said, "I do that all the time." So we went down the hill to the park and smoked a couple of joints. Oh my God. On my way back home, I felt like I was floating. That night was my sister's eighteenth birthday, and she was having a party on the first floor. You could hear the music coming from the window. She and her boyfriend were outside singing and trying to harmonize. As soon as my sister saw me, she said, "Black, what is wrong with you? Look at your eyes!" All night I just sat there and listened while they partied. I felt so scared and strange. "Oh boy," I told myself. "I ain't gonna do that thing no more." But soon, I wanted to do that thing again and again, as often as I could.

The rest of my life was going okay. I got into this wonderful work-study program at DeWitt Clinton High School—you know, where you work a week and go to school a week. I was placed at the Equitable Life Insurance Company on Fiftieth Street and Sixth Avenue. I think I worked as a mail clerk, and I was learning about computers. Oh, I loved that job. I was doing so well, and the people were so nice.

Then, one day, my mother had an operation. The cold must have gotten in her or something, because she got pneumonia and she passed. For years, I felt like my mother had abandoned us. I was really mad at God for taking her away. It took a long time until I got better with that. Throughout my mother's whole funeral, my father didn't cry. In the old days, they believed if a man cried he wasn't a man. But later, when I walked into my father's bedroom, he was crying. Like I said, my parents had built a retirement house in South Carolina. They never made it. Thirty years later, their house is still standing, but it needs a lot of work. I can't even stay in it when I go down South to visit family. My mother was about forty-seven when she died. I was sixteen or seventeen. But I might have the times a little mixed up.

About a year later, I was going home from high school, and this Spanish kid I hung out with said, "Come on, come on, let's go smoke a joint or something! You got some money?"

"Nah, I ain't got no money," I said.

"Well come on, we gonna rob somebody today."

So me, being a people pleaser, I went with him when he walked up to this white guy. "Give me your money!" the kid yelled, and the white guy just gave it to him. Now mind you, I didn't do the robbing, but I was with the kid who did. Okay. So we smoked some joints, went home, went to sleep. I went to school the next morning, and the teacher told me, "The dean wants you downstairs. Go down there right away." As soon as I saw the dean, he said, "You robbed somebody last night." I said, "Wait a minute, I went home last night. I didn't rob nobody. What are you talking about?" Then the door opened, and there was the Spanish kid, crying. His mother was in the room. "Yeah, yeah," the kid said. "That's who. He was with me, and we robbed this guy." The dean turned to me. "You're out of here! Right now." So I had to leave DeWitt Clinton High School and leave the Equitable Life Insurance job I loved so much.

They transferred me to Morris High School. It had all the people who didn't want to do anything. In class, they'd jump over chairs. My older sister said, "You gotta go there. Just go and finish up high school." But every day the kids would be cursing out the teachers, acting like monkeys in the class. We didn't do that in DeWitt Clinton. We sat there, we learned. I couldn't stand it at Morris High School. So I talked to my father. "Yo, can you sign me out of school? I'd rather work."

Dropping out of high school was a big mistake. I look back and see it now. At first, I had delivery boy jobs, and I did security for different buildings. I would go to work, come home, and get high on marijuana. Pretty soon I went from sniffing to shooting to mainlining drugs—mostly heroin. After a while, I had to have both cocaine and heroin. By age twenty-three, twenty-four, twenty-five, I was copping to support my habit. Let's say there was a dealer on Seneca Avenue and Faile Street, and I met this buyer on Garrison Avenue. I'd take his money and go get the drugs for him. All the buyer had to do was promise me, "I'm gonna give you some of this." Sometimes I got arrested. That's how I started to do my three or four days in jail.

Another time, some guys tried to rob me in my building, and they beat me up real bad. By then, lots of my family had moved nearby, and we more or less owned the block. My cousin E—— came and told my father. "You know what that beating he got was all about? Those damn drugs!" My father said, "E——, what can I do?" One day my father just grabbed my younger sisters and moved to Rochdale Village out in Queens. He left the apartment with me and my older sister and brother. How long did that last? Not long, because none of us knew how to pay rent, and we got evicted. But we could go to our other sisters' apartments anytime. We'd hop. I'd skip around. My name wasn't on any lease, but I never slept in the street. I never slept on the train.

I got into a government methadone program after a guy told me, "You'll get high for free there." So I ended up addicted to methadone too. In 1994, my father died, and after he went, oh my God. I went wild. I didn't care about anything. I was doing the methadone, I was doing the dope, I was doing the coke, I was doing the pills, I was doing the liquor. Sometimes the cops pretended to be buyers and gave you marked bills to buy drugs. Then they'd search the dealer for the money and arrest both of you. That's how I ended up doing eight months in Rikers Island. I remember waking up in jail and thinking how my father was flipping over in his grave. I was in my forties by then.

After I got out of Rikers, it wasn't long before I was right back in there. What happened was I got arrested in the Bronx so much—I think maybe seven times—I had this bright idea. Since the cops don't know me in Manhattan, why don't I go to Harlem? I found this dealer down there on 110th Street. All I had to do was feed him customers, and he gave me a bag or two at the end of the day. It was working fine until one night, a guy walked up to me like he was in withdrawal. "I'm sick, brother. I'm sick. Where's the drugs at?" Now mind you, I had already finished for that day. I had gotten my own bag, and I was ready to go home. But this guy was sick, and me, I couldn't stand to see that. I knew how bad it felt. So I pointed over to my dealer—that's what they call "steering." "Right over there," I said. "Go over there and ask him."

I started walking down Lexington Avenue toward the subway station. All of a sudden, I heard this sound like horses. I didn't even need to turn around. I knew who it was. The cops ran up to the back of me and knocked me down. "You going to jail." For three days, I was in the bullpen. When I finally got in front of the prosecutor, I thought he was going to say, "You do a week, and you'll be out." Instead the guy looked at me. "Four and a half to nine years."

I was shocked. Four and a half to nine years just for steering! "Can I just—?"

The guy said, "You ain't taking no short cut. Either you sign this plea, or we go to court."

So I said, "Okay, we're going to court then." Meanwhile, I had to go back to Rikers Island.

When I got there, they asked if I was in the government methadone program. I said yes, even though I had gotten kicked out of the program for not following directions. But I was getting methadone on the street, and I wanted it in jail so I wouldn't get sick from withdrawal. The unit at Rikers opened at eight o'clock in the morning. I sat there all night, waiting, figuring I'd get at least one dose of methadone. But when morning came and the Rikers doctor called the government program, he found out I was lying. "You ain't getting nothing," he said. So I was hungry now, and I went to have lunch. But my stomach was all messed up, and I threw up over everybody. "Yo," the inmates said. "Leave him alone. He is sick. Leave him."

After that, the Rikers hospital said they found a little spot on my lung. They thought I had TB. So they put me away from most of the population for about three months. That whole time, I was kicking the methadone and everything else. I was put alone in a little glass room called the bubble. Outside, the workers walked back and forth, ignoring me. For twenty-three hours a day, I stared at the ceiling. They put the lights off at 10:00 p.m., and they came on at 6:00 a.m. I couldn't sleep because I was in withdrawal. After about a week, they let us out to take a walk. Some other guys were going through the same withdrawal. "You have to get exercise! Get yourself real tired," they told me. So I would exercise—pushups, pull-ups, everything. And then I could sleep for about twenty to thirty minutes at a time.

After detox, I had a regular cell and got some inmate jobs. I used to work in the visitors' room. I'm telling you, there were more drugs in there than out on the street. Once or twice I got high in jail. I even crushed and sniffed the pill a doctor gave me for a cold. It burned my nose like drugs, but I wasn't getting high. I sat there crying in my cell, thinking life was over. That's when I knew I had to do better. The next time my boys visited me in jail, I said, "Yo, if you like me or love me, don't bring me no more drugs."

I wouldn't wish for anybody to go to jail, because that's like wishing him death. You can wake up one morning and somebody is slashing you. It can happen very easily. Nobody would give a hell about it. You don't know what it's like, sitting behind bars, wondering what was going on in the world. I had time to think, time for my head to clear up. I thought about my parents a lot. They didn't raise me to go to Rikers Island. They did not raise me for that. At Rikers Island, I hit rock bottom. There wasn't nowhere to go but up.

I got a job mopping the hallway. It was about a mile and a quarter long. I must have mopped every inch of that place. I mopped every corner and crevice. For that I made ninety-six cents a day. "When I get out of here, I'm gonna get a real job," I said.

One of my sisters brought me a Bible. I didn't know what it meant, but I read the whole thing. I started going to church every Sunday. Then I felt I could make it through another day. My sister said, "God will help you," and I decided I was going to help him along. So when they asked if I wanted to be saved, I said, "I'm going to try that." I went up there to the altar, and they dipped my head back in the water and brought me up again.

But I need to tell you I also turned Muslim in jail. And that's because the gangs didn't jump you if you were Muslim. They knew if they messed with one, they had to mess with all. The Muslims prayed on Fridays, so I could still go to church on Sunday. And I thought they were kissing the ground when they prayed, so I did it too. I started eating Muslim food. I ate so much tuna fish there in jail, oh my God!

For thirteen months, I went back and forth to court. They gave me a legal aid lawyer, a good lawyer, too. I remember telling him things like,

"If you get me out of here, I'll come clean your house." He said, "No, don't worry about it." I had a jury trial, and my family came to support me every day. Finally, the verdict came. The jury decided I was innocent! The judge said, "You're acquitted!" I jumped up, and my family was right there. When I left jail the next morning, a guard said, "Ha! You'll be back." I said, "Oh no I won't." How long ago was that? About eighteen years.

I was going to do whatever it took to keep it moving. "I'm not gonna shoot no more dope and coke," I told myself. "I'm just gonna drink some beer. That's all I'm going to do." Now, my brother used to be worse than me with the drugs. But he went to Narcotics Anonymous and he already had three years clean. It was my brother who showed me the way to my first NA meeting. The problem was I got there with alcohol on my breath. My brother put me in the corner. "You seem to be heading right back the same way you came from. Maybe you should sign up for some outpatient program." That's the first time I took a suggestion from my brother.

So I signed up for an outpatient program, and the morning I started, I bought me a beer. When I walked into the room, all the people seemed so happy. "Why the hell are they so happy?" I thought. "I ain't happy like that." Suddenly this girl sniffed the air. "Somebody's drinking in here!" I looked around, wondering who the hell she was talking about. About an hour later, I met with my program counselor. "You know, Black," he said, "you can't ever drink any more in life." And my heart went boom, boom—because what was I going to do if I couldn't drink anymore? I couldn't use drugs, and now I couldn't drink? The counselor said, "You gotta go to detox."

So he set up an appointment with St. Barnabas Hospital. But they told me I had to take methadone to get into the detox program. I was scared because of what had happened with that drug in my past. The nurse said, "How about if you take it for just this one day. If you don't want it tomorrow, then you don't have to take it." So I took the methadone that first day. The next day, the same nurse came around. "Medication, medication . . . Mr. Black, you want some?" I said, "Nope." And that was it for me. I never touched methadone or any other drugs or alcohol again in my life.

I remember H&I (Hospitals and Institutions) coming around. They're sponsored by NA, and they go into facilities like detox units. The people would be looking all clean. The ladies looked big and nice and smelled nice. The men looked good. Yet they said they used to do the same drugs I did. I decided I wanted what they had.

After detox, they put me in a holding shelter in Harlem. Pretty soon I was helping run that place. There were bums coming in, and I knew how to talk to them and be nice. I served the food. Finally, a bed opened up in Bronx Lebanon Hospital Rehab Center. I remember sitting there in rehab watching Martin Lawrence on the TV. And a man came in and cut off the TV. I said, "You know, you just cut off Martin, and I was watching it." So the guy said to me, "Man, I am here to save your life." And I realized he was an H&I representative. "Oh sure, that's okay." All I wanted was to hear that good NA message.

I met my first sponsor at Bronx Lebanon, and he said, "I will love you until you learn how to love yourself." I thought, "Oh shit, he's funny." I'm just trying to tell you how my thinking was back then. He told me to call him every day for the next thirty days. "Call you?" I thought. "I can call the women, but the men?" But I did what he said. For thirty days, I called him. And we talked about everything.

Then I was transferred to the Bronx Lebanon outpatient program, and I started living in their halfway house. It was good at first, but you can't get along with everybody. So there was this guy—let's call him Richard. I heard he was a little funny. You know what I'm saying? So listen, in the summertime, everybody stayed in the park, playing cards. In the middle of something—I don't even remember what—Richard came up to me and stuck his finger in my face. Everybody stopped, and they were looking at me. You know I had to retaliate now. So I just pushed him back a little bit. Next thing I know Richard ran upstairs to the counselor. Mind you, that counselor was gay too. When he asked what happened, I said, "That little undercover mother so-and-so was there and—." "Oh no!" said the counselor. "You're out of here!"

So check this out. They kicked me out of the halfway house and put me in the Greenpoint Men's Homeless Shelter all the way down in Brooklyn. But during the day, I was still supposed to go to the outpatient program in Bronx Lebanon. So now, for seven months, I had to go from Brooklyn to the Bronx every morning. And every time I came uptown, this guy Richard would put out his hand to shake and make up. "Oooh, I hate him," I'd say and keep walking.

It was like God was testing me, because one day I realized I couldn't be mad at Richard anymore. I realized we had both been a little crazy that day in the park. I did what I did. And I couldn't keep coming here hating somebody. That was defeating the whole purpose. So the next time Richard passed me, I put out my hand out and we shook. Today Richard is one of my best friends. I don't know if he's gay or not, and I don't have a problem either. He is really cool. Like, one day I was with him, and this guy on a bicycle was so drunk he fell off. This big wad of money rolled out of his pocket. "Oh," I said, "I'll take care of that money!"

But Richard stopped me. "No, Black, give the money back to him."

I said, "What?"

Richard replied, "'Cause if you don't give it back, you're gonna pay for it sooner or later."

I did what Richard said. I picked the guy up, put him back on the bike, and put the roll of money in his pocket. The guy rode on and fell off the bike again. Unbelievable.

Listen, let me tell you about the Greenpoint Shelter in Brooklyn. Back when I was young and had jobs, I used to work security in that place. And now I was living there. Some of the people I used to see had never even left. Lots of people were still smoking crack and doing other drugs. I asked them, "You wanna make an NA meeting with me?" You know what they said? "Oh, I'm going to go next week, don't worry. I got you." Me, I was trying to make a few NA meetings a day. The Bronx Lebanon program had an NA meeting, and there was another one in the same place at 6:00 p.m. By 10:00 p.m., I had to be back at the shelter in Brooklyn or else I lost my bed. By the end of my day, I'd be so tired, all I could do was go to the shelter, take a shower, eat, and fall down.

I decided to use Greenpoint as a stepping-stone. There was a housing unit where they took you after three months if you followed the rules—you had to leave by 6:00 a.m., be back by 10:00 p.m., and not cause any confusion. Tammy, my counselor from Bronx Lebanon, told me, "Black, you do this right. You go to housing every morning. You ask that man, 'Is there any housing yet?'" I did what she said. Every day at 5:00 a.m., I ran into the shower, ran and ate breakfast, ran to the housing man. "Anything come up yet?" He'd look at me. "No, Black, not yet." After a couple of months, the housing man got tired of me. He got me a place up in the Bronx on Webster Avenue—it was a brand-new one-room SRO, just opened up. That was all I needed. I was cool with that.

Soon after I moved into my new apartment, my counselor said, "Black, there's this life skills empowerment program downtown. And I nominated you for that. It's a spiritual program." Once she said "spiritual," I said, "I'm in there!" I loved the classes. We learned about building relationships, communication, and time management. Before the life skills empowerment program, I thought only poor people or black people had troubles like mine. Now I saw that everybody did. Other people came and helped us by telling their stories about homelessness. I told my story too. It was cleansing, because it came from the heart. I cried when I told it.

After I graduated from the program, Marc Greenberg invited me to go to the Speakers Bureau meetings. I was also a mentor for two or three life skills empowerment programs. The people I worked with knew one thing for sure. I was going to show up. If I had something to tell them, I would tell it in a loving and caring way. I wasn't perfect, because I had my stuff to deal with. But I was getting better. I got my friend Richard to join the program and also a man named Forster, who was in the Bronx Rehab Center. Forster was the type who was always locked in his room. I knew he wanted help, but he didn't want to ask for it. So I knocked on his door. "We need some more people down in the life skills empowerment program. Would you like to come?" "Oh no," Forster said, "I'm staying right here." Finally I talked him into it, and everyone loved him. Forster had some stories, oh my God. He'd tell you about the hillbillies and how he used to rob graves and take the rings off the dead people's fingers. Forster was one of the best guys I knew.

I got my job through the life skills empowerment program. Marc took our crew on a spiritual retreat, up on the tip of the Hudson River. A supervisor at a big law firm came with us. "Would you be able to help some of our people get back to work?" Marc asked her. "Yeah," she said. "Send them on down, we'll interview them." About three of us went for the interview, and I'm the only one still there. I started as a messenger, then moved to the mailroom, then moved to conference services, and I'm right now in maintenance. I handle the doors, lights, windows, and air conditioner. I paint and get supplies. I manage a lot of people, and they love me because I treat them nice. I just love it there. You know, I always missed Equitable Life, that company where I worked in high school. All I wanted to do was to get back there. The place I work now is only three blocks away. That's the closest I'm ever going to get back to Equitable Life. I've had that job working on sixteen years now.

Around the same time I started working, I met my wife in one of my NA meetings. She always asked me for cigarettes. "I'll give you a cigarette if you give me a kiss," I told her. Eight years ago, we got married. We both wore white and had a big church wedding right off Fordham Road, near Roosevelt High School. About 120 people showed up. The reception on East Tremont Avenue lasted all night. My wife is the lady that keeps me strong. We have our ups and downs, but I wouldn't leave her for the world. My wife doesn't cook much. I might get a spaghetti dinner every once in a while. Most of the time I cook on Sunday, and we have leftovers or eat out. We have a renovated house with two bedrooms. She has a son from a previous marriage. I have two sons and a daughter. I love the way we're living today.

Both my wife and my brother had gotten their bachelor's degrees. At my job, they give you stipends to go to college. I got my GED in 1999, and now my boss was pushing hard. "Black, you need to go back to school." So I went to Touro College and got my bachelor's degree in business. Believe me, it wasn't easy. There was a lot of studying, a lot of reading. I used to get migraine headaches. The last term, I wanted to finish up, so I took five classes. Oh boy. I would never do that again. But then graduation came. It took place at Lincoln Center. My son came, and my brother and my sister and my wife, and my niece on my wife's side. My sponsor came too. I loved it.

When I was younger, you could beat me up just by calling me "Black." I didn't have self-esteem. I guess that was part of the reason I gave up and wanted to do drugs all the time. Today I have more confidence, not enough for a lot of things, but I think I have gotten better. I owe a lot of my strength to my predecessors—my brother, people in NA, people in the life skills empowerment program and the Speakers Bureau. They showed me that I could shine. Now I try to show that to other people who need help. Some people get better, and some people don't. You have to have willingness and faith—something that's unseen.

I'm not going to lie. I haven't been to church in a while. But I talk to my God every day. I pray to him. I tell him, "Thank you for another day clean." I tell you, on this journey, God is powerful—so powerful. I don't see how a person can live without God these days. I'm so grateful to him and to my predecessors. And they say grateful addicts don't use.

Telling my story has been good. I didn't think I would last that long, to tell you the truth, because I get real emotional. Like I said, in the old days, they believed if men cried, they're not men. That's not true. Men do cry. There are a lot of things on my mind that are painful, but they have to be talked about. They have to be remembered so I can move into the future. I know it can only get better from here. At least that's what I'm hoping for.

Reflection
Stephanie Reid

Stephanie Reid has served as a mentor since 2014 for Riverside Coming Home, a life skills empowerment program for formerly incarcerated individuals at Riverside Church in Manhattan.

I was born in 1956 and raised in the Red Hook projects in South Brooklyn. I am the second of seven siblings. I have one sister and five brothers. We were a very close family until my parents separated and divorced. Once my father left home, he rarely came around us. We had to wait for him to bring money every Monday so we could eat.

The divorce affected my family tremendously. I noticed that we were getting more and more disconnected. My father had been strict when he was around. We had to be in bed early and keep the house clean. My mother was more lenient. Consequently, our lives changed for the worse when my father left. We started cutting classes in school and hanging out in the street. All of us had social and emotional problems. I was raped at age thirteen and had an abortion at age fourteen. By age fifteen, my sister had her first child.

My brothers really suffered the most. They still blame my father for their social problems.

The first of the siblings to go to prison was my brother Samuel. He was incarcerated from 1979 to 1981. During his stay, I visited once but never wrote to him. When my brother got out of prison, he lived wild in the streets. He would rob the drug dealers and then walk past them as if he'd done nothing. Six months later, a group of dealers decided to put the fear of God in him. My brother was beaten with bats and stabbed in his heart.

He died on the streets of Red Hook in 1981. That was devastating for the family; to this day, we are not at peace with my brother's death.

About five years ago, I discovered that my father himself had been in prison at the age of sixteen. He had vowed never to return and kept his vow. I also learned that my father's brother spent ten years in prison for impersonating a police officer. I have a nephew who spent ten years in prison and was killed on the streets about three years ago. Another one of my brothers has been in and out of prison for the past thirty years. His son, my nephew, went to prison at age eighteen. So prison has been in my family for over fifty years.

In 1997, Jesus transformed my life. I was called to become a minister. From the start, I knew part of my calling was prison ministry. As a result, I enrolled in Fordham University's graduate program in social work. My internship was at Providence House in Brooklyn, where I worked with homeless or formerly incarcerated women with children. I met women who had spent between three to thirty years in prison for murder, drugs, robbery, assault, and domestic violence. These women were smart and intelligent. They were beautiful inside and out and had potential to do better things in their lives. Most of the women had emotional, psychological, and mental challenges. Because of my own family's history, I immediately felt an affinity with them.

In September 2014, a friend of mine told me about Riverside Coming Home, the life skills empowerment program for formerly incarcerated people run by Riverside Church. When I began mentoring there, I had an emotional meltdown during a circle session. We were all sharing thoughts, and I talked about my brother who was the first sibling to go to prison. For years, I was guilt-stricken about not writing to him. When he came home from prison, my brother asked me, "Why didn't you write?" I had no valid answer. That evening in the circle session, I had an emotional release. One of the formerly incarcerated participants said he saw a change in me after that experience. I had a more humble attitude.

The participants in the program are trying to find their way in society. Just trying to stay positive is a serious struggle. Some of the people cannot read or write. Some are in their fifties and sixties and going to school for their GED. It is rewarding to tangibly help people by mentoring. Even after the program ends, I stay in touch with them. That's when the authentic relationship begins.

Being involved in this program reminds me that I am no better than anyone else. Unexpected things can happen that can land anyone in prison—a person's lifestyle, or a case of mistaken identity, or a simple fight between two people. None of us can stick our noses up and say, "Never, not me." We all have to be grateful for the little things in life.

Life Story
Dennis Barton

Dennis Barton was born on August 29, 1951, in the Bronx, New York. He graduated in 2002 from the Education Outreach Program (EOP), the original life skills empowerment program, run by New York Catholic Charities. Dennis's story includes details from a life story he published in CURA: A Literary Magazine of Art and Action, in 2012.

You know, if we had the time and paper to record the systemic injustices black people experience in this country, it would fill volumes. We've been marginalized, demonized, made to feel less than. Don't forget, we came here as slaves. When we finally won our freedom, we didn't get our freedom. My older brother Junior always said, "Boy, I want you to remember that if a 'nigger' does it, there's gonna be a law against it." So even with the gains of the civil rights movement, what happened in the years to follow? There came the stricter drug laws. Why? Because drugs were in the ghetto where black people lived, and we were more apt to get caught with drugs. What does it say about a society when somebody gets caught with powdered cocaine and gets a slap on the wrist, but somebody who gets caught with crack cocaine gets twenty-five years? Today there are more black men incarcerated than ever before. As a man and a father, I have cried some nights, wondering what my children are going through, knowing what I had to go through as a child. Even when I was on the streets, homeless, I cried for my children. I don't know where to begin talking about systemic racism and injustice. I really don't. It's just going to have to come through in my story.

So let's begin with a little family background. My mother was one of thirteen children in her family from the rural South—South Carolina. They were sharecroppers, and my mom never went past the third grade. Somewhere around the 1930s or '40s, she made her way north as part of the Great Migration. At that time, she had one child, my older brother. First my mother worked as a domestic in Washington, D.C. Then she lived in Long Island and worked in a laundry. Not having a great education, these were the types of jobs she could get—working for the white folks. In New York City, my mother settled in the South Bronx and worked in a factory for a ladies' novelty company. My mother never went back to the South, and she never sent me back to the ancestral home. I was born in 1951. In 1955, Emmett Till was murdered for allegedly whistling at a white woman. I remember my mom telling me, "Boy, if I send you down there you'll be killed."

I know my father's name was Marion. My mom said that he was from Virginia and he was in the Air Force. Sometimes, when she got mad at me she'd say, "You're just like your red-ass father." So that tells me he was a red bone, or a light-skinned black man. That's all I know. Did I resent my father? No, I did not know him to resent. Did I say, "Where my daddy at?" No, because I had my mama. By the time I came along, my brother was like seventeen, eighteen. He had already left home, and Mom could concentrate on me. I was my mama's baby.

My mom didn't need a man to provide for us. There were boyfriends, but she didn't need that. She was able to make it on her own. The only time I ever knew my mom to miss work was when she lost the tip of her index finger in a factory machine. They bandaged her up, gave her some pain medicine, and after a few days she was back on the job. If she hung out and drank with her girlfriends on the weekend, Sunday nights she would say, "I gotta take a physic—get this liquor out of me." Monday morning, hangover or not, my mother was back on that bus, rain, sleet, snow, or hail. She was going to work for hers, and she instilled that in me.

I had a roof over my head, toys to play with, clean clothes, and a TV. We were one of the few black families in the neighborhood with a washing machine, because my brother won it on a quiz show. And I ate every day. There were kids in the neighborhood that had their mother *and* their father at home, but they had to fight over food: "He ate my sammich! Why you drank all the milk?" In my apartment I'd go to the refrigerator and there was always milk; there was cereal in the cupboard. My belly was always full.

My mother had books for me, and I learned to read young. Don't forget, my mother didn't read that well—I used to have to read her mail to her—or that's what she told me so I would learn to read. My education was the most important thing to her. I'm not going to say I worked hard at school. My mother pushed so much that anytime I could get away with stuff, I did. But I was a smart kid. My school had black kids, white kids, Chinese kids, Irish kids, Italians, and Jews. Back then the South Bronx was a melting pot.

Before I turned one, I was baptized at Union Baptist Church in Harlem. When I was old enough, my mother sent me to Caldwell African Methodist Episcopal Zion Church with our neighbors. She didn't go herself. "Do what I say do, not what I do," she told me. That was the answer

Dennis in the Bronx, circa 1955–57

for a lot of things. Anyway, I liked getting dressed up and going to church and Sunday school. Plus, I knew my mother believed. In my house, there was a big family Bible that my godmother had given us and a big bust of Jesus on the dresser, like an altar. Mama taught me the Lord's Prayer. She taught me the Twenty-Third Psalm. The community we lived in, people drank and they partied, but everybody knew there was a God. There was no question about that. You knew when you did something your mama told you not to do, God was looking at you.

I listened to Mama because I had a healthy fear of her. If I did bad, I'd get a whooping with the strap. Was I always a good kid? On a scale of one to ten, I was like an eight. Some of the things I see kids get away with today, you never got away with when I was a child. You behaved. You respected your elders. You said, "Yes, sir" and "No, sir" and "Yes, ma'am" and "No, ma'am."

Mom was very protective, but she wasn't overprotective. She knew I was a man-child and that I was going to have to go out there in the world and experience it. When I turned eleven or twelve, she let me join the Boys' Club of America, down the street near Freeman Street Train Station. It cost like a quarter to join, and they gave you this real hard Boys'

Club card. The Boys' Club opened up a whole new world for me. I started hanging out, meeting new friends, kids from other blocks. Sometimes, when Mom was sleeping on the weekends, my friends and I went to the Freeman Street Station, squeezed through the bars of the elevated train, and rode the trains from end to end. I joined the Keystone Club for young teens, young men. We had jackets and everything.

Around that same time, I got a job at the Bernstein brothers' candy store. Arty was the first Jew I knew who had an afro. I loved those guys. They paid me nice, and they trusted me.

My older brother was a plumber by trade and worked as a super; he spent years working with coal-fired boilers. That, combined with his alcoholism and heavy smoking, led him to contract tuberculosis. When I was about fourteen or fifteen, he came home sick as a dog, coughing and spitting. My mother took him to Van Etten Hospital. I remember seeing my brother, his nose all packed with gauze and tubes. And I remember my mother finding out that he had passed away. Did she go in the living room and bawl and fall out? I'm sure Mama shed some tears. And I think she cried not only because her child was gone, but because she knew he was going to Potter's Field on Hart Island. We didn't have any insurance on Junior. There was no funeral.

After my brother died, we moved to 180th Street, about two miles uptown. I still went to the Boys' Club, but I was a teenager now. One night, an older group of boys rented the Boys' Club for a party. They asked my friends and me to work the soda machine for them. Because it was at the Boys' Club, my mother let me go. It was a barn dance, and the place was decorated with bales of hay. Eventually, the guys started sneaking bottles of Southern Comfort into our concession stand. That's how I had my first real drink of liquor. After the party, I got on the bus somehow, but as soon as I made it home, I had to puke in my closet. No time to make it to the bathroom.

The next day, my mother said, "You drinking, huh? I'm gonna kill you!" But she knew I was growing up and feeling my oats and stuff. I started sneaking around, going downtown to parties with my cousins. I drank on weekends and smoked a little pot. But I was not heavy into drugs. I was pretty much still a good kid.

When I first set foot in high school, it was the year of open enrollment. Until then my school had been zoned for white kids from Little Italy and Fordham Road. Now students like me were coming from all over the Bronx. Because the school was so crowded, they had to have split schedules. Juniors and seniors went in early. First years like me didn't have school until ten or eleven. While my mother was busy working, trying to pay the rent, I'd lay around at home watching *The Beverly Hillbillies*.

Sometimes I'd ride through Corona Park on the ten-speeder my mother had bought me from Korvettes. Spring semester, I was wearing my Keystone jacket from the Boys' Club and riding my bike over by the tennis courts. When I reached the crest of the hill, this junkie came over and stopped me. "Yo, can I get a ride?" I looked at him. "No!" The guy grabbed my bike under the seat. I tried to push him away and ride down the hill, but my dungarees got caught in the bicycle chain. Suddenly the guy pulled out a big hunting knife. I remember seeing an old lady on one bench and a smooching Hispanic couple on the other. I remember someone yelling and the junkie running away. By then, the blood from my chest had saturated my sweatshirt. I got dizzy and fainted by a tree on the hilltop—that tree is still there. It was only a sapling at the time.

They rushed me to what was then Fordham Hospital, which is ironic, since now I'm talking to a Fordham University professor. I remember the operating room and the people cutting off my clothes. All told, I had about fifteen stab wounds in my arms, back and chest. Good thing I was wearing my Keystone jacket, or the wounds would have been deeper. When I woke up I was in a ward with like forty other people in various states of trauma. I looked over the side of my bed, and there was a kind of plumbing fixture pumping bile out of me. I had a tube up my nose, and I could see the liquid dripping down. It was gross!

I stayed in the hospital for a couple of weeks. It wasn't like we had a whole lot of money to pay hospital bills. Once they released me, I recuperated at home, and then I was back to school. Everyone had heard what happened. Now I was the cool kid. "Yo, man, wow, you got stabbed! Let me see your wounds! Let me see!" The Boys' Club gave me another Keystone jacket.

I think it was the spring of 1967 that I went back to school. This was around a year before Martin Luther King Jr. was killed. It was a turbulent time in this country. You had the Vietnam War, the birth of the hippies, the drug culture, and the civil rights movement. You had Huey P. Newton, the Black Panthers, and Malcolm X. My friends and I were trading books like *Manchild in the Promised Land* by Claude Brown, *Down These Mean Streets* by Piri Thomas, and *Pimp* by Iceberg Slim. Back then, most of you college intellectuals knew nothing of these books.

My first bust was in my high school bathroom. My friends and I were smoking cigarettes when all of a sudden the dean and the school cop charged in. I had some weed in my pants pocket, but I immediately flushed it down the toilet. The school cop searched all of us, but he couldn't find anything. Then, just as I was picking up my books, the dean pointed at my coat. "Search his coat. You didn't search his coat." Inside my pocket, the cop found two roaches of weed. That was enough probable cause for the dean.

"You got a record now," the white cops told me in the central booking precinct that afternoon. They were laughing when they took my fingerprints. "Yeah, you got a record, now you can't drive a cab, you can't even get a barber's license." All the kids locked up with me in the bullpen, we all heard the same thing. "You got a record now."

There wasn't enough weed in those reefers to run a test on. When we got to night court, the judge turned to the school dean. "What kind of nonsense is this?" Right away, he acquitted me. But I had already been fingerprinted. I had already had mug shots taken. My mother was in the courtroom, and I had already disappointed her. All my life, from my mother, my aunts, my uncles, and my cousins, I had heard the same thing: "Boy, don't get a record, 'cause once you get a record you can't get a good job; you can't get anywhere in life." I felt doomed.

And it didn't happen just to me; it happened to all like me. Even as black people were fighting for their rights, there were those who said, "Okay, give them their rights. But along with that, give them a record. Marginalize them." In the world of academia, it might be described by that awesome term "social stratification." You stratify somebody. You put them on a level where they can't go any further. And how do you do that? You give them a record. I believe this was a conscious way of demonizing young black kids.

I'm not saying that my future was inevitable. I could have gone the other way. Some people made it out of the ghetto. But my story is no different from lots of other people's stories during that time. My mom did everything she could. She sent me to the Boys' Club, she sent me to Cadet Corps, she got me involved in the church. But just like with my brother, I think she knew, "He's gonna get old, he's gonna grow up, the streets is gonna get him." This was a fact of life for us where we lived. Children grew up, you tried to raise them, feed them; you did the best you could for them. Then you hoped they stayed alive.

Heroin was flooding our neighborhood, and heroin had become real cheap, like two dollars a bag. Every kid with lunch money had enough to buy a bag of heroin. There are a whole lot of conspiracy theorists that will tell you the government sent that heroin to our neighborhoods. All I know is that as long as the drugs stayed in Brooklyn, Harlem, and the

South Bronx, there was never any problem. "Let those people kill themselves" was the understanding. But as soon as heroin started hitting the suburbs, President Nixon got up and declared, "We have to have a war on drugs." What that filtered down to for people where I lived was, "You gonna get arrested."

In the South Bronx, crime went up. Dudes were running in and robbing stores. The Bernstein brothers and all the Jews on Jennings Street sold their stores to the blacks and Puerto Ricans, but they were also getting robbed. When the Woolworths on Wilkins Avenue closed, you knew things were really bad. Junkies were moving into buildings and not paying rent. So now the landlords were abandoning buildings or burning them down for insurance. Lots of people talk about white flight and the fall of the South Bronx. Well, I *lived* through that as a teenager. I watched the South Bronx disintegrate from a vibrant community where you could walk down the streets and hear different languages to where it looked just like those pictures of bombed-out Germany.

By the time I was in the eleventh grade, I was sniffing heroin. First, it was just at the disco or on the weekends. Then it was in the bathroom at school. Soon I was selling. I started selling "deuces" (two-dollar bags). I'd make ten dollars for every fifteen bags or "half load" I'd sell. Quick money. A lot of us fell into that, going around selling drugs. We couldn't just go down to a corporation and get jobs, because we'd already been arrested. What the hell! People get busted every day. If you got money, you can make an arrest record go away. But we were poor kids in a rich country.

One day, when I was about to make a sale across the street from school, the dean saw me and ran outside. To get probable cause, he threw a glassine bag of flour that looked like heroin at my feet. True, I had seventy-five bags of heroin hidden on my body. But without that bag of flour the school cop couldn't have frisked me. When we got to court, my mom and my aunt were there. This time I knew I was not going home. They tried to give me bail, but of course my mother couldn't afford it.

I got two blankets and a pillow and was assigned to Cell 3A19. Back then, inmates kind of ran the cell blocks. Somebody got in a fight, you fought, and you got bloodied. You'd hear the stories about dudes getting raped in the shower. Me, I was not a fighter, so what I did was write letters. First, I wrote them home, and dudes would see me. "Yo Homie, you know how to read and write?"

I'd say, "Yeah, man."

"Yo, can you write my girlfriend? I'll pay a couple of cigarettes."

"Sure, man."

So they told me what they wanted to say, and I would write to their girlfriends for them. This gave me a level of respect. "Yo," they'd say, "don't you mess with Dennis. He gotta write my letters." I didn't go in the TV room, because I wasn't about to get in any arguments over the television. I didn't gamble, because that was a trap. I didn't fuck with the dudes behind the steam table in the mess hall, because then they might spit in your food.

I was in Rikers Island for four months. About two weeks before my eighteenth birthday, I went before a three-judge panel in New York State Supreme Court. The dean of my high school got on the stand.

"What was the probable cause?" the judge asked.

"Well, he had a bag at his feet," the dean said.

My legal aid attorney jumped up. "According to the evidence report, the bag at Mr. Barton's feet was full of flour. The bags he had in his pocket, on his person, yes, they did contain heroin. But the one you found at his feet contained flour. So here's my question: Why was Mr. Barton throwing away a bag of flour?" The judges mulled it over, and they weren't buying the dean's story. I got out on probation.

The dean said I couldn't go to school, but the American Civil Liberties Union got involved and made him take me back. But by that point, I wasn't interested in my education. Pretty soon I dropped out. After that I was called by the draft board to go to Whitehall Street. This was 1969, the height of the Vietnam War. Even so, they decided not to draft me, because one, I was my mother's sole surviving son, and two, I was on probation. Who knows if that was a blessing or a curse? I've always wondered if going into the service would have changed my life.

Not long after that, I met G———. We dated and did what young people do, and somewhere along the line she got pregnant. That's the long and short of it. She was around eighteen at the time, a really smart young lady, working as an executive secretary for a major oil company that had offices in the Chrysler Building. Me, I was pretty much hustling for work, doing whatever I had to do. In September 1971, we got married in my mother's living room on 180th Street in the Bronx. We spent our honeymoon in the basement of her parents' home in Queens. After that, we found an apartment around the corner from where I grew up.

One night, sometime around November, a bunch of friends were over, and I went out to get cigarettes. On the way back, I stopped to buy a bag of weed in the building across the street. As soon as I did, someone ran up behind me and stuck a gun in my face. "Give me your money!" The gun looked so small and fake that I just punched the guy in the face. Bang! Even when he fired, the gun sounded like a cap pistol. Eventually, I started feeling a hot sensation in my stomach. I wasn't bleeding, but I was woozy. By then, I had dropped my money—I think it was ten dollars—and the guy scooped it up and ran. After I made it back to my building and up the three flights of stairs, I fell on my bed. "I've been shot, I've been shot." I wound up going to Van Etten Hospital, the same hospital where my brother passed away.

Turns out it was a small caliber gun—I think it was a .22—and the bullet had traveled through my stomach, my spleen, and my liver. They literally had to open me and stitch up everything inside of me. When I came out of the operation, the doctor said, "Not for nothing, I did my best work on you. You shouldn't have a scar." And truthfully, I don't. That doctor was a really great guy. I remember he wore a yarmulke.

In December of that year, my daughter Tannia was born. She was the cutest little thing in the world, and she had a sixth finger on each hand. They were just small appendages. After the doctor wrapped catgut around them, the fingers fell away. G——'s mother kept asking the doctors, "Do you think that happened because he"—meaning *me*—"was on drugs?" But my mother saw the extra fingers as a blessing. "That baby is born for luck!" she said. I think my mother was right, because the woman Tannia turned out to be today . . . I'm about to cry right now. She is a mom, a wife, the first lady of her church. She's had her struggles, but through it all she's beat the odds.

G—— and I went on welfare and found an apartment around the corner from my mom. During the 1970s it was just easier to go on welfare, but that's a whole other story. On the fourth floor was a guy named Jimmy. He and I became friends, and after a while we went into the weed market together. G—— got fed up with that, thinking about the baby and whatnot. "If you don't stop selling weed," she said, "I'm going to take Tannia and go home to Mama." And one day she did—packed up her bags, took the baby, and went. Jimmy laughed about that until his wife did the same thing to him. Evidently these two women had put their heads together and decided to leave us. What was I going to do, take G—— caveman-style and drag her back?

Somewhere around 1974, I met Sandy, and she got pregnant. My mom found her an apartment in her building and watched over the pregnancy like a mother hen. Meanwhile, I was living with another woman and taking numbers, making like a hundred dollars every day—this besides the money from welfare. The day I turned twenty-four years old, my mother waddled down the block and found me. "Boy, you got another baby. Born on your birthday!" I ran up to Fordham Hospital, the same hospital I was in when I got stabbed, and I got this second bundle of joy. One thing about me, I make pretty babies. I'm just going to say that. Tenisha weighed seven pounds, three ounces, and she was born at 6:54 in the evening. The next day, I played number 736 and I hit! It felt good to give Sandy some of the winnings for the baby.

With both these kids and later with my third daughter, my mother was always hovering in the background. She'd call up the girls' mothers and say, "Bring them damn children to me." And then she'd call me. "Your children gonna be here; bring your ass up here and see your children." Christmases and birthdays I was always there, no matter what drug I was doing or what I looked like. Mama would find a way to clean me up and put money in my pocket. G—— wound up having another child by someone else. Sandy, too. But Mom was the glue that kept us together. She accepted the mothers' other children in her grandkids' lives. This was our village—the kids, the extended families. The mothers and grandmothers, they accepted it for what it was, and we just rolled with it. This is how black people do.

By 1978 I was working at Hunts Point in a poultry processing plant. This was a big multimillion-dollar company. All the things that I knew about people and that my mom had taught me about hard work coalesced at this job. I was put on the boning floor, where lots of women worked. Whenever they'd yell, "I need more chicken," I'd run over and spill the chicken onto their stations. Flirt that I was, all the girls liked me, and they worked faster when I was there. One day the boss told me, "Dennis, I want you to learn all the operations in this plant, 'cause we're gonna be moving into bigger quarters and I'm gonna make you a supervisor." That was an incentive to me. I learned how to run a boning operation; I learned how to run the packing operations; I learned how to break down the machines, clean them, and put them back together. When we moved into the bigger building, I was put in charge of the breading and battering operation, and all the girls started running up to me: "Dennis, I wanna work for you! I wanna work for you!"

I met Linda at the poultry plant. She was cute and I was attracted to her, and when I got my own operation, I made her my assistant. It wasn't just wham, bam, and hop in bed with Linda. She and I actually dated, and eventually we moved in together. Everything was going right for me. I had a job, I had a nice girl, I had good place to live. But I also had a drug addiction. By the time Linda and I got our apartment, I was shooting cocaine.

Which is why one Saturday after payday, I went to get a haircut and ended up in a shooting gallery. At that time, the dealers were lacing the cocaine with speed. That kept you wanting more and more and more. Pretty soon I had burned through my whole paycheck, so I needed more money. For women, that was kind of easy. They'd go out there, and they'd get a trick. For guys it was harder. Some guys went out with guns and stuck up stores. I went out there with a little pocketknife and tried to rob somebody. Robbery was out of character for me. The cocaine and the speed played a factor in that. People chased me and caught me and held me for the cops.

For the first time in my life, I was accused of a felony. My bail was set for $75,000. Well, that wasn't bail for someone like me—that was ransom. While awaiting sentencing, I got locked up in the Bronx House of Detention. There were dudes in there who had homicides; there were dudes who were planning to break out of jail. Truthfully, they had hammers and picks and ropes to climb out the windows. It was crazy in there—people fighting over the television, people fighting over commissary, all that shit. I started going to church in jail. I started reading the Bible. I was looking for help wherever I could find it. I took GED classes just to get away from it all.

After months of playing games, the DA finally came back with a decent plea bargain—two to six years. My legal aid lawyer said, "This is about as good as you're gonna get." So I said, "Yes, I'll do this." A few days later, they handcuffed me and shackled me and gave me my number: Barton, 80A★★★★. For the rest of my incarceration, that's what I was known by. First they sent me to Sing Sing, where I saw the Death House out the window. About a week later, they called out, "Barton, 80A★★★★! Pack up." They put me on a bus to Downstate. About thirty days later, I heard it again: "Barton, 80A★★★★! Pack up." This time the bus went to Otisville, about an hour and a half from New York City. Otisville was nothing like Sing Sing, nothing like Downstate. This was a campus spread out over sixty acres and enclosed with a fence, not a wall. I got assigned a cubicle in a forty-man housing unit with a full kitchen, a nice dayroom, and nice showers. Everybody was friendly.

They gave me a battery of math and reading tests, and I scored so well they decided to give me the GED right away. I got a 302 or 304 on that test, the second highest mark in the state for that particular period. That was because of all the studying I had done in the Bronx House of Detention. "Mr. Barton," they said, "we're gonna sign you up for our program with Orange County Community College. It will be paid for, and the courses are right here in prison." I couldn't wait to call home: "Mom, I'm going to college!" My mother was over the moon. She went around telling everybody, "My boy going to college!" I was the first person in my family—of all my cousins—to go to college. I had a 3.5 or almost a 4.0 grade point average.

When I wasn't going to college, I worked on the forestry crew outside the prison fence. Once we fought a fire for three days and nights. In the summer, they gave us chainsaws to cut down trees. When it got too hot, my gang officer would take us to the reservoir to go swimming. Then, in August 1981, right around my birthday, the crew was eating lunch, and a sergeant drove up in a jeep. "Barton. Pack up. You were approved for educational release." The guys got all excited. "Yo, D, you going home, you going home!" Back in my cubicle, I packed up all my textbooks and other crap. The next morning, I was on the bus back to the Boogie Down Bronx. I was going to Fulton Correctional Facility, right across from Crotona Park.

Here's how educational release worked. During the day, I attended Bronx Community College. By 10:00 p.m., I had to be back at Fulton for curfew. On weekends, I could leave and spend time with Linda or my mother. Bronx Community College was great for me. I went to class, made friends, and had fun on campus. The Admissions Office gave me a job as a file clerk, and I worked my way up to interim assistant to the director of admissions. In June 1982, I was paroled.

That's about the time I met Billy in a summer school math class. He had a car, and during those long hot days, we would sit in there during our break and smoke weed. Over the next year and a half, Billy and I grew very close. Our girlfriends got to know each other, and whenever we were late, they'd be on the phone: "Where they at?" "I don't know, they riding around in that damn car somewhere."

Sometime in the fall, Billy called and asked me to meet him in the cafeteria the next morning. He had something to tell me.

"Yo, D," Billy said when we sat down. "I got that new shit."

"What you talking about?"

"Yo, haven't you heard about that AIDS shit?"

"No," I said. And I really hadn't. At that time, there was very little known about the virus, and there was a lot of stigma about it.

"Yeah man, they say there's no cure for it. Yo, D, I'm gonna die." This was a guy who had been through 'Nam and had struggled with drugs. "They think I got it because of dirty needles. Yo, D, I'm gonna die. D, what am I gonna do?"

Billy and I went to his car, we rolled up a joint, and all the time I was thinking, "Fuck it." We smoked a joint together.

That night I went home and prayed: "God, what do I do?" And God revealed himself to me. "Dennis, Billy needs you. He needs you as a friend."

In October, when Billy went to the hospital for the first time, our little crew of friends kept asking, "What happened to Billy? Why's he in the hospital?" Billy had told only three or four people the truth. He didn't want anyone else to know. "Tell them I got leukemia from Agent Orange during the war," he told me. And I did.

"Yo, D," Billy said when he called me in March 1984, "I gotta go to Puerto Rico, my grandmother died. Please can you go with me?" The next day I was on an airplane for the first time in my life. Billy's father picked us up at the airport, and when we got to his house, Billy told his family, "This is my friend from New York. He paid his way to come down with me." His mother and father looked at each other. "You did that for our son?" I said, "Yeah, that's my friend." That night after we went to the viewing for his grandmother, Billy's father said, "Take the van, take your friend, show him around Puerto Rico." Billy and I wound up going to a club called La Riviera. It was actually a whorehouse, and we went and did what we do in whorehouses. Yeah, I had a good time that night. Fortunately, we had sense enough to use condoms. The next day we buried Billy's grandmother. The day after that, Billy's father took me to the beach in San Juan. It was so beautiful.

Soon after we came back to New York, Billy went into the hospital. The day he died, it was snowing so hard the campus was closed, and there were no classes. No, wait a minute. Back up. I got it confused. We were all in school that day and it was a payday—I remember that. It was sometime during late spring or early summer after we went to Puerto Rico.

I didn't cry so much at my own brother's death, but I cried at Billy's death. I don't know why that is. I'll let the shrinks do that one. Anyway, I wasn't the same after Billy died. I would be at my job at the Admissions Office, and I'd think, "Fuck it. I'm gonna go get high." I began thinking about selling the computers at work to buy drugs. That scared me so much I left my keys on my desk and quit. I stopped going to school. I forgot one meeting with my parole officer, and the next time I walked in there, he handcuffed me to the chair. I wound up doing ninety days in Queensboro Correctional Facility and four days upstate before my parole was restored.

When I got back, I started working for the Neighborhood Work Project run by the Vera Institute of Justice. They taught parolees how to rehab apartments for the city. I learned how to hang Sheetrock. I learned how to paint. I learned how to do tiles. I took a test, and they made me a supervisor with a beeper and a crew. Every payday, supervisors would go out and party and do coke.

One day in like 1984, my foreman and I were sitting on the stoop of a building in Brooklyn waiting for a supply truck. A girl we knew came out, and we said, "Yo, where can we get some coke?" The girl took us around the corner, got some coke, brought us back to her apartment, spilled the coke in water with some baking soda, and started cooking it. We were looking at her. "What the hell are you doing?" I had heard of crack before, but I'd never done it. The girl pulled out a pipe, and we started smoking it. And I smoked, and I smoked, and I smoked up all the money I had in my pocket. I didn't even have money for carfare. I walked home from Brooklyn that night, across the Brooklyn Bridge, into Manhattan and up Second Avenue, halfway to the Bronx, until I got to a train station where I felt comfortable enough to hop the train.

That was the start of my crack addiction. Needless to say, I lost my job at the Neighborhood Work Project. Meanwhile, my girlfriend Linda was pregnant. Linda had never done drugs, and during her pregnancy she stopped drinking and smoking, too. She wanted this baby to be healthy. If I called to say I'd be late, Linda told me, "You're high. I know you're high. Don't bother coming home." My mother also knew. You couldn't lie to Mama. "I know you going out there to do them drugs," she said. "I know what you doing." Some nights I'd sleep at her house. Some nights I was sleeping on the streets.

Still, I managed to get myself over to the hospital on that night in October when Nicole was born. It was the only time I was ever there to see my child's birth. It gave me a whole new respect for women. And to see that life start, and to hold that little life in my hands was just amazing. Yeah, it was great. But after they took the baby from me, what did I do? I think I went and got high somewhere.

By then I was pretty much living on the streets. Crack kept you out there. I've often described it, even while I was smoking, as the most insidious thing that ever happened to me. There was a rap song that said, "Six minutes and the high is gone"—or something like that. Crack cocaine was a real quick high, and then you wanted more. If you were working and getting a paycheck, it was nothing to sit up and spend your whole paycheck. If you didn't pay your bills first, they didn't get paid. And every time you got high, the instant you lit the lighter and put the pipe to your lips, at least in my case, you were thinking, "Where's the next high coming from?"

I started staying far away from my family because I was around some treacherous-ass people. People were going around cutting their own family's throats. That's what the high did to you. And I knew. I knew if I went to my mother's home, I'd be looking at the TV and thinking, "Well, I can get fifteen dollars for that." Or I'd be looking at the toaster, thinking, "I can get ten dollars for that." I didn't want to be that person who said, "Yeah, I went to my mama's house and I took the TV and I sold it." I didn't want to be that person. My mother didn't raise me for that. And I didn't want to be around my kids and have them see me as a crackhead. I made sure none of their little friends could say, "Your dad is a crackhead, I saw him out there on the avenue." I stayed away from my family, because I knew the dangers that came with my addiction.

I could tell you stories of other crackheads who didn't make it, who aren't here today. I remember one white girl who lived across the street from Aqueduct Park. That was where people hung out and smoked crack at night. You could walk through that place and see nothing but empty vials. I think this girl lived alone or with her aged father. She had cerebral palsy, so she was getting a government check. This girl, I'm not going to name her, somebody introduced her to crack. If you can imagine this, she would get her check and smoke it up and then go out there and try to catch dates or tricks. Well, one day they found her in Aqueduct Park. Somebody had beaten her up. Killed her.

One night I was sleeping in a park right off Fordham Road and University Avenue. It must have been about nine or ten o'clock, and I woke up to these teenage kids punching and pummeling me. "Oh, you fucking crackhead," they said. They were kicking my ass, but I was able to jump up, fight them off, and run away. I could have lost my life. A few years later, a man was sleeping in the doorway of a church on 103rd Street, and some teenagers came by, sprayed him with lighter fluid, and lit him on fire. This is man's inhumanity to man.

For a while I paid for my addiction by collecting bottles and cans. It was hard work, because the stores limited the amount you could recycle. But I found a Manhattan supermarket on 207th Street and a beer warehouse across the street that each gave you up to twelve dollars a day. I spent a lot of time in that neighborhood in the 1980s and 1990s. A group of us built shacks out of the wooden pallets near the warehouse. I actually built myself a three-room ranchero with cardboard and a tarp for a roof. I had a foyer, a living room, and a back bedroom. My electricity came from the street lamp outside. I even had a TV that I found in the garbage. After about three and a half months, the city sanitation came and cleaned us all out.

Then I happened upon a super of a building who was knee-deep in garbage near an alley. I went up and asked him with my broken Spanish if he needed help. Within about an hour, we had all the garbage bagged up, and the alley swept and cleaned. The super gave me ten dollars and said, "You did such a good job I want you to come back on Monday." Meanwhile the super next door saw what happened and asked me in Spanish, "Can you help me also?" Pretty soon I was helping three supers take out their garbage and clean out their alleyways. They paid me a few dollars each.

For the next thirteen or fourteen years, this was my life. I worked my way around the neighborhood. People called me Moreno, a name I chose for myself. If anybody needed help with an odd job, they'd say, "Call Moreno. He'll do it." The supers paid me to sweep in front of their buildings, take out their garbage on collection days, and sweep and mop their hallways. In doing so, I got to know the tenants, who also asked for my help. I washed their cars and took out their garbage at night. Some people gave me money to shop for them in the supermarket. People even gave me keys to their houses.

My mama raised me to help people. You helped the old lady up the stairs with her packages. I'd been doing that since I was a kid. One lady named Miss Elsa did domestic work or something. I'd see her coming down Davidson Avenue at the end of the day looking so tired, and I'd run up to her and say, "Come on, Miss Elsa, let me take your bags." She would always find a dollar or two to give me. One night when I was sick and coughing, she said, "You can't stay outside like this. Come, I will make a place for you to sleep on the floor of my apartment." Miss Elsa allowed me to take a shower. She made me a hot bowl of soup and gave me some cough medicine. Then she prepared a place on the floor of her foyer so that I could rest for the night. In her actions, I saw the love of God.

Another woman named Jackie managed a building on Grand Avenue. She always had odd jobs for me to do. One snowy night in February, she said, "I don't want you staying out there in the cold." She gave me a blanket and let me stay in the sheltered area by the door on the roof landing. For while, I made a home up there. I had a two-drawer file cabinet and a chest of drawers that somebody had thrown out. I had a plastic lounge beach chair as a bed. I had one of those pocket-size New Testaments I always managed to keep with me throughout my homelessness. I was getting light from an overhead socket in the ceiling. The building super had a pigeon coop up there, and I watched his birds overnight.

Lots of people gave me their used clothes, and one day somebody gave me a nice suit. "Damn," I said, looking at it. "I'm going to save this suit."

I wrapped it carefully in plastic, and Jackie and the super gave me a little space in the basement to store it with a good pair of shoes and socks I had.

People in that neighborhood were very kind to me. They knew me. They knew my heart. But they also understood I had a drug problem. Did I know I had a problem? Yeah, I knew I had a problem! I was living in the park. I was living on rooftops. I was sleeping on trains at night. I was not with my family or kids. I smelled so bad that one time I tried to hop the train and the cop who saw me just said, "Get out of here." I couldn't even get arrested, I smelled so bad. Yeah, I knew it was a problem!

In 1997, it was like October 11 or 12, I was working for the super on Aqueduct Avenue, and one of the tenants who knew my oldest daughter, Tannia, saw me pulling the garbage cans. "You need to call home. There's some news for you." That's how I found out that my mother had passed away.

Tannia said, "Daddy, where can I come find you?" That afternoon, she drove up in a little minivan. I didn't even know my child could drive. Tannia looked at me. "Daddy, you got any clothes?" My mother had always had a sort of running joke. Sometimes we'd go to funerals, and people would be showing up raggedy with a bad-looking suit. Mama would turn to me and say, "Boy, when you come to my funeral, you better have a nice suit on." So I went down to the basement of Jackie's building and un-wrapped the suit I'd been saving there.

My daughter found a barbershop, because I was looking like a wooly mammoth. She got me a haircut and a shave. The next morning, I woke up early, and one of the tenants let me take a shower. Somebody gave me a clean dress shirt. I walked down the block with the money my daughter had given me to take the train to the funeral home. I had on a nice suit, clean shoes, clean socks, clean underwear, everything. As I was walking, people in the neighborhood were going to work and looking out their windows. "Who the hell is that? Yo, is that Moreno?" When I turned onto Davidson Avenue, people said, "Oh my God, look at him! Moreno, you look so good! Oh my God!" Everybody in my family knew about my addiction. "Oh, Dennis," they said, "he out there, he out on crack." But that day, I showed up at the funeral home with a nice, clean, fitting suit. I think I made my mother proud.

This was the first time I'd seen my mom in a couple of years. I went up to the casket and touched her and kissed her. Mama always told me when you touch the dead they won't bother you at night, they won't come back and haunt you. Then I sat down in the front, and my oldest daughter handed me my youngest grandbaby. My daughter Nicole and her mom

Linda were on my left, Tannia was on my right. We sat there at Mama's funeral. When it ended and they put Mama in a hearse, Tannia drove us in the minivan to the cemetery in New Jersey. Up until then I hadn't shed a tear. But when we got to the gravesite, and they started saying the words over my mother and lowering her into the ground, I lost it. I walked away and started crying. And I cried, and I cried, and I cried. I told Mama I was sorry. I asked her to forgive me. When I finished crying, I wiped my eyes, walked back to my family, got back in the car, and we left.

The next day I was back out there getting high.

For three more years, I kept smoking like a runaway train, like someone left the stove on and something was burning. Wherever you saw me, you saw a cloud of smoke. Then, on November 29, 1999, I was helping another super clean out his boiler room. The super was in the crack game too, and his girlfriend was selling it in the building. When I went outside for a cigarette break, he was lollygagging with his friends. This young lady walked up to us. "Yo, anybody know where I can get some crack?" she said. I'd never seen her before, so my antenna was up. "You know her?" I asked the super. "Yeah man, I seen her around before," he said. So I made the crack run to the super's girlfriend, and the lady gave me five dollars for the job. With ten dollars I could buy some crack, so I asked the super to advance me five dollars. He gave me a ten-dollar bill, and I gave him my five-dollar bill from the lady. Turns out that lady was an undercover cop and that five dollars was marked money. This was what they called a "buy and bust" operation. It was a Giuliani policy.

The next thing I knew, this undercover cop came charging into the boiler room, screaming, "Put your hands up!" He dragged me outside, and they had the super up against the wall. The cops put us in the van and drove us all around the area, picking up other people. "What am I charged with? What am I charged with?" I kept asking.

"You're charged with sale," they said.

"What? I didn't sell anybody no drugs."

Nobody listened. They just kept riding around, picking people up until the van was full.

That night I went into the bullpen dirty and nasty from the boiler room and looking like a crackhead. "Oh my God," I thought, "here I am again." It was a big bullpen with everyone sitting on a bench that went all the way around the wall. The toilet had only a little half-screen on it— no privacy if you had to take a crap. I actually crawled under the bench to try and fall asleep. But all I could think was, "Damn, they're booking me on sale. I'm going to be sent upstate again." I was looking around the bullpen, and it was full of young dudes in their twenties and thirties. They were singing rap music. I was still singing ballads from the 1960s. They were talking about LL Cool J. I was still talking about James Brown and the Temptations. There were kids in that bullpen that were the same age as my children. I realized how old I was, how long I'd been doing this crap. I couldn't do it anymore.

About two days later, they packed me up and sent me to a big barge they had converted into a jail. It was sitting off the bottom of Hunts Point. At Rikers, it was like fifty guys in the dorm and you were practically breathing each other's farts. This place was more spacious and clean. I said to myself, "If I gotta do time, I wanna stay here." A guy came downstairs and said, "Does anybody want to sign up for the substance abuse intervention program? You'll get to stay on the boat until you are sentenced." My hand was the first one up.

On Monday, I met my counselor, and her name was Miss G.

"Wait a minute," I said. "Do you have a brother named Charles?"

She said, "Oh my God, yes!"

"Did you used to live in the so-and-so projects?"

"Yes."

"What's your first name?"

She told me and I said, "I remember when you were just three years old. Me and Charles would be in the living room getting high and always shooing you out!" Charles had died from HIV. Now his younger sister was going to be my drug counselor. What were the chances that somebody I hadn't seen since she was a baby would wind up being my drug counselor all these years later? This is how God works in our lives.

For the next year, I went back and forth to court waiting to be sentenced. Miss G. almost got me into a drug rehab program as an alternative to incarceration. But then my codefendant, the super, turned state's evidence on me, and I was sentenced to Ulster Correctional Facility. After the sentencing, I actually saw the super in the bullpen, and guess what? He had the nerve to ask me for a cigarette. I looked him square in the face. "You're going home, and I'm going upstate 'cause of you. And you're asking me for a cigarette? Fuck you and the horse you riding outta here."

As it turned out, about a week after I got to Ulster, they sent me before the parole board. Three people sat in front of me, looking at my record. They saw I had been to college. They saw I had been busted on a minor sale. So they asked me a simple question: "Mr. Barton, if we decide to let you go, what are you gonna do?" I knew just the answer they were looking for. "I'm gonna seek and maintain employment, and I'm gonna continue with my drug therapy." And they said, "Good luck, Mr. Barton. You'll be going home soon."

Six weeks later, I started the substance abuse program at Bellevue Hospital and was given a bed in the clean and sober unit at Bellevue Men's Shelter across the street. Through my window I looked out on the East River—a view that people are killing for right now. Over the next two years, I took care of all that business of getting my benefits like welfare, food stamps, and Medicaid. I finally took an HIV test. When the results came back, I was expecting them. It was kind of ironic that I wound up getting HIV all those years after my friend Billy died of AIDS. A lot had happened since then. Now there were medications for the virus. I take them every day, and I've been fine and healthy.

In the winter of 2002, Ms. K. interviewed me to become a participant in New York Catholic Charities' life skills empowerment program. At some point, I reached into my pocket for something and pulled out my little green Bible. "Oh, do you go to church?" Ms. K. asked. I told her I was looking around for one. There's a personal contract you have to sign before starting the program, and Ms. K. wrote these words in mine: "Mr. Barton will find a church and attend regularly." I was fine with that because I had already told God, "This time around I'm just listening to you. Whatever I have to do, just let me know." He was guiding me through his word and through his spirit. A few months later, I was a member of Middle Collegiate Church, which is part of Collegiate Churches of New York, the oldest church in America.

I saw the value of the life skills empowerment program right away. I liked that you got to read something and reflect on it at the beginning of each session. I liked that it met in a nice space at New York Catholic Charities. I just have to say, I also liked that I would get a stipend at the end of the program. Early on, James Addison came in and did a session on Empowerment for Change and told us about his recovery from homelessness. I looked at him and said, "Damn, if he could do this, I can do this." And the facilitators, Ms. K. and George Horton, were so great and understanding. George had a habit of sitting there with his hands together and his head down, listening so carefully. George and Ms. K., they made you feel like people.

And I have to add this, because it will be important later. Ms. K. made these place cards with our names—"Dennis Barton" or whatever—which we put in front of us every session. And every session I kept seeing these three girls coming in as part of their high school service. They would wheel the dinner in on a little dolly and set it out for us. They were always giggling and laughing—the same three girls always together, one black and two white.

I was given a mentor, and he was something like the head fundraiser for New York Catholic Charities. The day I met him, he took me to his office, and I went to sit in the chair at the side of his desk.

"No," he said. "You go over there and sit in my chair."

"You sure?"

"Yes."

Why was this so important? Because I was used to dealing with the Bellevue Shelter guards, who would look at you like you were a piece of crap. When you went to welfare, they looked at you like you were piece of crap. My new parole officer was great, but the other parole officers looked at you like you were a piece of crap. Now here was my mentor, telling me to sit in *his* chair behind *his* desk. It was a sign of respect. My mentor made me feel like a person.

He asked me about my goals, and I said, "I really want to find my kids and see where they're at." "Well," my mentor said, "You could search for them online." My last experience with computers had been back at Bronx Community College, when there were green letters on a black screen. I wasn't used to the whole new internet thing. Fortunately, there was this Russian guy in the shelter who was an expert in computers. That Saturday, he took me to the public library and showed me how to work a mouse and type on a keyboard. He helped me set up my first email account. Week after week I went back to the library and practiced my skills.

When I graduated from the life skills empowerment program at New York Catholic Charities, that was a real accomplishment for me. Until that moment, I had never finished anything in my life. When I was going to school, I never finished my homework. I had my GED, but I hadn't finished college. After the ceremony was over, George handed each of us our hundred-dollar stipend. I used some of it to get my first cell phone.

Back at the library, I found a website called Anywho.com. It was a people finder and it was free. So I said, "Well okay, let me start with G——, my first wife." I typed in her name and I put in South Carolina, because somehow I knew she was living down there. Up popped a phone number. I copied it down. That night, I went back to my seven-man room at the shelter. For a long time, I stared at that phone number. Finally, I went into the shower room, away from everybody, and I made the call.

"Hello, G——?"

"Who's this?"

"It's Dennis, your ex-husband."

"Oh my God. I thought you was dead."

"No, sweetheart, I'm not dead. I'm in a shelter. Where's Tannia?"

G—— gave me my eldest daughter's phone number. Tannia was living in South Carolina too.

"Hello, Tannia? It's your daddy."

"Daddy? Daddy, where you been? Where are you?"

"I'm in New York City in a shelter and a drug program. Things are okay."

"Daddy, don't go nowhere. I'm gonna drive up. I'll bring the kids. We'll come up there and see you."

On Christmas Eve, I was at the shelter and my cell phone rang: "Daddy, I'm downstairs." And there was my eldest daughter with her husband and my grandkids. The little one, who I had held in my arms at my mother's funeral, was like five or six now. My daughter had grown up and become a wonderful woman. She was married to a pastor, and we all went out to dinner at his mother's house in Brooklyn. It was a great night for me.

From Tannia, I got the phone number for Linda, the mother of Nicole. "You should know where Nicole is," Linda said when I called her up, "'cause you were passing her every day at Catholic Charities."

"What?"

"Yeah. Nicole saw you every day at that life skills program."

Remember the three giggling girls who I kept seeing at New York Catholic Charities? Well, one of them was my own daughter! Linda put her on the phone.

"Hi, sweetheart. Your mama said you saw me at the program at Catholic Charities."

"Yeah, Daddy, I saw you with your name tag. I didn't say anything because I was with my friends."

"Okay, I can understand that."

"I saw you lots of times. In fact, one time you was on the elevator and you was talking to this white lady named Janet about how much you loved me."

Today I have all three of my children in my life. I have five granddaughters and a newborn great-granddaughter. Over the years, I have asked each of my daughters the same question. "After all that I did, why are you showing me so much love?" And each of them has said pretty much the same thing: "Daddy, we knew you had a drug problem. But you didn't bring that bullshit around us. We look at the man you are today, and we love you."

Somewhere around 2004, I disclosed my HIV status to Ms. Ballard, the director of Bellevue Men's Shelter. "Oh my God, Dennis, I wish you would have told me this earlier, because you would have been out of here!" If you're HIV positive, the law says you're not supposed to be in a shelter like Bellevue. You are supposed to have your own apartment with its own bathroom, and you are supposed to have air conditioning. Once I disclosed my status, all the bells and whistles started going off. Through her connections with Volunteers of America, Ms. Ballard got me an interview with the Horizon Program of Volunteers of America.

Pretty soon I was dragging my four garbage bags of crap out of Bellevue Men's Shelter and into an SRO building on Ninety-Seventh Street and Riverside Drive. I dragged my bags up the elevator, down the hall, and over to my new front door. I put the key in the lock. Click. I saw a bed, a bathroom, and an air conditioner. There was a place to hang my stuff. There wasn't a table or dresser, but that didn't matter. I fell on my knees and thanked God. I had a place of my own.

That night, when 10:00 p.m. came, I got up, took my keys, locked the door, and went outside. It was curfew time at Bellevue Men's Shelter, but I didn't have a curfew anymore. I walked a couple of blocks and bought ice cream. Then I went back around the corner and walked down Ninety-Sixth Street. In the Church of the Holy Name an AA meeting was taking place. I went to that AA meeting. At 11:30 p.m., the meeting ended, and I got up and went home.

After graduating from the life skills empowerment program, I became a mentor, a member of the Interfaith Assembly on Homelessness and Housing Speakers Bureau, and eventually the Speakers Bureau coordinator. In 2008, I began facilitating the Panim el Panim life skills empowerment program. I wanted to do the same thing for the participants in my group that George and Ms. K. had done for me. But I also wanted the participants to be able to look at me and say, "Hey, wait a minute, he was homeless too." I never puffed myself up or stuck out my chest. "No, dudes," I'd tell the participants, "I'm just like you. I came through this and you can too. If some people look down on you, it doesn't make your value any less."

My God tells me to feed the hungry, clothe the naked, and be with the sick and suffering. Well, sometimes people are hungry for a meal. And sometimes they're hungry in their spirit. In the life skills empowerment program I wanted to feed the people's spirit. I wanted them to feel good about themselves. I wanted them to know that they were worth something, just like when I walked into my mentor's office and he said, "Here, take my chair."

Over the years I've met so many people. I have sat in so many rooms. Today, I am a peer educator for Planned Parenthood. I am a parent workshop facilitator for the LEAP for Girls program at Love Heals. In 2006 I was ordained a deacon in the Middle Collegiate Church of New York. I have served on their consistory and as a member of the Benevolence Committee, which oversees grants to worthy organizations. This is a fiduciary responsibility. Among our many contributions, our church has built two or three classrooms in Africa; we've helped support the IAHH. Twenty years ago, I was trying to scrape together five dollars to buy crack. Today, I have sat in rooms and helped make decisions about how to distribute a six-figure budget to worthy causes. I'm respected as a person regardless of my history. Deacons are also the pastor's assistants in care. We visit the sick and grieving and help the pastor with the needs of the congregation. I think my pastor recommended me for this because she saw in my spirit the spirit of care.

I got that from church, from God, from my mom. My mom would feed anybody. Whenever she saw one of my brother's friends on the street, she'd say, "Boy, you hungry? Come on upstairs and get something to eat." My Aunt Bill lived with six kids in a one-bedroom studio in Harlem, but when she cooked, everybody on 129th Street ate. That's how black people do. We take care of each other. People talk about blacks killing blacks, but nobody talks about how when you don't have a pair of shoes to go to your mama's funeral, somebody goes and gets you a pair of shoes. They don't talk about how when you don't have anything to eat, somebody will go in their cabinet and get you something to eat. When you need a bath, somebody will invite you in their house and give you a bath. Nobody talks about that.

So where did I get my spirit of care? I got it from the people that raised me. Yeah, I did my crap, I did my shit, I was a drug addict, I was homeless and all that. But you know what? At the end of the day, I was raised right! Today I live on the values that my mother and my aunt and all my family taught me. I'm no perfect angel, but I do believe that there's a house in heaven for me someday. I only hope that I can continue to do what I do to make myself worthy of it.

Reflection
Dawn Ravella, DMin

Dawn Ravella, LMSW, DMin, is the director of Mission and Outreach at the Reformed Church of Bronxville, where she created the Coming Home prison ministry program, a life skills empowerment program designed for formerly incarcerated individuals.

Soon after we exited the plane, I found myself in a scene of chaos: we were surrounded by people begging for money. I clutched my dad's hand as I came face to face with a child my size who was gripping *his* father's hand, and I noticed a stump where his father's other hand should have been. As I made eye contact with the child—his face now vividly etched in my memory—I recognized injustice. Through pure luck, I had a father who could afford to take our family on a fancy vacation to Acapulco, while this child had a one-handed father who had to beg in the street. I was deeply disturbed by these differences. At dinner I wondered why I was served the same amount of food as my dad, a grown man. Why couldn't we each take some food from our plates and share it with the people who were begging? I was heartsick. This is my first memory of recognizing inequality—a recognition that developed and later led to a two-decade career of organizing faith communities to respond to poverty and injustice.

Seven years ago, after I began my position as director of Mission and Outreach at the Reformed Church of Bronxville (RCB), we began a Coming Home prison ministry program to support formerly incarcerated and now homeless individuals in the reentry process and to build community and relationships in a way that few Bronxville residents had ever experienced. What happened at RCB shocked us. In supporting the program, our whole congregation came alive. Members were eager to help cook meals; mentor; and teach computer skills, resume writing, financial literacy, job interviewing skills, and more. The enthusiasm and support from congregants was so great that I had to adjust the program to allow for more volunteers and add a community meal with spiritual reflection.

In the program, those returning from prison had the chance to process and reframe their personal narratives. The church community heard tragic childhood stories about young people who lacked supports in life and wound up in a punitive criminal justice system that causes further damage by breaking up families and creating more traumas. As congregants listened to the stories and challenges facing the returning citizens, we recognized and celebrated their strength, intelligence, hard work, grit, and determination. As one congregant and retired business owner put it: "If I had to be in a lifeboat with ten guys, these are the ones I would pick, because I know that they would have my back."

One participant had a particularly profound effect on my life. After he was accepted into a PhD program at John Jay College of Criminal Justice, I was excited for him and told him I'd always wanted to earn a doctorate degree. He looked me right in the eye and told me that I could do it and should do it. His courage and attitude inspired me to apply for the doctor of ministry program at New York Theological Seminary, which provides education inside Sing Sing Correctional Facility. I couldn't think of a better place to study, since the school's values and beliefs so closely matched my own.

In many ways, the returning citizens were great role models who were creating change. Yet despite this, and even after some of our participants completed higher education, no one wanted to hire them except the administrators of reentry services. "They supposedly paid their debt to society," a volunteer helping with resume writing observed. "But they continue to pay." As church community members recognized this injustice, they saw things differently. Alexis, the church school director explained, "My husband is a cop, so I only thought of one perspective, but I've had a change of heart. People have paid their dues to society and deserve to be welcomed back in a loving way."

Because of the program, the congregants and I started exploring the root causes of poverty and an unfair system. We faced tough issues, such as poverty, race, class, and human rights violations against youth and those with mental illness. Today, the Reformed Church has developed a more informed community that engages deeply in its work with impoverished people. An inspired group of congregants is spearheading restorative justice projects and working to create systemic change. In Yonkers we have hired a community organizer to help residents break the cycle of poverty—the "pipeline to prison"—and create the change they want in their community. In addition, a community member is now spearheading restorative justice processes throughout Westchester County.

More than two thousand passages in scripture mention poverty and justice, the basis of the work I believe we are called to do. I believe in the unique and sacred dignity of every individual, and I want to help create a just world where there is hope, opportunity, compassion, and inclusivity of all. God calls us first to love God and love our neighbor as ourselves. When you really love someone, you don't just put a band aid on their wound and keep walking. As the Good Samaritan illustrates, we are called on to care for people until they are brought back to health and to support them so they can share their gifts and be fully connected members of the community.

With hope and faith, we can continue to take strides forward to a more just society.

Life Story
Michelle Riddle

Michelle Riddle was born on June 14, 1962, in Brooklyn, New York. She graduated in 2003 from the Education Outreach Program (EOP), the original life skills empowerment program, run by New York Catholic Charities.

My father served three tours as a sergeant in the army. He worked in the burial detail. He was the one that handed the flag to the family. The day I was born—June 14, 1962—he said it was time to come home. I am my father's fifteenth child, and I'm the only girl. That's why he retired from the army, because he had a daughter and not a "rock head," which is what he called my brothers. I miss my father, I do. He came home just because I was born. He came home to make sure I had a daddy.

My mom was the oldest of thirteen children. She had four children— my older sister, my older brother, me, and my younger brother. My older sister had another father. My parents weren't married, but I didn't know that until I was a teenager.

We lived in St. Albans, Queens, in a house off 201st Place and Linden Boulevard. It was a beautiful two-story house with a stained-glass window in the living room. My father used to make a big deal about Christmas. One year, he painted our house and the picket fence all white. Then he built a cross and painted it white, put blue bulbs on it, put it outside our window, and turned the lights on. We had the best house on the block. I remember Christmas with toys stacked high over my head.

My mom couldn't do so much as boil water, so my father did all the cooking. He was a Southern man and would fry fish and chicken. During

the day, he was a mechanic at a Mobil station out in Corona. At the station, he had three red boxes of tools stacked on top of each other, and he also had tools at home. When my father wasn't working at the gas station, he was working at home.

My mom was a custodian for St. John's University. We never called her Mom, only Jenna, which was her nickname. My mother didn't show any emotion; she never hugged us. From the time I was six, I don't remember ever hearing the words "I love you" coming from her mouth. At the dinner table, my father would say, "How was school today?" In the third grade, I was reading at a twelfth-grade level. If you did well, my father made a big deal. He'd be like, "Oh, I'm so proud of you. Come here, Shellie!

Give me a hug." My mother was never like that, and I couldn't under-stand why.

"Dad," I said, "am I adopted?"

"No," he said. "Unfortunately, that is your mother."

I said, "You sure? I don't think she is."

My mother favored my younger brother and my sister because they were fair skinned.

There was a color issue in her family. When we visited our grand-parents' house, my father wasn't allowed inside because he was dark. My older brother and I had to sit in the living room with my grandfather, but the other kids could run through the house. My grandmother was light, but she wasn't the mean one. It was my grandfather. He came from St. Troy and had blonde hair and blue eyes. When my mother got mad at my father, she would call me and my older brother "Blackie" and "Darkie." If my father did not come home at night, she would wake up my older brother and make him stand in the dark, in the corner, down in the dining room. One night, my brother told my father, "Jenna told me to stand here and wait till you come home." Of course, when I woke up the next morn-ing, my mom was walking around with a black eye and sunshades. But my father was a tender man—he was real compassionate. My mother—I hate to say it—she instigated a lot.

David, my younger brother, was born in 1969 on the same day that Neil Armstrong walked on the moon. It was pouring rain when David came home, but my mother didn't come with him. She wound up going into a psychiatric ward for three, maybe six months. My grandmother came, and she and my father kept us going.

After my mother returned, she used to ask me to watch David. One time I fell asleep, and when I woke up he was sitting in a high chair scratching his tongue. My mother said, "I asked you to watch him, and you let him get my cigarettes, and he's sitting there chewing on my cig-arettes!" That scratching was the tobacco that he had in his mouth. My mother was like, "You did that on purpose." I didn't, but I thought it was funny.

A few years later—I was about nine or ten, and David was two or three—I told him, "We're going to go to the basement and catch roaches and burn them." We found matches, and I gave them to David. "Take these downstairs and I'll meet you in a minute." By the time I got to the basement, the drapes were on fire. David was standing up.

"Look, Shell! Oooh, look, it's a fire!"

I yelled, "What did you do? You were supposed to wait for me!"

Michelle in fourth grade (circa 1971)

We all got out of the house, but the firemen had to knock out the windows on the porch and in the dining room and the stained-glass window in the living room. There was a lot of water damage. My mother used that as an excuse to pack us all up and run us to Brooklyn, where she had a lot of relatives in the projects. Even though my father worked real hard to get her that house, she always wanted to be in the projects.

My father stayed in Queens, trying to fix the house. But without my mother's income, he couldn't keep up with the mortgage. They came and cut the lights off, but my father found the source for putting the power back on. They came and cut the water off, but he found a way to put the water back on. My father was very, very skillful. The problem was he drank. Before my parents' separation, he was always the level-headed one.

After my mother left, my father was on a "pity pot," and alcohol became his life.

In Brooklyn, we went from family to family. My mother would leave us and not come back from work and not pay bills, not help with anything. Whenever a family got tired of my mother's crap, they'd put us out. My Aunt Paige did that, and others too. My sister went to stay with her father and his mother, but my brothers and I used to walk around until two or three o'clock in the morning, sleeping on park benches, waiting for my mother to come out of bars. It was horrible. Sometimes the neighbors or friends of so-called friends would let us in, and the older kids would try to molest us. I know some people had it worse, but I had it rough. I had to learn young. I fought most of my life.

We used to go to a bar in Flatbush and say, "Would you please ask Jenna to come out? Say that her kids are out here." My mother would come out raising hell. "Why the fuck are you out here?" Twice, the bartender let us go to his house, and my brothers and I slept in his bed. Even though my father was a full-fledged alcoholic, he was still trying to help. At the end of sixth grade, I said, "Daddy, I'm graduating. I need a dress." I remember him coming and taking me and David out shopping. I didn't go anywhere without my younger brother. I felt I had to protect him.

Our homelessness lasted around a year. In January, my mother finally got an apartment in a tenement on Gold Street, on top of a store. She hooked up with this cat named Jimmy. He was real nice to us kids, gave everybody money, bought everybody junk. He gave me a little extra, but I didn't pay it any attention. Then he and my mother started drinking, and Jimmy would come to my room at night. Why was he watching me? I could feel him staring. I used to wake up my older brother in his room and tell him, "Listen, you go sleep in my bed and let me sleep in your bed." So when Jimmy came in to fondle me, he found my brother instead. He got so mad.

The store next door to us caught on fire, and the building was abandoned. The two buildings had connecting roofs, and we used to climb out our kitchen window and go inside the burned-out store. We would play with my dolls and drink the soda that hadn't burned. One day, I got out of junior high school early, and when I went into our apartment I could smell Jimmy's cologne. I thought, "Damn, he was just here." He had to be watching, because I heard the front door open. I went out on the roof and ran down the stairs of the abandoned building. Jimmy followed behind me, running from room to room. "I know you in here. You wait till I catch you!" I hid behind the boiler and got stabbed by a rusted nail. I've still got scars on my body from hiding from that man.

Later, I told my older brother what Jimmy did, and we got in touch with my father. My father wasn't working at the time. He had no means of transportation, so he walked in a snowstorm all the way from St. Albans, Queens, to where we lived in Brooklyn—with a gun. We were like, "Daddy, why are you over here?" He said, "I've come to see Jimmy." My older brother and I had to take that gun, because my father would have shot Jimmy if he saw him. My mother kept telling my father, "She lying, she lying!" I was like, "I'm lying? Look at these scars on me! I'm lying?" She thought I was ruining her good thing. But after that my mother gave up Jimmy. She had no choice. My mother knew my father was not playing.

Pretty soon our own building caught on fire, and the Red Cross put us in the Brooklyn Arms Hotel shelter for a few months. From there we moved to the Marcy Projects. I was in the eighth grade and going to I.S. 33. I've been an asthmatic all my life. Today, if I broke a bone, it couldn't be repaired because of all the prednisone and different medications I took as a child. But I still ran track in elementary school and junior high school. I won the 200-yard dash and the 400-yard dash. My coach taught how to breathe and run at the same time.

I breezed through my classwork, but I was always acting out. In ninth grade, the teacher said, "Michelle, you could be on the honor roll, but your behavior, young lady!" I thought, "Ah, who wants the honor roll? For what?" Nobody at home made a big deal of it, so I stopped making a big deal of it. It might have been different if my dad had been there, cheering me on.

The summer after ninth grade, I met and fell in love with Hank, who also lived in the projects. His mother was a barmaid, and she had everything to drink at home. Because of my dad, I didn't really care for alcohol. Instead, Hank and I smoked weed. His mother didn't mind. By my sweet sixteen, I was pregnant, and I didn't go back to high school. I had my oldest son, who I love. He was our first.

I was still living with my mother, but her mental health problems started again. At home she was entertaining not only men, but also kids; they included my brother's friends and some of the guys I had gone to school with. It was so humiliating. My mother would buy them beer, buy them weed. We didn't know at the time that she was blowing all her rent money on that. My older brother had to leave, because he didn't appreciate what my mother was doing with his friends. I would have left with my baby, but I didn't want to leave my younger brother. David was about twelve at the time. My mother used to do him wrong. She let these drunks cut his hair, and one guy gave him bald spots. I came home and David said, "Shell, look what she did to me." We laugh today, but I was too scared to leave him with her. I had to make sure David was taken care of.

I needed my dad to step up and petition for custody of my brother. "Jenna is not in her right mind," I said. "If you get the papers, I'll serve her myself."

And I swear to God by my right hand, that's what I did. "These papers are for you from family court, because you shouldn't have David," I told her. My mother was furious, but my father got David. Then he and the mother of David's best friend made an arrangement. My father paid her a set amount of money so that my brother could live with her and stay in his neighborhood school. She was a good lady. My brother made it through high school and everything.

I started living between my girlfriend's apartment and Hank's mother's house. Hank and I were together on and off, and we started doing cocaine. Our daughter was born on Easter Sunday in 1984. She was real light skinned—a "red bone." At first, I thought her color came from my doing so much cocaine. But there were no toxins in my baby's system. She was fine. When I got ready to take her home, they kept checking the identification bracelet to make sure she was my daughter—I was checked three or four times because she was so light skinned.

Six months after my daughter was born, I found out that Hank was talking to this other chick. When he told me they were getting married, I didn't want to live near him anymore. My father came by car to pick me up. "Where you going to go?" he asked. "I don't know," I said. "I guess I'm going into a shelter." My two kids and I were placed in the Prince George Hotel shelter.

By this time, I had started seeing Darnell, and I was pregnant with our child. Darnell was like a one-night stand that kept on going. The only reason I married him was to save face with my dad. My father had accepted my first and second children, but he said, "Michelle, before you have your third one, please be married." I married my baby's daddy to honor my dad. When Darnell wasn't messed up, he was really handy. He got a lot of work landscaping and painting. Around the hotel room, he cleaned and was great at fixing stuff. I could cook, but I mean Darnell could *cook*. Oh my God, I put on so much weight!

We got married a month and two days before our daughter was born in the summer of 1986. The baby was supposed to come in September, but I had her at seven months. Shellie was a very loud child. The prenatal ward let her go at four pounds, ten ounces instead of the usual five pounds because she kept crying and waking up everybody. When I took the baby home, she was all head and stomach, but there was nothing wrong with my second daughter. I had sampled crack by then, but my drug of choice was still cocaine.

The Prince George Hotel shelter was on Twenty-Eighth Street between Park Avenue and Madison Avenue. I always joked, "It took *this* for me to get a Madison Avenue address?" It was ugly, horrible—the whole ordeal! We were all in one room. Crack ran amok up there. The woman next door had a little girl and a little boy. When Darnell cooked, those kids would knock on my door. "Miss Michelle, my mom said can we borrow two slices of bread to make us a peanut butter sandwich?" They could smell the food. I fed them once or twice, but soon I told the mother, "Listen, they're hungry. They've got food pantries, you can go and get something from the pantry." It hurt me so bad. Your baby is knocking on my door to eat. You have your welfare check, but you only feed them two good meals a month and everything else goes to crack? The Bureau of Child Welfare (now the Administration for Children's Services) was in the shelter, but they were missing stuff like that. I was happy to leave the Prince George Hotel, so happy.

By January 1987, I was in my apartment in Harlem. I took the first thing they offered, because I wanted a place to call my own. The Department of Housing Preservation and Development (HPD) had renovated the building, but there was no elevator. My fourth-floor apartment had two bedrooms and a living room.

One day, while I was doing laundry, I found Darnell's crack stem. I knew that stuff had been missing from the apartment—change and bracelets—but I didn't want to believe he was selling them for crack. Mad as I was about it, I soon got addicted to crack too. Darnell didn't put a gun at my head to make me smoke, but he didn't stop me. Cocaine made you numb, but crack would make you feel like you couldn't move, couldn't talk. The first high was such a rush. You never got it back again, but you kept chasing. You chased a cloud. You did anything and everything to get that first feeling again. You became a slave to it. Crack was my downfall. It was my worst enemy, my rock bottom.

I never smoked around my kids. Getting high was a weekend thing for me. During the week, we didn't have the time or money. My son needed to go to school, and we had to make sure the girls had Pampers. On the weekend, I would send my son and older daughter to Hank's mother and send my younger daughter to my mother-in-law. Then Darnell and I would hang out, but not near my family.

My mother was homeless, going from one kid's house to another. Around Easter, she came to stay with me for a while. She kept telling me I wasn't raising my kids correctly. She told me how bad I was because I was addicted to crack. She even started the color issue with my younger daughter, who was darker than the first two. One day, my mother bought toys and stuff just for the lighter kids. My younger daughter was in a walker trying to catch up with them, and I said, "Y'all share with her."

"Oh, they don't have to share with her!" my mother said. "Come here, Darkie, come here, Blackie." That's what she called my younger daughter. The light clicked on in my head. I thought, "Whoa—slow down—wait a minute."

"What did you call her?" I asked my mother. "We're not going to do this again. This is something I carried with me throughout childhood. Thanks to you and your family, I'm all screwed up, thinking one child is better than the other. I treat my children according to their worth, not their color. If you come with something for these two and not this one, I'm going to have to ask you to leave. If you stay, you're going to have to treat them all the same across the board." My mother apologized, but she also called me defiant. She stayed with us until October.

During that same time, Darnell became a little snake. He started stealing out of our children's mouths. Every month when the food stamps came, I would buy groceries for my kids. Even if it was just a package of franks and beans, they had something to eat. I always ripped up the receipt, so I wouldn't be tempted to take the food back to the store and get money for crack. Yes, I ripped up the receipt so I couldn't do it. Then I found out Darnell was taking the groceries out and selling them on the street. I actually caught him outside selling the sugar cereal. Darnell was about six foot one, like a buck ninety, and I was about 135 pounds, but I snatched the bag of food he was trying to sell and I fought him. "Listen, I don't know what kind of shit you're smoking, but I don't steal from my kids. If I didn't want my kids to eat, I wouldn't have bought the damn food. How dare you! I bought it so my babies could eat! If you need to get crack, go suck a dick. I don't care. Go sell yourself. But stop stealing from my children!"

Another time, I gave that bastard money to buy a meal from the meat market in Brooklyn, across the street from his mother's house. He didn't come back. I called his mother's house—he wasn't there. I called the meat market—he never came. Finally Darnell came home with two catfish and a frozen chicken. I almost beat him with the frozen chicken. I threw a hammer, aiming for Darnell's head, but he ducked, and the aquarium

I bought for my kids got smashed. Yeah, I killed the goldfish. We were scuffling so bad my mother or the neighbors called the police. They handcuffed me and asked what the fight was about. "He smoked up my children's money. And now he's coming back here with two catfish and a frozen chicken thinking that's going to last for a month? He got nerve."

My father came by and saw I was unhappy. I said, "Daddy, my marriage with Darnell isn't working." By then my father had turned his life around. He was a genuine, solid citizen with a girlfriend and a Lincoln Town Coupe. When I told him Darnell was stealing from my children, my father said, "Come on, let's go grocery shopping." After he saw me put the food back in my house, my father gave me money for myself. He knew I would get high, but I was taking care of my family. He promised to come back on Saturday and give me money for a divorce.

A long time after my father left, I looked out the window, and he was still sitting in his car. "Well damn," I said, "Why Daddy ain't leave yet?" I went downstairs to check on my father, and he didn't look right in his face. "Wow, Daddy, you don't look good. You okay?" He said, "Yeah, I'm going to go to the bank and bring the money, and I'll come give it to you for a divorce."

By this time, when my father said he was going to do something, he did it. But Saturday came, and he didn't come by. He didn't come by Sunday either. I was like, "No, something is wrong." So that night, I took my oldest daughter over to his house in Queensbridge. When we got there, the house was dark. Turns out my father had had a stroke that night he left my apartment. Nobody in my family thought enough of me to let me know. By the time I got to the hospital, my brothers were fighting over my father's stuff and his car. I was so mad. "Y'all act like he already dead." My father wasn't dead. And only I knew about his bank accounts. "Michelle," he always said, "even if you marry, leave your name as Riddle, because if anything ever happens to me, it's going to be like you hit lotto." When my father went in the hospital, I could have run through all his bank money, but I didn't touch it. What was I going to do? Smoke up his life savings?

After my father got sick, my world unraveled. He was my backbone, and I realized he wasn't going to be around much longer. When I sat in the house with the kids, I didn't feel like I had anything left to live for. Part of me was at the hospital in the bed with my dad. The other part of me just didn't want to feel. That's when my addiction really took off.

But before I allowed it to take off, I made arrangements for my kids. I took my two oldest to Hank, their father, who had just gotten married, and I wrote up an agreement. "Here," I said, "I don't want them to go to the Bureau of Child Welfare, and I don't want to go to court." I signed over the welfare checks because they needed it for the children. I took my youngest daughter and gave her to Darnell's mother. I worried about my kids, but I thought the farther I stayed away, the better chance they had of a good upbringing. I had become a loose cannon. I knew I couldn't help or nurture or protect my kids. I wasn't the best mother—I pushed off my responsibilities to someone else—but I tried the best I could by putting my kids in places where I thought they would get the love and attention they needed.

After that, I was just running from one place to another. For a while, I rented my apartment to other people. Then the marshals came and put everybody out. They put all my stuff in storage, and I never went back. I lost a lot of stuff. I didn't look at myself as being homeless, because I always had a place to sleep. But if there wasn't a lease in my name, I was homeless, and that's the gist of it.

For money, I would go out on the stroll near a project in Brooklyn. I didn't want to steal—didn't have the heart to rob anybody. So the only thing I had to offer people was me, and that's what I did. One particular evening, I made about a hundred dollars in a car. When I got out, there was this white van, driving real slow. At first, I saw one guy get out of the van. I was walking, and he was walking behind me. Then the van came around again, and two more guys got out. I started running, and I had three guys running behind me. I felt them reaching for my body. They grabbed my hoodie, so I unzipped it and ran out of my clothing. I kept running. I crossed the street. I reached the G train station on Flushing Avenue. They were across the street. By now there were four of them, and the van was parked on the corner. But they couldn't catch me. Thank God for track in junior high school! Later that day, a dead girl was found in the lot nearby. She probably fought back, and they killed her. I followed my instincts and saved my life that night. I know I did.

That was not the only time. I also had this kid run up on me. He wanted a blowjob, so I told him, "Give me the money." He put the money in my hand. Then he pulled out a gun and put it to my head. "Now you're going to suck my dick and my four other friends' dicks. Otherwise I'm going to shoot you!"

Well," I said, "you better get to shooting me then because I ain't sucking anyone and you ain't getting your money back."

When I started walking away, the kid said, "Yo! I'm not playing with you!"

I said, "Shoot me! I'm going to die anyway. Kill me tonight!" And I walked the hell away with his money.

It was during this period that I contracted HIV. I found that out when I was in Phoenix House for a few months. When I got the word, I'll never forget: it was May 7, 1992. Charles, the coordinator who ran the staff meetings, said, "Come here, Michelle. Listen, you know what you did and the risk you took when you were in the street. You know about that, right?" From what he said, I knew I was HIV positive. I was so upset. It was eating at me, and I wanted to run. I wanted to die almost, just knowing what I was going to have to live with. Other people with HIV were trying to explain to me, "You can live with it. We're living today." They were right. Today you wouldn't even know I was HIV positive if I didn't tell you. I take my medicine like I breathe.

The good thing about rehab was that my father got to see me clean. Before that, I couldn't bring myself to visit him. I wasn't good for anybody; my life had become worthless. But after I got clean at Phoenix House, I walked into my father's nursing home. All the nurses said, "Oh, you must be Michelle!" They told me my father used to ask for me all the time. "Where Michelle at? Why she ain't come?" By the time I finally got there he wasn't talking anymore, he couldn't move, he had been in the fetal position for two or three years, and he wasn't even fifty-seven. To see this man who used to be almost two hundred pounds look like he was eighty-eight pounds broke my heart. His hands were so confined and restricted. They just let him lie there, and nobody helped him. He was in diapers, he started crying, I was crying. His money was gone, nobody was visiting. It was horrible.

One Friday at Phoenix House, I asked for permission to visit my dad, and my counselor wouldn't let me leave. The next morning, the staff coordinator told me, "Your father passed last night." My father had a stroke on August 1, 1988, and he died, I kid you not, four years later, on August 1, 1992.

Next thing I knew I was in the funeral parlor, but there was no viewing and no casket. I was like, "What's going on?"

My brother David started crying. "They did an autopsy, and since there wasn't much of him left, we had him cremated."

I lost my mind. I was furious. I started hitting the table with the box of ashes on it. "You had him cremated before I could say goodbye? Why didn't you let the military pay for it? We could have got a picture, and we could have got the flag."

David kept crying. "I'm doing the best I can, you wasn't here."

About a week later at a Phoenix House meeting, I kept raising my hand to share, and my counselor kept passing by me. Finally I just took the floor: "You're going to listen to me! I asked you, could I go see my dad. You knew what was going on. And your fat ass wouldn't let me go see him. And now I'm looking at ashes." I was fit to be tied, I was so lonely. There were about 325 people in that Phoenix House building, and I was the loneliest thing in there.

I was upset with God for a long, long time after that. Nothing mattered any more. All bets were off. I just wanted to run and medicate. In 1993, I left Phoenix House and relapsed.

Now that I was HIV positive, I wouldn't sell my ass for money anymore. Even though I got the virus through one of my sexual partners, I didn't think it would be fair to give it to anybody else. That's how I felt. It just didn't sit right with me. So I started pitching—selling crack for different dealers. That's how I was taking care of my habit.

They couldn't put me in a shelter because of my HIV status, so I ended up in a hotel for people with the virus. That's where I met the father of my next child. They called him CD and he was a piece of work, I'm telling you. I didn't realize what I signed on for with this guy. I went through a lot of verbal abuse. He even took a piece of umbrella and jammed the lock on my door, so I couldn't get into my own place. Then some chick started coming around. CD tried to tell me it was his cousin, but the next thing I knew, they were in bed. Sleeping with your cousin? That stuff didn't even look right. My son David, I'm going to be real honest, he shouldn't have been born. I should have taken care of that. But I was so caught up in my addiction that I couldn't do anything about it.

On May 10, 1994, David was born premature. He weighed maybe a pound, and he had to stay in the hospital after I left. The hospital gave me an identification bracelet so I could visit David any time. They told me that little boy needed to feel my love and hear my voice, because he was having trouble. "Hey, David," I would say, and I'd play with him. But I found myself getting attached, and I knew I wasn't going to be a part of his life. So I went out and brought CD and his so-called cousin up to the hospital. I told the people there that CD was David's father, and I made sure he got an identification bracelet. I pointed to the girlfriend. "And give the ho one too. Let her have it." Then I held out my bracelet. "Now cut this one off." Once they cut off my bracelet, I knew I wasn't coming back to see my baby.

After I got rid of CD, I met Jerry, who also had HIV. He was a tall drink of water, and I'm attracted to that. One Christmas, I was dodging somebody and needed a place to stay. Jerry let me sleep in his bed, and after that we got together. About a year later, Jerry got arrested for robbing an old lady's apartment when she was in the hospital. That same old lady had once handed Jerry and me a bag of pennies. We used them to buy like thirteen dollars' worth of groceries. On the way back, I saw this mother begging with her little boy, who was crying and hungry. Jerry and I must have had half a bag of pennies left. "Here," I said, handing the mother the bag. "Go buy him something to eat." Jerry said, "Why you do that? I could have used—" I said, "Let her have them. That child is hungry."

After Jerry went to jail for the robbery, I found out I was pregnant. Bethany was born September 3, 1996. She wasn't even seven months yet, and she weighed a pound and a half. As soon as I was able, I got out of my hospital bed and left my baby in the hands of God. It seemed the only thing proper was to pray that somebody else would come along and take care of her. And that is what happened. When Bethany was three months old, a lady named Daphne saw her and fell in love with her. She became Bethany's foster mother.

It was so easy to leave David and Bethany in the hospital, not only because I didn't have a place to take them but also because I couldn't take care of them. I was in another ratty welfare hotel for people with HIV. Both kids were born with the virus, and both had toxins from the crack use. By the time she was two years old, Bethany had grown out of her HIV, and she has never had any physical problems from the crack. David died of complications when he was four and a half. The social worker who was handling both of the kids' cases told me, "I have good news about Bethany and bad news about David." I said, "No, it was good news both ways around," because my baby boy was not suffering any more, and I was very grateful for that. I had a picture of David, but I lost it when I got arrested. I won't ever have any more pictures of David.

When I went to prison in 1998, I was considered the world's smallest drug dealer. I weighed all of eighty-eight pounds. My hair was so matted that they had to cut it all off, because we couldn't even comb it. They told me that if I did the prison's substance abuse treatment programs, I would get work release and then I could do parole. The prison treatment programs were good, because you actually got to work on yourself. Narcotics Anonymous came in, and I was required to attend that. I remembered hearing about NA when I was on the street, but I didn't have time for it then. I was too busy trying to make that next dollar and get that next hit. When I was in prison, NA helped me realize that I had a disease, that the driving force to get the next hit was my disease. Until then, I just thought I was going to die using. I thought I was going to be an addict for the rest of my life. When I came home from prison, I had been clean for four years. Today I have been clean for sixteen!

In prison, there were four cliques. You had to join one, because if you kept to yourself, the inmates would gang up on you. Either you were "gay for the stay," you were Muslim, you were a commissary ho—meaning you did anything and everything for somebody else's commissary—or you were a Christian. So I became a Christian. I started going to church, and I became an usher. That's when I came back to God. After I got out of prison, I was baptized at a Baptist church. It took going to prison for me to get my life together. I always say I was rescued, not arrested.

The bad thing about prison was the doctor, Dr. H——, the only doctor they had up there to give out medicine. He wanted to give all the women hysterectomies—young, old, HIV positive, HIV negative. He was trying to genocide us so we couldn't reproduce. Dr. H—— was a nasty doctor. There wasn't a woman doctor or nurse in there, just him and me, and he was always touching me. Because I was an inmate, there wasn't very much I could do, although I did refuse to have a hysterectomy. After that, some inmates who came to prison after me started leaving before me for work release. I asked one of my captains, "Why am I still here? I should have gotten work release six months ago." Sure enough, it turns out Dr. H—— had put a medical hold on me because I wouldn't do the hysterectomy. Not too long ago, I found out that he's still there! He needs to be put out.

In 2000, I got out of prison and went to the Department of Corrections' Phoenix House. It was there that I saw my daughter Bethany again. Daphne, the woman who adopted her, wanted me to be part of my child's life. I call Daphne my angel. In prison, she sent me a picture of Bethany's first Christmas; she was in a rocking chair, and the candy cane she had was bigger than she was. First thing Bethany said when she saw me in Phoenix House was, "Hi, Mommy."

Daphne told me that when Bethany started kindergarten, the little girl sitting next to her pointed to Daphne and said, "Is that your mommy?" Bethany said, "God gave me two mommies." That answer melted my heart.

We all started getting together at McDonald's for Christmas and birthdays. I would bring toys and stuff. One Christmas we did a big brunch at IHOP. We had like twenty-six people—my family, Daphne's family—my daughter Shellie and my brother. Daphne invited me to her house. I went there for Thanksgiving, I went there for Christmas, I have been there for birthdays. In August 2014, I went to see my oldest daughter Evette down South, and guess who came with me? Bethany!

After I left Phoenix House, I needed a place to go during parole, and my mother said I could stay with her, in her building for seniors. This is how I found out that my mother really did love me, and she did do the best she could. She saw that I always went to my NA meetings and I was a changed person. My mother said, "I would hate to see somebody or something hurt you, because you're doing so good!" After a few months, I moved into an SRO; after that, I moved to a place run by the Volunteers of America.

I did everything I could to recover and get help. I joined the Women's Prison Association. No matter what my counselor there asked me to do, I did it. I might gripe, but I did it. She said I was one of her best clients and gave me a Phenomenal Woman certificate. After that I went to Women in Need, where I was tutored for my GED. I worked hard, and when I got my diploma, I was so freaking happy.

People at Women in Need told me about the life skills empowerment program at New York Catholic Charities, run by George Horton and Ms. K. In 2003, I joined the twenty-ninth class of the program. My mentor was named Lucille, and we connected spiritually. She was Catholic and I wasn't, but God is God no matter what religion he is under. The program gave me the opportunity to hear stories from different people. When they shared their lives, I felt their pain, and that response told me that they were telling the truth.

On Speakers' Night, I got picked to tell my story. I was really nervous, but God helped me and took over. I shared about what I had done. I shared about prison, and I shared my experiences coming back home. After I finished, I got a standing ovation. My class had sixteen people, and we didn't lose anybody. We all graduated in December. I wore a winter white suit that a friend bought for me, and it looked really nice.

I'm telling you, I got me some certificates. I got my certificate from the life skills empowerment program, my GED diploma, my Phenomenal Woman certificate, I got my baptism paper, I got my drug treatment certificate, I got certificates from Volunteers of America, I got a certificate for anger management, too.

In 2001, I met Calhoun on an AIDS walk. Everyone called him CL. He was born in Augusta, Georgia, in a family of two girls and five boys. He was third from the youngest, the middle child. When I met him, CL was a snappy dresser and just all-over colorful. It took this man two hours to get dressed in the morning. And he had a kind heart—oh my God! If you were feeling bad or depressed, CL would get you out of it. He'd tell everybody he saw, "Good morning, young man, good morning, young lady, how you doing." I'd ask him, "Why do you keep doing that?" He'd say, "Come on, baby, if I can put a smile on their face, let me put a smile on their face." I got him to do the life skills empowerment program, and he loved to be around George and Ms. K. CL was nice to everybody— the opposite of me. I can be nice, but I can be nasty too—not selfish, but I've been through so much that I can smell bullshit at the door. I don't have time for bullshit.

Still, CL loved me, man. I really got a chance to find out what love was besides what I had with my dad. Through my good and bad, CL put up with me unconditionally. And I loved him back.

One day, a few years later, my mother didn't call me in the morning like she always did. It was July 8, 2004, a day before her birthday. I got worried and raced over to her apartment. When I unlocked the doors, I found my mother on the floor. She was blue, she couldn't talk, and she had urinated on herself. She smelled so bad the EMS people wouldn't pick her up. My mother weighed like three hundred pounds, and my brother had to pick her up and put her on the stretcher.

In the hospital, my mother kept calling me "Madame Rat." She said it in front of my Aunt Paige—the one who put us out when we were kids—my Aunt Betty and everybody else. "Where Madame Rat at?" It hurt my feelings.

Finally, my Aunt Paige turned to my mother: "You need to stop calling her that 'cause if it wasn't for Michelle, your ass be dead. She came because she didn't hear from your ass. You need to be saying, 'Thank You, Madame Rat!'"

My mother called me over to her bed. "Shell," she said, "listen, I know I don't say how proud I am of you, but I am proud of you. And whatever happens to me, I don't want you to use it as an excuse to go out and get high." It kind of threw me off, kind of spooked me. On July 16 she slipped into a coma, and on July 27 she died. The day she died was the day I was celebrating six years of sobriety.

My mother died surrounded by my older brother, my son, and my younger brother, who came with my oldest daughter, Evette. Since age nine, Evette had been living down South with her father's wife, and my mother had always kept in touch with her. It was my mother's death that actually opened the door for me to get to know my daughter again. She's a teacher today. I am so proud of her.

In the past, I always dealt with death by getting high. When my mother died, I was together with CL and I had my NA meetings, but I was afraid of idle time. I got in touch with Ms. K. at New York Catholic Charities, who told me, "Come on in and help with the EOP's fifteen-year anniversary." That was ten years ago, and I'm still volunteering at Catholic Charities. On any given Tuesday, you can find me there; after that I go to my NA home group. It's like tea before the cake. You can bank on it. I do whatever Catholic Charities asks. At Christmas, I run their store—we sell coffee, chocolates, and handmade stuff from around the world—all fair trade. I have also been a life skills empowerment program mentor several times, and I have facilitated a couple of programs with the Board of Education and in transitional shelters.

On June 9, 2007, CL and I got married at the Grace Congregational Church of Harlem on 139th Street and Edgecombe Avenue. My older brother did the service, and my younger brother walked me down the aisle. My son was CL's best man. My daughter Evette filmed it. My other daughters, Shellie and Bethany, were there as my ushers. I'm telling you, I was so blessed. I looked at all I had done and where I came from, and I could honestly say that I had done the best that I could for all of them in their own time.

Everything is for a reason. Before we got married, CL had a tumor on his neck, but they said it was benign. Around 2010 he lost a lot of weight, but he had just lost his brother Robert, so we thought it was depression. Then CL started getting weak; he was walking slow. I insisted that we go to the doctor. "We gonna find out what the hell is wrong with you, 'cause something's wrong." It was February 7—I'll never forget because my grandson was born on the fifth. Turned out CL already had stage four lymphoma. Chemo just opened the door on the damn thing. CL ended up in the ICU. They tried everything, but his immune system was not as great as mine—his T-cell count was around two hundred.

It was the hardest thing in my world to not be selfish and keep this man around, knowing his organs were shutting down. They took him off the respirator. They gave him the morphine drip. The last time CL was conscious, I went to his bedside. "Baby, I'm not going to let you go alone. I'm going to be right there with you." He was bleeding from his gums. He was turning blue. I didn't want him to die without me by his side. I didn't want them to call me from the hospital and tell me I missed it. I stayed right there until my husband took his last breath—on March 9, 2011.

I'm so glad that he had life insurance, because when it came time to send CL home, we had the best funeral going. The room in the funeral parlor held 250 people, but there were people in the foyer and in the street; that's how many people came to honor CL. I put him in the suit he wore for his wedding. Back when he bought that suit, he said, "I won't be wearing this again." I said, "Shit, if you don't, I'm gonna put your ass in that suit." And I did. He looked so handsome.

After CL died, I was so thrown. I had to stop doing as much for other people, because I had to take care of Michelle. It was a process that I had to learn, but I learned it. I never gave up, and I never got high.

I used to have a big grievance with God, but now I know he never left me. I'm not going to lie. I have some lonely periods at times. My husband is gone. There's never going to be another one like him. He loved me unconditionally, and he was the sweetest, nicest guy. But I know he is still with me. And every day I talk to God. I talk to him when I get up in the morning and before I go to bed at night. I thank him for all I have been through. If I could go back and change something, I don't think I would, because I wouldn't be the same. I'm not a bad person. I made some bad mistakes, bad decisions, and there were consequences to pay. But I have worked really hard to be who I am, and I love myself. I'm still dealing with the grieving, but I'm also still living—not just existing. Today I have a reason to get up and be happy.

I have eleven grandkids and one great-grand kid. God has done a good job in preserving me. When I went to get disability for my bad knees from the asthma drugs, the judge said, "Miss Riddle, given your condition, we don't know how you're walking around." I said, "I'm walking around 'cause God got me walking around." I am a very active person. I am employed as a companion and coach for sick people, I am very much active in the fellowship of NA, I go to New York Catholic Charities, I am a life skills empowerment program mentor, I'm a good friend, I'm on the Board of Directors of the Interfaith Assembly on Homelessness and Housing, and I'm on the advisory board for this book. I actually have places where I'm needed. I know what it is like to be hurt in life, so I have a lot of compassion for people.

To me it's just like having a conscience—doing the right thing because it's the right thing to do. Coming over here, I ran into three homeless people. One guy was playing a saxophone on the train. Great music. He played, "My Favorite Things," one of my favorite songs. I gave him three dollars. When I came out of the train, there was an Asian lady standing there. I gave her two dollars. Coming up Sixtieth Street, there was another lady with a dog. I gave her a dollar. I know that if I stop doing what I'm doing, I will be that person in the street. I don't give to see what I'm going to get back. I give because I have it to give.

Today I live in an apartment in Brooklyn. I have been there for five years now. My landlord is a doctor, and she only rents to women. I'm on the first floor in the front. I've got four steps. I have a nice bedroom, a closet for all my clothes, a bathroom, a nice-sized living room, a nice kitchen where I can cook and serve the people I have over. God is good all the time. I am in here with my dad, my brother-in-law Robert, and my husband CL. I have everybody's ashes. So I'm not alone.

Reflection
Hope

In 2012–2013, Hope helped start Riverside Church's program for formerly incarcerated individuals, known as Riverside Coming Home, as part of her internship for the master's program in social work at Fordham University. She then served as program director for Riverside Coming Home and for L-STEP, the life skills empowerment program at Xavier Mission, from 2013 to 2015.

When I was born, I was placed for adoption. In my first parents' minds, it was the best decision for me based on their life circumstances at the time, but I never could wrap my head around that. I would sit alone in silence in my pink bedroom surrounded by my dolls and dream about what life would be like living with my first mother in what I imagined was a tiny studio apartment in Philadelphia. We looked exactly alike; everybody could tell that she was my mom. We didn't have much, but we had each other; that was what was most important. Of course, this was all a fantasy, but it gave me comfort.

When my parents adopted me, they named me Hope, because they hoped for me and they got me. I didn't always feel like a Hope. It was a name that had a lot of power and significance, something that I felt I couldn't really live up to. In fact, in middle school, some of the older kids on the bus used to call me Hopeless. On the worst days, I believed it.

When I was a child, I was in my own little world. I rarely spoke to anybody outside of my immediate family. I was always afraid to share my thoughts or feelings with others because somebody might reject me—again.

127

My parents are absolutely wonderful people, but I still felt a deep sense of hurt, anger, and rejection. It made me question whether I was worthy of love. Maybe I'm a horrible person. Maybe that is why my first parents left me. Maybe these parents will leave me too. These thoughts would race around my brain, over and over again. I was paralyzed by them.

As I grew up, the romantic relationships in my life suffered as I tried my best to sabotage them out of fear that these people would leave me too. Eventually I began to open up more, but I never talked about my sadness and anger. I held it in. I was ashamed. It was programmed into me by society that I should feel grateful to be adopted and be with a wonderful family and that I shouldn't feel this sense of loss. But I felt it. It was in the little things, conversations with friends about how much they look like their family members and stories about the days they were born. Nobody could see my pain.

From an early age, I wanted to work with people who were returning to the community from incarceration. I felt a deep connection to people who had experienced incarceration. I didn't understand it, but I went with my gut feeling that something was calling me.

In my second year of the master's program in social work at Fordham University, my internship was to help start a life skills empowerment program at Riverside Church for men and women returning to the community from incarceration. I will be forever grateful for this opportunity, because it has been the most healing and impactful experience of my life.

It is hard to explain the magic that is created in Riverside Coming Home. I step inside the room and suddenly I belong somewhere. I am surrounded by people I care about and who care about me. I am surrounded by family. There is a magical element that transcends space and time and has a spiritual aura to it. You can smell the delicious food—rice and beans, chicken, a fresh pot of coffee. Beautiful faces join hands together as we begin with a prayer. We eat together. We share in this moment.

Then we move to our circle. A poem, a song, twelve different views of the same piece of life, a pat on the back, a round of applause, a wink, a chuckle, a grin, a tear. Stories are shared. Stories of pain, laughter, courage, triumph, regret, rebirth. A hug, a tissue, a kind word. We are in this together. We are welcome here. We are safe. We are important—each of us. You can see people in the group—mentors, volunteers, and staff—all changed from this experience of having a safe space where they can finally be themselves, be honest, and genuinely belong.

One night at Riverside Coming Home, when members of the group were sharing their stories, it finally dawned on me why I felt such a deep connection to them. The members shared stories about their anger stemming from adoption—never knowing their first parents or being abandoned by a parent—holding it in for their whole childhood, feeling like nobody understood. I listened to their pain, wisdom, insight, and bravery. And I understood. In hearing their anger and pain, I heard my anger and pain. Our paths were different, but our feeling, our humanity, was very much the same. By telling their stories, they liberated me to tell my own story—to tell my parents, my friends, my community my story.

After this experience, I gained the courage to begin the process of reconnecting with my first parents. This has been very hard emotionally, and things haven't always gone the way I wanted. But the confidence I gained and continue to gain from my experience with the Coming Home family has helped sustain me. At Coming Home, I saw the weight lifting off people as they told their truths. It gave me the strength to tell my own truth. It still does.

Life Story
Edna Humphrey

Edna Humphrey was born on April 12, 1954, in New Orleans, Louisiana. She graduated in 2005 from the Life-Skills Training and Empowerment Program (L-STEP), the life skills empowerment program at St. Francis Xavier Church. Edna's story includes details and quotations from a StoryCorps interview she had with me in June 2010.

There were six kids in my family—three brothers and three sisters. I was the oldest girl. Beatrice was next after me, and then Sharon. We were born in New Orleans, Louisiana. When I was very young, my mother took my three brothers and brought them here to New York. "I can't take care of the girls," she said. She only wanted the boys. We are still trying to figure out why.

We were left with my Grandma Leah and my Grandpa Teddy, not with my father because my mother said he was no good. But I liked my father. He worked at a gas company down in Louisiana. Sometimes he told my grandmother, "Don't cook tonight. I'm takin' y'all out." We all went— my sisters, my grandmother, and my grandfather. It was a good restaurant, a buffet, all you can eat. I had chicken, rice, sweet potatoes, collard greens. You could go around two or three times and take something home if you wanted.

Grandma Leah and Grandpa Teddy lived in a nice house in Baton Rouge. They fed us all the time and made sure we had clothes. We couldn't miss church down South, not a single Sunday. We stayed there from morning till night. My grandmother said, "Y'all gonna just keep

130

praying that y'all gonna get where y'all wanna go to." I knew God was watching over us.

In my grandparents' house, my sisters and I had our own room. We kept it clean. We did our homework. We did everything my grandmother told us to do. Then we could go outside and play with our friends. My sister Beatrice was good at jump rope. I was good at stickball. We used a mop as a bat. I could hit the ball straight across the street to the neighbor's yard. Our street was rocky. It wasn't cement like up here in New York City. My grandmother sat on the porch and kept an eye on us. My grandfather too. When we came from school, my grandfather would say, "I'm making y'all a sandwich. What kind of sandwich y'all want?"

One day my grandmother said, "Come on, let me take you to the store, buy y'all a toy or something 'cause there are no toys in the house." We thought she was playing, because my grandma never went to the store much. I said, "Grandma, we don't need nothing." Still, she took us to the store. I picked up a paddleball with jacks, my sister got a puzzle, and my other sister got a jump rope. My sisters and I got along good. We never fought.

We didn't have a mom because she didn't take care of us. Whenever we called her, she would hang up. My grandma said, "I'm gonna call your mother's sister, tell her to tell your mother to call y'all." But my mother didn't call, didn't say nothing about nothing. My mother didn't want us girls, only the boys.

My grandmother was nice to us girls. I never wanted her to let me go. When it was time for school, I used to stand right underneath her, holding on to her skirt.

"You gotta go to school!" my grandmother would say.

"No! No!" I thought something bad was going to happen to her while we were gone. "Somebody has to stay here with you."

My sister laughed at me. "She gonna be okay, Grandma gonna be okay. Come on."

But my grandmother wasn't okay. When I was about eight or nine, she got cancer. For a while she was going back and forth to the doctor. Then she couldn't pay for the doctor anymore because her insurance coverage stopped. My grandmother's face started swelling up. My mother wouldn't send her any money. Finally we called my father, and he sent money to take my grandmother to the hospital. They kept her there. "I'm not gonna make it," my grandmother said. "Don't say that to us," Sharon said. "'Cause you're gonna make it."

My mother didn't come down for my grandmother's funeral. My father was there, and my mother's sister came with her daughter. They were in dressy, movie star clothes. My sisters and I had only our school uniforms on. We didn't own dressy clothes like that. All three of us were just hugging each other. There weren't many people at the funeral.

Two months later, my grandfather died. He had cancer too.

That's why my sisters and I had to go stay with my aunt and her daughter. My father gave my aunt money to pay our school tuition and to buy us food, clothes, and shoes. We saw a check for $2,000 and a note saying, "Stuff for the kids." But as soon as my aunt got that check, she bought her daughter all these beautiful clothes and shoes. She said my father didn't send her anything. My sisters and I ate breakfast and lunch at school. But when we got home my aunt would say, "I'm not cooking, and I'm not feeding nobody." Then she would feed her daughter, not us. Sometimes the sisters at the school would put an extra sandwich in the bottom of my book bag. My aunt would search my sisters' bags but not mine, because I told her I had too many books. At night, I'd sneak the sandwich out and share it with my sisters.

My aunt sent us to school with no shoes on our feet. We had to walk on the rocks all the way. The sister who ran the school got all heated up about that. I think her name was Maria. She asked us what size shoes we wore, and then she went to the store and bought us some nice, brand-new shoes. She asked where our mother was, and I told her, "New York."

"You know her number?"

I said no.

"Where's your father?"

Sharon said, "I'm gonna try and contact him"—because this was crazy. Our tuition wasn't paid.

Sharon had seen my father's address on the envelope when a check came, and she had written it down in her book. Sharon knew everything. She wrote my father a letter: "It's an emergency, Pop. You gotta come and see Sister Maria at school. We need you bad." The day after he got the letter, my father came to our school. My sister Beatrice was so skinny my father barely knew her. "We ain't been eating," Beatrice told him. "I didn't know your aunt was doing that," my father said. He paid up all our back tuition. He asked Sister Maria, "How much I owe you for them shoes?" But she wouldn't take any money for that.

We had been with my aunt nine, going on ten months. "Let me take y'all away from her," my father said. Since he was working a double shift at the gas company, we couldn't go live with him. So we all got on a plane to go to my mother's house in New York City. My sisters liked the plane, but I thought it was scary. When we got off in New York City, I looked around at all the buildings. Some of them looked so nice. "Boy," I said. "I'll bet the rent is expensive here."

My mother lived in a brownstone in Brooklyn. She had the first floor and the basement. When my sisters and I got there, she didn't open the door. My brother did. "What you want?" my mother asked. My father said, "I'm bringing the girls to you." My mother didn't hug us.

"The girls go in the basement," was all she said. My father gave us a kiss, put some money in our pockets, and told my mother, "Don't you take their money, 'cause that's their money to spend." Then he told us, "Bye. I'll come back and see y'all again."

He never came back. The day after he returned to New Orleans, my father got killed in a gas explosion on the job. I don't know how many other people working with him died; I just know my father did. All my mother said was, "Your father's just passed away." She had no kind of reaction, just my sisters were crying. I cried a little bit.

"Well, I gotta go to the funeral," my mother said. "But I'm not taking the girls, only the boys."

"Why you ain't taking us girls?" I asked. "That's our father."

"'Cause I don't have the money," my mother said.

Then somebody—I think it was the president of something and his wife—read about the explosion in the newspaper. They told my mother, "No, you're going to take the girls to the funeral too." They paid for our plane tickets and bought us clothes. They even paid for a hotel room where we stayed down there.

I wore a white dress, white tights, and white shoes to my father's funeral. Before it started, my sisters and I wanted to see his face to make sure it was the right person in the casket. So my mother asked the undertaker to open it for us. That was him in there.

Lots of people from my father's job came to the funeral. My aunt and her daughter came. They had a big picture of my father on top of the casket. My father had taken out life insurance for us kids, but my mother took the money and spent it.

After the funeral, we came back to New York City. My mother said she had to get back to her job—she did sewing work. At first, my sisters and I went to a Catholic school on Eastern Parkway. That didn't last long because my mother wouldn't pay the tuition. After that, I went to public school at 167 Northeastern Parkway. It was a nice school. I liked doing my math and reading and science.

When my sisters and I came home from school, we had to go straight to the basement. We couldn't hang out upstairs on the first floor like my brothers. My mother gave us food, but she told my brother to bring it to us. Sometime he would just throw it down the stairs. There were two twin beds in the basement, and we put them together. My little sister Sharon slept in the middle, and Beatrice and I slept on the ends. That's how it was.

On Sundays, all my friends went to church, and we had to stay in the basement because my mother didn't like us girls going out. She locked the door and made sure every window gate was locked. My sisters and I would get on our knees and pray that she would open the door so we could go to church and go outside and get some air. We'd stay on our knees for hours. It didn't work.

Sometimes, when she left the house, my mother would chain me and Beatrice to a pole in the middle of the basement. Otherwise, she said, we would get out and leave. There was this big old chain going around and around us. We couldn't move. To go to the bathroom, we had to use a pail or do it in our clothes and things.

When I was around twelve, my mother kept us from school a few times. Sharon wasn't on the chain. She tried to get me and Beatrice loose, but she couldn't do it. I think the third time we missed school, a truant officer came looking for us. Sharon wrote "Help Us!" on a piece of cardboard. When the officer knocked, she held the sign up in the basement window for him to see. The truant officer called the police, and they came and broke down the door and unchained us. A detective came too—I don't remember his name, but he was a nice guy. He got us out of there. Later, at the police station, he told my mother, "You do that again, you're going to jail." My mother took us home, and after that we went to school.

Still, things got worse, because my mother had a boyfriend. When I was fourteen or fifteen, he started abusing me and Beatrice. Our youngest sister, Sharon, he didn't touch. We tried to tell my mother what was happening, but he said, "I didn't do nothing to them." My mother believed him, not her own kids. One day my mother left the house with him. She never did come back again. Her boyfriend came back a few times, though. He raped me and Beatrice. "Why are you doing this?" we asked. He said, "Because your mother ain't going to believe you all."

During the last rape, he kept punching us. He didn't beat me up that much, but he was stomping and stomping on Beatrice's chest. There was so much blood coming out all down her leg, some from her back, her nose. She had a black eye, and her whole face was swollen on that side. I think the neighbor upstairs heard a lot of noise and called the ambulance. Or maybe my youngest brother called the cops. My mother's boyfriend left the house on the run. All us girls went to Kings County Hospital. They said Beatrice had broken ribs and things. The people in the hospital believed we were telling the truth about the boyfriend. But when my mother came, she still didn't believe us. They were looking for him to lock him up, but my mother said, "Y'all ain't gonna find wherever he at. He gone." I don't know if the police ever caught up with him or not.

My sister Beatrice died from her injuries. At the funeral, she had a white dress with a black belt around her, like a ribbon. She had stockings

and little shoes on her feet. We buried her down South with my grandmother, grandfather, and father. I wore my hair back.

After that, my father's sister, Aunt Ruth, took us in as her own kids—
me, Sharon, and my youngest brother. The other two brothers stayed with
my mother. My Aunt Ruth and her husband were very nice. They had
a big house in Queens with a big yard, and they gave us everything we
needed. My aunt owned a religious store on Ocean Avenue, and sometimes Sharon and I went there and helped her.

In school, I met this guy. "Oh, I like you, you look nice," he said. A
girl told me, "Don't trust him 'cause he no good." I didn't listen, and after
a while the guy said, "I wants to marry you." I said, "I'm not going to
marry nobody. I'm gonna stay single until I find the right man." When I
was seventeen or nineteen, one of those ages, I got pregnant for the first
time. I ended up having two kids, a girl and a boy. I named my kids after
my grandparents, like I always said I would. Aunt Ruth told me, "Don't
worry. I'll help you with them." She bought my kids clothes, diapers, and
things. She did mostly everything for them.

After a few years, I wanted to get my own place, so I went into a shelter. That was the only way for me to get an apartment. Aunt Ruth said,
"You're not taking them kids to the shelter. You leave them right here.
They'll stay with me." So she took them, and I saw my children on the
weekend. They did well with my aunt.

First I went to Brooklyn Women's Shelter. That's the intake shelter. If
they don't have a bed, you sit in the chair and sleep. It wasn't a good place
to hang out, because there were too many drugs and people fighting. Security always checked your bag to make sure you had no knife or scissors.
After thirty days, they transferred me to a women's shelter at 85 Lexington
Avenue in Brooklyn. I was there a long time. It was okay, but they had bed-
bugs. The workers would get you up at six every morning and throw you
out of the shelter at nine. I would go walking or go to the library and read.

Next I went to the Bowery Residents' Community (BRC). They were
nice there and had different programs. I took a computer class and got a
B. I also saw a medical doctor and a psychiatrist at BRC. I started getting
therapy and was referred to the International Center for the Disabled. I
don't know what my disability is. I really don't. I still go to therapy once
a week, but now I go somewhere else.

Altogether, I was in those three shelters for fourteen years. Finally, I got
an apartment in Brooklyn. My daughter and son left my aunt's house and
came to live with me. It was a three-bedroom apartment, and they each
had their own room. It was good having my kids with me.

One weekend, my cousin's three kids came to visit us. Nobody knew the electrical wire in the closet light was broken, because the landlord said everything was fixed. I think it was my son who turned on the switch. Everything went up in fire. Just like that. The landlord had put a tall, locked gate on the fire escape. Nobody could get out. The firemen had to tear down the gate and break the window to rescue us. My cousin's kids were still alive when they got to the hospital. They died about an hour later of smoke inhalation. I lost one, two, three kids that night.

My daughter and son lived, but they had smoke inhalation and their legs were burned. They were in the hospital for two or three months. After they got out, they went back to Aunt Ruth's house, because I said, "I don't want anything else to happen to them." I was homeless again and went back to the BRC shelter to wait for transitional housing. Eventually I got moved to an SRO. I'm still in an SRO today.

I think it was after the fire that somebody came by the shelter and talked about the life skills empowerment program at St. Francis Xavier Church. I went with some other people from the shelter. The program let us out in time for our shelter curfew, so we didn't lose our beds. I liked the program. It was good mingling with the participants. In the life skills workshops, I learned how to budget my money. I'm still saving my money. My mentor was very nice, and she helped me set goals. I graduated in 2005, and I told my story at the ceremony. Afterward, a lady came up to me and said, "You went through all that? I don't know how you could make it, but you did."

When the ceremony was over, I asked Marc Greenberg, "Got any work for me to do around the office?" Since then, I have volunteered at the IAHH every single day, Monday through Friday. I help with the filing and typing, look up things on the computer, and run around doing errands. I go to the post office and the bank. I'm also a member of the IAHH Speakers Bureau. I've gone with Dennis Barton to different synagogues, churches, and schools. It's good telling your story to people. I remember one little girl said, "You made it through." I said, "Yeah, baby, but when people ask for money, don't reach in your pocket and give it to them, because you don't know if they gonna hurt you or what."

Every third Wednesday, there is an alumni meeting for the group from my life skills empowerment program. I go to that too. They say, "Come and keep yourself out of trouble."

I'm always glad to get away from my SRO in the Bronx, because it's bad around there. People will rob your apartment if they know you aren't home. They know when I'm leaving and when I'm coming back. I had to

Edna at work at the IAHH

get my lock changed, because some people were going into my apartment. My church paid for the locksmith. Once, the building manager didn't let my son see me on my birthday. My son had called and said, "Mom, I'm gonna come and take you out." But when he got to the building, they wouldn't let him or my granddaughter up. She is only six years old. I don't want to stay in that building. I told BRC I want another apartment, but nothing is happening.

On Saturdays and Wednesdays, I help the homeless people at my church. We give them clothes. On Wednesday night, they get a hot meal, and on Saturday, they get bag lunches and juice and coffee. On Sundays, I greet the people coming to services at my church, and I work with the kids in the Sunday school. I don't miss a day unless I'm sick. On Tuesdays, I work in a soup kitchen at another church on Seventh Avenue and Thirteenth

Street. On the weekends, I take care of my cousin's two boys. They come to church with me on Sunday.

Down South, my grandmother used to take us to help people. Three or four ladies were real sick, and one was dying of cancer. My grandmother would say, "Come on, let's go and see what we can do." We'd go to the ladies' houses and comfort them and pray. That's something I still love to do. At church, I keep telling my pastor, "Let's go to visit somebody." One of my best friends keeps falling in the street. I go see her in Brooklyn, go to the store for her, wash her dishes, and see what else she needs.

I love doing things to help people. My grandmother brought me up that way. And I love going to church. I love to hear the Word of God. I thank God every evening when I get home. In the morning, I thank God for waking me up and starting me on my way. That's how I have survived.

Reflection
Ira Ben Wiseman

Ira Ben Wiseman has volunteered since 2011 with the Panim el Panim life skills empowerment program and has served six times as a mentor. At one of the graduation ceremonies, Ira was chosen to give a short speech on behalf of the mentors. This is what he said.

I am honored to share some sentiments and ideas at this graduation ceremony. As you know, the life skills empowerment program pairs mentors with people who are or who have recently been homeless here in New York City. We mentors enter into this endeavor with an open heart and the desire, not to do the critical work of recovery and rebirth for our mentees, but to listen to their stories and to do our best to guide and support them in their very personal struggles to achieve their stated goals. It is easy within this framework of mentor/mentee, helper/helped, contributing member of society/those struggling to take their first steps toward this state of being to assume that we mentors have never experienced any of the issues currently facing our mentees. I can tell you from my personal life, from my own story, that this is simply not the case.

Often we only see what is on the outside, the face we present to the world today. One might look at me and say, "Well, here is a middle-aged, middle-class, Caucasian man who has practiced both law and social work. And oh, yes, let's not forget that he is a Jew (with all the attendant stereotypes that sometimes attach themselves to this designation). It is nice that he is here helping these downtrodden, unfortunate folks, but, come on, what could he possibly know of their struggles?"

140

Well, I am not ashamed to say that I too have struggled with depression and substance abuse, like some of the program participants. While possessing many positive attributes, my family also came with a healthy dose of abuse, which deeply affected both my sister and myself. Somehow, with the help and grace of God and the kind assistance of many generous souls, I was able to survive. Unfortunately, my sister did not. As a young woman, she felt there was no way out except to take her own life. I can also share that for me, recovery and rebirth are not like a light switch, which when turned on banishes the darkness completely. I toil daily to recognize and lessen the effects of the deep anger and sadness, which I know will never fully leave my side.

So, my friends, my message is that we are all fragile children of God and that there is no such thing as "the other," but only each other.

Life Story
Deborah Canty

Deborah Canty was born in June 1954 in Sanford, North Carolina. She graduated in 2005 from the Education Outreach Program (EOP), the original life skills empowerment program, run by New York Catholic Charities.

I grew up thinking I was the sacrificial lamb, thinking that I didn't matter. Maybe you have heard the story about the eagle and the chicken. Well, this man found an eagle's egg, and he put it in with his chickens. So the eagle hatched and grew up thinking he was a chicken, pecking on the ground for food and carrying on. One day he looked up in the sky, and there was an eagle soaring. He said, "That's such a majestic bird. I wish I could be that." Then somebody said, "Naw, man, you're just a chicken. Just stay here with the chickens." So the eagle lived and died as a chicken because he didn't know who he was. Isn't that something? It's like my mother always said, "It's not what they call you, it's what you answer to."

I was born in 1954, in a quiet little town called Sanford, North Carolina, the same town where both my parents grew up. My mother, she had seven brothers and sisters. My father had seventeen brothers and sisters. My grandmother, when she died, had seventy-eight grandkids and 158 great-grandkids. So it was just cousins all over the place and always somebody to play with. I knew everybody in the neighborhood. When I went back to visit Sanford as a teenager, my grandmother would say, "If you meet a boy you like, you better let me see who it is because you might be related."

My mother's name was Deborah, and my father was Willie James. I had two older brothers and a younger sister. We lived in a little white

house, and when we looked outside, we saw the road that my brothers used to take to school. My mother was a great cook. She always did everything from scratch. When she made bread, my younger sister and I used to roll it up. My mother would put it in the oven, and we would give it to my brothers when they came back from school. Church was a second home for us. My mother sang in the choir, my grandmother sang in the choir, my aunts too. Everything happened in the church. Nights, they would give us parties like for Halloween, and everyone was always cooking great food. My father's family lived on the country side of town, so we were able to ride horses, milk the cows, and feed the chicks and the pigs.

My oldest brother, Garland, he had blonde hair and gray eyes. My baby sister was fair too. My second-oldest brother, Kenny, was a year and four months older than me. He was a little darker than me. I had a big birthmark on my face, but I never even noticed it when I lived in North Carolina. My father would always tell his friends, "My daughter, she look just like me." And it would make me feel pretty. I was Daddy's little girl.

To other people, my father was just bad. He killed a couple of black men. He was sent to the chain gang more than once. One of his fingers was burnt down to the stub from smoking cigarettes. I remember when my sister was a little baby, I clipped some clothespins on her ears because I thought they would make nice earrings. When my mother spanked me, I told her, "As soon as my daddy come home I'm gonna have him beat you up." Evidently I must have seen this happen before. I remember the look on my mother's face. "Come here," she said. "I'm gonna give you something to tell your father." And she tore my butt up.

When I was in first grade and Kenny was in second grade, my mother left my father for good. She moved to New York City and said she'd be back soon to get us. My grandparents took Garland, and the rest of us went to live with my Aunt Millie, my mother's baby sister. My aunt's husband used to hang out and play in a band all night. Money was short. A lot of times, we didn't go to school. Our clothes were all dirty. A couple of times, we had to go pick cotton just so we would have something to eat that day. It was hot, and we would go picking this little white stuff out there all day.

My aunt didn't have indoor plumbing. So when she gave me a bath, she would put me outside in the tub with all these little boys running around. She would just walk off, and then here they would come taunting and teasing and carrying on. I hated that. Kenny and I had to do all the menial work, like emptying the chamber pot. We thought it was because we were darker skinned than the others. We thought we were the black sheep of the family. That was our reasoning because it seemed like my baby sister and older brother always had it better.

When the school year ended, my grandmother told us our mother was coming. We got all dressed up, and I had this big, brand-new doll with white, silky hair. I was lying on my grandmother's bed when I heard, "Your mother is here!" So we all ran outside. It seemed like ten minutes later, we were all in the car. There was my mother's new boyfriend, my mother, and four kids. I remember not being able to get comfortable. The whole way we were saying, "Are we there yet? Are we in New York?" Later, I realized I had left my doll lying on my grandmother's bed. I had just gotten it for my birthday. She still had that new smell on her. I begged for my doll for two or three years, but by the time I got back to visit North Carolina, my cousins had destroyed it.

My mother lived in Brooklyn on Atlantic Avenue, which was an eight-lane street. I was terrified. Even holding my mother's hand, I didn't want to cross that street. I had never seen so many cars in my life, and they were all going so fast. I saw so many people die in traffic accidents, hitting those posts. Every Saturday or Sunday, the fire trucks would be out there hosing down a mangled car. I saw my first dead body when I was around eight. We were playing hide-and-seek in a little alley around the corner. First there was a lot of argument, then a man ran out the door and another man ran after him in the alley, and we heard, "Pop, pop!" When the cops asked if anybody had seen something, my mother said, "Don't you ever say anything. You don't know who those people are."

In North Carolina, I had family everywhere. I was allowed to be a kid—to play. And I was fearless. My aunt used to tell me, "I couldn't take you to nobody's house 'cause you used to beat up their kids." In New York City, I didn't want to go outside. I didn't want to go to the park. I didn't know anybody. My brothers, sister, and I would just go to school and come home.

My mother worked two and three jobs, just trying to make a way to feed us and carry on. She was cooking and cleaning people's houses and working in a place where they made watches at night. My oldest brother, Garland, was eleven, and he was in charge of us most of the time. Since my mother was too busy to take us to church, she said it was up to Garland. "If he want to take you to church, y'all can go to church, but you can't go alone." So that's how church left our life.

I saw more prejudice in New York City than I ever saw in North Carolina; I guess because I was sheltered from it. Down South they knew what stores and restaurants to take us in, where we were allowed to go. We all went to one segregated school, and it was from first to twelfth grade. My mother went to that school. In New York City, a Hispanic family lived next door to us, about eight or ten of them in one apartment. They always harassed my brothers when they were outside playing.

And in New York, I started noticing the birthmark on my face. The kids in school used to tease me about it, my brothers and sister too when they got mad at me. They would call me "two-tone." Little kids don't really look in the mirror, but in New York City I got older. I started to think I was the ugliest thing that God created. My mother was a beautiful woman. I kept praying, "God, if I could just look like my mother . . ."

Meanwhile, my mother was changing. She was swearing, drinking, partying. I had never known this woman. I remember hearing the first curse word come out her mouth when I was seven or eight, and it shocked me because my grandmother didn't allow anything like that around us kids. No. My grandmother, she was a small lady, but she carried a big stick. One time, my father was trying to fight my mother, and my grandmother came out there with a belt and beat my father.

Every Saturday, my mother would give Garland money to take us to the movies so she could be alone with her boyfriend. Whenever we came back home, her eyes would be black. My mother would be wearing sunshades or have choke marks around her neck. I loved that lady more than any woman that I know of. But we couldn't protect her. My brothers were too young to stop her boyfriend. You saw the bruises that he put on her. What is a kid going to do to protect her from that?

When I was about ten, I woke up one morning and the boyfriend's face was dead in my face. I thought, "Why is this man breathing on me, and why is he that close?" He smoked and he drank and had this odor that was just horrific. Even now when I smell that combination, I have to start praying about it. Later that day, I was so angry that I took our dog Princess into the backyard, and I just beat her and beat her and beat her. Then I looked in my dog's eyes, and they were so big and soulful, I started crying. I grabbed Princess and I swore to God, "I will never, ever hit you again. Never mistreat you again." Princess didn't run away from me or anything because she knew I had to get my frustrations out. I never hit that dog again, and she always slept in my bed. Animals, they understand you.

The first time my mother's boyfriend penetrated me, I was around eleven. My grandmother was sick, and my mother went down South, and we were staying with my aunt in Brooklyn. One day, my mother's boyfriend came and dragged me back to our empty apartment. To this day I wonder why my aunt let me go. What did he tell her? After he was finished, he took me back to my aunt's house, and nobody asked me what happened. Nobody. When my mother came back, I couldn't have a decent sleep at night because I never knew when he would come into my bedroom. I started wearing my pants and girdle and bra to bed. I shared a room with my sister, so my sister probably saw, but what are you going to say? You hear your mother scream when he's beating her, so what are we going to do.

I thought my mother knew what was happening to me. Like I said, I thought I was the black sheep. I thought she was sacrificing me so her boyfriend didn't mess with my younger sister. My mother even cornered

Life Story: Deborah Canty   147

me one time and said, "What goes on in the house stays in the house." Two weeks after that, she took me to the police precinct, but by then I was too damn scared to say anything. Later my Uncle Fred came and put the boyfriend out of the house. My thing was I planned to kill him. That's what I said. "I'm gonna kill him one day."

Meanwhile, my life wasn't going right. My grades in school started to decline. And the nightmares started coming. I would wake up crying from a recurring dream: I was a little girl, back in North Carolina, and I saw this man and lady—I couldn't see their faces or their heads. They were dancing to a song. My baby sister was lying at one end of the couch, and I was lying at the other. And you know how when you pull a sheet over your head, you can see the lights from under the covers? Well, we were under the sheets, and you could see the lights. You couldn't see nothing but the lights. And suddenly I felt this terrible pain.

After that the dream changed. My mother was lying on the bed at my grandmother's house, doing a crossword puzzle. I had to use the chamber pot, and when I urinated I started crying because it hurt so much. My mother started screaming, "What's wrong with you?" She threw me on the bed and opened up my legs. "Who did that? Who did that?" I couldn't tell her who. The next thing I knew I was in court, and a black judge had me sitting on the desk with his gavel. "Who did that?" he said.

I mentioned the dream to my mother, and later I heard her tell my aunt, "I was hoping she never remembered that." I didn't remember. I just knew the dream kept popping up in my head, waking me every night, like something happened, something else happened besides the boyfriend. When I tried to talk about the dream or the boyfriend, everybody just said, "We don't talk about that." But what they were not talking about was killing me. Even a girlfriend who was molested said, "You're just saying that same damn shit! Forget about it." And my thing was, "Tell me how. Tell me how you forgot so I don't have to deal with it no more."

You know, it happens to a lot more people than you think. I had a white girlfriend, and the things she used to say—the inappropriate way her father acted around her—led me to believe she was being sexually abused. The girl who taught me to smoke said her father had molested her since the time she was eight years old. Another girlfriend said that when she was like nine, she told someone, "My sister and I gotta go home and have sex with our grandfather." And that person looked at her like what planet are you on? "And that was the first time I realized it was wrong," my friend said. It happens to little boys too. Lots of the men in jail, something happened to them when they were kids. Someone took their lives away from them. They took away their childhoods. And then you don't know where you stand in society. Am I a whore? Am I a jezebel?

And let me tell you another thing that happened. When I was thirteen, the sister of my mother's girlfriend came from Georgia. That woman took one look at my birthmark and asked my mother, "What did you do to mark the child like that?" My mother didn't say anything to her, but two or three days later, she told me not to call her "Ma" anymore. I said, "What? Why?" Her answer was, "People say I look too young to be your mother." But I knew she felt ashamed of me because of my birthmark.

"If I'm not your daughter, who am I? If you're not my mother, who are you?"

From that day on, I never called my mother "Ma" again. I only called her "Miss Johnson"—or "Nana" after she had grandchildren. Pretty soon my mother changed her mind. She wanted me to call her "Ma" again. When I visited North Carolina, my grandmother would say, "Call your mother 'Ma.'" My uncles and aunts tried to make me say the word. But in my stubbornness, I refused. I refused to call my mother "Ma" again, until the day she died.

By thirteen, I was drinking a lot. I hated the taste of alcohol, but I liked the effects. When I was drunk, I didn't have that dream—I didn't have to think much when I was drinking. Sometimes my friends and I would drink a pint of wine before school. I would turn the bottle upside down and pour as much in my mouth as I could because I didn't want to feel anything anymore. On the weekends, my mother's new boyfriend would bring five or six gallons of Scotch, and the whole neighborhood would party at our house. I'm telling you, we'd have glasses full of Scotch sitting around the house. I would drink till I couldn't drink anymore. My brother Kenny said, "Debbie, by the time you fifteen you gonna be an alcoholic." I remember him saying that to me.

In 1969 my mother threw a going-away party for my oldest brother, Garland. He had just finished boot camp for the Marines, and they were shipping him to Vietnam. I was fifteen and Kenny was sixteen. My girlfriend and I were out on the stoop, and the guys next door were feeling her up and touching her. When Garland tried to stop them, the guys jumped him. My mother, Uncle Fred, and Kenny were in the kitchen. I ran in shouting, "They're trying to jump Garland." Kenny started cursing. "Ain't nobody gonna f— with my brother like that." Then my uncle turned around and got mad at Kenny. "How dare you curse in front of your mother?" I think my mother told my uncle, "Yeah. You need to whip Kenny's butt." Next thing you know, Uncle Fred and Kenny went outside and started fighting. All of Kenny's friends were there, and I remember one of them saying, "His uncle is a grown man, he shouldn't be fighting Kenny like that." But none of them would help my brother, I guess because it was family. They fought even around the corner. My uncle was kicking and stomping my brother. When the fight finally broke up, my brother came home, and he turned to me and said, "This is my sister and I love her."

Kenny had a fever that night, and the next day my mother took him to the hospital. Every day after work, my mother went to the hospital to see how he was doing. One day the hospital called after she got home. Kenny's appendix had erupted, and he was dead. I tell you, when we buried him in North Carolina, I just wanted to crawl up and die. I asked my mother, "How can you leave him sitting in that cemetery by himself?" After that we never discussed Kenny's death. We never discussed anything. It was a family that just pushed stuff away.

My relationship with my mother was never the same because she forgave her brother. I couldn't understand it. I said, "Nobody's ever gonna hit me again. Ain't nobody ever going to tell me what to do." From then on, everything my mother said, I did the opposite. When she said no, I said yes. She said, "rain," and I said, "sun." When my mother cursed me, I cursed her back. When she hit me, I hit her back. I dropped out of school. I had sex with a lot of boys. Afterward I felt so dirty and unclean that I would be scrubbing, scrubbing, and scrubbing myself.

My mother took to drinking. She had seizures when she drank, but that didn't stop her. Back then, I never saw my mother's pain. All I saw was the pain I was going through. Now, more than forty years later, I ask myself, "But what did you put her through? What did you put your mother through?" Every day I ask God to forgive me for the way I disrespected my mother. Oh yes. I'm telling you. My mother was the love of my life, but I always said, "I don't want to be nothing like her."

A year after Kenny's death, my father got murdered by his girlfriend in North Carolina. The story is he was banging on her door and shouting, "When I get in there, I'm gonna kill you." The girlfriend shot a gun through the door just to scare him away. The next morning, they found my father in his brother's yard across the street. In the newspaper, they had a picture of him on his hands and knees. My father must have been smoking when he crawled because he was still holding a cigarette. My mother told us, "Don't hate that lady who killed your father. She did it 'cause she was afraid of him."

Soon after, I met a handsome guy at a party in Brooklyn. When we dated, he used to open the car door and let me out, let me in. He was the perfect gentleman. The only one who wasn't crazy about him was my mother. She saw him try to turn me away from my best girlfriend. "That's the first thing they do. He's gonna mess up your friendships. Then, he's gonna take you away from family. And then he's gonna take you away from the state." My mother was telling me to be aware, but she knew I wouldn't listen.

I'm going to tell you why I married my husband. I was looking for somebody to fix me because I was all broken. And I thought marriage would make me a different person. I decided, "This is my new life, and I'm gonna try to be the best wife I can." I gave up drinking. I stopped fighting with people. And yet, as soon as I married my husband, I couldn't stand to have sex with him. Every time he touched me, my skin would crawl and I'd suck in my teeth. I was so lost and I had no idea what was wrong.

The day of the wedding, it was pouring down rain. My husband had an umbrella, but this time he didn't get out and open my door like before. "I got you now," he said, like, "I don't have to be a gentleman anymore." Not too long after that, my husband took me out of the state. Next thing I knew, we were on our way to South Carolina. If my mother or anybody wrote me a letter, he had to read it first. If I wanted to mail a letter out, he had to read it. I couldn't have a key to the house or to the mailbox.

Because I didn't want to have sex, my husband called me frigid, and it frustrated him so much he became abusive. I always said I gave drinking up at the wrong time. The old Debbie would have fought back, but now I was too afraid. My husband beat me up at home. He came to my job at the convenience store and kicked me and stomped me. I thought I would lose my teeth. He used to take medicine for his post-traumatic something from his time in Vietnam. Then he'd drink and want to go driving on the highway. In the newspaper, there was an article about a man and woman who died from carbon monoxide poisoning. My husband looked at me and said, "That's the way I want us to go."

Three times I went back home to my mother, and each time she sent me back to South Carolina, saying, "That's your husband, you married him till death do you part." I thought, "Whoa, wait a minute, she left my father like how many years ago?"

Finally, my husband put a shotgun to my head. "Just tell me I won't pull this trigger."

I prayed, "God, if you get me out of this, he will never see me again." And I kept my word. In August 1977 I went back to New York City for good. My mother said, "Debbie, you left your job, you left your house, you left your bank account."

I said, "He can have it. I left with my life."

I stayed with my aunt and uncle, got a job at a meat-packing house, and went back to school for my GED. But I also started drinking again because my husband kept trying to find me. My mother said he had been at her house four times. I was terrified, and the alcohol gave me courage. Finally my husband got tired, and I never laid eyes on him again. Still, I always thought I didn't do right by him. I figured if I had been more sexually accepting of my husband, it would have worked out.

When I was around twenty-four, the doctor told me, "I don't think you will ever be able to have kids because you have pelvic inflammatory disease." That broke my heart. I kept telling God how unfair that was. "My brother has a child, my sister got three, and you won't give me any." Soon after I met a tall, dark, and handsome guy at my sister's house. I was twenty-five and he was twenty. I usually never dealt with younger guys because they were so immature. But this guy made me laugh, and we hooked up. Three months later, the doctor told me I was pregnant! I was ecstatic. I had been praying for that child—just praying for that child.

It was a complicated pregnancy because I kept bleeding. The doctor wanted me off my feet, so I went to my mother's house and stayed on her couch for two months. The labor was seventeen hours. I'm telling you, I thought I was going to die. Finally I had to have a C-section. My daughter was a day old before they brought her to me because I kept getting a fever. When I finally saw her, I thought they gave me the wrong child because she was just gorgeous. I couldn't believe it. I kept thinking it was the wrong baby and checking the ID band. Oh my goodness! We named her Monique Nicole and called her Nicki.

Nicki's father and I were together on and off. Besides him, I refused to let another man live in my house. I'd say, "You can visit but then you gotta leave," because what happened to me was never going to happen to my baby. Not on my watch! Then one night, one of my cousins came over. Nicki was three years old and already asleep. For ten minutes I left my cousin there with her while I ran to the store. When I came back, my daughter was awake, and my cousin left. Later that night, my daughter came into the kitchen. "Mommy, he tried to put his thing in my mouth." I thought, "Wait a minute, calm down, Debbie, 'cause what does she know about a *thing*?" I turned to my little daughter. "What thing you talking about?" Nicki said, "You know, the thing you pee-pee out of."

I tell you, I was ready to commit homicide. For months I couldn't sleep, I couldn't eat, I was just miserable. I took my daughter to the precinct, and the detectives came to my house. They said, "Because of the child's age, the DA doesn't want to pick up the case." I said, "But if I kill my cousin's ass, you'll come and get me, right?" I was separated from Nicki's father at the time, but I got him back in her life. I told him, "You gonna kill my cousin." I went looking for him at night, and my aunt got so scared for his life that she shipped him to North Carolina. Then I started drinking more and more and more. One morning, about a year or two later, my daughter crawled up in my face and said, "Mommy, what my cousin did wasn't nice. But I still love him." I just broke down and cried. That child taught me a lesson about forgiveness that day.

When Nicki was in the second grade, her father and I broke up for good. My mother used to say, "If he can't have the cow, he don't want the calf." Once he saw that I wasn't going be with him, he decided not to be in his daughter's life. I never asked him for child support, and he moved to Ohio. By then I had already gotten involved with Eddie. He was twenty years older than me, and he had a good job fixing laundry machines. I worked on and off throughout the years—mostly as a cashier and stuff like that, but Eddie helped support us. He would help me with the rent. He bought all my daughter's school clothes. He paid for her trip to Canada with her class. With Eddie, my daughter got to get out of the neighborhood—she got to see better places. Eddie stabilized us for a while.

Eddie drank, but he knew when he had enough. Me, I would just chug-a-lug, and I only knew I'd had enough when I was throwing up and getting sick. I never drank for joy. I drank to not remember stuff—like the lights under the bed covers, the terrible pain between my legs, and my mother throwing me on my grandmother's bed. "Who did that? Who did that?" she said.

Alcohol was the great eraser. By the time my daughter got to be eleven or twelve, she would have to go pay the light bill or the gas bill because I was too hung over. My mother lived downstairs with my niece, Garland's daughter, and most of the time Nicki stayed there too. If it wasn't for my mother, I don't know where my child would have been.

Garland lived in the apartment next door, and he was running a crack den and hotel. He would steal from my mother and let people get high in her house. When I wasn't home, my brother told people to have sex in my house. He even tried to pimp me out. We were fighting all the time. Once I grabbed my mother's butcher knife and stabbed Garland dead in the neck. If he had moved a little, I probably would have hit the jugular. Another time Garland started choking me, and I beat him with a baseball bat. But there were also times when my daughter would scream, "Mom, Mom, the drug dealers are beating up Uncle Garland." I'd have to run downstairs to save my brother. Now when I look back, I realize there was something wrong with Garland. He wanted to fight everybody. I never recall having a conversation with him. We never talked about his days in Vietnam or said, "You remember Kenny, the things we used to do?" I bet Garland was molested too. I'll never know because he died four years ago.

So, you understand, with all of us in the same building, my daughter was being raised in chaos—the arguing, the fussing—pure mayhem. The cops were in and out all the time. And I was just hanging out, drinking. I blame myself because my daughter started going with a boy named Angel. Soon she was stepping in my house at three in the morning. I hauled up and punched her dead in the face. "How dare you. You think you grown?" I hit her, and I just kept hitting her. One of Nicki's girlfriends called ACS (Administration for Children's Services) and the next day, the ACS worker came upstairs saying, "You can't hit your daughter like that."

I said, "My daughter can't step in my house at three o'clock in the morning and think that's okay. She's fourteen years old. Something would have happened to her, you'd have been on my case."

That night my daughter went to my niece's mother's house, and the next day my niece's mother came over. "Debbie, I don't know what's wrong, but I see Nicki throwing up this morning." So I brought Nicki home. "You know what?" I said. "Tomorrow I'm taking you to the doctor." She spent the night with my mother, and the next morning she was gone! It turns out my sister drove all the way up from North Carolina and took my daughter back with her because Nicki said I was going to kick that baby out of her. I went insane. I kicked my door down, I busted the windows out my apartment, I was just so angry. "God," I said, "I don't want my worst enemy to ever feel like I feel."

After three months Nicki came back home, and she got on her knees and cried. I said, "Nicki, I don't believe in abortion. Every child has a reason to be here. But I know one thing, you gonna take care of that child." So my grandson was born on my daughter's fifteenth birthday. They had a birthday party for her in the hospital. After that, while my daughter was in school or at her part-time job, I would take the baby and watch him. Then I would leave and let her be a parent.

In December 1995, three months after my grandson was born, my mother was sitting on her couch, and I could tell she needed a drink because she had the shakes. So I walked to the liquor store and bought her a pint of vodka, and I bought me a pint of wine. When I came back, my mother said, "Debbie, spend the night with me." I said, "I live right upstairs. I'll be down in the morning." She said, "No, I want you to spend the night with me, and we'll go shopping in the morning." So I ran around the corner, I kissed my grandson good night. Then I came back, and I crawled into bed with my mother. It was very cold that night.

When I woke up in the morning, it was bright outside. I got up, put my mother's slippers on, and I went to the bathroom. I washed my face, and I was brushing my teeth, thinking the sound would wake my mother up. But when I went back to the bed, I thought, "She's sleeping too good. I'm not gonna wake her." I crawled back into bed, but something was just not right. I nudged my mother. "Nana?" My mother was always a light sleeper, but she didn't answer me. I nudged her again. No answer. I crawled to the bottom of the bed and I grabbed her big toe. It was kind of hard.

My brother had come in during the middle of the night, and he was sleeping on my mother's couch. I went to the door and told him, "Go in there and wake Nana up." Then I got on the phone and called 911. "I can't wake my mother up!" The guy told me to do CPR, so I told my brother, "Do what the man say." But my brother just walked out of the bedroom and sat on the couch.

"Debbie, she's gone."

I said, "What you mean?"

"She's gone," my brother said.

And now I was putting on my clothes and running down the stairs. And I didn't realize, but I was screaming. All the traffic had stopped, and people were looking at me. I ran to my grandson at his other grandparent's house. "I can't wake my mother up. I can't wake my mother up," I told them. Then I heard a fire truck coming, and I went back out the door, and the son of my mother's boyfriend stopped me. "Debbie, she's gone." I looked across the street, and I saw Garland's daughter coming. "Nana's gone. Nana's gone," I told her. Like twenty minutes later, my daughter came home from her school in Coney Island. "Mommy, I was sitting in my first period class and something in me said, 'Go see about your grandmother.' I just walked out of class and got on the train and came back here."

They didn't come get my mother's body until about ten o'clock that night. I just couldn't go back up there. My niece and my daughter, they combed her hair.

I so admire that woman today, the sacrifices she made that I didn't see. My mother made sure we had a roof over our head. Sometimes we were a little hungry, but she always made a way. If we had friends over, my mother would make soup and say, "Just add some water to it. Everybody might not get full, but everybody's gonna have something in their stomach." After all us kids ate, I would see her sopping the pot with a piece of bread. She could have gotten her food first. She cooked it, she paid for it. But she never did. Sometimes we had to get our clothes from the secondhand store. But my mother wouldn't even buy herself a pair of shoes. She had to hold her coat together with her hands because there weren't any buttons on it. I remember one day my mother came home with this beautiful dress. "Debbie, I saw this in the boutique, and it looked just like you." Louise from *The Jeffersons* was wearing that same dress. My mother would do things like that, and I would think, "She do love me. She do." Holidays, everybody wanted to be in my mother's house because she was such a great cook. To this day, I don't know how to make a biscuit because I thought my mother would still be here to make me one.

After my mother died, I started drinking even more. Two or three times I went to the doctor and he put AOB on his chart in red ink—Alcohol on Breath. He said, "Debbie, have you ever thought about suicide?"

I said, "No. A couple of homicides."

The recurring nightmare came back. I still couldn't put a face on who was hurting me. If I woke up in the middle of the night, I had to have a bottle there. Strange things started happening. One night I woke up and there was a plate of chicken, rice, and cornbread on my table. When I went to my daughter's apartment to thank her, she looked at me funny. "Mommy, *you* cooked that food. You brought *me* a plate." I had no clue I had done that.

Then, on January 12, 2002, when I was forty-seven years old, I went to my niece's house so she could braid my hair. I got so drunk I must have fallen asleep. When I woke up the next morning, I was looking at the walls and the ceiling, and I had no clue where I was. I was thinking, "Where are you? Where are you?" There was a body lying beside me. "What did you do? What did you do?" I didn't want to roll over because I didn't know who was there. I had to go to the bathroom, but I didn't know where the bathroom was. Then I heard a voice: "Aunt Debbie, are you ready to eat?" I looked up, and my niece was standing there. I looked down, and it was my grandson lying beside me. That was the body I hadn't recognized. First thing the next morning, I checked myself into rehab because I had never been so scared in my life. Today I have thirteen years of sobriety.

As soon as you enter rehab, you have to join Alcoholics Anonymous and go every day. I hated AA. I thought it was a cult because everybody kept talking about prayer and meditation and God. As a little kid in North Carolina, I used to say prayers with my grandmother before going to sleep, but the last time I did that was the night before my mother came to take us to New York City. My grandfather was always telling us, "You're gonna go to hell," and I remember thinking, "So long as I'm already going there, let me bust it open."

"AA is a crock," I told my counselor at the rehab. "All I ever hear about is 'God, God, God!'" When I told him what my grandfather used to say about hellfire, the counselor asked, "Well, Debbie, if you did believe in God, what would your God be like? Not your grandfather's God, not your mother's God, not your father's God. A God of *your* understanding. Just talk to God like you're talking to me. Just talk to God." And I looked my counselor dead in his eyes, and he was so sincere that I just busted out crying. "Just look at what God did without your permission," the counselor said. "Imagine what he'll do with it."

When I went back to AA, I realized that the people sharing their stories were sharing my story, and they were talking about forgiveness. My uncle who killed Kenny had been gone for five years. But all of a sudden, I saw his face right in front of me. There were tears in his eyes, and he was saying, "I'm sorry, I didn't mean to do it." And then I noticed the other people around Kenny's death. You had a brother who lost a brother. You had a sister who lost a brother. You had a mother who lost a child. How painful that must have been. For all those years, I felt only my own pain and hatred. Now I saw why my mother had to forgive my uncle. Hating him would have eaten her up like it ate me up. And my mother became an alcoholic after that.

That night I got on my knees, and I said, "God, forgive me for holding onto this hatred for so long." I asked my uncle to forgive me. I even asked my mother's boyfriend, who had molested me for three years, to forgive me. I started thinking maybe somebody did the same thing to him. That's no excuse, but I just saw forgiveness all over the place. And I swear, I was on my knees, and I felt the weight of the world lift off me. I was so light I had to hold on to the bed because I thought I was floating away. I ran to the phone and called my AA sponsor. "That's what forgiveness do," she said.

I stayed at the rehabilitation center for eighteen months, and I learned a lot. It was the first real stable home I ever had. When it was time to leave, I had no place to go. Eddie said, "Debbie, I can rent you a place," but then he would make all the rules and try to control me: "I don't want this person in the house. Don't wear that dress, it's too short." I refused to live like that. For maybe three weeks I stayed with my daughter, but that wasn't going to work. My grandson was six, and I saw myself intervening too much. The final straw came when my daughter got so mad at me she spilled my pills all over the floor. I have hepatitis C, and I was taking interferon at the time. I really wanted to hurt my daughter for that. Instead, I left the next day and walked to the Brooklyn Women's Shelter (BWS).

My daughter ran after me. "Mommy, you don't have to go to the shelter."

I said, "Yes I do, because if I stay with you I'm going to end up in jail, and I'm not going to jail sober!"

Brooklyn Women's Shelter was surrounded by factories. It was a dangerous area to walk through, even in the daytime. They used to find dead bodies and stuff up there. I was terrified, and the tears were just pouring down my face. "God, why me? Why me?" Then I remembered how a lot of people said, "Why not you? God would never give you more than you can handle." All of a sudden, I heard a spirit speak to my heart. "Be still and know that I'm God. You do you and I do the rest." The tears dried up, I walked in that shelter, and I have never had any regrets. Later at my AA meeting, I said, "Hi, I'm an alcoholic, and I became homeless tonight." People in the room said, "Debbie, you can come stay with me." I told them, "No, God put this walk in front of me. I have to walk it for a reason." I didn't know the reason but I walked it.

I used to put down homeless people. "Oh, they homeless because they don't wanna work," I said. "They lazy." So God said, "Let me put you in a shelter so you can see what's really happening." When I walked into BWS, I saw the elderly. I saw young kids. I thought, "Where is your family at?" I used to think the pain was all about me, but that wasn't true. Unjust things were happening everywhere, and nobody should have to live like that. Three months later, when I was transferred to New Providence Shelter, I saw women in their sixties and seventies, looking so lost. My daughter and grandson were near enough to visit, but some of these people were far away from home. A couple of ladies died in that shelter. How sad to die and have nobody there to claim you. It just changed my way of thinking. Everybody should have somebody. Empathy filled my heart.

Still, living in a shelter was hard. For the first three months at New Providence, I didn't want to know any of the women because I saw a lot of arguing and fist fighting. The residents called you the "b" word and never used your real name. I signed myself out for the day as much as I could. I went to my AA meetings or to my doctors' appointments. I visited my daughter. Then one day I was signing out and I heard some people singing "Amazing Grace." My mother and grandmother used to sing it when they were in some of their hardest times. Pen in hand, I looked at the security guard. She said, "Go back there, Miss Canty, you'll like them." So I went back, and this little lady came up to me.

"Hi, I'm Sister Dorothy. Would you like to join our Life Experience and Faith Sharing (LEFSA) group? We're not church. It's about your lived experience and your faith, whatever that is." Sister Dorothy's presence made me feel so welcome. In the group, the people shared their real names, and everyone said, "God loves you and we love you too." From then on, I started hanging out with the LEFSA women. In there, I met some friends that I still have today.

Before in my life, I always thought things were black and white. I never saw the in-between. But the shelter and LEFSA changed me completely. For instance, one morning two women at the shelter got in a heated argument, and one of the ladies tried to throw a pot of scalding coffee at the other. When I saw that woman later, I said, "You stay away from me because I don't trust you." She cussed me out. Next thing I knew, the shelter gave me that woman as a roommate. At first, I wanted to have nothing to do with her. Before bed, I'd say goodnight, but I did not talk with her. In the mornings I'd just get up, make my bed, and leave. Then one morning, I came in the room, and she said, "Look, Debbie, I made my bed." It was the first time she had done that. After that she told me she had been in foster care all her childhood—and now she was in a shelter. It never ended for her. Right then and there, I got up and embraced that woman. We spoke every day after that. No wonder she was so violent. Hurt people hurt people. I know because I hurt a lot of people with my pain. Pretty soon the people in security and on the staff were saying, "Miss Canty, something changed about your roommate. She started watching you."

Another time, Sister Dorothy took us to a church in Yonkers where undocumented immigrants were going for protection. The government had just filed charges against the church for that. They told us a story about a Mexican woman the government wanted to deport. She was going to have to leave her husband and child behind. How can you take a mother from her child? We stood outside the church and asked people to sign petitions. There are so many unjust situations, not just in the United States but all around the world. Back when all I cared about was self-preservation, I was unaware of that. Now other people's problems touch me, and I realize that God is in everybody.

Next, Sister Dorothy suggested I attend the life skills empowerment program at New York Catholic Charities. Sister Dorothy, whenever she asked me something, I couldn't tell her no. So I met George Horton and

Ms. K. Ms. K. was tough and no nonsense. I respected her for that. And George—George was the compassionate one. He was just a sweetheart.

My mentor was hands-on. She listened to me, and she urged me to be all I could be. She said, "Maybe you can go and get a higher education." When I faltered, she would tell me a little piece of her story. My mentor was a white woman, and she was kind of obese. People would make fun of her and put her down and degrade her. "But they don't even know me," she said. When she was young she lost her husband and had to raise her two boys as a single mother; now her sons were grown and she was alone. My mentor's story made me more aware of what I said to people. It made me be more mindful. Before I spoke, I thought, "How would I feel if somebody said that to me?"

George says, "Everybody has a story worth hearing." In the program, I wrote about how I had been sexually abused. I told my story at graduation, and I told it at other places after that. Sometimes when I finished, I heard people say, "I can identify with that," or "Something like that happened to me," or "Thank you for bringing the monster out of the closet." Maybe my words were setting them free to tell their stories. What they thought was their shame was not their burden to hold onto. We think the sexual abuse was our fault, and that's what keeps us quiet. But what does a child have to say about a grown person taking advantage of him or her sexually or mentally? Get the guilt back to where it belongs.

I also started seeing a therapist once a week. That was because Ms. K. told me I should. My therapist allowed me to express myself, to let the anger come out. I had to get it out, whatever it took, screaming and cussing or hitting things. I had to do that until I was too exhausted to be angry anymore. It took a long time.

In the past, I was a nasty, mean drunk. I couldn't even look myself in the eye in the mirror. I would never look into my soul because I didn't like what I saw. I would fight at the drop of a hat. If you said two or three words I didn't like, I was going to swing on you. During recovery I started asking, "Why am I so sore? Why am I hurting so bad?" I put myself in other people's shoes, and I became the first one to apologize. People who knew me before were shocked. Once I was with my daughter, and someone said something nasty to me. My daughter backed up, expecting a fight, but I just kept on going. "Mommy, you're not gonna say nothing?" she asked. And I said, "What? There's nothing to say."

For a long time, I had been trying to get housing. Some of the places were so scary and run down. I wouldn't allow my dog to live there. We want affordable, decent houses—some place where you can feel safe. Finally, an organization called SUS—Services for the UnderServed—offered me a room in an SRO called New Life Homes, only six blocks from my daughter's apartment. When I first went to see it, I wasn't sure. It was a little studio, and it had a stove but no oven. At the shelter that night, I got on my knees. "God, let your will be done 'cause you know what's best for me." The next day I looked in the paper, and Macy's was having a sale on toaster ovens. So I went and bought one, and I also bought three nonstick frying pans—small, medium, and large. I gave the large frying pan to my daughter. And I said, "I'm claiming that apartment in the name of Jesus." That's where I've lived ever since. They have twenty-four-hour security, and I love the people who work there. I have my own bathroom, my own little kitchen area. If I need to cook something big, I can walk six blocks and use my daughter's oven.

After I got my apartment, Sister Dorothy called me. "Debbie, we have been talking, and we want to give you a job on our LEFSA team."

I said, "I can't do what you're doing."

Sister Dorothy was feisty. "Weren't you homeless? Of course, you can do it." That was nine years ago, and I'm still working for LEFSA today. Two days a week, I go to the shelters to sponsor hope. I let people know that what God did for me, he can do for them. I tell them they're entitled to affordable, decent housing. Did Sophia Worrell tell you she was in my LEFSA group? At first she didn't want to talk about the abuse that she went through. I told her not to be ashamed and that 90 percent of the women in the shelter had probably been through it too. "You need to talk about it to get over it," I said. "And if you tell your story, maybe other women can let theirs out." We referred Sophia to the life skills empowerment program—we do that for a lot of people.

Every Wednesday the LEFSA team gets together. We pray for each other, we pray for others, and we read a scripture and elaborate on what it means to us. On Fridays, we talk about how we can improve our work in the shelters. LEFSA also does advocacy work. We have gone to Albany on policy day and to protest the Rockefeller Drug Law. I have also mentored for the life skills empowerment program five or six times.

In all this time, with all this recovery, I still couldn't forget the nightmare. Certain sounds or smells would bring back the memories: I was a little girl on a couch. There was a man and woman dancing and then a terrible pain between my legs. "Who did that? Who did that?" my mother said. "Who did that?" the judge said.

Well, every year I go back to North Carolina around Mother's Day, and I always see the Lee County Courthouse on Main Street. It's a nice,

Deborah and her grandson, circa 2011

neat building, the only courthouse in our little town. Two or three years ago, I was riding by, and I remembered being on that judge's desk. It was time. I knew I needed to know what had happened to me. I walked in and told the clerk my name and said I wanted to have her see if there was a file on me. Two weeks later, I gave the clerk my birth certificate, and she gave me a microfilm file about a case with my mother and father. I didn't read the whole file. I couldn't at the time. But I know it said something like this: "Willie James Johnson, convicted to serve four years on the chain-gang for molestation of daughter." Then I remembered something else. My father had said he was going to kill my mother when he got out.

I could never understand why a woman with four kids would leave all her family and all her school friends behind in North Carolina and go to New York City. I didn't realize that my father had molested me and threatened to kill my mother. She was protecting her kids, like mothers do. In AA they told me, "Your mother did the best with what she knew how." That stuck with me. And she was a beautiful woman, my mother. She had a beautiful spirit. Sometimes that could be beaten out of her because that happened to me. But my mother persevered. Back before my mother died, my daughter and I once got in an argument, and she said, "You just like Nana." I really wanted to slap my daughter for saying that. But today, it's an honor to hear that I'm just like my mother—or that I look like my mother, because people say that too. If I could be just half the woman—or one-third or one-fourth the woman—my mother was, I would know I'm a woman.

I hope my daughter can say that about me one day.

Reflection
Jane Griffin

Jane Griffin served as a mentor from 2010 to 2015 for the Education Outreach Program (EOP), the original life skills empowerment program, run by New York Catholic Charities.

I was brought up in in a left-leaning family in England, where our house was constantly abuzz with Labour Party activities. We had no formal religion, but a very strong humanitarian and ethical feeling was dominant in our house. I trained as a physician in London and then came to the US. In those days (the 1960s), the health department sent doctors out to child health stations, day care centers, and some schools. So I traveled all over the city to areas that I might not otherwise have ever seen and worked with families and all the problems that went with them. These were pretty harrowing circumstances in many cases. As a result, I felt comfortable working with people who'd been through everything that life deals out— positive and negative. At that point, I thought I'd heard and seen everything; however, I was to learn otherwise when I became a mentor in the life skills empowerment program.

Until then, I had always thought of myself as a pretty sympathetic and empathetic person. But getting to know some of the program participants and hearing them talk about the horrors they had been through made me realize that I had more to learn. These men and women had been dealt such a poor hand. They lived for years on the street and in shelters, and if they finally found housing it was usually in the most troubled neighborhoods. But through it all, they demonstrated an amazing resilience that

163

was truly remarkable and really awe-inspiring. Hearing their life stories was extremely moving. The great willpower and bravery that brought each individual to the moment of telling his or her truth filled me with admiration.

I've often wondered to myself: Could I survive like that person and share my story like that? I'm not so sure.

Life Story
Lisa Sperber

Lisa Sperber was born in 1954 in Newburgh, New York. She graduated in 2007 from the Education Outreach Program (EOP), the original life skills empowerment program, run by New York Catholic Charities. Lisa's story includes details and quotations from a StoryCorps interview she had with Dennis Barton in June 2010.

I was born in a rural town called Newburgh, sixty miles north of New York City. My parents were very well-educated. My father, who studied the oboe at the Juilliard School of Music, became a tenured professor of music at SUNY (State University of New York) New Paltz. He founded the university's jazz program and also taught courses in music therapy. My father played in many orchestras, including the Philadelphia Orchestra and the Buffalo Symphony. He even played on a record that Charlie Parker recorded live at the Apollo Theater. My father really touched a lot of lives.

So did my mother. She and another woman started a great preschool called the Valley School. You could say the Valley School began the day my mother found me sitting in the "bad girl's chair" at Mrs. Snyder's nursery school. I was being punished for wetting my pants. This happened when I was four and now I'm sixty, but I still remember sitting there in that terrible chair. Immediately, my mother withdrew me from Mrs. Snyder's school and started her own playgroup. Eventually, that playgroup became the full-fledged Valley School. The school incorporated music, dance, and movement, and I loved going there. My mother also went back to school and earned a master's degree from the Bank Street College of Education.

I have always loved the expressive arts. From a very young age, my family took me to Broadway musicals, like *Mary Poppins*, *The Sound of Music*, and *Pippin*. At age seven, I started playing the piano and then the clarinet. My father said I should play the oboe instead: "There are a million and one clarinetists, but there are never a million and one oboists." He gave me one of his extra oboes, and he got me an oboe teacher. When my father played in the Hudson Valley Philharmonic, I played first oboe in the training orchestra. To play the oboe, you have to make your own reeds, and there is an art to it. I loved shaving the reeds and using cane to tie them together.

Lisa at age three (1957)

Music is almost like therapy—like an adult pacifier; it has a soothing, calming effect. To this day, if I get upset or I have an argument with someone, I go home and turn on a CD and just lie on my bed and relax. I love Bach, Beethoven, Tchaikovsky, Mendelssohn, and Haydn. I've always liked jazz. I listen to gospel music, like Kirk Franklin.

I love the visual arts too. When I was growing up, my parents paid for me to go to the Talented Art Program in Newburgh, where I learned pottery. We'd press leaves and weeds into clay to get images. When we baked them in the kiln, it came out like raku pottery, which is traditional Japanese pottery. I did ceramics in high school and got a potter's wheel as a birthday present so I could continue doing it at home. My parents loved my pottery. They loved my music. They loved to come see me in school plays. They applauded me when I went from one grade to another.

But in school you don't get graded on arts. Unfortunately, I wasn't that great academically. Writing was very hard for me, and reading was very hard for me. At the time, nobody knew I had a learning disability. Learning disabilities are well known now, but they weren't then. I was very quiet in school. I was always the one who was withdrawn, who didn't have any friends. I sat in the back of the room and never raised my hand to talk. The kids called me "the cootie bug." People said, "You're stupid."

My parents didn't say those kinds of things, but I felt like they insinuated it. They were always putting me down, asking, "Why can't you read?" and sending me to my room without supper. When we went to restaurants, I wanted to stay in the car because I couldn't read the menu. My parents would ask me, "What do you want to order for lunch?" And I didn't know. I was so embarrassed.

I had no trouble reading music because music is concrete. If there is an F note on the page, you see an F and you play an F. If it's an E, it's always an E. And when you play an A—because the oboe always has to tune the whole orchestra—there's only one A, the 440 hertz A. But with reading and literature, you have to interpret the words on the page, and I couldn't interpret them. When I tried to tell people I couldn't read, no one would listen. "You come from a well-educated family," they would say. "Of course you know how to read. Your mother can read and your father can read, and your sister does well in school."

My sister Meg is three years younger than I am, and our early years were filled with rivalry. When I was six and she was three, I used to pull her out of the crib and swing her around. I think unconsciously I wanted to see her get hurt. One time I dropped her, and she had to go to the hospital and get six stitches in her chin. In school, my sister always did better than I did. She had friends, she was good in sports, and schoolwork came easy for her. My sister never had to study, and she always got straight As. I was very jealous of her. She had a better relationship with my parents than I did.

My parents tried to be loving to me, but I guess they felt overwhelmed by a child who was difficult. They told me I was very irritable, very demanding. They even said that I shouldn't have been conceived.

I felt more loved by my grandparents—my father's parents, Jack and Lucy. They were more than special people. The word "special" would not do them justice. My grandparents took my sister and me to the library on Forty-Second Street, and we fed the pigeons. They took us to the theater, the circus, and the Bronx Zoo. If we wanted something, they would simply say, "How much?" They really spoiled us, but me especially. I was their first grandchild, and I think deep down my grandparents knew I had special needs. When we went to my grandparents' apartment, my grandfather used to fry up *grievens*, which is like Jewish bacon, and we all used to fight over it, as bad as it is for you, because it's the fried fat of the chicken. He used to make this rice pudding in a pan and matzo ball soup that was absolutely delicious. Toward the end of her life, my grandmother thought I was her daughter. Instead of trying to correct her, I almost liked it. It was really nice.

Still, my grandparents and I had some rough bouts. When my parents went on vacation, my grandparents stayed with us, and I did everything I could to make their life miserable. I let our dog, Grizzle, run loose outside, and he got sprayed by a skunk. "Not only do I have to worry about Lisa and Meg," my grandfather said, "now I have to worry about that bastard dog getting sprayed."

The truth is that I loved that dog dearly, but I was just so mad that my parents went away that I acted out. Grizzle was a shaggy dog, like an overgrown Toto from *The Wizard of Oz*. He did everything too much. He sniffed too much, and he peed too much. One day, when my father was giving a piano lesson, my mother invited the student's mother into the kitchen to have a cup of tea. Grizzle picked up his leg and peed in that lady's pocketbook. Oh my goodness! Luckily, the lady took it in good spirits and kind of laughed about it. Years later, when Grizzle started dying, he ran away. I still really want to believe he did that because he didn't want me to see him getting sick.

I really relied on my pets for company. Over the years, I had many turtles and hamsters and lizards. People called me "Lisa's Museum of Natural History." From the time I was six, I had a blue and white parakeet that I named Lenny, after Leonard Bernstein. Lenny used to say things like, "One, two, three, four, Bubbie." My father and his cronies would play poker at our house and when they bet, the bird would say, "Are you sure? Are you sure, Marty? Are you sure, Paul?" One night, Lenny said, "Oh my God, you're kidding." Then he dropped dead in the middle of my father's poker game.

When I was in tenth grade, my parents got me tested and found out I was reading at a third-grade level because I was dyslexic. The people at the testing center asked, "How did she get passed through all those grades?" The answer was that I was a good listener and I could give back the information verbally. I might not have been able to read, but I amazed the teachers because I could remember everything they did and said. My memory helped me compensate. After the diagnosis, my parents became very empathetic. I think they felt bad and were overwhelmed with guilt.

They got me a tutor, Nell Stevens, an older lady, who worked with me every day after school. We would work on making inferences, and she helped me prepare to take my PSAT and SAT exams for college.

But then I started having my big, big downfall. In high school, I did everything and anything to be accepted by the other kids. I kind of forgot my morals. I started hanging out with the wrong crowd, started drinking and using soft drugs like pot. For the first time, I had a few friends in school, but I was very confused. On the one hand, I was finally getting academic help, but on the other, I was drinking and smoking.

My parents didn't know any of this. They were just worried about what I was going to do with the rest of my life. Soon they heard about Curry College, a private college in Milton, Massachusetts, for people with learning disabilities. I applied and got in and went there. For a whole year, I stuck it out at that school. But there were problems. My roommate had all these people coming in and out of the room. I asked her, "What is going on?" "Here," she said, "let me show you." So we took a walk in the woods, and she turned me on to cocaine. Until then, I didn't know what cocaine was—I'd never even heard of it. I lived a very sheltered life in the suburbs. But after that walk, I was off to the races. I must have lost like thirty pounds. I stopped going to classes, and I stopped getting help. I don't know how I kept my drug use from my parents, but I did. My mother's and sister's mouths are going to drop open when they read this book.

At age nineteen, I dropped out of Curry College. When I moved back home, my parents said, "We're going to have to establish some rules." So we went to family therapy, and the therapist said it wasn't going to help my growth if I stayed stagnant at home with nothing to do. She said it would be a good idea for me to go out on my own. So my parents, being well-off, gave me $3,000. I already had a car, and I moved out to Westchester. I don't really think that was the best decision for me, but my parents swore by this therapist.

I think I started off in White Plains. Then I moved to Ossining, then Tarrytown, then Port Chester. I would spend six or seven months at each place, trying to find myself, still dipping and diving with drugs. I went back to school and got my associate degree, but I don't remember the year. I do know that in 1984, I got my degree in recreational therapy from Lehman College. I loved recreational therapy. As a therapist, you can work at nursing homes and therapy centers to help people improve their fine motor skills and gross motor skills and set goals. You help them develop to their full potential. But even though I loved the work, I couldn't keep a job for longer than a year. When I got into a conflict on the job, I didn't know how to deal with it in a socially appropriate way. Either I'd get fired or I'd quit. This went on for almost fifteen years.

One day in 2000, I just fell apart at my therapist's office. I remember we were talking, Dr. Hugh and I were talking, and I must have completely overwhelmed myself. The next thing I knew, I was in the psychiatric unit of the Westchester County Medical Center. I remember waking up in the emergency room. There were machines hooked up to me. I had an oxygen mask on to make sure I was breathing okay. They had an IV in me because I was a little dehydrated. Then they started asking me questions about who I was and my family. Thank God I had Medicaid.

Turns out I had bipolar disorder. I was anxious—I was depressed—all at the same time. That's what makes you bipolar. In one day you can sway from being extremely manic and extremely excited to being very depressed and very lonely, and you can burst into tears. They think I was depressed when I was a little girl. That's why I would stay in the car when we went to restaurants. Back then I couldn't label my feelings "depression." I only knew I didn't want to order any food. Then I would get anxious and withdraw.

I stayed at the hospital almost seven months while they tried different medications to see which ones worked. I was on Neurontin—that I remember. I was on Haldol. I was on Buspar and Prozac. I was in intensive individual therapy and intensive group therapy. I had no access to alcohol or to any kind of drugs, and I've been clean ever since. I went to NA meetings and AA meetings, but I didn't make friends there. Those places were transitory, and I was still kind of keeping to myself because I was ashamed.

After I left the hospital, I settled down and got a job. I think I was working as a mental health worker for a group home for physically disabled kids; I also worked at Stop & Shop just to make ends meet because the rent and food were so expensive. I even got a cat—I went the whole nine yards. Finally, I found a furnished room in a house on a side street in Ossining. I had to pay the landlord a month's security, and then I was paying him weekly. I didn't have a lease. One night, after I had lived in the house for maybe a week, or maybe three weeks, I came home from Stop & Shop and pulled into the driveway. I got out of the car and walked up the driveway and went into my room. It was empty! I almost freaked out. I went back out to the car, looked on the front lawn, and there was everything I owned—my papers, my books, my clothes—in plastic bags on the ground. I was just devastated. Absolutely devastated.

I pounded on the landlord's door. "Why is all my stuff out on the street? I paid you a week's rent just yesterday!"—plus the month's security deposit. He proceeded to tell me that he had gone into my room and found my bipolar medication. What he did was illegal, but I didn't know this at the time. "That medication is for 'crazy people,'" the landlord said. He used air quotes. "I don't want anybody crazy living in my house." What could I do? I didn't have a lease. I didn't get a Con Edison bill. I didn't get a telephone bill. I had no document saying I lived there. I didn't know whether to laugh or cry.

I called a girlfriend, who came over and helped me, but all we could take was what would fit in my car. I think I had a small Toyota at the time. I went to my girlfriend's house that night. The next morning, I had to work with the physically disabled kids at seven o'clock. I had just started that job and was trying to follow the work ethic. So I worked a full day, and then I checked into a Westchester County shelter that was at the old airport. I felt too much pride to tell my parents what happened. If my father could read this book, he would turn over in his grave.

The old airport shelter was horrendous. It wasn't clean, and the food was horrible. All the women were in one room, and all the men were in another room down the hall. The beds were lined up in a row, literally, just like the beds in the *Madeline* books for children. You had to keep all your stuff in a pillowcase and sleep on it. How much can you fit in a pillowcase? I had to go and get storage. Plus the airport shelter was suburban and like fifteen miles from anywhere. I lost my job, and I couldn't afford to keep the car. My parents would probably have given me more money, but I was too prideful to ask. I said to myself, "Three thousand dollars is enough."

After about a month at the shelter, I got into a fight with somebody, and they kicked me out. But I have some brains. I had already been thinking that I wasn't going to be able to get around or better myself at the airport shelter. It was too isolated. "I have to get to New York City," I said. So I took a backpack and two suitcases of clothes, and I got a train ticket. At that time, the fare was only a couple of dollars.

I arrived at Grand Central Station. After walking around aimlessly, I bumped into these two homeless men. One was white and one was Spanish. "Where can I get something to eat?" I asked them. "Come with us. We'll show you," they said. This was right around the holiday times, and people were giving out free meals—I don't remember if it was in the Bowery or Madison Square Park, because we're going back twelve years. The guys showed me where I could eat, and then we rode the A train, because it's the longest train ride in the City. It goes from 207th Street in Manhattan to Far Rockaway in Queens. We rode it three times that night and slept on the train.

That first week, those two guys showed me the ropes of being homeless in New York City. There were enough places like soup kitchens where you could eat. You could go to the bookstores and the libraries, to Grand Central and Penn Station. Madison Square Park was my favorite hangout. At night, I slept sitting up on the subway, my arms wrapped around me. In the dead of winter, when the cold hit, I would go to Franklin Shelter. It was the pits, but at least I had my own locker, and it was urban and easy to get to transportation. Still, I preferred being street homeless because it is safer. You could get beat up in a shelter.

On the street, homeless men protected me, because when you're female they gravitate toward you. In the past, I never had many friends. Now it was just the opposite. I found out that you have something in common with people when you're homeless. It's like having a community. You're both out there on the street, you're both trying to make it, and you don't want to see each other get hurt. You have a mutual interest in staying safe. I remember helping this one homeless person in a wheelchair and this other person who was blind. I helped a hungry person get to a soup kitchen. Today I have no problem making friends.

Being white also helped me out—I hate to say it like this, but it's true. Because of my skin color, I was able to walk into a lot of big hotels, make believe I worked there, and take a shower. Like, once I said to an employee at the Penn Station Hotel, "Can I walk in with you? I'm applying for a job, but I need to take a shower first." I just made up this lie. She looked at me like I was crazy, but she said, "Okay, come with me." Little stories like that get you over other people. If you were black and you tried that at a hotel, you'd be stopped. When I was homeless, I even taught for the Board of Education two days a week as a substitute teacher. That gave me the money I needed to survive on the street. Once in a while, I would sleep in a hotel. The whole time I had Medicaid, and I never stopped taking my bipolar medication.

I did not want my family to know I was homeless, and my mother still doesn't know what happened to me at that time. I saw my parents on Thanksgiving and holidays. I never brought up that I was homeless, and they never asked. It just wasn't said. I'll never forget the day I was sitting in Central Park, and I got the call on my cell phone about my father passing away. I felt like a part of me had died. But I can't talk about his death. No, I can't.

My homeless period on the streets lasted about three years, from 2002 to 2005. In 2006, while I was at a drop-in center, an organization called Beacon of Hope, which was looking for homeless people with a psychiatric diagnosis, rescued me. After they interviewed me to see if I would qualify for supportive housing, I got an apartment. During my first month there, I was so unused to having space that I never left the bedroom. I was afraid to branch out to other parts of the apartment. I literally didn't enter the kitchen or the living groom. At night, I never used the bathroom. The little things we take for granted when we're housed—I was not used to them.

Soon after getting my apartment, I got a dog that I named Blackjack. Blackjack was very loving and caring, because I treated all my pets in a special way. Animals can't talk, but they deserve as much love and respect as human beings. When I had all my teeth pulled because of an infection in my mouth, Blackjack lay next to me in bed and would not let me get up for anything. If I asked him to go get me a piece of paper, he would go to the living room and get it for me. He was an unbelievable dog. When he got a kidney problem, we had to put him to sleep, and I was so hysterical you might think my son died.

That same year, I woke up one day and suddenly had no feeling in my legs. I absolutely couldn't get out of bed. The doctors in the hospital first thought it was sciatica, but eventually they diagnosed me with spinal stenosis, which you can never cure. The doctors think the problem started when I was homeless, because sleeping on park benches and on the ground hurt my spine. On top of that, in 2011 I fell on the stairs and had to have a hip replacement. Now, I am physically disabled, and I always use a walker outside. I'm on strong pain medications because some days can be really bad. Still, I am determined to walk a mile every day. I decided to do that on my own, and my physical therapist says it is an excellent idea.

When I was homeless, I had gotten involved with the Life Experience and Faith Sharing Associates (LEFSA) and met Sister Dorothy, Sister Teresa, and James Addison. Through them, I found out about the life skills empowerment program at New York Catholic Charities, and in 2007, I met the leaders, George Horton and Ms. K. The love they created in the program gave me the freedom to love myself.

The life skills empowerment program taught me the skills I needed to manage my money. It helped me get my Social Security Income and Disability. It helped me establish priorities to put my life on a better path and to set short-term and long-term goals. I was asked to think about whether I wanted to go back to school. Did I want to work? I decided to go to Easter Seals where I got training, and I now work part-time as a recreation therapist at senior centers. I teach all the things I love to my seniors—music, art, dance, culture, theater. Another one of my goals in the program was to mend relationships with my family. The first step was to call them once a week. That was such hard work! I had to set an alarm clock to remind myself to do it.

Writing my story for the program was the first time I'd ever taken a good look at my life. You start writing and you're reviewing your own pain. But the beauty is you've overcome it. You've lived through it, and you can see where you are now. The class picked me as one of four people (out of twelve) to tell my story in public on Speakers' Night at Fordham University. George had to put his arm around me before I got up in front of the audience. "Lisa, you can do it." We said a little prayer. Telling your story in front of people you don't know with the lights on you is nerve wracking. Exposing some of the things that happened, exposing your inner self, not knowing how the audience is going to interpret it—that was hard. I fumbled through the words, but I got through my story. Everybody clapped for me, so I guess it went well.

That night, Dennis Barton from the Interfaith Assembly on Homelessness and Housing heard me describe my mental illness and how all my belongings were put out on my landlord's front lawn, and he wanted me to join the Speakers Bureau. A lot of people think homelessness only happens because of drugs and alcohol. Dennis wanted me to help get rid of that myth. The first time I told my story for the Speakers Bureau, I couldn't stop crying. Now I can pretty much tell my story without bawling. Since 2007, I have gone with Dennis and told my story at least twenty-five times. Dennis and I know things about each other that people don't talk about on a day-to-day basis, and that makes for a special bond between us.

It wasn't until I participated in the life skills empowerment program and wrote my story that I proved to myself that I was worth something. I could form relationships, and I could be a happier person. I have made so many friends through the program and the Speakers Bureau: I know just about every author in this book.

In 2010, when I told my story to a life skills empowerment group at All Angels' Church, I met Eric Mull, the director of Community Ministries. He invited me to come to a Sunday service. So I did, and immediately I felt like I was home. I loved the service. I loved the gospel choir. I just felt the love and acceptance in the room. Now I go to All Angels' at least three Sundays out of four—not for the Episcopal religion per se, but for the love that I feel there. I'm in the gospel choir, and I've gotten a lot of friends through that.

To this day, if someone asks me about my religion, I always say I'm Jewish. But religion was never a big deal in my family. There were maybe five Jewish kids in my school, and I never went to religious school. On Passover, Rosh Hashanah, and Yom Kippur, we had big meals at the house of my nana—my mother's mother. We read the Haggadah and the Torah, but the meaning of the holidays was never explained. So I really didn't have a notion of what being spiritual meant.

Back when I was still homeless, I had a feeling that spirituality was missing from my life. In the LEFSA women's group, when people talked about God, I had no concept of what God was. When I asked Sister Dorothy, "What is God?" she said, "It's a very special spirit, a very special feeling, that God made you. God keeps you grounded. You can lean on him." I'm paraphrasing her. "You can put all your troubles on him. He will guide you. You can focus on him."

I haven't quite sorted it out, but I definitely believe there's a God. After all the running around I did with abusing substances and homelessness, why didn't I get killed? Something must have been watching over me to keep me alive. I definitely believe Jesus died on the cross for us. Then again, I also have the menorah—I have my past Jewish culture too. I celebrate Hanukkah with my family, and I celebrate Christmas with my friends. I celebrate Easter with my friends, and Passover with my family, so I really have the best of both worlds. I speak to God each morning: I ask him to let me live, to continue my relationships with people, to go to the Bible group—things like that. Today I asked to have a good interview for this story. I don't know if I'd call it prayer, but I do talk to God.

At All Angels' Church, I'm very involved with the community ministries. Every six to eight weeks, I volunteer overnight at the homeless shelter. After the five o'clock service, I go downstairs and sleep on a cot with the women. They often argue with each other because a lot of them have mental illness. I tell them that I have mental illness too; I share with them that there is hope in life.

I also run one of All Angels' wellness groups for homeless people. First we pray, and then we ask the group questions like, "How do you deal with anger?" or "How do you ask for help?" Last week we asked, "What are you thankful for?" A lot of people in my group were thankful for All Angels' Church. They were thankful they had a place to go on Thanksgiving. They were thankful they had a mother, they were thankful for their last breath. All of them said they were thankful for me. I can't even put into words how much it has meant to me to be a wellness leader. Giving back to others is necessary for my own psyche.

I'm thankful that I have friends and that I have reestablished relationships with my family. Recently, when my sister Meg came to pick me up for Thanksgiving, she gave me an early Hanukkah present of gorgeous new curtains. She knew I had just moved into a new apartment and was fixing it up. My sister and I are very, very close now. We speak three times a week. Because Meg is a psychiatric social worker, she jokes about giving me free therapy.

I have two nieces, and I'm getting closer to them. In fact, I just emailed one this morning because it's her twenty-first birthday. I also have three godchildren who call me every day and leave a message on my machine.

To this day, I'm living in a supportive apartment. My counselor visits me twice a month to see how I am doing, make sure all my bills are paid, and to negotiate with the landlord if I have a problem. I have three lizards, three turtles, and three cats—Marvin, Bianca, and Jackie Gleason Sperber. They all give me unconditional love, but the most special one is Marvin. He sleeps at the foot of my bed. Whenever I tell him my problems, Marvin just listens and never interrupts and never gets bored—he's that sensitive. Marvin is almost like a therapist.

Yet, now that I have people in my life, I know that they are more important to me than animals. Animals were all I had growing up. Today when I get down and out, I have a different way of coping. I have friends I can rely on. I have family to lean on. I have a therapist I can lean on. I have more of a sense of community, and I have a better self-concept.

I have always wondered what would have happened if I didn't become homeless, or take the life skills empowerment course, or join the Interfaith Assembly on Homelessness and Housing. Would I have gone to church and become articulate? Would I have become giving? Would I have become loving, caring, and compassionate? Would I have become the person that I am today?

I don't know, and that is my story.

Reflection
Reverend Alistair Drummond

Reverend Alistair Drummond is the pastor at West End Presbyterian Church in Manhattan, which has hosted the Panim el Panim life skills empowerment program since 2013. He was coordinator and co-facilitator of Panim el Panim in spring 2016 and has since become a consultant for programs with Fordham University's Bertram M. Beck Institute on Religion and Poverty, which is collaborating with congregations to initiate and embed programs in the life of their communities.

In the Gospel of Mark, we are told that when Jesus entered the synagogue he found a man with a withered hand. People were watching Jesus to see whether he would cure the man on the Sabbath, so that they might accuse him of breaking religious law. "Come forward," Jesus said to the man. "Is it lawful to do good or to do harm on the Sabbath, to save life or to kill?" he asked the others. Then he said to the man, "Stretch out your hand." The man stretched it out, and his hand was restored.[1]

Christian faith and practice are centered on the character and example of Jesus as depicted in the gospels and reflected elsewhere in the Bible. All these sources point to a holy preoccupation with the well-being of the most marginalized and otherwise least-supported members of society. The life skills empowerment program is in perfect alignment with the character and example of Jesus. Participants are invited quite literally to "come forward," and they are invited and nurtured to experience their own empowerment, to "stretch out their hand," and in so doing to discover significant recovery and healing.

My whole life I have been learning to "stretch out my hand" and express faith in action. I was raised in the highlands of Scotland by parents who did not hesitate to bring children and families who needed care and encouragement into our home. During my years of married life, my spouse worked tirelessly for international women's aid and refuge for victims of domestic violence in Edinburgh. Now I am the pastor of West End Presbyterian Church, a predominantly African American and Latino congregation in New York City. Like others living in this neighborhood, I have often been at a loss to know how to help the homeless individuals I encounter on the streets of the city or sleeping on the church steps or subway cars. I have been in a long search for ways that the congregation and I can serve and lower the threshold for building a trusting and collaborative relationship with people in the most vulnerable circumstances.

In 2013, through a fresh mission study undertaken during my congregation's 125th anniversary year, we identified the goal of making a more meaningful presence in the community. And shortly after that (be careful what you ask for!), Marc Greenberg told me that the Panim el Panim life skills empowerment program needed a new home for its workshops. I seized on the idea of providing space as a real contribution our congregation could make. The church board readily agreed, and from there we have not looked back. I added my own direct contribution as an occasional presenter with the participants and as co-chair of the Interfaith Assembly on Homelessness and Housing's Steering Committee and Advisory Group.

With minimal organizational complexity and overhead cost, the program affords many homeless and formerly homeless people the opportunity to empower themselves week by week and semester by semester. At West End Presbyterian, the church community has also benefited. By providing a workable and safe environment within the church building, we enact the ministry of care to which we all feel called. Our shared internal sense and experience is that when are engaged in this work, the church is functioning as it should—through collaboration with others. Here, each program participant finds resources in staff, volunteer mentors, and church volunteers providing wholesome meals.

From the beginning of providing a home for the program, I have felt actively engaged. I gain spiritual encouragement by being of service. I exercise leadership in an area of ministry about which I myself am still learning. And I feel fulfilled when I can see the positive effects of my collaboration with other congregants and other program leaders. I am so grateful to have found an avenue by which my church community and I can be of service to our program participants.

In this day and age, when the church is too often associated with power and establishment interests and the most vulnerable feel little sense of sanctuary or support within its walls, the life skills empowerment program provides an important stepping-stone by which we all can grow toward the beloved community.

Life Story
Rodney Allen

Rodney Allen was born on September 22, 1954, in Raleigh, North Carolina. He graduated in 2009 from the Panim el Panim life skills empowerment program, which was designed by Congregation Ansche Chesed and the Interfaith Assembly on Homelessness and Housing. Rodney's story includes details and quotations from a StoryCorps interview he had with his daughter, Roxanne Stephenson (then Roxanne Allen), in March 2010. Roxanne also transcribed Rodney's speech from her wedding video.

In 1962, when I was seven years old, my parents split up. My father stayed in Raleigh, North Carolina, and my mother moved me and Stanley, my younger brother, here to New York City. In the summertime, Stanley and I would go back to North Carolina and stay with my mother's parents. That's when the reality of segregation set in. A perfect example was at the movie theater—blacks upstairs, whites downstairs. I could not fathom that. I told my uncle, "In New York City you can sit any place you want." He tried to explain, but it was very hard for me to accept. When we would go to Woolworths, we had to use the "Negro" side, and the other side was where white people shopped.

Besides the segregation, summers were great. You had a chance to get out of the city, you had the wide-open spaces. My grandparents were poor, but there was always food on the table because they had a farm. I remember watching my uncle wring a chicken's neck. First he swung the chicken in a circle maybe eight or nine times, and then he chopped its head off. That particular chicken, he cooked it. I ate it, but I felt funny, to

be honest with you. My grandfather grew corn, tomatoes, blackberries. Once he hooked me up to the mule to do the plowing, but the mule didn't want to move. I said, "Come on! Let's go!" The mule took a couple of steps and stopped. Couple of steps and stopped. Oh my God!

To go to the bathroom, you had to use the outhouse. "I don't understand," I would tell my mother when I came back to the city. "There's no running water, you have to walk outside to go to the bathroom, there's no gas or electric. You got to chop wood and put it in the stove and light the wood up for heat." My mother would just say, "Rodney, that's the way they live. That's the way I grew up."

Maybe twice out of the month, my father might come by my grand-mother's house. I had heard stories about how he used to hit my mother and stuff like that. Whenever he would visit, I didn't really talk to him. I actually walked out of the house—tried to keep my distance. My brother was the opposite. He spoke to our father. Stanley didn't care. But there was nothing my father could say to me because my mother was my universe. She was my rock. She was the person I could always turn to with everything—when things were going good, when things were going bad.

The next thing I knew, my mother got remarried. I don't remember the exact year this happened. We moved from the Bronx to Long Island City, Queens. I remember vague bits and pieces of the first time I saw our house—bedrooms upstairs and kitchen, dining room, living room, everything else downstairs. I was kind of upset because Stanley and I got five new stepsiblings. Until then, it had always been just me and my brother. Now all of a sudden I had all these other people to share things with. I was trying to figure out why the family had to change. But all in all, I must admit, we had a good time growing up. No animosity with the siblings. We were very close.

My stepfather, on the other hand, I really didn't care for him. He was—how should I put it—very old school. If you did something wrong, he wouldn't try to talk to you. All he said was, "Come here! Come here! I'm gonna grab my belt." So I got hit a couple of times. That drove me away from him. I thought about how a father should talk to his kids. Hitting wasn't the only answer. I said to myself, "If I ever get married and have kids, I'm going to be the opposite of him." Still, after the marriage, I always called him my father. Yeah, I called him Dad.

My parents worked very hard. My father was a shop steward for Midland Steel. My mother was a dietitian and the manager of a diner. I would say we were almost middle class. We never got the electricity turned off or got kicked out for not paying the rent. And when holidays came, I always got a new suit. So life wasn't bad.

I still remember the day in second grade when another teacher ran into our classroom: "Oh my God! President Kennedy was shot and killed!" I was in shock. It's like the world stood still. You looked up to the president, and somebody took his life. Then Jack Ruby shot Oswald on TV. Here was Oswald in handcuffs and the next thing you know, some guy takes out a gun and boom. I said to myself, "There is too much violence in the world." I asked my teachers, my parents, my friends' parents why all this was happening. They just said some things are unexplainable. But I thought there had to be a reason for everything. That's the way I looked at it when I was growing up.

Five years later, it was April 1968, and my mother, brother, and I went Easter shopping on Delancey Street. And when we got home, my father said that Martin Luther King Jr. got shot. "Oh my God," people said. "Martin Luther King Jr. is dead." Some even said, "Malcolm X was right about white people being the devil," even though Malcolm X changed his mind about this before he died. To me, Martin Luther King Jr. was another situation. Here was a guy trying to do the right thing, trying to bring people of different colors together, and he lost his life. That was something else I didn't understand. There was no reason.

Other than these events and my father with the punishments, I had a good childhood. Just like in everybody's life, you're going to have your problems. Nothing is perfect. But I was a happy person growing up, basically.

For high school, Stanley and I went to Holy Cross, a Catholic high school in Flushing, Queens. My mother worked another job and my father worked a lot of overtime to pay the tuition. All the other siblings went to public school. I have no idea if my mother just wanted her two oldest sons to go to Catholic school. Matter of fact, I think my mother favored me personally. Maybe because I was the oldest—I don't know—I was her firstborn.

At Catholic school, I didn't think about following the religion. I knew that I was baptized, and the nuns and priest would talk to us about God, but I didn't much think about it. I believed in God, but I didn't really talk about him. History was my favorite subject because it explained why things happen.

As a sophomore, I tried out for the football team. My coach said, "Allen, you're pretty quick. I'm going to put you in the position of free safety." From the moment I got on the field and started practicing, I just fell in love with football. My teammates and my coaches became almost like a second family to me. That's the best way of putting it. After the games, especially if we won, we would go out bowling or have pizza, or the coach would take the team to the movies. On the field, we all believed in each other. And off the field, when one person had a problem, we would talk to him.

Once I taught my mother the rules of football, she loved coming to my games. My father really didn't care about sports. If I asked him to come see me, he would say, "Yeah, maybe I can come." Then, when it was a day or two before the game, he'd say, "I gotta work," or "I gotta do this,

I gotta go here, gotta do that." I would rather he had just said, "I don't want to go." In my whole life, my dad only came to see me play football once. My mother came to every game, even when she was sick. Like I said, my mother was everything to me. She was always happy, always trying to help everybody else.

When I started playing football and associating with the team, I hung out with a lot with white people. My brother Stanley was just the opposite. "I would rather hang out with my own kind," he said. Once I invited him to a party after school, and he asked, "How many black people are gonna be there?" I said, "I couldn't tell you that. I don't know." So he said, "No, I don't want to go." Just like that. As we got older, Stanley was more of a militant type. We didn't argue about things. We were still close. But Stanley liked to read about the Black Panthers. He always loved to read about Malcolm X. Our mother said, "Don't judge people by the color of their skin. Martin Luther King Jr. didn't. Judge people by their heart." And that's the way I judged people. I judged if you were a good person. I didn't care what color you were, or religion. I just liked all different types of people.

After high school, I went to Hunter College and lived at home for a year. Soon it was time to move out because my father and I didn't see eye to eye. I had to abide by his rules, be home at certain times, different things. I just didn't want to hear it anymore. I remember the classic line: "As long as you're in this house, you're going to do what I say or leave." So I left and got my own apartment in Rego Park. I also left college and started working. I worked at a pizza store, at a messenger company, and as a phone operator. Eventually, I got a job as a dispatcher for a dispatching business and did the trucking accounts. Estee Lauder was one of our clients; we also had J&R Music World and Colgate Palmolive. There was a lot of money being made back then, and dispatching was a big business.

In June 1977, right before the big blackout, I met Carmen at a newsstand on Park Avenue and Fiftieth Street. At lunchtime, I would always go up and read *Sports Illustrated* magazine. There was a big sign at the newsstand: "Unless you're going to buy, do not read the magazines." Being the person I was, I said, "Yeah, okay, you're right," and just kept reading. It was all right because I knew the newsstand's manager. But Carmen had just started working there. One day, she said, "Sir, you can't read the magazine unless you're gonna buy it. Take it or leave it."

I was polite: "Yeah, okay, you're right." And I just kept reading.

"Well you know what?" she said. "Next time you come up here I'm gonna take the magazine out your hand and put it back in the rack."

I said, "Oh really?" But then, I don't know, we just started talking. The next thing you know, we hit it off and started going out. We got married on February 3, 1978. And my daughter Roxanne was born on October 29, 1978.

Roxy was the best thing that ever happened to me. I can't explain the joy, the happiness. I said to myself, "Wow. I helped bring this living human being into this world. I'm gonna treat her the right way, not the way that my father treated me." She was going to have love, caring, and acceptance from me. As a child, my daughter would run around, and I'd run around after her. She was always an outdoors person. The park was my daughter's heaven. Whenever it was time to go home, she would scream and hold onto the swing.

"No, Daddy, no!"

"Roxy, let the swing go!"

"No! No!" Oh, my God. I laugh about it now.

My brother Stanley started hanging out with the wrong people, and he got involved with heroin. He hung out in the street and would say things like, "Yo, what's going on?" We weren't brought up that way, so our relationship wasn't as close as it had been. I worried about him all the time. Fortunately, by 1979 Stanley was coming off drugs. His wife was pregnant, and he was working at Midland Steel. We had a great relationship again. On weekends, we always got together, hung out, talked about family, old times, stuff like that.

On Friday nights, Stanley and his coworkers would shoot dice up in Hunts Point. One night, this other guy that came by every now and then was playing with them. The guy lost a couple of games, won a couple of games. Then he put most of his money in what they call the pot, and he lost. When everybody went to get their money, this guy just grabbed all of it. "I'm leaving," he said. "I don't want to play anymore." My brother and his three coworkers were angry.

"You're not taking our money."

But the guy pulled out a gun. The coworkers backed up, but not my brother.

"Stanley, let it go, he's got a gun. It's not worth it, blah, blah, blah."

But my brother said, "No. To you it's not worth it, but he's not taking my money"—it was like twenty dollars. When my brother started walking toward him, the guy pulled the trigger. Shot him. And then ran.

Only thing I remember was holding the phone, listening to my mother cry. "Your brother got shot," she said. Stanley was rushed to Lincoln Hospital in the Bronx. The doctors did surgery. My brother had lost so much blood they almost had to bring him back to life. He ended up in a coma. Even if he came out of it, the doctors tried to explain to me, Stanley might be a vegetable. He was hooked up to a ventilator, lying there with his eyes open, moving back and forth, back and forth. After a week, my brother died. I can't explain the feeling. It was like everything stopped. It was like being in a time warp. This was October 1979, one year after my daughter was born.

I went to the trial, and the guy who killed my brother went to jail. I don't know how much time he got. I think it was like five to ten, or five to twenty-five.

It took years for me to get over my brother's death. The loss hurt so bad because I was thinking about the memories, thinking about his birthday. We were so close. A couple of times I went to North Carolina where the family plot is, where Stanley is buried. It was very heartbreaking. I felt like a part of me was gone.

I started doing crazy things. On Friday nights, I would go out drinking with my coworkers. With me, no matter what, there were always sports involved. We'd watch boxing, baseball, football at bars or people's houses. After we left one place, we'd go to another, saying, "Oh, I'm going home at one o'clock." Next thing you know it was two o'clock. "Oh, we'll go home at three o'clock." Next thing you know it was four o'clock. Then it was five o'clock in the morning. When the next Friday came, we would go out and do the same thing all over again. It became a routine. Even though I was still in love with my wife, I started taking her for granted—I'll put it that way. Things went from bad to worse. Pretty soon my coworkers and I were meeting up with different girls. One time this lady got my phone number and called the house. After that my wife didn't believe anything I said. At that particular point, I didn't care what happened with us.

Soon after my brother died, my mother developed breast cancer. After she was diagnosed, she would always cry and cry, thinking about "when Stanley was here." She started getting radiation and chemotherapy at Sloan Kettering. My father—even though he knew she had cancer—was never there for her. It was like he cared but he didn't care. So my mother would call one of my sisters or me: "Rodney, come pick me up at the hospital? Rodney, can you take me to the doctor, can you take me for my chemo?" Obviously, my father and I had a strained relationship from the beginning. Now I was really, really angry at him.

When my mother died, it was real, real tough. I didn't want to live anymore. First of all, there were two wakes. I had to see her in a casket in New York and then again in North Carolina for the burial. I was very, very angry at God and thought, "Why did you take her away?" That was before I understood God like I do now. Now I would know that we all have our time. I was mad at the doctors because they said she was getting better and a week later she died. I was mad at my wife too. I would come home late from work, and we would argue. She would nag me and get on my nerves.

By then, my coworkers and I were using cocaine. We started using it little by little until we were buying a whole lot. The next thing you knew, your money was disappearing, even though coke was cheap back then. A gram was like twenty-five dollars. Now I was staying out more and more—I'd leave on a Friday and come back on Sunday. My temper got bad, because the drugs can really change you. I didn't throw things or hit, but I used to raise my voice. Afterward, I had a tendency to shut people out. That's one thing I learned from my mother, the silent treatment, because that's what she did with my father. I don't know. Maybe that was inherited or something. One thing about my daughter, I never got mad at her. But when my wife would argue with me, I'd just get up and leave the apartment. Or when the aunts and uncles from North Carolina would say, "We hear you're using drugs," I'd tell them to mind their own business. If my siblings explained how I should change my life, I'd say, "When I need your opinion, I will let you know."

I didn't think my wife understood the pain I was going through from the deaths. That was how I used to explain what I was doing. But if you asked me now, I'd say that was just a crutch. The same thing could have happened if my brother and mother were still alive. Maybe I was just being selfish. Whatever I did, I just did; I didn't think about the consequences. You know how they put it? Hindsight is 20/20. I should have told my wife, "Do you realize the hurt that I'm dealing with right now?" Instead, to make a long story short, I took the marriage for granted. I assumed I could go out, get high, come back home, and the person would still be there.

Until one day, that person was gone. In 1984, I put the key in the door, walked into the apartment, and saw a note on the table. "Rodney, I can't deal with this marriage anymore. I'm gone. And I'm taking Roxy with me. You might not ever see her again." I just sat there—sat there for a long, long time. I kept saying to myself, "I really screwed up this time." The first few weeks, I was numb. "She wanted to leave, so she left," I thought. But as time went on and I didn't see my daughter for months, I started getting angry. My wife was not going to keep me from my daughter! Until then, I had seen Roxy every day since she was born. Now it was like the Twilight Zone. I had a hole in my heart. I called my wife's relatives, but they wouldn't tell me where she was. Finally, one of the aunts, who liked me through all the craziness, gave me Carmen's address. I went over there, and of course we got into a big screaming match. Her brother had just come back from Panama, and we almost came to blows. My wife called the cops to get me out of the apartment. At that time, my daughter was out with my wife's sister.

About two weeks later, I went back. "Okay, I'll be calm," I told my wife. "We don't have to get into a screaming match, but I want to see Roxy. I want to see my daughter."

Finally, Roxy came running out. "Oh, Daddy! Daddy!" She was about five years old. She hadn't seen me in such a long time. In her mind, it must have been like, "Where have you been?" I picked her up, and I was crying, and she was saying, "Daddy, Daddy, Daddy, I love you, I love you, I missed you, I missed you!" After that, I started seeing my daughter little by little. It was hard. Very hard.

My wife took me to family court. She could have said, "Let's work out some type of financial arrangement." Instead, I had to pay $1,000 in arrears. Then they were taking money out of my check. I was coming home with barely ninety or a hundred dollars. It was crazy. I told Carmen, "Let's sit down, and you can tell me what the money is going for." She never wanted to explain that. You talk about being angry? That was a nightmare.

But after we got the payments going, I started seeing my daughter every other weekend. One Saturday, I kept Roxy until Sunday because she didn't want to leave. Her mother went ballistic—called the cops and everything. With all my craziness, I don't know why Roxy loved me so much. Remember, she was living with her mother, so she was hearing stuff like, "Your father's no good." Some kids living with one parent almost become brainwashed against the other. But my daughter was the opposite. "I don't care," Roxy told her mother. "It's between you and Daddy. I just love my father." As she got older, I got to see her more, like a couple of times during the weekdays.

The rest of my life wasn't too settled. I was still working, but I shared a type of rooming house in Brooklyn with some coworkers. I had a couple of girlfriends, but one thing about me, it was no commitments—even today. As time went on and reality sunk in, I wished that I was still with my wife. But I knew in my heart that we weren't ever getting back together.

I was doing more and more cocaine. It just took a lot of the pain away. You could say it was sadness. Or I just needed something to lift me up.

That's a better way of putting it. In your mind, you think it's euphoria. You could be up all night. But then you come down. That is the tough part. You're tired, and you're sleeping, and you're irritable and all that stuff. I was like—what's the term—a functioning addict. I still had a steady job.

Obviously, I wasn't using drugs when my daughter was around. But when she was in tenth or eleventh grade, Roxy found out about my use. I don't remember the actual event. But I know my daughter looked at me in disbelief. "Dad! You're using drugs?"

"Yes," I said. "I'm sorry." That didn't solve the problem, but that's what I said. I was hurt and angry at myself. And it really made me sad. Even then, with all the shock, Roxy kept on loving me. I have no idea why. To this day, every time I ask her that question, she just says, "I love you, you're my father. I can't put it into words." And I laugh. "Four years of college and you can't put it into words?" Roxy graduated from Fairleigh Dickinson University. I was super happy when she walked across the stage for her diploma. With all my craziness, my daughter had enough sanity to keep herself together. To this day, I thank Jesus Christ for her.

For over twenty years, I kept working as a dispatcher. Matter of fact, I got promoted to the job of office manager. Eventually I left that job to make more money at another service—$800 a week. The problems started when my boss decided to expand his business. We moved from Thirtieth Street and Fifth Avenue to Sunnyside, Queens. The boss hired his own fleet of drivers and stopped paying the rest of us. We went from getting paid every week to getting paid every two weeks, to getting paid once a month. My boss said, "I'm not gonna be able to pay you guys this month 'cause we got to buy computers—we gotta do this and we gotta do that." But that has nothing to do with paying your employees. You want people to work every day? Nine, ten hour days, but you're not paying them? Meanwhile, he had three cars and a big house in Cranford, New Jersey. That was crazy. I quit that job.

I tried to get another job, but I didn't want to dispatch anymore. I did piecework for a while, but that didn't pay enough. Pretty soon I gave up. I can't explain why. After about six or seven months, all my money in the bank was gone. I couldn't pay my rent. At the time, I was sharing an apartment with a guy in Brooklyn. He was having his own problems, and he stopped paying rent, too. I had no idea where my roommate even was.

In July 2007, the landlord put a notice on the door: "If you can't pay such-and-such amount by such-and-such time, we're going to evict you. You have seventy-two hours to clear out all your belongings." I moved out as much stuff as I could. One of my brothers kept some—so did a neighbor downstairs. I didn't have time to take everything out. The third morning, I came back to get some clothing and personal stuff. My key didn't work, and there was a lock outside the door. A big sticker said "Marshals."

That's the saddest feeling in the world, to know you don't have a place to go. It's true I had plenty of family, but being the type of person I was—Mr. Independent—I didn't want them to know my situation. You can call me embarrassed. To this day, people from church and other places say, "Why didn't you go to this person or that one?" I could have called my daughter, because she was grown-up and living in New Jersey. I could have called my brother and my sisters. The brother who took some of my stuff said, "You can stay here a little while." But I didn't want to burden myself on anybody. "Nope," I said. "Until I get another job, I'm just gonna have to be without an apartment." But what was my next move? What was Plan B? There was no Plan B.

"Let me go to Manhattan," I decided. "Then I'm going to sit down and think this thing through." I took the R train to Twenty-Third Street, came up the stairs, and Madison Square Park was right there. I saw people on the benches with all these suitcases, carry bags, and duffel bags all in front of them. "Who are all these people?" I asked one of the guys. "Oh," he said, "all these people are homeless. This is where they stay at." I just looked at him. "Wow. You know what? I'm homeless too."

I sat down next to him. This was about two in the afternoon. I had like ten dollars in my pocket, maybe fifty dollars in the bank, nothing more. At night, the Coalition for the Homeless came, and the guy where I was sitting got two meatball soups and gave me one. Everybody loved the meatball soup. Around nine o'clock, I got up and went to the bathroom at McDonald's. Then I came back to the same spot on the bench. It was like being in a daze. I couldn't say, "Oh, it's such-and-such a time, let me go home now." I didn't have a home anymore. Eventually, the other guy on the bench left. I sat there by myself, all night long, dozing on and off, looking around. Just thinking, saying to myself, "Wow. How did I get myself into a situation like this?" No answer. No answer. Then I thought, "Thank God it's the summertime."

For months I sat in Madison Square Park. I got up and stretched my legs. I sat on different benches. On Twenty-Third Street and First Avenue, you could take a shower twice a week. But everything else I did was in the park. I ate the soup from Coalition for the Homeless. The people from Midnight Run brought food and clothes. During the day, the regular people who came with their kids used to leave newspapers. I would read them and talk to some of the other homeless people. But for some reason, I didn't venture out of the park. I became glued there. I can't even explain. I didn't call my daughter—I thought about it, but I didn't. I didn't have money to buy minutes, but I could have gone to a public phone and dropped in two quarters and called collect. I didn't. I shut down. That's a better way of putting it. I shut down.

When I became homeless, I stopped using cocaine. I couldn't afford it anymore, and I have never used it since. That's something to think about.

Weeks went on. Months went on. It started to get colder. One day in October, a big white guy—270 pounds, white hair, white beard—came up to me. He looked like Santa Claus. "How are you doing?" He sat down on the bench next to me. My answer was very curt. "I'm not doing well. I don't have a job, I don't have a place to live." The way I was talking, I showed that I didn't want to be bothered. But he just said, "My name is Bob Moore. I'm homeless too, but I have a job." Later I found out Bob did security at All Angels' Church. Pretty soon I started talking, and we just hit it off. When he left, Bob said, "I'll see you tomorrow. I'll get some sandwiches from my church and bring them to you."

From then on, every day around six o'clock, Bob would come to the park. We would talk. Whatever food he had from the church, he would bring. He told me about all these places where I could eat—an egg place at a church on Eleventh Street and Avenue A, a meatloaf place on Second Avenue and Second Street. Bob wrote this down and gave me a Metro-Card to travel. When I asked why he was singling me out, he said, "Don't ask me a lot of questions."

Then one day, he said, "Listen. I'm gonna take you to the five o'clock service at church."

I wouldn't go. "I don't want to go to church. I don't want to go to the service. I just want to stay right here." So that particular Sunday, I didn't go with Bob. But the next Sunday, it was colder. "Rodney," Bob said, "you're going to church!" Oh my God. He didn't literally pick me up or grab me. He just stood there. "We're going!" I was like, "Okay, okay, we'll go, let's go."

And that was the first time I left Madison Square Park since becoming homeless—except for getting food and going to the bathroom.

"This is All Angels' Church," Bob said when we got to the Upper West Side. "The service starts at five o'clock. After that, they have the community meal. So now you can get acclimated to another place where you can eat." To my surprise, some of the homeless people who sat on the benches at the park were at the service. One of them came up to me. "I

see you in Madison Square Park." I said, "Yeah, I see you there too." Seeing other homeless people from the park made me feel much better. After
that, these same people, when we went back to the park, had something
to talk about. We could chat.

For about five weeks in a row, I went to All Angels' Church on Sunday.
I actually began going on my own. I used the MetroCard Bob gave me to
come up and go back. At first, I would not really listen to the sermon. A
lot of the homeless people would sleep through it. You had people snor-
ing. Oh my God. Reverend Milind would get angry: "This is not a place
you come to sleep! This is a place you come to find God, to change your
life." After a while, I started paying more attention to him. Just hearing
Reverend Milind's voice made me start to feel a little sense of—I don't
know—joy. I started to feel more relaxed, more comfortable. After the
community meal, I would tell Bob, "See you later. I'm going back to the
park." And the next day Bob would meet me at the park.

Eventually Bob said, "I can help you get a job at the church as long as
you keep the job. Make it last!" Well, I needed a job, and about a month
later the church hired me for two days a week to paint and refinish the
chapel's wooden floors. Once I got my own money, I started saving it. I
didn't have a bank account, so I just kept it. Bob kept some of it for me
too. It wasn't much.

All this time, I was still sleeping in Madison Square Park. Bob brought
me some blankets. I never spent a single night at a shelter. People at the
park said, "The shelter system is the worst you could ever do. They rob
your stuff, they beat you up, they want to fight all the time." Some homeless
people say, "Oh yeah? Let me go and find out for myself." But I just said,
"You know what? I'm going to stick it out in this park as long as I can."

"You can't keep staying here," Bob told me at about the end of November. "I'm going to get you a MetroCard so you can sleep on the train."
By then I had two bags of clothes. The first time I slept on the train, I
woke up and one of my bags was gone. It was scary. My favorite train was
the E line, because they had a bathroom at the last station that stayed open
until 1:00 a.m. But at night, the cops would come on the train and bang
their sticks on the side of a seat. "Wake up! Get up!" Even though you
were dead tired, you had to wake up and switch trains. Penn Station was
tough, too. If you sat in the Long Island Railroad section, they'd come
around and ask, "Tickets? Tickets?" If you didn't have a ticket, you had
to get up and go to the New Jersey Transit side—you could stay there
until they came around and checked for tickets. Then you would go to
Amtrak. So that would be a vicious circle: Long Island Railroad to New

Jersey Transit to Amtrak. "You don't have tickets? You gotta get out." It was constant. You had to change your seat all night long, and that's why so many homeless people were tired at church.

Once I started working at All Angels', I bought minutes for my phone, and maybe once every three weeks I called my daughter.

"Dad, where are you?"

I would just answer, "I'm going through a not-good period in my life." I didn't go into details or anything.

"I want to see you!"

"Okay, Roxy, but right now, I want to try to get my life a little bit more under control." I don't know why I didn't want to see my daughter. I guess subconsciously I was embarrassed to be in the situation. I was hoping I could get a better job, get an apartment, anything, before I got to see her. By September 2007, I hadn't seen my daughter in over a year. Finally, I agreed to meet her in Madison Square Park.

When Roxy saw me, it was instant gratification. We hugged, we cried. But my wife had come, too. Roxy was ecstatically happy. "Daddy! Daddy! Daddy! Why did you wait so long for me to see you?" She was really overjoyed. I was extremely happy, but I was—how should I put it? I was a more reserved happy. That day, we went to the movies and talked. "Next time," I told my daughter, "just come by yourself. Then I can tell you a lot of stuff that's happening in my life—why I didn't wanna see you in the situation I was in."

The following week, my daughter and I met at the Museum of Natural History. "I'm homeless," I told her.

"Oh, you can come stay with me. Why didn't you call me? Why didn't you tell me?"

"Roxy, you know how I am."

"Yeah, that's my point. You shut people out. But I didn't think you would ever shut *me* out."

"I didn't really mean to—I just didn't want you to see me in this situation."

My daughter and I talked and talked and talked. Finally, Roxy said, "Daddy, if you're going to stay one night a week, what night would you like to stay?"

"Stay where?"

"Don't start this! Stay with me." Roxy had her own apartment in Teaneck, New Jersey. She had a job as a vocational counselor for mentally disabled adults. To this day, she still works there.

So I started staying with my daughter on Monday nights. We'd rehash the whole week—what was happening in the world, what was happening in New York City. My daughter asked me about my life, and I asked about her life. Sometimes Roxy made chicken and macaroni for dinner, and sometimes we ordered Chinese food. On Monday nights, *CSI*, a show I loved, was on television. Later I slept inside on the couch and had the whole living room to myself. Tuesdays were sad because I wouldn't see my daughter for a week. Roxy would have been happy for me to stay longer, but I wanted to stand on my own.

As time went on, change started happening. When Mondays came and my daughter asked how I was doing, I could tell her how I was bettering myself step by step. I got a social worker at a place called the Open Door, and I began the long process of trying to get housing. By spring 2008, I got a couple more days of work at All Angels' Church. One day Christine Lee, the director of Community Relations, came up to me. "How's your spirits, Rodney?"

I had no idea what she was talking about.

"Listen," she said, "you probably don't read the Bible, and maybe you don't believe in all the scriptures, but I want you to read a couple of psalms every day." She wrote down five or six chapter numbers for me. The next day, she said, "Did they make sense to you?" I said, "Some made sense, some didn't make sense, to be honest with you." After that, Christine kept showing me different psalms. I noticed that I started feeling better when I was having a conversation with her. The way she would sit down and take the time to explain these little things just helped me. A spiritual belief would come over me. My whole outlook started changing. I said to myself, "There is hope out there."

Then Eric Mull, who ran the Community Ministries, said to me, "Christine Lee tells me that you are starting to open up more. I see progress from the time you first came here." Eric started showing me shortcuts to parts of the Bible that make you feel better about life. He really helped me get closer to God. I can't give a date or timeline for it—it just happened. Eric just told me simple things. "There's a little good in everyone. Even when it's the darkest and you're in despair, God is still with you." Eric and I, we got very, very close. I was totally uplifted. Faith changed my whole personality and my whole outlook on life. I started to talk to God and worship God. I thought of everything that Jesus Christ went through up on the cross, how he died and then rose again. I said to myself, "It's like changing your life." It was something to think about.

A year later, 2009, Bob Moore started getting very thin. You could see it when he sat at the security desk. "Rodney," Reverend Milind said one day in May, "we had to put Bob in the hospital because he's getting worse and worse." He had bladder cancer. Bob did the chemo, did the radiation. When I visited him at Harlem Hospital, Bob kept saying, "I'm going to beat this thing. I'm going to beat this thing." I didn't even have a chance to see him in the hospice. After a week there, Bob was gone. I was very, very sad that I couldn't help him the way he helped me. "Rodney, I believe in you," Bob would say. "Even though you may not believe in yourself, I believe in you. Don't give up, don't give up, don't give up, no matter how dark and gloomy things are." I will always be grateful to Bob Moore. They have a picture of him at All Angels', in the sacristy.

A few months later, I got housing in South Jamaica, Queens. The first night I took the elevator upstairs, put my keys in the door, and went inside my own apartment, all I said was, "Thank you, God." I walked around, turning on the water, making sure everything worked. I made my bed with some sheets I got from All Angels'. It's like what they say, you don't realize what you have till it's gone. Being able to stretch out in my own bed, oh man, what a feeling! I didn't want to get back up again. I could have slept on that bed for a whole month. South Jamaica is a long way from All Angels' Church. It's the last stop on the E train, then you take the bus. Ninety minutes each way. But it's good to be away from the sirens, the fire trucks, and everything else in Manhattan. I like the peace and quiet where I live.

That fall, Eric came up to both me and Akira, who was the church's assistant chef at the time, and said, "There's a program that can help change your lives. It's called the life skills empowerment program. It's going to take place right here at All Angels', so you don't have to travel. Oh, and by the way, you will receive a stipend if you go." Akira and I looked at each other. "Okay, we'll try it," we said.

I remember the first couple of weeks of the program. I loved the facilitators, Dennis and Naomi Goldman, and I appreciated all the different people—Marc Greenberg, the session leaders—who gave their time to help us better ourselves. And I loved having you as a mentor, Susan. Here was this person who didn't know me from Adam but who cared about me and vice versa. My daughter kept asking, "Who is this Susan?" You walked on water as far as I was concerned.

As for writing my life story, I never knew there was anything like that in a program. I had to go back, to reflect, to see where I was, where I failed, where I picked myself back up, and where I had people who supported me and believed in me. When I wrote about everything I went through to uplift myself, I started believing more and more because I was living proof it could be done.

After graduation, Akira and I told our stories at St. John's University and the high school where Lady Gaga went. Oh man, I remember that. The audience's response was like, "Wow. We thought most homeless people are people that don't want to work, that are on drugs, that just gave up on life." They were amazed because we were wearing clean clothes and looked nice. "*You* were homeless?" one student said to me.

"Anyone can become homeless," I told him. "You can have a fire and become homeless. You can have a flood. Anything can happen. Homeless people are not bad people. They're not stupid people. They're not lazy people, and they are not all drug addicts." So it was good—it was good to tell my story.

In spring 2012, my daughter married her college boyfriend, Kimani. From the moment I met that guy, I told my daughter, "I want you to marry him." There was something about Kimani—he was polite, well spoken—that I liked. When they broke up after college and Roxy would tell me about other boyfriends, all I'd say is, "How's Kimani?" She would look at me. "Daddy, get real." Then one day, when I was still homeless, she called me on my cell phone and said, "Dad, I'm here having dinner with somebody you know very well—Kimani."

"Kimani! Let me talk to him."

When they got engaged, Roxy said, "I know you are extremely happy now, and you're probably going to say, 'I told you so.'" I didn't say anything, but my dreams came true.

Walking my daughter down the aisle was the highlight of my life. A lot of my friends came to the wedding—you and your husband, people from church, Reverend Milind and his wife, my brothers and sisters, my niece and nephew. Some people knew my struggle; some people didn't. To feel the journey I came from, to see all these people I hadn't seen for months and months, and years and years, to sit down with them and share the day of my daughter's marriage, I just felt overjoyed. I stood up and gave a toast.

My daughter is the person that, when I had no one standing beside me, when I was going through my own personal trials and tribulations, peaks and valleys, she was the only one that stood by me, stood by my side, right or wrong. She always said, "Dad, no matter what, I will always be there for you. . . . No matter if you hit rock

Rodney and his daughter, Roxanne, at her wedding in 2012

bottom or you're at the top. I will stand by your side." That's what she has done. She is like an angel, an angel that has really brought me back and kept me on the straight and narrow. So I want to say God bless Kimani and Roxy. May you have a great life forever and ever. Amen!

Now I am a happy, lucky grandfather too.

All Angels' Church is also like my other family. During the week, I work forty-five to fifty hours doing maintenance and security. Tuesday nights, I volunteer at our Wellness Circle for homeless people. We have dinner together, the director does a religious teaching, and then I lead one of the study groups. One of my recent questions to the group was "Do you believe in God?" Some people said yes, and some said no. The ones that didn't say anything were the ones I had to push to speak. As far as I'm concerned, not saying anything is almost like giving up. A lot of people are lost and afraid when they come to All Angels'. I tell them they can get their lives back together again. "But you gotta keep fighting for it, keep talking about it, keep trying to find people that will help you. They're out there, but you have to talk to them. You can't just do nothing and say nothing and think your life is gonna change."

And the lives of some of the people in my group have changed. They come up to me and say, "Rodney, I read this in the Bible, I read that in the Bible." And they feel totally uplifted. They just feel better every day.

Every Sunday at 10:00 a.m., I come to All Angels' to pray. The ushers greet me at the door. I put my coat and belongings away. Then I walk into the chapel and focus on God, focus on the Word, focus on the day's sermon. When the service ends, we come downstairs and have snacks, coffee, and cake. You mingle, and you talk to different parishioners. About 12:30 or 12:45, we go to lunch, and afterward, I go with a couple of parishioners I call my "Sunday crew" to watch the games at Brother Jimmy's Restaurant. During the baseball season, we watch baseball; during the basketball season, we watch basketball. I still love football best. I have my own particular group of Jets fans from All Angels'. Watching football is a thrill—you get all pumped up and crazy.

Religion is more subdued. It's a quiet uplifting of the mind. If I had to choose between religion and football, I'd have to choose religion. Today God is the driving force in my life. I believe Jesus Christ is the reason that everything happens. If you were to take that away from me now, I don't know, I might be lost again.

Life Story
Akira

Akira was born in 1950, in Saku City, Japan. He graduated in 2009 from the Panim el Panim life skills empowerment program, which was designed by Congregation Ansche Chesed and the Interfaith Assembly on Homelessness and Housing. He was a mentor for Panim el Panim from 2010 to 2014.

My father was born in Tokyo. His name was Shigeju. "Shige" means *prosperity*. "Ju" means *tenth*, because my father was the tenth child in his family. Always in Japanese the first name has some kind of meaning. My mother was born near Ueda City. Her name is Yukiko. "Yuki" means *snow*. That's why I love snow.

After their marriage, my parents went to Manchuria. They were young and ambitious. My mother was a nurse. My father worked at the national railroad company. Manchuria was a colony of Japan before World War II, and there were big railroad projects there. My eldest sister was born in Manchuria. She's the first of our five brothers and sisters. My eldest brother was born in 1944, also in Manchuria.

At the end of World War II, Russia invaded Manchuria, and my parents lost everything. They had to move back to Saku City, Japan. They couldn't take any property. They started with nothing, just surviving, so it was a miserable situation. It was horrible in Japan because all over was bombed. Not just the atomic bombs in Hiroshima and Nagasaki, but conventional bombing every day, all over Tokyo. It destroyed the whole city. Roughly six million people died during the war, young men mostly.

In Japan, my parents had three more children—my next eldest brother, my younger sister, and me. My name—Akira—means *clear*, *bright*, or *light*.

Japan's baby boom started in 1947. The country was restoring all its industrial and commercial business. We don't just need "man power," the government said. Also, we need "mom power." As in the United States, Japan emphasized that every family had to help. When I was in elementary school, junior high, I remember so many neighbors the same age—so many kids. And we all had to do community service. That was an obligation. All kids, every Sunday morning, had to clean the public streets, not only your own garden. There were also festivities and annual events, like

Boy Scouts, with everyone the same age gathering in one place. It was kind of exciting. Japan was in the process of recovering.

We had a very traditional Japanese home. When dinnertime came, my father sat at the end of the table, drinking some sake or some whiskey. In the meantime, my mother and big sister were working in the kitchen. The boys sat down next to my father, listening to his war stories. That's what I remember vividly. I was fascinated when my father spoke about Manchuria because it was so big and so cold. I think during their stay there, my parents had a very good life—a big house, a couple of Chinese servants. My father also mentioned the discrimination against the Chinese people. The Japanese very much looked down on them. Listening to my father—that's maybe when I started my interest in history.

Even at a young age, I started reading a lot of history books—and not only Japanese history, but also European history. What fascinated me most were great heroes like samurai warriors but also Napoleon, Alexander the Great, and Julius Caesar. As a little kid, I admired what they had done. In elementary school, I raised questions with my teacher. "What happened in the Roman era? How did the United States get independence from England?" They taught us about World War II, but they didn't say Japan lost the war—they called it "shusen," which means *ending the war*, not "haisen," which is *lost the war*. They did not teach us about the Japanese atrocities in Nanking or Beijing, killing civilians and Chinese people. I remember a movie about how the atomic bomb ruined Hiroshima and Nagasaki. It was black and white—a very old movie. The school children watched together in the gym. It showed how a victim was corroded because of the heat. The skin was horrible.

My father continued to work for the national railroad. My mother, after having delivered all five children, needed more income because we were growing up and needed higher education. So she went back to nursing. My mother was quiet. My father dominated all conversation. He had a kind of machismo. Later, I realized my mother brought in more money than my father. She was the one paying all the high school and college tuition.

The concept of love in Japan is hard to express. The husband and wife never say, "I love you, I love you" five or six times like on Hollywood TV. But I felt love, especially from my mother. For example, when I was about ten years old, I fell off a roof and broke a bone in two places. For almost two months, I had to go to the hospital every day. From the beginning, my mother always took me, even though she was busy. We had many children in the family, so this was like a special occasion. My mother also took me to the restaurant for ice cream. I felt her love indeed!

My father was always emphasizing competition among the brothers and sisters and also with the neighbors. He wanted his children to be the best academically and also with sports. At the national railroad, he belonged to the company baseball club. He played catcher. He wanted my brothers to play baseball, too. My eldest brother excelled, and he became a professional baseball player. After college, he was drafted number one. My father was very happy, very proud of his son. I could not compete with my eldest brother in baseball. I was more interested in studying. Almost every semester, I brought an excellent report card from the teacher. I was very proud, showing that to my father and mother. My father always said, "Akira, you have to be the leader. Do not be a follower. You have to compete the fair way, not by cheating. But you have to fight, you have to study hard, and try to be the leader." Always he said that.

I remember my father brought home a new TV. Of the neighbors, only our house had one. My father was very proud of it. A lot of kids would come to watch TV at dinnertime. Mostly they were farmers' sons, so there was not much income in their families. At 7:00 p.m., the news or some program like *Shane*, *The Three Stooges*, or *Lassie* would come on. All the neighbors would sit in our living room, watching. I wanted to come to the United States because I was so much influenced by the television.

I was into movies too, both Japanese and Western. There were many great Japanese movie directors when I was young. I remember Akira Kurosawa's movies. *Seven Samurai* is a very good one—also *Tokyo Stories* by Yasujiro Ozu. I liked them as much as *The Alamo* with John Wayne. I remember *My Fair Lady*, because after college I wanted to excel in English like Audrey Hepburn with Rex Harrison. I went to see that movie so much, like maybe ten times, the same movie. In the 1960s the Beatles started booming and also the Rolling Stones. I listened to them all the time. My two-years-older brother excelled in the saxophone and joined a jazz band. My mother bought an upright piano, and my sister would play it. There was always a lot of music in the house.

After high school, I went to Seijo University in Tokyo. I wanted to be independent—away from the family. Tokyo was much bigger than Saku City, more exciting, with more opportunities to see a high level of culture.

I majored in economics. We studied *Foundations of Economic Analysis* by Paul Samuelson. I took economics because I was thinking about the future. What should I do after college? How do you make money? I never dreamed about getting rich, though. I just wanted to compete and to be the winner. I was not always the best student in college. But I felt my future was not limited—I felt I could challenge anything. I started reading

Nikkei, the Japanese economic journal. That's like the *Wall Street Journal.* I dreamed of working in international business.

I'm pure heterosexual, but I was not so much interested in women. It would be too much time consumed. I hung out mostly with men. We would go to the movies, go to the theater. I had a lot of friends who lived in wealthy, nice houses—they even had a pool. They invited me over so many times. Compared to them I was less wealthy, but I didn't think about it. Maybe I was too optimistic. I never had an inferiority complex.

My family, especially my mother, sent me money. I lived in a regular apartment, not a cheap dormitory. My mother rented it for me and paid the normal market price. So I very much appreciated my mother, who took care of me for four years. She was constantly calling me on the telephone, asking how I was doing.

In Japan, college seniors can't just take a job interview. You have to look for work in a certain period in April. First you pick a couple of companies. Then, if you pass a written examination, you go to the interview. I took the test for Taiyo Fishery Company (now called Maruha Nichiro Corporation). That was one of the biggest fishing companies in the world at the time. They began with whaling over a hundred years ago. Then they diversified into all kinds of fields—shipbuilding, transportation, cold storage, international trading, manufacturing. About three hundred students came together for the written examination—all were men. I got tenth best.

Next was the interview. I sat down in front of eight or nine directors. I remember one old man asking, "Do you know the blue whale? Are you allowed to catch it?" The blue whale is the largest living animal in history, including dinosaurs. At that time, whaling was very controversial because Japan caught so many whales. We used every piece of meat. But the International Whaling Commission tried to ban whaling. I answered, "Probably no." I passed the interview. As a matter of fact, I was the third best.

In April 1972, when I was twenty-two, I started working at Taiyo Fisheries with about sixty other college men. In Japan, the twenty-fifth of every month you get paid. The first salary was like 50,000 yen. That means, at the current rate of exchange, about $500. Most people brought the salary home to show their parents: "Look, Mother, this is my first earning." Since I was living by myself in Tokyo, I couldn't show my parents. But I called on the phone. They said congratulations to me. "Be careful how you spend the money." For four years I had lived within the allowance my mother sent. I knew how to be careful.

I was placed in the foreign exchange section of the Financial Department. This was a very busy department because the volume of international transactions was growing. We got telephone calls from around the world, and I had to speak English. I excelled, and after a few years, my boss picked me to send on an overseas assignment. I was only twenty-six years old at that time. Usually the company was afraid of sending a young, single man abroad. Maybe that person would fall in love with a local woman or not concentrate on the work. Usually, well-experienced and older, married men were sent. But I was lucky. My boss thought I had talent. I was going to the New York City office.

So I had to make a decision about a girlfriend I had. Japanese companies traditionally recommended marriage inside the company. I had fallen in love with a woman who worked there. Her first name was Rie, and she entered Taiyo two years after me. When a woman joins the company, she usually does bottom-level work. She is kind of like a secretary; that's the system in Japan. So Rie was constantly bringing documents from the Foreign Trade Department, where she worked, to the Financial Department, where I worked. We started chatting. She invited me to her parents' home a couple of times. When 1976 came and I was being transferred to the New York City office, I told Rie, "In one year, I'm going to come back and marry you and bring you to the New York office." She agreed. I introduced her to my father and mother and everybody was happy.

In the 1970s, there were big farewell ceremonies in the airport for overseas assignments. We rented a special waiting room. A lot of people came to say goodbye to me—my bosses, my coworkers, my friends, my family. In front of like one hundred people, I introduced my girlfriend: "This is Rie. I'm engaged, and hopefully I'm coming back next year to marry her." Everybody celebrated.

On June 20, 1976, right before the bicentennial, I arrived at JFK Airport. Taiyo's New York City office was on Park Avenue at Forty-Seventh Street, in what used to be called the Chemical Bank Building. Chemical Bank was the most prestigious building at that time, two blocks away from the Waldorf Astoria Hotel. I checked into the Lexington Hotel, just across the street from the Taiyo office.

New York City was not what I imagined. Today everything in New York City is clean, everything is new. In 1976, the city was so dirty. The first Saturday, when I walked from the Lexington Hotel to buy the *New York Times*, I was called three times by street women. This was the center of the business area, and it was full of prostitution! Broadway was horrible. All the theaters had XXX movies, garbage was all over, drugs were all over. But I mostly loved New York City because it was so energetic and exciting.

However, I decided not to live in Manhattan, because one year later my bride was coming. So I found a nice big apartment in Bronxville. I bought furniture and started preparing for life with my future wife. She sent me letters every week, and I called her on the telephone. All of a sudden, September came and there was no letter at all. But I was so busy learning the US business that I had no time to worry about it.

Then one day my mother called me, crying. "Akira, it looks like your girlfriend tried to break the engagement." Maybe it was my fault because I was too concerned for business and not a good communicator. My girlfriend felt so far from my presence that she started dating some other person. It was a severe blow for me at that time, but I recuperated anyhow. Maybe I was not serious, not deep in love with my girlfriend. I can tell that now. After the breakup, I decided to move back to Manhattan. Why live a single life in Bronxville? I rented a big studio in a new high-rise apartment on Fifty-Third Street between First and Second Avenue. I decided to concentrate on my work in order to forget my broken heart. I had no time for romance.

Meanwhile, my father stopped coming to the telephone when I called. Always I asked my mother and my brothers, "Where is Father?" "Oh," they would say, "he is out of the home." At first, I didn't think about it. But by December, I started worrying. Still the family would say, "He is just busy." In March 1977, I went on the company golf outing in the Poconos. Monday morning, when I arrived at the New York office, I had a phone call from the Tokyo office. "Your father is in a coma. Come back immediately." I went straight to JFK. My boss arranged the ticket. I took a twelve-hour flight through Anchorage to Tokyo, arriving at midnight. Some company people drove me to the railway station. Then I took the train to the hospital. The whole time I didn't know what kind of sickness my father had.

The reality was the day after he said goodbye to me at the airport, my father started suffering some pain in the intestine. My father was still young, sixty, I think, and always strong and healthy. He hated to go to the doctor. When he finally went, they found pancreatic cancer. The cancer cells had spread throughout the whole body, so the surgeons closed him without taking out the tumor. My father had been hospitalized since October 1976. My mother didn't tell me the truth because I had just moved to the New York office and my engagement had broken off. She didn't want to give me another shock.

When I arrived, everybody was waiting in the hospital room, totally silent—my mother, all my brothers and sisters, my relatives, uncle, aunt.

The last time I had seen my father he was healthy, tall, good-looking, with a full head of hair (I didn't inherit that!). Now he was skin and bones, like a skeleton. His face was so dark, I didn't recognize it. And obviously, my father couldn't recognize me. I think his brain had stopped functioning. My family was just keeping him alive until I came. I was so physically exhausted and mentally blank. Nine months after I said goodbye at the airport, there was my father, almost dead. I couldn't even cry.

A couple of days after the funeral, my mother called all her children and their husbands and wives into a room.

"Please," she said, "never pain your partner with an extramarital love affair. Please know that your partner will suffer. Do you know why? Because my husband, Shigeju, your father, had an extramarital love affair for long time. He hid it from you, me, and everybody."

It turns out, after my father was hospitalized, some woman started coming to take care of him. My mother asked, "Who are you?" And the woman said, "I'm this man's lover." My mother got more shocked than when my father got cancer.

My father had been with this woman for twenty years! He had a house with her, *and* he had our house. So he was taking care of two houses and wasting money. That's why he didn't bring much money to the family. That's why my mother had to go back to work. My mother never suspected that her husband was doing such a criminal thing. And she couldn't even express her anger because my father was already gravely ill. Imagine how my mother suffered. She told me she cried a lot, but she also felt sorry for the man who lay dying in the hospital. So after he died, she reminded us, "Do not have any love affair. Do not let your wife cry."

The company let me stay in Japan for two weeks, and then it was back to New York City. In a little time, I reestablished myself at work. I was appointed treasurer of the office, and I did the finance and the budgeting. The Japanese business is a twenty-four-hours-a-day commitment, especially when you are on an overseas assignment. I got so many phone calls at night, because Tokyo is twelve hours ahead and Europe is six hours ahead. When the Tokyo office needed capital, the New York office did the financing. I borrowed money and got credit lines from Japanese banks and American security companies like Merrill Lynch and Morgan Stanley. If the Tokyo office bought one thousand tons of shrimp from some South American country, I signed the promissory note for the credit and the payment to these suppliers. For one transaction, I could borrow up to two or three million dollars. After two years, I started doing the office's accounting and payroll too.

I was also involved in physical transactions with bluefin tuna. They are the most beautiful fish you've ever seen—so much aerodynamic power and so big—up to one thousand pounds. For sushi, bluefin is the best tuna in the whole world. But Americans didn't eat it at the time. In the early 1970s, Taiyo found out that Boston fishers were throwing the meat in the garbage. We started buying from local fisherman and sending the fish by air to the Tokyo market. Taiyo was the pioneer in this transaction. From June to September, my boss sent me to New England to set bluefin prices and deal with the shipment.

In 1980, I met a girl at a private party. Her name was Regina. She was of Spanish heritage and so beautiful. At that time, Regina was twenty-five or twenty-six. I was thirty. Regina had graduated from junior college and was a student at Columbia University, living with her mother and stepfather in Chelsea. I didn't know then that he wasn't her real father and that Regina came from a broken family.

When I started seeing Regina, I had no intention of marrying her. In Japanese companies, everything was business first. There is not so much private time. Even on the weekend, you cannot take care of the family. If you married someone from a different culture, she might not like this. You would have to do double effort. You would have to struggle. But after six months together, Regina wanted a commitment. So I sent a letter to my mother. "I'm dating an American girl and I want to marry her." My mother responded, "That's very problematic for your future and your business life." But I had already decided. Finally, I convinced my mother. "Okay," she said. "If your decision is so firm, I accept it."

Regina was a devoted Catholic, but I was typical Japanese—nonreligious, so we couldn't marry in a church. In October 1981, we went downtown to civilian court, signed the marriage papers, and had a small gathering with Regina's family. The next day we flew to Japan. Everything was new for Regina, and she was excited. My mother arranged a reception in some hotel in Saku City. All my relatives came. Then Regina and I visited Kyoto and Nara, the ancient capital of Japan, on kind of a honeymoon. I was in love with my wife—deeply. I cared about her, believed in what she said, trusted whatever she did. And I hoped she could accept my Japanese culture and be able to take the very different type of lifestyle.

At first it was not so hard because I was working in New York City. My wife and I moved into a two-bedroom apartment on Park Avenue South, near Gramercy. The rent was expensive, like $1,500 a month. Still, I could afford it because the New York office had good pay—so no problem. My son was born in June 1982—he was almost a honeymoon baby. Before he was born, my wife and I went to Lamaze class. This was a strange thing to do in a Japanese company. When I left the office early, the others did not understand. From the Japanese standpoint, I was a weird person. I was also in the delivery room when my son was born. In Japan, the husband never even went near the hospital. That was the wife's job. He kept doing the business. That was one of the best moments of my life, when I was able to share this happiness with my wife.

But problems had started. A few months before the birth, an order came from the Tokyo office. My assignment was over. It is always a cycling rotation in Japan. Nobody sticks to one department. In April, usually people start shuffling. To stay in New York for the delivery, I had to get special permission. In August, I returned to Tokyo without my wife and son. Two months later, they joined me.

Now I was in the Trading Department, buying seafood, including tuna fish, from around the world. A lot of time I was on business trips—to the US, South America, Korea, Taiwan, Italy, and Spain. I worried about leaving my wife by herself. She didn't speak Japanese. Obviously she felt very lonely. One day I received the telephone bill. It was like $4,000, more than my monthly salary. My wife was talking to her mother for two hours almost every day! I told her, "Honey, you can't do this because I cannot afford to pay." Sometimes, when I was not travelling, I had to entertain clients after work. On the weekends, the company group went golfing. Everything was business first. One time my wife got so fed up that she cut the telephone line with a scissors when I was talking to an associate. I started sending her and my son back to New York City when I had a long trip.

In April 1986, I got another overseas assignment. "You have to go to Taiyo España in Madrid." That was the company's order. Either you accept it, or you have to leave the company. Now I was going to be vice manager of the subsidiary. My wife was excited because she spoke Spanish fluently. I studied Spanish at the Berlitz Language School.

We rented a 3,000-square-foot house in a wealthy suburb called La Moraleja. It was a gated community with a big swimming pool. Most of the people were European and American—very few Japanese. I still traveled forty to fifty times a year, but my wife was very sociable with the neighbors. I paid about $3,000 a month for the house. My salary was high—about $10,000 a month. In Spain, Taiyo had a different payroll system. My son went to a private international school. My wife had a maid coming every Monday to Friday. She bought clothes, jewelry, everything. She was a materialist, and I was the same as her. For business, I drove the company's Mercedes. I had another car for personal use. I could afford this luxury life on my salary. I didn't borrow any money, but I couldn't save at all.

In 1989 my wife got pregnant again and went back to New York City. When the due date came, I flew there too. Again, I was with her in the labor room. The funny thing is my son was such a pretty baby when he was born. But my daughter came out reddish, looking kind of like a monkey. I was a little disappointed because I worried, "Oh, what's going to happen? This is a girl." But one month later, my daughter became very pretty. Very early she started talking. She was very mature and very sociable, so I was happy.

We went back to our luxuries in Spain, but I knew this kind of lifestyle could never last. In 1993, the order from the company came: I had to move back to Japan. My wife didn't want to go, so I had to make a decision. That was my first big mistake. I went to New York City and rented a big apartment near the United Nations. My wife and children lived there. Then I went back to work in Tokyo. The living expenses for my family were $5,000 or $6,000 dollars a month. That was more than the income I was getting in Tokyo. I also had to go back to New York City frequently to see the family. That cost too much money, and also the Japanese corporate culture did not allow so much absence.

So, after one year, I was forced to make another decision. A job offer came to sell insurance through a financial subsidiary of Sony Corporation. At Taiyo I had a lifetime appointment, seniority, and a $100,000 salary. The Sony job was on a commission basis. With the talent, experience, and networks I had established in my previous business, I believed I could make double or triple my current income. So I left Taiyo after almost twenty-three years of working there. That was my second mistake.

The first couple of years at Sony, I made the salary I wanted. I could afford the two livings in New York City and Tokyo, though barely. But in 1997, my sales started going down. I tried as hard as in the previous years, but results didn't follow. So my income started decreasing. The first couple of months, I used my savings to fill the gap. Then I started borrowing from the bank. The money was supposed to be for a business purpose. Actually, it was going to my personal expenses, so I was lying.

The third mistake was when I breached a contract I had signed in 1996 to buy a condominium on the Upper East Side. Obviously the owners were angry, and we were faced with a serious lawsuit. One day in 1998, my wife went to the bank to withdraw money, and the teller said, "I'm sorry, but your account is frozen by the court order." We started panicking. By now, the bank was not lending me extra money. So I started borrowing from trusted friends and my family in Japan, mostly my eldest sister. "This money, I use for business," I told them. It was a lie. Altogether, I borrowed almost half a million dollars.

Common sense said my wife and I had to downsize. But she kept demanding the same amount of money, and I kept trying to keep my family happy. I was very optimistic. The fantasy was my business was coming back. This was a total denial situation, an unrealistic dream. It was like a drug. My relationship with my wife started to deteriorate. My wife didn't believe I was struggling financially, and she started getting suspicious about my life in Japan. Maybe I couldn't send the money because I had another woman.

It was all piling up and getting worse and worse. In 1998, I was already delaying the monthly rent in New York. One time I was almost six months late. The landlord sued us.

By December 1998, I decided I could not continue to have the two households. I had to make drastic changes, so I quit my job at Sony. Without a concrete idea about how to get a new job or income, I left Japan. I didn't give my Tokyo landlord notice. I didn't tell my mother or sister I was going. I just kind of escaped. On January 1, 1999, I arrived in New York City without savings, in debt, and with two lawsuits against me, one for the condominium and one for the rent. It was all under litigation.

The family was glad to be living together, but I was preoccupied with how to get a job, how to restore the apartment, and how to settle the lawsuits. Despite such a disastrous situation, the best part of the day was picking my daughter up after school. She was a very good, very clever girl. My son was sixteen, and our relationship was kind of rocky because I had been absent so much. But my daughter was nine and extremely happy because finally, "Father is always coming to get me."

One nice spring day, I went to the school to get her. On the way home, we stopped at McDonald's. My daughter wanted some chicken nuggets. We talked, and at that moment I was happy. Then we came back to the apartment and took the elevator up to the thirty-fourth floor. My daughter was holding my hand as we walked down the hall.

On the door was a yellow sheet of paper. It was an eviction notice. I tried to insert the key, but the landlord had already changed the lock. That was the biggest embarrassment in front of my innocent daughter, the biggest disaster, and she was a witness. My daughter immediately realized the situation. Maybe she had overheard my conversations with my wife. She started crying. We could not get into our apartment. That was the worst moment in my life.

We talked to our lawyer, and we talked to the building's lawyer. But they just said, "Pay the bill. That's the only solution." It was $30,000. And obviously I called all over the world, but my friends, my family, nobody responded. Meantime, we begged the superintendent, "Just let us get in for our passports, some money." The superintendent gave me one or two hours: "Just get your papers, absolutely necessary things, do not take any clothes, no children's schoolbooks, nothing." He was there and watched me the whole time. I couldn't find my passport, Social Security card, or driver's license. I took only some money and got out. Within two days, the landlord arranged to clear the apartment, and he dumped all our furniture in a warehouse.

My family had to intrude on my wife's mother and stepfather. It was a small apartment. Can you imagine one bedroom for six people? I already had a rocky relationship with my mother-in-law. Plus my wife and her stepfather had a bad relationship. And every day, from the time I got up, my mother-in-law was bugging me. "You are a failure. You are putting my precious daughter in such a miserable situation." She called me a loser. I used to have a very bad temper. So my mother-in-law and I were kind of a disaster. Meantime, I got interviews for jobs, but something always prevented me getting an offer. We had no money because I wasn't working, the savings were gone, and we were in debt. We were living at the mercy of my mother-in-law.

Finally, after nine months, I borrowed $10,000 to get our furniture from storage. But where to put it? My mother-in-law was subletting her apartment in Chelsea. My wife convinced her to let us live there. It was a very small apartment. The condition of our furniture was horrible. The china was broken. But we tried to squeeze it in, find a space to live in, sleep in, eat in. Every day it looked like chaos. But the children were performing very well in school. My daughter was so innocent still. My relationship with her was very good.

My wife started making money, but she didn't go to work. "How do you get the money?" I asked. "Just don't worry," she said. Then one day she showed me the bunch of tickets. Do you know where she went? How do you say it? Pawn shop? My wife had luxury tastes. So I used to respond, buying a lot of jewelry, fur coats, that kind of thing. Now everything was gone.

The summer of 2001, the final moment came. My mother-in-law moved back into the Chelsea apartment. Her intention was very clear. She didn't want anymore living together. Sometimes, she would not let me into her apartment—not only me, but also her granddaughter. The neighbors could hear the sweet, young girl knocking: "Grandma, please let me in." They thought that was child abuse. The neighbors called Child Protective Services. A social worker came and took my daughter away. That time, I was not there in the apartment. I didn't see this happening.

And do you know what she did, my daughter? Two days later, she told the social worker, "I want some clothes. Would you take me to Bloomingdale's?" And they went there, and my daughter escaped back to my mother-in-law's apartment. A few months later, my daughter told me the story. Listening to her was another worst moment in my life. My daughter did it for an adventure. She was proud of herself.

Obviously, the social worker came back to the apartment. But this time, an arrangement was made for emergency shelter for my daughter and wife in the Bronx—some motel, one room. My son stayed at my mother-in-law's place. I was not there when the arrangement was made. I had already been kicked out of the apartment.

The first day I was kicked out, I just walked along, drifting. At night I went to a familiar place—some park near the East River, on the Upper East Side. It was summertime still, not that cold. I stayed on a bench sitting, not sleeping, not laying down. After that, I sometimes slept in the basement of my mother-in-law's building. I had the key to the entrance, and sometimes at midnight I could sneak in. I never went back inside my mother-in-law's apartment. Also, I stopped contacting my family in Tokyo. That came from pride, my stupid pride. I had so much shame for what my situation had become.

I still saw my wife and daughter. I didn't have a cell phone, but we promised to meet at Grand Central Station after school. I rode with my wife and daughter on the train back to the Bronx. Then I came back to the city because in the motel we could not be together—only mothers and children. On 9/11, I waited in Grand Central, but my wife and daughter never came. I was totally alone that day.

Around one month later, my wife and daughter stopped showing up at Grand Central. Maybe they changed their route. Obviously, this was intentioned by my wife. The last time on the train, my daughter had told me about escaping from the hands of the social worker. Maybe that's why my wife stopped the meetings at Grand Central. I don't know. I wanted to go to the motel to find them. The problem was I had absolutely no money, and I could not even get the MetroCard.

I never saw my daughter again—or my son. The last time I saw either of them was fourteen years ago.

I saw my wife once in 2003. I was near Grand Central, and somebody called my name. I looked back, and there she was. That encounter was by accident. We went to a cafeteria and talked. My wife told me she had been working as a cashier in an Italian bakery shop. She calmly explained what had happened the past two years. My daughter was going to a Catholic school. She was an honors student, and the tuition was exempted. They were living in some project on the Upper East Side—my son too. While I was listening, my wife called my daughter on the cell phone. "Are you okay? Did you eat?" My wife didn't let me talk to my daughter. "Oh, she ate pizza," she said after hanging up. Then she took the bus uptown.

By that time, I could not even sleep in my mother-in-law's basement. They had changed the key to the building's entrance—maybe for security reasons. Now I lived on the street night and day. I was totally homeless, but I was in denial. Before I became homeless, I had always despised poor and homeless people. Years ago, in 1990, when I had started seeing homeless people in Tokyo, I thought that homeless people equaled losers. I hated losers, so I despised homeless people. I thought they were lazy and had a weak will. I had the same concept in New York City. So when I became homeless, I pretended not to be. I didn't mingle with homeless people. I never went to a drop-in shelter. I never went to a soup kitchen. If I saw people getting free food at a church, I never joined the line.

I was getting much skinnier because I had maybe five dollars a day to survive. That was from the small cash I made after midnight. A very nice nighttime superintendent offered me a cleaning job in an Ivy League Club building. No strangers were supposed to get inside the building, but he let me in through the service entrance. There was a kind of awning at the service area. After cleaning, I would bring some UPS boxes and newspaper and sit in that space. According to the rules nobody could stay there—not sit, not stand, nothing. But the security guard let me do it. At five or six in the morning, I got up and left. That was usually my pattern. I never slept for more than three hours a night.

During the day I had nothing to do because it looked like every day was Sunday. Before I was homeless I was so busy, so occupied with business, with family. Now I was sitting for long hours on a bench. I had no appointments, nobody depending on me, nobody expecting me, nobody waiting to see me. I had no friends, no family, no money. It looked like I was dead. Some days I thought maybe that would be better. I felt I was not worthy to live anymore. I felt like I was nothing, so it would be better to die. Nobody would know. Nobody would hold a funeral for me. It would be more like a piece of garbage, just disappearing in the world.

Other days, I loved going to the library. The midtown library with the lions in front had a big, quiet reading room. Their biographies were very thick. I read about all kinds of historical figures, such as General Franco, Theodore Roosevelt, Stalin, Mao Zedong, and Napoleon. The book about Winston Churchill was a couple of thousand pages. I used to think Churchill was a genius, Superman-like. After the biography, I realized he was not Superman. He was a born aristocrat and definitely a racist, and almost everything Churchill did was wrong politically. But at the right moment, he was correct. Churchill insisted that Germany had become our enemy. Also, I read Japanese books because I had plenty of time. Sometime I fell asleep, and the security guards would wake me up, but very gently.

Not the police. For example, early in the morning I would go to the Grand Central basement, buy a cup of coffee, and stay there for a couple of hours. When I fell asleep, the same policeman always came by, harassing me. I used to think the police, the authorities, were our protectors, that they were on our side. Now I realized that the police were the enemy. It was easy to pick on poor, weak, homeless people. I was trying to be as normal as possible, but for the police I was homeless. That's when I first realized I was one of "them" in their eyes.

Still, I refused to use any homeless services. So obviously I didn't take a shower for a long time. Before I was homeless, I took a shower twice a day. Now I started cleaning myself in the bathrooms of luxury hotels— not during the day when the bathrooms were busy. But when nighttime came, I would walk like a guest into Barclay's, or the Hilton, or the Waldorf Astoria. The bathrooms had huge, spacious stalls with their own sink inside. I carried a bag with a towel and soap. I would get in there and very carefully clean my whole body—wash my hair too with shampoo. Then I would clean the floor as if nothing had happened and come out.

Maybe once a week I did this before my midnight job. But usually I was just walking downtown, uptown, west side, east side—just walking and listening to the radio. For my only amusement, I had a small Walkman.

With the money I made, I could pay for cheap clothes. But the heavy coat necessary for winter I couldn't afford. This was another thing I realized when I was homeless. Besides that the police were the enemy, I realized the difference between inside and outside. Outside in the wintertime, it was freezing cold. Inside the apartment, you could even live in your underwear. Obviously I knew this difference before, but I physically realized it during my homeless time. When the winter came, I was very worried about clothing. So I went into the Macy's and put on a nice coat. It was pretty expensive because it had to protect me all winter. Then I went to the bathroom, cut off the security tag, and walked out of the store. I did this for three years in a row.

In 2006 I took a pair of thick pants as well as a new coat. I went into the—how do you say it—dressing room?—and I put the pants on double, inside the ones I was wearing. On my way out of the store, I also picked up a box of chocolate. Suddenly a security guard came out and questioned me.

"Excuse me, did you pay for this chocolate box?" Then they took me downstairs and handcuffed me in a room. They already knew. "You stole the pants. Take off your clothes." A manager came to me. "Why did you do this? I could call the police to put you in jail." I had to tell him the truth: "I'm homeless. I need a coat because it's cold." For a couple of hours, I was detained there. Finally, the manager said, "We are letting you go. This is mercy because it looks like you are not a criminal. But never do the same thing again. If you are homeless, why don't you go to a shelter?"

That was the day I decided to make a change. For years I had thought nobody could help me because I couldn't help myself and my life was already over. So many times I had been approached by the social workers. They saw me sitting on the bench and asked, "Are you homeless?" Always my answer was, "No, I'm okay." Still they gave me a "street sheet" with resources for homeless people. After the time at Macy's, I decided to read the sheet more carefully. I visited a few service places and watched from a distance. Some places I was too afraid of because the lines of people looked so rough. I liked All Angels' Church because it was small and not so crowded. It was on the Upper West Side, and I thought that would be a safe location. Also, two days a week you could go take a shower there. That was good because I didn't want to sneak into hotels anymore.

I came to the church on a day of the Pathways Program. The program is for basic needs, like a shower and medical services. That is every Tuesday and Thursday, from ten to two o'clock. The first day, I still remember, people lined up outside the church at eight o'clock in the morning. I was one of them. It was my first experience among all the homeless people. About 80 percent were black, and there were a lot of Mexicans and some women. I tried not to talk to anybody. When the church door opened, I just sat there quietly, having coffee until my turn for a shower came. I still remember when the security guard gave me some underwear. I got in, took a shower, and left the building because I was afraid of all these rough people.

But after a couple of weeks, a couple of visits, I said to myself, "Akira, why don't you stay?" Because they also gave you lunch. Then I was sitting down, looking, observing. There was a volunteer named Joy who was like the angel of the church. At every Pathways Program, she was cutting the bread, taking care of the coffee, talking to all the homeless people. So tirelessly she was working from ten to two o'clock. Sometimes the people would fight. But Joy's love was incredible. That changed things for me. I had never done community service in a church in my life, but I said, "Joy, can I help you cut the bread or with lunchtime serving?" "Yeah," she said, "why not?" After that I started serving at lunchtime, going to the kitchen, picking up the food, bringing it upstairs. I was a homeless person—a guest, but I was also helping. I was doing both. I have been volunteering at All Angels' ever since.

On Sundays, All Angels' has a community dinner and a shelter. So I started coming on Sundays too. One night I stayed at the shelter in the church. That was maybe 2007. In the early morning, I helped with making the coffee and setting up all the cleaning things. In 2009, I started supervising the Sunday shelter. I also started assisting the cook for the community dinner. I had basic knowledge about food from my previous business experiences, and I had experienced eating different cuisines during my travels to like sixty countries in my life. My family used to love what I cooked. So I got a New York Food Handlers License, and today I am the in-house chef at All Angels' Church.

In September 2009, Eric Mull, the director of Community Ministries, told Rodney Allen and me and a couple of the shelter men about the Interfaith Assembly on Homelessness and Housing's life skills empowerment program. I had no idea what he was talking about. But I met Dennis Barton, and Marc Greenberg gave the introduction. "This is a place for opening your mind, sharing whatever reason you became homeless." Until that time, I had not told anybody my story—maybe I had mentioned a little bit to Eric, but nobody else. I thought I had the worst case of failing because I came to New York City as a foreigner and lost everything—my business, my family and friends, my money.

Then, one by one, the people in our life skills empowerment class started telling their oral story. Everybody else's experience was worse than mine. That started convincing me, you don't need to be ashamed. We were homeless for different reasons, but we had the same experience. For the first time, I started feeling a sense of camaraderie with the other homeless people. Rodney and I were becoming friends. When my turn came to tell my story, I didn't tell the whole thing. But I told a little bit, and it let me open my mind.

I was wishing for a mentor older than me, because always in the past my boss or whoever influenced me was an older guy. I was lucky. Doug Mastin became my mentor. He had a lot of years of business experience. He did not try to preach to me. He did not look down on me—he respected me. And Doug was a good listener. That gave me the opportunity to tell the whole truth about my life. Almost every week, Doug invited me out for dinner or lunch. Of course I couldn't pay my portion, so he paid, and I appreciated it. He treated me as a friend. Besides a few of the people at All Angels' Church, this was my first personal relationship after I lost everything. I didn't take advantage of it. I never asked to borrow money from Doug. I had learned my lesson about that.

While I was in the life skills empowerment program, I got transferred, through a social worker, to temporary housing in the YMCA. Before then I sometimes stayed at a sanitation worker's apartment. He was a beacon to me. But at the YMCA, I had my own individual room with a key. That was a relief. I also got a cell phone.

One day, after he checked on the computer, Doug found the number and address of my wife and children. I was so excited. Finally, after so many years, I could call them. They didn't pick up, so I left a message. "This is Akira. I'm your husband and father. I have been homeless after we separated. And now, at last, I'm moving to a temporary room in Harlem. Here is my cell phone number." Nobody called back. Then I realized, "Oh, they don't want to talk to me." So I started writing letters, so many pages, about all that happened to me. Almost every week I sent a letter—maybe twenty, thirty letters during that period. No letter back. Never. Then I realized, maybe my wife dumped the letters in the garbage. So Dennis and Marc let me use their return address. Even Eric Mull sent a pastoral letter in an All Angels' Church envelope. No response. Nothing at all.

So I went to the building, waiting outside, late at night. Even I went one day to the renting agent. First, he refused to see me, saying, "No, I cannot disclose any private information." But finally, he met me. I explained what my wife looked like, how old she was, and the ages of my son and daughter. After hesitating, the agent told me, "Looks like exactly that family living in apartment so-and-so." But I couldn't get into the building because I didn't have a key. Every way I tried.

I wish I could talk to my son and daughter. I'd say, first, "I'm very sorry." I would ask them to forgive whatever happened. And I would try to offer help. I still love them.

Somebody, maybe Eric Mull, asked, "What are you doing with your family in Japan?" Now I wrote a long letter to my family there, explaining what had happened. "Please forgive me," I said. My bank debt might have expired because of the statute of limitations, but I still owed a lot of money to my family, especially my eldest sister. My sisters and brothers wrote back. Everybody signed the letter. "Whatever happened, we forgive you. Just start reestablishing your life as soon as possible." Then they explained, "We are sorry to say that your mother, our mother, passed away. There was no way to inform you. She died very calmly, peacefully, of natural causes." Somehow I had expected this because my mother was old, but I felt so guilty that I had not been able to be with her when she died. My sisters and brothers also wrote, "Your mother worried about you until she died." I had no words, and I felt so much pain, but I was happy for my mother's unlimited love. After that, we all kept writing. My brothers and sisters are well-off. I have a lot of nephews, nieces—a lot. If one day I get money, I will try to compensate my sister.

Because I was volunteering so many days at All Angels' Church, a lot of congregation members became my friends. There were all kinds of people—homeless people, young people, old people, bankers, lawyers, architects. And everyone loved Jesus Christ. I had an interest in Jesus Christ from a historical point of view, because he was one of the most influential people in the history of humankind. But now I was being influenced by the congregation's strong faith. What was this? I started more digging, started reading the Bible. Then I started attending the Sunday morning service. I could not take Communion because I was not baptized yet. That was kind of uncomfortable. But I started listening to the sermons, started singing the worship. I always stayed there until the end. Every service.

One day Reverend Milind said, "Akira, when are you getting baptized?" I said, "I'm not ready." Always I was not ready. "Akira. You'll never be ready. There is never the perfect time to become Christian. So let's do it." I was baptized in, I think, 2011.

Although physically and mentally I had already recovered from homelessness, Christianity has helped me recover spiritually. I have learned that you cannot carry the past, and you cannot carry heavy burdens all the time. You have to let go. And besides, we are powerless. We are not God. We cannot do anything. We have to be humble. I used to be too overconfident and egocentric. I thought I could do everything myself, and I tried to control everything. Most of the disaster that happened in my life was because of me. That's true. But I cannot always think about it when there are more important things to do, like ask forgiveness, ask pardon, then move

Akira and Gillian

on to the future and try to give back. Whatever I can do, wherever I have some talent to utilize, I'm trying to give. That's why I do so many things at All Angels' Church. I have also been a mentor for the life skills empowerment program six times in a row. I try to give back what I received from Doug. I try to be a role model for the homeless people.

From my giving, I have recovered myself. My character and personality used to be very sociable, very caring. But I gave up on relationships once my married life ended. I gave up on loving somebody, on romance. It was never coming back. I was too old. "It's okay," I thought. "I married Jesus Christ. So I got a new life. I don't need a girlfriend anymore."

Meantime, I became friends with Gillian at All Angels' Church. She was always helping with community ministries. We had lunch a couple of times. Then, two years ago, I got free tickets to see *Faust* at the Metropolitan Opera. I invited Gillian to join me. It was a long opera, and the ending was very moving because everyone was singing that Jesus Christ has risen. Gillian was crying, and I was also crying. Afterward, we went for some late dinner, and I kind of confessed: "I gave up on relationships. I thought it was never coming back. I took it as a punishment because of my disaster. But I can't help but say—" So much emotion was coming. I couldn't express myself. But Gillian understood, and we started dating.

Two weeks later, I told her I loved her. This was the start of a new happiness in my life. After long, long years, it was like a personal joy came from the inside. Gillian and I have been dating ever since. I feel like it is God's gift, more than I deserve because I never expected it. Gillian is my biggest support. She supports mentally, emotionally, and spiritually what I'm giving to the community and doing at the community ministries program, and she is my soul mate.

I think I tried to always be a giver in my life. It was maybe something I got from my mother. Even when I was very materialistic, I found it easy to give. But somehow I did it in the wrong way. I thought I could become a very successful businessman, which I couldn't—I lost. Today I want to be successful in a different way, not in a material way, but as a human being. Today I want to be successful not for what I have, but for what I do.

Reflection
Doug Mastin

Doug Mastin has been a mentor many times, mostly with the Panim el Panim life skills empowerment program and once with L-STEP, the program at St. Francis Xavier Church.

I grew up in a small suburban town, the youngest of eight children. My father was always concerned for all eight of us, and he took an interest in the welfare of the town. I remember he once bought an ambulance for our volunteer fire department. After college, I went to work for a bank in New York City. Within a few years, I became a computer systems analyst, usually working for or with banks, almost always on securities processing systems. When I retired, I had more time to contribute to my church and community.

I was brought up to care for people in need. Anyone who is homeless obviously has huge problems and needs an opportunity to figure out how to find housing and get back into society. Some people huddle in doorways under blankets on the coldest winter nights. There are more than 60,000 homeless people in New York City. It is very upsetting that so many people are so uncared for, and it is depressing to live in an area where you are walking by homeless people every day. The problem feels overwhelming, and our society is clearly not addressing it adequately. For an individual who wants to help the homeless, it is very difficult to know what to do. With so many people in trouble, any personal response can seem futile.

At least that's how I felt until I began contributing annually to the Interfaith Assembly on Homelessness and Housing. In 2008 I became a life

222

skills empowerment program mentor for the first time. As a mentor, you can respond to the needs of one person in a small group and try to have some beneficial impact on this person and this group. Mentoring is easy. All you have to do is listen, with an ounce of common sense. We all know that when you have a problem, it helps if you can talk it out with someone you can trust.

One of the participants I mentored, Akira, has become a personal friend. He is intelligent, personable, and scrupulously honest. When I met Akira, he had been sleeping on the streets for over three years. Nevertheless, he was able to maintain his appearance and look like a successful Japanese businessman on foreign assignment. We have maintained our friendship and usually see each other every month or two. Sometimes Akira uses my computer, and sometimes we have dinner together. I have met Gillian, the woman he has been dating, and I like her too. Recently they invited me to dinner at her apartment. It was very nice to be the guest of people who are such good cooks!

To this day, Akira is living in a shelter with a difficult 10:00 p.m. curfew. His ability to confront and handle his problems is impressive. I particularly admire Akira's tenacity and the continuing work he does at All Angels' Church. I am enormously pleased and heartened by his progress but do not know when he will be able to have a home of his own.

Mentoring is always rewarding but in varying degrees. If you can help get someone off the street, you can be very pleased indeed. If you can at least establish a trust relationship, that can be a major accomplishment. Of the four other people I have mentored, two have clearly benefited from the program and now have a wider network to assist them. There are two others I no longer have contact with. One of the participants I was assigned to dropped out of the program before I ever met him. I doubt if he has recovered, but it is possible he has found other avenues, connections, or contacts to assist him.

The difficulties the program participants face seem overwhelming, and yet most of them are able gradually to make progress. Their courage is an example to all of us, and it can teach us to persist even when the obstacles seem too difficult to overcome. Most important is the realization that we are all in this together. We all need each other to make our lives meaningful.

Life Story
Sophia Worrell

Sophia Worrell was born in October 1963 in Barbados. She graduated in 2010 from the Education Outreach Program (EOP), the original life skills empowerment program, run by New York Catholic Charities. Sophia has also served as a facilitator for the Living Well program for survivors of domestic violence.

Some people's lives are always bad. Some people's lives are always good. My life has been a combination of good and bad. I have always had a lot of friends who didn't know what was happening to me. On the outside, it seemed as if my life was beautiful, but on the inside, I was falling apart.

I was born on the lovely island of Barbados more than fifty years ago. Let's see if I can make you see my island. We have the bluest waters in the world. When you're at the beach, you can look down and see the whitest sand there is. You can travel around the island in one day—it is that tiny. Culturally, we're a proud people, community oriented and very gentle. We are a people who like to help. When other islands have had devastating hurricanes, people come to Barbados for relief.

Until I was nine, I lived with my mom and dad, my brothers, and my sister in St. James. My father was a carpenter by trade who built our house with his own hands. It was a chattel house with four rooms and a bathroom outside. My mom and dad shared a bedroom and all the other kids shared one. My dad loved the hi-fi system, and on Sunday afternoons he would play the golden oldies; there were particular songs or a certain beat that made my parents look at each other in a loving way that made me

feel very secure. He and my mom would start to dance, and we would sit and watch them. That memory just stays with me.

I just loved my dad. He was tall, athletic, dark, and very gentle. I thought he was the most precious man in the world. I liked to go with him to his carpentry work. People were impressed. "Your daughter is with you?" I worked alongside him and banged in nails; yes, I did. My dad was not aggressive. He would never tell you what to do. If there was an issue, he would give you both sides and allow you to come to your own conclusions.

My mom would tell you what to do. She was very assertive, always aggressive. My mom was more of the dad in the family. When my father came home, he'd give all the money to my mom. She was the one paying the bills and everything. She was an excellent cook and took care of all of us. Our home was a well-oiled machine.

My mom worked outside our house as a maid in a private home in Oyster Bay, a couple of blocks away. It was a vacation house, so families would come and stay. I would go to help my mom, and I often ended up having dinner, sleeping over, going to the beach, and going out with the kids. They were always white, always. Sometimes I felt bad having dinner while my mom was serving and then going to the beach while my mom was cleaning.

When I was around eight, my mom made a decision to leave Barbados and go to America. Her idea was to get more money to send back so my father could extend the house. Eventually, the house expanded from two bedrooms to three bedrooms. Then it extended some more, so finally, after many years, we had a real wall on the back and a shower and toilet inside.

Obviously, we didn't want my mom to go away. My dad had to come home and pick up where my mom left off—cook, take care of us, and everything. He said it was too much, and he decided to take a lady in to help out. Again, we didn't like it. There was no way this woman could compare to our mother. But we were children—we had to respect our parents. Eventually my father and the lady got involved with each other, and the lady got pregnant.

When my mom heard about that, she was livid. She came back to Barbados, and everything went downhill. Every night, I heard my mom and dad fussing, crying, quarreling, arguing. Of course they argued before, but now you could feel the tension in the air. I remember vividly the day my dad walked out with his suitcase. I ran behind him, begging him not to go. He said, "It's for the best." The best? "How could your leaving be for the best?" I cried. But my dad just left, walked out, and that was it. The island is too small to be far away, and I still saw my dad a lot. But my life went downhill from there.

I don't have a memory of the days after my dad left—that's a blur. But if I take up my story three years later, I remember telling my mom I wanted to go to church. I was just devastated, and I needed something to believe in. My mom said to ask my aunt if I could go to her Seventh-day Adventist church, and my aunt said, "Sure!" So I became a Seventh-day Adventist. Just to be in church eased the pain and taught me that there was something more to life. In the Seventh-day Adventist church you have to know the Bible. This is not just a talk, it's a walk. They would elect you for different tasks, and you didn't get to say no. I was assistant Sabbath-school teacher, assistant secretary; I was part of the choir, part of a church path-finder group, and Advent Youth leader for the evening service. The activities gave me something to hold on to, something solid and structured that I lacked, and took my mind away from life at home.

Around the same time, I took the secondary school exam and passed. I was the first of my mom's kids to get accepted to a public secondary school. Because I did so well on the exam, my mom decided to send me to a private Seventh-day Adventist school. My school was beautiful. It was church oriented. The emphasis was on Christian principles and being spiritual, but we still focused on the academics. It was a wonderful community, a wonderful experience. We wore a burgundy uniform with a tie. I loved that. It made me feel official.

My principal was Miss Bain. I loved her. She was tall with brown skin. Her hair was part silver and part dark. She was so ladylike and so pious, so Christian. She never married and didn't have children. I wanted to be just like her. She was a woman who commanded respect without saying a word. When we were lining up for assembly and chattering and she walked in, all of a sudden everyone stopped talking and it got quiet. This is something that happened without fail every single day.

Because we were a Seventh-day Adventist school, we believed that the Sabbath was on Saturday. On Fridays we had to go home and prepare for the Sabbath. We were not allowed—and I mean it—*not* allowed to go into our town on Fridays. That was a distraction danger zone. Everybody in town knew the Seventh-day Adventist uniform, and at every assembly, especially on Fridays, we were reminded that we must not disrespect our uniform.

One Friday, instead of getting on the school bus and going home, a group of popular girls were going into town. I decided I would go too, so I went into town. We went into a store, but we should not have been in there. The girls began to steal. Did I walk out or did I stay? I wanted to be with the cool girls, so I stayed. I saw them take things. Did I say something? Did I stay quiet? I was scared. I didn't say anything. Some of the girls put stolen pens in my pocket. The pens were pink—that color has stayed in my head to this day.

We went to school the next Monday. Assembly was at eight thirty. Everything went as usual until Miss Bain got up on the podium and called out the names of all of us who were at the store. One by one she called us into her office. I was the last to go in. Miss Bain looked at me. "I know you didn't take those pens. I know how you were raised"—because Miss

Bain knew my mom. She told me everybody else on the list was being punished—everybody except me. "I'm not putting you in detention, and I'm not going to lash you. No. Your punishment is that you're going to go home and tell your mother what you did."

I was terrified. "Please, punish me, give me detention, lash me! I don't care, but don't make me have to tell my mom because my mom don't play around."

"You will!" Miss Bain said.

I don't remember what my mom did when I told her, but from that day I made a decision—no one was ever going to pull me into anything again. This resolution was burned into my psyche. When I got older, I thought about the wisdom of Miss Bain. I asked her how she knew who was in the store. She never gave me an answer. I don't know how she knew to call out every one of us, and I don't know how she knew to give me that punishment, but it had an impact on me for the rest of my life.

Life at home was really bad. My mom had many relationships after separating from my dad. Stepfathers would come and go. In my heyday, I was really beautiful, wonderful to look at. Too beautiful. Too wonderful.

One of my mother's boyfriends had a shop with a place to cook and a room with a bed to rest in. My mom worked in the shop, and as usual I would go to help. One particular day, I was on the bed, reading a book by Agatha Christie, and he came into the room—he said he was a little tired and lay on the bed. I was still thinking my mom was out in the shop. He asked me about the book I was reading, and I was in the midst of telling him the story when suddenly he rolled on top of me. He was a big-bellied guy—a heavy roller. So I was taken off guard. I was confused. I remember asking God, "Just give me some strength. Don't let this happen." Then I bore down, and I was able to give one push and get him off. I ran and hid in a shed out back. Finally, I heard my mom call and I snuck out. She asked me where I was. "Just playing," I said. I was twelve years old, maybe thirteen.

Another time, another guy came to our house in the middle of the day. I was on my mom's bed, and I was the only one there. There was something he asked me to find. So I was searching over the bed, I was searching on the bed, and then he just attacked me from behind, pushed me on the bed. This guy was not as big as the first one. I thought, "God! How could I be so stupid?" Finally, I managed to get away and run into the road.

I promised myself this would not happen again! But it did. Again I was on my mom's bed. An older gentleman she was dating came in. By the time I heard the door open, I was too afraid to move. I remember him forcing me on the bed, and I remember fighting him off.

The men never penetrated me, but just the attempt—just having it re-played over and over—it was disgusting and it messed with my head. These events affected my school life and ability to study. They affected my church life and desire to read the Bible. They ended any hopes of my trying to live a holy life. Every time an event occurred I felt my pureness slip away. I went through a whole set of emotions—blaming myself, being angry, not being able to share any of it. I couldn't tell my mom. I don't know why.

The last straw was one particular morning when I was standing with a group of children waiting for the school bus. A cute bus driver who I had a crush on came by in a big car and picked us all up. It was probably his day off, and it just happened that he was driving by. The car was so big it held six, seven, eight of us. It was a long time before I realized that my school was the one farthest away. I was going to be the last one dropped off: this only dawned on me after the last kid got out of the car. I prayed that he would just drop me off at my school. But he passed right by my school. "This can't be good," I thought. "This is not going to be good." I was saying Hail Marys and trying to beg—don't, don't, don't—not now, another time when I don't have my school uniform on. I decided when he stopped the car or slowed down I would jump out. But there was no stopping, there was nowhere to jump out. Finally, he drove deep into an open field. He stopped the car.

I ran for dear life, but a man determined is a man determined. He caught me and raped me, and then had the nerve to drop me off back at school.

When I got there, I was a mess. By chance or by God's design, my mentor, Douglas, saw me, and I broke down crying and told him everything. Douglas snuck me down to a basement area and took my uniform and cleaned and ironed it. Later, he asked me if I wanted to press charges, but what did I know about pressing charges? He said to tell my mom, but I couldn't—I don't know why.

From that day on, I just went crazy. Life wasn't supposed to be someone coming to rape you. That was not true life. It happened, but that was not life. I didn't want someone who was involved with my mom trying to have sex with me. That was not life. My mom should have been with my dad. I should have been able to go to school and study. I couldn't concentrate on my studies. I could not. I tried.

After graduation, those of us who did well went to college. Those who didn't do so well went to work. I went to work at a place that inspected the little chips and dyes that go into electrical products. The problem was that I had to work on Saturdays when there was church. I asked the pastor and elders what to do, but they just said, "Pray to God." I prayed to God, and he didn't show me the way. I got really angry and said, "I am done with God, done with church." I gave up on my life.

Then I started doing secular things. I got into relationships with men, drank, smoked, partied. I loved alcohol. When I got drunk, I could just pass out and not worry about anything. I'd move in with a guy, and when it didn't work out, I'd move back in with my mom. She was angry with me. I was angry with her. I began moving from house to house because I hated my mom so much. I was very confused, and I had all these messages in my head. I felt like the good life kept eluding me.

Maybe psychologically I thought that if I wasn't busy, I would die. So I was always active in community groups. I had a netball team, I played volleyball, I rode a bicycle, I lifted weights, I ran. I started a community group for fashion modeling. I loved—absolutely loved—roller skating because it put me in a different space and time. I skated on Tuesdays and Thursdays.

One Thursday I remember vividly. After skating, I went to a bar with a poolroom. That night, a whole crowd was watching one guy play pool. I was trying to look through the crowd of people. At first I couldn't get close enough to see. Then someone shifted, and I saw this tall, dark, and handsome guy bent over the pool table. I was like, "Yes—Mmm hmm! That is the guy I'm going to have my son with." Just like that. We started talking. We started dating, and I decided I wanted to settle down with him. I had a miscarriage with twins when I was twenty-five. Two years later, I gave birth to my son, who I call my Bean.

I was very happy with my son's father until I wasn't happy with him anymore. He was a professional gambler and pool player; that's why he was so good at pool. After we had our son, I thought it was time to settle down. I told him to get a day job, but you can't force someone to do what you want. He loved gambling and made a lot of money from it. The last straw was the night he turned our house into a gambling room. The next day, I packed all his things up and drove them to his mother's house. I changed the locks on our house. He got really, really mad with me.

What made it worse was one night, after we separated, I asked another guy to take me to a party on the other side of the island. My son was just over a year old, and he was staying with my mom. My son's father either saw the guy pick me up or he was told about it. I came home the next morning. Obviously I had been drinking. I heard the door open. It was my son's father breaking into the house. He unleashed his fury on me. I was so out of it, I couldn't even fight back. There were too many injuries to describe. He kicked me, there were punches, there were scars. The police had to be called, but I didn't press charges. I kept saying, "This is my son's father."

My mom was livid. She wanted to press charges—she wanted to go to his mom's house and take his head off. But my dad was still his usual gentle self. "Just learn from this. I told you he wasn't the person for you." I wanted the roles changed. I wanted my mom to soothe me and my dad to be aggressive. So I got very mad with my dad, and I wouldn't talk to him for what seemed like years. Then one day the phone rang, and it was my dad. He said he was sorry if I was angry and he didn't mean to hurt me. That moved me, that touched me for the rest of my life—just the fact that he said he was sorry that he hurt me. That really solidified my respect for my dad.

Once again, I was going from relationship to relationship. I realized I needed help to settle everything in my brain. So I started going to a Pentecostal church called Abundant Life, and I prayed, "If you are God and you do love me, you need to open a way for me to get help." This is where things changed. At church, a group of women made an announcement about a T. D. Jakes Ministries conference called "Woman, Thou Art Loosed," taking place in Atlanta, Georgia. I knew I had to go, and I raised the money. In October 1999 I went to Atlanta. The conference was beautiful, and I felt loosed from all the pain and the sexual things that happened, at least for a little while.

When I came back to Barbados, everything started flowing. I worked as a waitress. I would serve white people and overhear conversations at the dinner table. The children were actually talking about their day. The parents were talking to their kids. It was so foreign to me. I started to linger at my tables and listen to the conversations. My customers asked me questions about local attractions like Harrison's Cave, and I couldn't answer because I had never been there; those were things we said only the white tourists could enjoy. But my association with white people pushed me, and I started to enjoy the cultural events on the islands. I would take my son with me.

After waitressing, I started a cleaning business. I also started to volunteer with different organizations. One day, when I was volunteering at the Barbados Association for the Blind and Deaf, the director, who was a blind gentleman, saw something in me that I didn't see in myself. "You seem like a perfect person for a job opening here," he said. The salary was much less than I got from my cleaning business, but he persuaded me to do the two-week training session. "Then you can make a decision."

During the training, we learned what it was like to be blind. We had to cook under a blindfold, eat under a blindfold, wash and sort our laundry under a blindfold. Under a blindfold, we had to walk across the streets with canes and go shopping. After the two-week training, I gave up my cleaning business and started working at the association. It was like meeting your lover for the first time and saying, "This is the one!"

My job was to teach persons without sight to have independent living skills. I absolutely loved it. I would go to people's houses and train them. If they were elderly, they might want to learn how to prepare food. I taught blind children how to get to school. My job was very interesting and gave me new skills. It was also beautiful—an eye-opener, no pun intended. I stopped stressing about life. I realized I had no problems. A person who cannot see has problems.

My clients were isolated because of their loss of sight, so I started to take them to attractions every month. I would take them to museums and arrange for them to feel and touch the artifacts. They went to Harrison's Cave, and I explained what they were seeing. Once we went to a kind of zoo; my son came, and he explained everything about the animals there. I was floored that he had all this information.

Unfortunately, I was fired because of these trips. My managers didn't like the fact that I had such a good relationship with my clients. They told me I was trying to form my own organization. It wasn't true, but my bosses were adamant, so they fired me.

Around the same time, Calvin, an old boyfriend who was living in America, invited me to come be with him. I was always seeking a better life and realized that I could never have it in Barbados. In Barbados, if you don't start college as soon as you finish high school, that's it—you're doomed. Plus I was involved with a married guy who was really abusive, very terrible. When Calvin called, I was in a moment of desperation, of wanting something better. My mom said she would keep my son so he could complete his schooling and graduate from high school the next year. Without saying anything to the married guy, I packed up and left. I got Calvin's call in October 2006, and by December I was on a plane to New York City.

Calvin said he lived in a wonderful place, but it was not wonderful. It was in the basement and it was horrible. That was my first red flag. But what could I do? I had given up my apartment, sold my car, closed up my bank accounts, all without even thinking. After I came to New York, Calvin told me that he was taking care of a seventeen-year-old girl who was in foster care. Later I found out that she was pregnant with his child, and he was paying for her apartment. I realized he was not even documented. He was working as a tow-truck driver, and they were short-paying him. I also learned that he was married to someone who was helping him file for his green card. Because Calvin beat her up, the wife stopped filing.

Sometime later, I came across a document that said Calvin had a sexually transmitted disease (I'm not sure the document was authentic as I am completely free of disease). When I confronted Calvin about it, I got my first hit. After that, anything could set him off. Whenever he got violent, I saw how the cycle would go. He would beat me up, then he would apologize; he'd buy me flowers, bake a cake, be extremely nice. Then it all started all over again.

One day, he was home on his off day. It was a Wednesday. Some days I remember. I decided to do the laundry just to be away from him, but no, he insisted on going with me. And I was thinking that this is not going to be good. We were talking on our way to the laundromat, and something aggravated him. When we got back home, he stopped talking, and I knew this was not good for me. I was trying to be silent, but only *he* was allowed to be silent. If I didn't talk, it was like I was acting as if I was too good for him. I said, "I don't know what to say because whatever I say is going to upset you."

That was the wrong thing to say. This beating was really, really bad. He ripped my clothes, and he punched my head so much that I had ringing in my ear for over a week. I remember asking God, "Please don't let him have damaged anything in my head."

To make things worse, I became pregnant. So Calvin proposed to me. When he was still married, he proposed to me! "This is the family I've always wanted," he said. What family? He had gotten this little girl pregnant. He had all these children scattered throughout New York—for that was something else I had learned.

At the time, I was working off the books at a real estate agency. One day after work, I started to walk and to cry and to pray. "God, I cannot have this kid. I will absolutely die." I looked up and there, right in front of me, I saw Jamaica Hospital. I took a breath and I walked inside. The receptionist sounded Caribbean, so I went up to her and blurted out everything. "I'm in an abusive situation, and I'm pregnant, and I can't have this baby. But I don't have immigration status. I don't have money." She referred me to a clinic a few doors down. I went and scheduled an abortion.

When I told Calvin about the appointment, he didn't want to drive me there. I said, "You will!" And this time I didn't even care. "You can beat me down, but you will take me because I'm not having this baby." I wasn't playing. He took me and I had the abortion, and from then on, I used protection.

It was coming up to June and my son was graduating from high school, but when I told Calvin I had to see my son he said no. He thought if I went back to Barbados I would leave him. I told him not to worry. "The plan is for me to get my son and come back to America. And I *am* going to come back because I don't want to live with my mom and I don't want to see that married guy again." Eventually, he bought me the plane ticket.

I went back to Barbados, but of course I didn't tell anybody about the abuse because I was extremely embarrassed, extremely ashamed. My son and I had a wonderful relationship, but I just could not warn him about the situation he was coming into. After a month, Calvin raised the money to pay for my son and me to fly back to America.

When we got to the airport in New York City, Calvin was nowhere in sight. An hour or so later he turned up, and he seemed to have aged ten, twenty years. It turned out that while I was gone, he brought the seventeen-year-old girl and their new baby into the house. Now he was trying to get rid of her and clean up. The second I walked into the apartment, the stench hit me. The very next day, I was cleaning and finding baby stuff behind chairs and the girl's panties in the sheets. When Calvin called from work, I said, "How dare you!" and I shut the phone off for the rest of the day.

When he came home, he did not even hesitate. In front of my son, he beat me down, ripped my clothes. He got his gun, put it to my head, and said he was going to kill me. I closed my eyes and braced myself. In the background, I heard my son begging him not to shoot me.

Finally, Calvin turned away in a huff and walked outside. When he came back he did the usual thing—apologized to me, apologized to my son, locked the gun in the safe, said it would never happen again, put me on his lap, and said he loved me, always loved me. The next day, my son said, "This always happens to you, Mom, because you're desperate. Always rushing." I said, "You know what? You're right. But after we get out of this—'cause we are going to get out—your mom won't be so desperate again."

At the end of August, I had to go back to the abortion clinic for a follow-up appointment. They gave me a form for the pap smear release, and I turned it over to continue. Right there, on the back of the form, was a survey about whether you were in a domestic violence situation. I couldn't even believe it. I filled out the questions quickly: "Yes, Yes, Yes, Yes, Yes, Yes, Yes."

Fifteen minutes later, a counselor took me into her office, and I told her everything—every single thing. She gave me a safety plan. She told me how to pack my bags in a special way so Calvin wouldn't know that I was planning on leaving. She told me how to hold back a little of the grocery money so I could save it. Then she gave me the Safe Horizon hotline number. I went back home, and I told my son everything. As I saved the grocery money, I gave it to my son.

A few weeks later, Calvin and I were in bed, and I heard this knocking at the window. I looked out. It was the young girl with her baby. I said to Calvin, "Your little girl is here." He jumped up and went out the door. I told my son, "This is it." I didn't know where I was going to go, but I knew I had Safe Horizon's number. Eventually the girl left, and Calvin walked back with the baby and told me to come and lie with them. "No," I said, "I'm not lying with you and that baby." He got angry again. He beat me again and put the gun to my head again. My son said, "Mom, go. Go lie with him."

I took a deep breath, and I listened to my son, and reluctantly, I lay with Calvin and the baby. But I didn't sleep. It was three o'clock in the morning. And I knew when it was a minute past three. And I knew when it was three thirty and four o'clock. I watched the clock ticking. At six o'clock, Calvin got up, got dressed, got the baby dressed, and left. At nine o'clock, I called Safe Horizon. They said they would call back at three o'clock. I cooked. I put everything in a bag. As usual, Calvin called me and apologized. He loved me and he was sorry. And I decided that I was going to be the best actress today. "I love you too. It's all right." At three o'clock on the dot Safe Horizon called and said, "We've accepted you." They told me to meet them at Harlem Hospital. I hung up and Calvin called. "I'm on the highway. I'm almost home."

I ran to the young man that lived upstairs and begged him to drive me to the train station. I had fifty dollars and everything I had cooked and packed. I started writing a note for Calvin, but my son said, "He don't deserve a note, Mommy. He deserve you to take off that engagement ring and take the cell phone he gave you and leave it on the table. That's what he deserve." I took off the engagement ring, and I put the cell phone beside it. I was out the door and I never looked back.

I remember my first night in the Urban Women's Retreat domestic violence shelter. I felt ashamed and so alone. I felt really terrible for everything I had put my son through. I think I eventually fell asleep because I knew the shelter was a long way from Queens. It had two security doors, and you couldn't get in unless they buzzed you. Even if Calvin could find me, he couldn't get in the doors. I just lay there and thought of the two doors, and that's how I fell off to sleep. The staff at the shelter were really wonderful. I met with an on-site immigration lawyer and a caseworker. I saw a shelter counselor and started to look back on my life. What went

wrong that I made so many mistakes and landed in such an abusive relationship—almost killed and now homeless? I traced it back to when my
mom and my dad separated. Everything was fine, and then my life went
out of control with the men my mother brought home. Why couldn't I
do well in school? Why did I keep failing? Because I couldn't concentrate,
that was why. My childhood drama affected everything. I listed all my bad
relationships with men. It was so hard to face all those relationships—it
was painful, but I did it. I realized that I gravitated to all those situations
because I felt so worthless. I realized how angry I was. I was angry at my
dad, at my mom—and extremely angry with myself. I realized it was not
Sophia who was going from man to man and house to house. It wasn't
Sophia doing this. There was something that caused me to spiral out of
control.

The shelter counselor sent me to the St. Luke's Crime Victims Treatment Center. Lisa, my counselor there, was fantastic. She told me to write
down all the things I was thankful for. The thing I was most thankful
for was that Calvin hadn't shot me. I kept coming back to that when I
learned how many abused women are killed. Twice Calvin had put the
gun to my head, and once he had put a knife to my throat. That exercise in writing changed me. I went to the St. Luke's Treatment Center
for two years.

My son was traumatized by the experience and did not like being in
a shelter. This was his Barbadian pride. He was extremely annoyed and
angry, and he wanted to go back to Barbados. I didn't want him to go,
but eventually my mom paid for his ticket. I eventually told her what had
happened with the abuse. I had to disclose it. She didn't like the idea of
my being in a shelter, but I said, "I need to be here and I need to get help."

After my son left, I was transferred to Franklin Women's Shelter, a
shelter in the Bronx that is like an armory. It was a nightmare. By then, I
no longer had priority as a domestic violence victim. I went from having my own room in the domestic violence shelter to sharing a dorm
with twenty-three other women. We had to leave the dorm at nine in
the morning, and we couldn't come back until five. During the day, the
women would sit in a large area, and because they had nothing to do,
there was always some kind of scene: there were fights; there was sex and
drugs. The police were always called. I had never seen so much police
presence in my life. If you went out of the shelter, you had to be searched
when you came back, and that was demoralizing. They would search your
bag, your clothes, and your person. The beat-downs were constant, and it
was like being in prison. Then you went for dinner. I couldn't eat some

of the food. Once when I was on the food line, a lady threw up right there in front of me.

What saved my life was a group called Life Experience and Faith Sharing Associates (LEFSA) that came on Thursdays. I loved it because it was so intimate. I also became involved in VOW, the Voices of Women Organizing Project, which works to change systems that re-victimize the women that turn to them for help.

In my LEFSA group, a Barbadian woman named Lucy told me about the New York Metropolitan Martin Luther King Jr. Center for Nonviolence ATTAIN Lab, where you could learn technical skills. At the center, you chose a course and moved at your own pace. I went to the lab and did the customer service course first. I got 90s on all the tests. It was the most amazing thing! In school I never had a 90 in my life. When I did so well, the man who worked at the lab, an African gentleman, said, "There's a Microsoft Unlimited course on computers. You can do that." He admired how disciplined I was and saw my frustration with the shelter. At one point, when I started going crazy again because the Microsoft Word course was a lot of work and I had to study at the shelter, he invited me to attend his cousin's graduation in Boston. I think he wanted to motivate me. I went with him to Boston, and the graduation was fantastic. I came back renewed, passed the course, and got my Microsoft Word Specialist certification.

The higher floors of the Franklin Shelter were better, but only documented people lived there. Undocumented people like me stayed on the first floor. Somehow, a mistake was made, and I was moved up to the fourth floor. The first three floors were noisy, crazy. On the fourth floor, it was like heaven. The first thing my new case manager said was, "How did you get to the fourth floor?" When she realized I was trying to behave myself, she decided to work with me. "The only way you could have gotten up here is because of God," she said. As an undocumented person, I was never supposed to be transferred out of Franklin, but my case manager got me a spot in a transitional house. When she told me, I sat there and cried.

The transitional house was an actual house with different rooms. It was a lot better than Franklin, but it was supposed to be for women who had been incarcerated. I just happened to be put there. When our supervisor learned that I was Christian and knew the Bible, she asked me to lead the worship services. At first I said, "Nope. These women are badasses, and I'm not telling badass women about God." But eventually the supervisor convinced me. So I said, "God, if I'm going to do this, I'm going to do it Sophia's way." I wanted the Bible to come alive for the women, so I made them part of the services. Some of the women had written stories and poems that I incorporated in our worship. One time, I researched the meaning of all the women's names, and I read the definitions out to them. The women were just floored that that their names had meaning. They began to change. It was really wonderful.

My mom died in August 2009. Years earlier, I'd realized I'd been angry with her for too long. One of the things that made me realize this was my dad's funeral in 2000. When he passed away, I didn't know how to plan a funeral, and I turned to my mom. She was there every step of the way to get the funeral done. I realized that every time I left home, she never said no when I asked to come back. She always took me in. After that, I decided to forgive my mother and made it my business to hug my mom and tell her I love her. When she was dying, I couldn't leave the US, but I called her and said, "Although I can't be there with you physically, I'm there with you in spirit. I love you and I always will." My mom couldn't even answer me back, and she died two days later—but I feel good that I made amends and she didn't pass without knowing I love her.

My son had been with my mom in Barbados, and now he needed to come live with me. A few months earlier I had received my U Visa and had started to look for work. "God," I said, "I need a job to drop from the sky so I can bring my son back." A week later my cell phone rang, and I got an interview to work at a domestic violence shelter. I got the job in October 2009 and still work as a residential aide to this day.

That same month, I began the New York Catholic Charities life skills empowerment program. Sister Dorothy from LEFSA recommended me for it. It was wonderful. We learned about money management and goal setting. My first goal was to get my own apartment by December. I found a $600 studio in Queens. My son and I still live there, but now he has a full-time job and we plan to move to a bigger place very soon.

The most impactful thing about the life skills empowerment program was getting to put my life story together with the help of Mr. Horton and Ms. Kelsick. My life was in pieces and it was scary to imagine writing about it, but I heard that doing so was good and therapeutic. Finally, I just wrote everything down from beginning to end. When I had to share my story with the group, I was a bunch of nerves. That's when I coined the phrase "It is difficult but it is necessary." And it *was* difficult to share my story, but it was necessary because I wanted to get my past out in the open and get rid of it. I was determined to clean out my house. I was tired of my secret life—it was too much to carry.

Sophia in New York City

In 2010, Marc Greenberg asked me to facilitate the first Living Well life skills empowerment program for domestic violence survivors. I thought, "Me? What do I know?" My meeting with Marc and the social workers for the program was surreal. I couldn't believe I was part of this group and I was giving input about developing the program. I realized I had something else to offer.

Now, whenever I talk to domestic violence survivors in the life skills empowerment program and the shelter, I tell them that phrase I coined for myself: "It is difficult but it is necessary." If the women say how hard something is, I look back at them. "I know it's hard because I know my own journey. But it's necessary for your kids and you. I'm not just saying you can get through it. I can tell you how because I understand your struggle."

I believe you can be fully healed. It can be compared to getting a cut on your hand. At first, there is the wound. Then later, you can see the mark. Then there is just the scar, sometimes noticeable, sometimes not. But then it goes away. That's the same thing with trauma. I believe you can be healed from trauma if you embrace the help you can get. I've gotten a lot of help, and I don't want that help to be wasted. America did a lot for me. This country took me into a shelter when I was undocumented and had no place to go; it gave me counseling for free. I was able to get my GED and become legal and get my green card. Now that I have achieved my goal of starting college, my future goal is to get my credentials and work with child survivors.

In America, I was able to find Sophia. This is a new Sophia. I'm different, I'm better, I want to help people, and I have a lot to offer.

Reflection
Terry Michaud

Terry Michaud has served as a mentor since 1996 for the Education Outreach Program (EOP), the original life skills empowerment program, run by New York Catholic Charities; as she points out, she has worked with thirty-seven participants.

My experiences as a mentor in the life skills empowerment program began in the fall of 1996, more than eighteen years ago. Since then, I have worked with thirty-seven remarkable individuals, all of whom have enriched my life.

One woman named Phoebe had a rough and difficult existence. Her face alone conveyed her misery. Born to a single mother with a drug problem, Phoebe had, by her mid-teens, engaged in a life on the streets that lasted more than twenty-two years. During that time, she gave birth to many children and lost custody of them all.

In contrast, I was surprised upon first meeting Grace. She was a very poised, well-spoken young woman in her mid-twenties who looked like a model. On the surface, it wasn't clear why she was in the life skills empowerment program. Gradually, as time progressed, more of Grace's story unfolded. As a young girl, she had been placed with a loving foster family who cared for her as a daughter. But emotional problems related to something in her early childhood were unresolved, and Grace had turned to substance abuse. Her life had unraveled from there.

Between meetings, I often found myself wondering about Grace, Phoebe, and the many others I met in the program. Clearly the details of every person's story are unique, but the very long work ahead of each participant

241

suggested that the rebuilding of lives is not as simple as following a well-crafted plan of steps from "a" to "b." In many cases, there were great barriers to overcome, and as a mentor I found myself in unfamiliar territory. For example, I didn't understand why so many of the participants had such difficulty with expressing long-range goals or dreams.

I often thought about beginnings. Each of us has been dealt the life and circumstances in which we find ourselves from birth through childhood. I knew that for some the cards are much more favorably stacked than for others. In my own life, I was so fortunate to have a father and mother who never stopped adoring each other. I especially remember how my father's love of his work and pride in his children gave us the foundation for a good start in life. Somewhere along the way I was inspired to believe that I could accomplish anything I wanted.

But what about Phoebe? Her life had been a struggle from birth. Did she receive any nurturing and guidance from her mother? Did she ever have any positive role models? And what had happened to Grace in her early childhood that couldn't be remedied by a loving family? I recalled how many program participants spoke about being alone in terrible situations without guidance, long before they had developed the necessary skills for handling difficult problems. It took time before I was sensitized to the injustices and emotional barriers they were struggling with.

Turning to my faith in Catholic social teaching, I realized that the common thread linking many of the participants' stories was dignity. I was reminded that each person has immeasurable value from birth, as each of us was formed in the image and likeness of God. I reflected on how in our human condition, we all have the same basic needs: love of self; a sense of belonging to a family or community that nurtures, loves, and supports us; and a sense of purpose through meaningful work. Dignity can be robbed by life events or illness or when certain skills are no longer valued in the workforce. In my heart-to-heart conversations with Phoebe and Grace, I realized that parents suffering from a loss of dignity were often unable to instill self-worth in their children. In situations like Phoebe's, the problem seemed to be perpetuated through several generations of the family.

Helping someone is a delicate balance. Attempting to solve another person's problems can rob him or her of dignity. So can imposing our own expectations on others. I realized that I often measured the choices of other people through a lens that was formed by my own beginnings, experiences, and background, instead of theirs. But interjecting the right help at the right time is key. This requires a continuum of caring people who are available to listen and provide support. Every one of us has had help along the way. No one achieves success in life on his or her own.

Through the life skills empowerment program, I have witnessed many graduates heal and use their new-found empowerment to assume important leadership roles in their communities. As individuals are empowered, one person at a time, whole communities—once marginalized—gain a voice and are restored to dignity. Of all the people I have encountered in my life, the program graduates are among those I hold in highest esteem. Being a mentor has shown me that we can all be God's instrument in the lives of others.

Life Story
Cindy (Pseudonym)

Cindy was born in spring 1972 in Trinidad and Tobago. She graduated in 2011 from Living Well, the first life skills empowerment program for survivors of domestic violence, which was run by the Interfaith Assembly on Homelessness and Housing. Cindy's story includes details and quotations from two oral history interviews she had in fall 2013 with Shelia Gilliam (then a student in Columbia University's master of arts program in oral history); it also includes details from a life story Cindy published in CURA: A Literary Magazine of Art and Action in 2012.

I was born and raised in the beautiful tropical islands of Trinidad and Tobago, known for the sound of steel pan music, beautiful beaches, and tasty foods. You can actually pick the coconuts off the trees and drink the juice from them. I know that my parents went through a lot of trials and hardships to see a better lifestyle for their family. My father used to work for the government as a night watchman. Eventually, he was able to build a big enough house to accommodate every one of his kids. My mom stayed at home. In the evening time, she would prepare dinner for my father, and I would put it in a bag and give it to him. Then I would watch my father ride his bicycle down the street and go to work. My parents stuck together as husband and wife for over fifty years. We had a very stable home, a very happy home, dedicated to our spiritual background, which was of Muslim faith.

I am the youngest of nine kids, with six brothers and two sisters. Growing up were the happiest days of my life. I was the spoiled child in the

A photograph of Trinidad taken by Cindy in 2016

family, and I am still the spoiled child in the family. My brothers would take me to soccer games, the zoo, and beaches, and we would climb the mountains; they had me having so much fun. One of my brothers played cricket, and every Sunday, I would tag along to see his game. I grew into playing cricket too, and I now go to watch the games in Queens during the summertime.

There were big celebrations on Friday nights. My mom's house had a big yard, and everyone would cook and talk and laugh a lot. Holidays were so much fun. At the end of the forty days of Ramadan, we had this celebration called Eid al-Fitr. We would go to services and give donations to the needy and then go back home and cook. My family was very large with all the grandkids, and there were so many friends in and out of the house. We ate my mother's *sivayyan*, which is like vermicelli with milk and raisins and spices. When you went to a Muslim home, you always looked forward to it. We also celebrated Christmas in a nonreligious way. On the first day we went to my eldest brother's house, and the next day to another brother's house, and every single day until New Year's, we visited another house. During the year, we would cook early in the morning, pack everything, and go to the beach, or we would rent out a beach house and go for the whole weekend. So we had a lot of family times. It was really, really enjoyable.

My family's Muslim background doesn't mean they didn't drink alcoholic beverages. My father used to drink a lot on weekends, from Friday until Sunday. But he was never an argumentative person or violent toward any one of my brothers and sisters or my mom. I liked it when he drank because he was such a funny person. And oh, how my father enjoyed the Indian dance. I used to sit down and watch him. I remember when I was small, he would pick me up in his arms and dance with me. There was a song by Luther Vandross—I loved that song. During the week, he would put me on his bicycle and take me to school.

But my father was also very strict. As I grew up and became a teenager, I wasn't allowed to do anything on my own. If I was going somewhere, my sister was right there with me. No way I was allowed to go outside alone. Even after high school, I was very sheltered.

In 1991, I went back to school for a Microsoft Office course. This is where I met Brandon, who was taking a welding course. Brandon was such a talker—such a well-dressed and good-looking guy. We exchanged phone numbers and started communicating secretly. When my parents found out, they made me stop the computer course. They didn't like Brandon because he was not working and he was two years younger than me. Plus, my family was Indian, and Brandon was Indian mixed with black. I tried to sneak and call him when my parents were outside. We never could meet, but Brandon would pass on my street like he was going to a friend's house. My parents, especially my mom, noticed everything, and they disciplined me so much. They stopped me from using the phone, they never let me go past the gates, and they didn't want me to go outside.

I hated what my parents were doing to keep me away from Brandon. I never disrespected them, but I cried and started demanding that they let me marry him. My whole family thought I was getting crazy. I remember one of my brothers saying, "She's being so rebellious. What does she want?" They thought I was on drugs or this guy did something to me. My father even sent me to the doctor to see if I was pregnant. He was happy when the doctor said, "She hasn't lost her virginity yet." But they still thought I was crazy. I wanted to get married at the age of twenty, and this guy was not working. So it was like, "Who is going to take care of you? What are you going to do, come back home for food and money?"

But after my continuous forcing and crying and pleading, they decided to meet with Brandon's parents and maybe try arranging for him to marry me. Well, we did get married, in December 1992. Though Brandon was Christian, we got married under the Muslim rites. I wore a pretty, white wedding dress, and my father walked me down the aisle. It was a beautiful, huge wedding. I was told there were 500-plus people there. In Muslim rites, the bride returns home for three days before the marriage is consummated. Then she goes back to the husband with everything she owns. That was the tradition. My three days back home passed by fast because I was packing and everybody was together, and my mom was talking to me. After three days, all my belongings were packed, and Brandon came and moved me in with his family. We had known each other for maybe six months. Because I was never allowed to go out, we had not spent a lot of time together.

So I had never seen the other side of Brandon.

I found out about that side right before New Year's. Brandon had some friends come over, and he asked me to prepare meals. He drank, he was angry, he was moody. In front of his friends, he started treating me like a slave, yelling and embarrassing me all because I was not bringing what he asked for immediately.

I said to myself, "I never had this before. Why should I be treated like this?" Away from his friends, I yelled, "Come on, I'm trying my best! Wait!" That's when Brandon called me outside and smacked me in my face. I couldn't believe it. I sat down on the stairs, and I cried. I thought, "I forced myself into this marriage, I can't turn back now. That would be a big embarrassment for my parents. I have to make this work."

Brandon's mom came out and told him: "Why are you hitting the girl? You don't put hands on anybody's daughter." Brandon was like, "I'm sorry. I'm sorry." So I got up, and I washed my face, and I did what I had to do. Brandon hadn't left a bruise or anything, so I said, "It won't happen again." But I was wrong. From then on, I was being yelled at every day, I was being cursed at. Every week I was being hit.

Brandon *was* very nice when I got pregnant a few years later. He was a sweetheart. He would help, do as much as he could, bring home fruits for me. We spent a lot of quality time together. But after the baby was born, Brandon changed. He started to hang out a lot with friends and drink, and I think he used to smoke because his eyes would become red. When he came home, he would be very angry and upset. I didn't want my family to know about the beatings I was getting from him. They had begged me not to marry Brandon, and then they spent so much money getting me a huge wedding.

Meanwhile, Brandon borrowed money from my brother. He bought his own welding machine and started doing private jobs for people in the yard. One day while he was welding, he smacked me so hard in my eye that some of the blood vessels popped. Oh, how he smacked me! My eye became swollen and blood red. For days I couldn't do anything with it. I couldn't be outside. The glare would hurt too much. When I went to the doctor, Brandon's mother begged me, "Don't tell him what happened. Tell him that the door or something just hit you in the eye." I followed directions. I did it because I had grown up in a family-oriented home, and I wanted that for my baby. I did everything in my power to keep my family together. But when my eye healed, the abuse didn't stop. It just continued and continued and continued.

Finally, after Brandon bruised my hands and mouth, I called one of my brothers. "Come and get me. I can't stay here no more." When my brother saw the condition I was in, he almost punched Brandon. He told my mother-in-law, "She's not coming back here. Cindy is not coming back here. Do what you all want with the furniture"—because my brother had bought us that—"do what you all want but she's not coming back." I packed my clothes and the baby's things, and I went home. But about a week later, his parents told my parents that Brandon was very apologetic and that they didn't know what had gotten into him, but he was never going to hurt me again. So I went back with him.

In 2000, my father went to use the bathroom, and he saw blood when he urinated. We took him to the doctor, and they told us he had pancreatic cancer. Around the same time, Brandon's work got slower, and he decided to go to America to see what it was like. He went to New York for six months, and I stayed in Trinidad. Then Brandon came back and told me he wanted us to move here. I said, "Really?" So we talked about it, and I went and told my brothers. They were very disgusted because they knew I was being abused.

But I thought in America things would change for us. Plus I was excited to come see it—this big place everybody dreams of coming to. Everything amazed my eyes as I travelled. Wow! All these trees and these big buildings everywhere you turned. There were so many different classes of people in New York, so many white people, so many mixed cultures, the Spanish, the blacks. How busy the place was! Trinidad was nothing like this.

After six months, my family called me back to Trinidad because my father was worse. It seemed like one minute he was well and the next day he was flat down on a bed. His body just deteriorated in the flash of an eye. I actually saw my father wind down from a happy, running-around, jolly, hard-working man to a child lying in bed who could not do anything. We had to do everything for him—everything. My father couldn't even use the bathroom on his own. It was horrible. But I know at least now he's resting in peace. My father took care of his family, and I was with him at his bedside when he died. I was also pregnant. My second son was born in Trinidad in 2001.

Brandon was with us in Trinidad for part of that time. That's when I realized he was seeing someone in America. How I found out is that he had a bank card under the lady's name. Once when he withdrew money, the bank card fell, and I noticed it. Brandon would also go outside and make a lot of phone calls. I was nosy, and I checked his phone log when he wasn't there. But I never said anything to Brandon when he was in Trinidad. Instead, he went back to America, and I decided to follow him. "Don't go, please. Don't go," my brothers begged me. But I said, "I'm going because that's my sons' father, and I don't want to steer my sons away from their father. I don't want that. I just have to follow him."

The very night we arrived, Brandon was drinking out in the backyard with one of his friends. He had rented a basement apartment out in Jamaica, Queens. After the friend left, I asked him about the cheating.

I said, "Who is—?" and said the lady's name.

Brandon said, "How you know that?"

I said, "You left things back in Trinidad, and I saw them."

So he started to curse and yell at me. He took all the belongings that I came with—all my clothes—and threw them over the fence into a parking lot. I had to go all the way around the block to get them. Brandon wouldn't even take care of my older son when I went. The baby was sleeping inside, but I had to walk with my older son, who was four then. He was so young and tender. He called me Cindy, because that's how he heard everybody calling me.

"Cindy," my son said, "why did Brandon throw your clothes over the fence?"

"I don't know," I said. "But don't worry about it." I was trying to hide everything.

"But now you have to walk," my son said. He was small, but he was explaining to himself.

I was walking, trying to cover the tears flowing from my eyes. I said, "My God. What did I get myself into? Why did I come? But now I can't turn back and I have no one." So I stayed.

Well, after Queens, we moved to an apartment in Bedford-Stuyvesant, Brooklyn. Brandon had a very good job in welding, so he was able to support the family and I wasn't working. But he was still going out and drinking and coming back in the morning time. The abuse got worse— my eyes blue-black, mouth busted, hands blue-black, legs blue-black; my neck had squeeze marks on it.

One day my youngest son said, "Mommy, you look like you were in a boxing fight. What happened?"

I told him, "The door hit me in my face." It was all lies to my kids, continuously—lies, lies, lies to both of my boys. Brandon would never apologize for what he had done. He always said that I caused that to happen to me. I blamed myself, like I must have been doing so much wrong to be treated like this. Later you had sex, you made up for a few weeks, and then it happened again. Then sex again, and you made up. It was like a pattern now. I knew I was being abused, but I had no one to turn to. Brandon wouldn't allow me to have friends in America. He wouldn't allow me to talk to anyone. If I went out of the house, he would time me until I came back.

I couldn't call my family in Trinidad to tell them I wanted to come back home. Why? Because I didn't want to take shame back to my family. They had begged me not to get married. Then they spent so much money getting me a huge wedding. How could I be the first one to get a divorce? My six brothers were all married and living well, and one of my sisters was married and living well. Why should I bring shame to my family? My family wasn't going to appreciate this.

I did call the cops on numerous occasions, but most of the reports were just classified as verbal abuse. I never reported the hitting because I was scared Brandon would somehow get to take my kids from me. I didn't know better because I was new in this country. I didn't know about the shelter system; I didn't know about anything. The officers advised me to go to family court and get an order of protection. But where would either of us go if I did that? I wondered who would take care of my kids. I was also scared to go to family court because I had no legal status in the United States. Once I asked a cop if I could take my children back to Trinidad. He said, "If the father is still here, that would be kidnapping. They'll arrest you wherever you are." Now I had that fear as well.

As the years went by, I saw that Brandon was not bringing in the same amount of money. Financially, things were becoming harder, the rent was starting to back up, and we got an eviction notice. I had a tax identification number, so I became a childcare provider through the Human Resource Administration (HRA). That meant I could have up to five kids in my home and the HRA paid for it. This was the first time I ever worked in America. Now that I was seeing other people, Brandon stopped hitting me in the face. He would hit me in the arms where I could be covered, or in my chest. He would go out to parties and come home, beat me up. Meanwhile, I was learning about the system through the HRA classes I had to take. I learned that the Administration for Children's Services (ACS) could take my kids away from me because of the abuse. So I kept hiding what was happening.

In 2005, Brandon started doing welding for this white lady twice his age. Her name was Cathy. One night, he came back from her house drunk, and when he went to take a shower, I heard him fall. Yes, Brandon was abusing me, but that was my kids' father, that was my husband in there. So I opened the bathroom door to see what was wrong. Brandon was down in the tub with his underwear on. I helped him stand up, and when I took off his underwear, my God! The thing was filled with sperm. I said, "Oh my God, he is sleeping with this white lady." At first, Brandon didn't admit it, but then Cathy started to pick him up in the mornings. I would see him texting her in the nighttime. Finally, he said that Cathy had offered to marry him and help him get his green card. "We gonna get divorced," Brandon told me.

Cathy wrote me a letter saying that this was all business, that after Brandon got his green card she would divorce him, and the kids did need a green card to continue their schooling and go to college. So I gave him the divorce with ease because I was thinking of my kids now.

But when I was signing the paper, I told Brandon, "I don't want you to come back to me after I divorce you. You can move on, 'cause I know that you are having sex with Cathy and you lied to me. And I don't want any green card from you. So if you decide to divorce Cathy, don't come back to me."

He said, "Why? Are you seeing somebody else?" He was always worrying about that. "No, I'm not seeing anyone else. I have no intentions of seeing anyone. You go."

I'm saying it smooth now, but I was crying when I told him this. In 2006, around March or April, we got divorced.

But even after Brandon married Cathy, he used to come back to the apartment and force me to have sex. My body would just want to push him away, but it kept happening. At this point, I had a cell phone from my babysitting money. All day long Brandon would call and track where I was at. My younger son's kindergarten teacher was also from Trinidad. When I confided in her, she actually had the courage to talk to him.

"If you're married, why don't you leave Cindy alone?" she asked my ex-husband. "Let Cindy do her thing. Leave her alone. She's not seeing anyone, leave her alone." But Brandon wouldn't stop. He threatened to call immigration on me if I tried to leave him. I took that as a serious threat. I had heard about and seen people being deported, and I didn't want to get deported and have to leave my kids.

In August, one of the girls upstairs had a birthday party, and Brandon came to that. There was this guy looking at me, but I paid no attention. When we got downstairs, Brandon said, "I saw you watching that man." I said, "You're crazy!" But he punched my left ear. It started bleeding and someone called the cops. When they came, Brandon fled the scene and went back home to Cathy. The police made a report and took me to the hospital. Now the domestic violence unit took over, and they investigated Brandon. The following weekend, we had to go together to the precinct.

But by then, I had promised Brandon I would say that everything was fine. So when the detective sat us down, I asked, "Are you all going to arrest him?"

"No," the detective said. "I just want to know what happened."

"It was just a little misunderstanding, but we talked it over and he's sorry, so it's all right."

"Okay," the detective said. "Just sign the police report before you leave." It turns out I had never signed the police report from the night of the party. So I did what he said.

The minute I finished signing, the detective stood up. "You can leave," he said to me. Then he pointed to Brandon. "But Mr. B—— has to stay." And right there and then, the detective arrested my ex-husband. Brandon hates me to this day for signing that report.

For six months after that, I had an order of protection from Brandon. During that time, he kept calling me on the phone. "Can you please don't follow up with pressing charges against me?"

"Why?" I said. "You continue beating me, and you say that you'll stop, and you're not stopping."

"If you continue with the case, they're not gonna give me the green card." Immediately I thought of my kids. If Brandon didn't get a green card, then they would not get a green card. So when the DA called, I insisted I was not pressing charges. He tried persuading me, but I said, "No. He's the father of my kids, and I don't want my kids to be without their father." The charges were dropped.

After the order of protection ended, my ex-husband started coming back to the apartment. In June 2008, I found out I was pregnant. Brandon sent me to get an abortion, and I went and signed up to have one the next day. But when I came back home, I said, "No. I can't do this. This is not what my mother taught me. I came from a Muslim home. I can't do this."

When I told him my decision, Brandon said, "I don't want nothing to do with that child." He didn't want Cathy to find out I was pregnant. She was aware that her husband saw the kids at my house, but she didn't know we still had a relationship.

I went through my nine months with a lot of depression, a lot of crying at night. Brandon still wanted to be around me, but he wouldn't ask how the baby was doing. One day he threw the phone at my stomach, and my stomach was pretty big. Another time after drinking, he took a kitchen fork and stuck my hand with it. He had boots on, and he kicked me on my shinbone. He started to pull my hair. But that night I grabbed back at him and pushed him against the wall. He was so drunk he hit his head.

In the wintertime, I became sick, and the doctor did a number of tests on me. One showed that my daughter was going to be born with sickle cell anemia. The doctor also said I had walking pneumonia. I called Brandon and asked him to keep the kids while I was in the hospital. At first he refused, but then he came and watched them. I also said, "My daughter is going to be born with sickle cell." Brandon was mean. "I told you not to have the kid. I told you I didn't want no more children."

I had my daughter in March. Later, Brandon came to the hospital and saw the baby. And what happened is she was so beautiful that he fell in love with her. He didn't sign her birth certificate because he didn't want to jeopardize his marriage with Cathy and getting his green card. But when I came home, Brandon set up the apartment so pretty to welcome us. He put up the bassinet, he made the beds, and he cleaned up the house so well. He even cooked dinner. He was scared to hold the baby, but he did it anyway.

"She's very beautiful," he told me. "Thank you," I said. Brandon stayed a few days and came back on the weekends. Things were nice for a little while.

And then the abuse started again, and he beat me to a pulp. I mean, really beat me to a pulp. I was blue-black, my mouth was bursting, my eyes were blue-black. I said to myself, "Okay, that's got to be it. I can't stay here no more. I can't do this no more. Not for my child, not for my daughter. I can't be breastfeeding my daughter under stress, crying while I'm breastfeeding my daughter. What is that going to do to her? My kids seeing this all the time. Every time they see me, I'm bruised somewhere, or my lip is swollen, or my face, tears running out my eyes."

Soon after, I met Matt, the father of a boy who was playing with my kids in the park. After talking a few times, I ended up telling him what I was going through. Matt said, "I'm going to help you." Later he told me it was because he saw me as a beautiful person inside and outside, and I didn't deserve what I was getting. "I see you as a very good mother. You take care of your kids. You're one of the most respectable young ladies living on the block. And if I can help you, I will help you. I've never done it before. I want nothing in return. I just think I need to help you because it seems as though you want to get help."

Matt told me that a domestic advocate named Danielle was going to visit me. "Okay," I said, "but I don't want Brandon to find out because he's going to kill the life out of me."

"Brandon doesn't have to know. I'm never gonna tell him anything. You just gotta do what you have to do for yourself and your kids."

I became very scared because I was living on edge now, trying to get Matt's help. Shortly after that conversation, Danielle drove to my apartment, and I went out to her car. The baby was sleeping inside, and I left the boys with her. My older son questioned me: "What are you doing?"

I told him, "Mommy wants to speak to that lady in the car. You'll see Mommy go right in her car to sit and talk with her."

My son said, "You want to leave Brandon?"

"I do want to leave him, but I don't know how."

"Oh." My son was about to finish the fifth grade and start junior high school.

"I'm going to give you a number for a domestic violence hotline," Danielle told me. "You call, and they are going to tell you to come to a homeless shelter." I had heard that homeless shelters had so many different races and cultures of people and that they were full of sickness. I was really fearing where I was going to take my kids, especially my daughter who had sickle cell. "But I don't want to be homeless," I told Danielle. "I have a home."

"Cindy, if you want to get this help and come out of this situation, you gotta do it. I promise you, you gonna get out." I was scared. I didn't want to leave. I didn't want the kids to leave their father. Weeks passed and I didn't call.

When the summer was about to end, that's when I got a little more serious. I called Matt. "I can't take this no more. I'm being beaten almost every weekend, and it's horrible." Matt told me he was going to go to consult a lawyer about getting an order of protection. I think Brandon realized that I was talking to someone now because he took my phone away. I had to go out to a pay phone and warn Matt and Danielle not to answer if he called. Back at the house, Brandon kept calling the landline. When nobody answered, he called my son's phone. "Do not answer him. Please do not answer Brandon," I said. I felt bad putting my kids in this dilemma to be fearful of their father.

The last Thursday before school opened, Brandon showed up with my phone. When he came—this is shameful—he wanted sex before he would give it back to me. And I didn't want to have sex with him. So I took a red marker and painted a pad, and I put it on, so he would think that I was having my period. Just not to have sex with this man. Then he asked me to jerk him off. I went to the bathroom and I—I was crying, but I was doing it because I needed my cell phone back. I was really determined to get away. I jerked him off, I got back the phone, and then he left later in the evening time. I sat down and I cried in the house, late in the night.

That weekend, my ex-husband hit me in front of the kids and cut my feet because I bought sneakers for my older son that cost $110. He said I could have bought two pair of shoes for that money. But I think Brandon was really upset because I paid for the sneakers with my own money, and he couldn't afford them. I was doing everything financially now in that house. He was not being the boss anymore.

The next week, a young, pretty black woman named Miss Grant came to my apartment. She said, "I'm from ACS. Someone called and said you're abusing and neglecting your kids."

"Me?" I called my ex-husband. "Brandon, somebody called ACS on me." The next thing I knew, he was at the door. Miss Grant and I sat down in living room.

"But I do babysitting for HRA," I told her. "How can I abuse my kids and neglect them if I'm watching other people's kids?" I was babysitting three siblings that day. Their mother knew about the abuse. She used to advise me, "Get away from that. You need to get away from that."

Miss Grant questioned my sons individually. She also questioned me individually. She looked into the cupboards and the fridge to see if there was food. When she was about to leave, Brandon said, "How can I get in touch with you? I would like to speak to you alone." That's when I realized. *He* must have been the one that called ACS on me. He must have suspected I wanted to leave. So he called ACS to trap me and take the kids.

As soon as he left, I called my friend the kindergarten teacher. She said, "Cindy, you get on that phone right now, and you call Miss Grant and tell her what you are going through." I was crying furiously. "Cindy, I mean it. Call her now." So I hung up with my friend, and I called the ACS number.

"Miss Grant, there's something I need to tell you."

"I'm listening," said Miss Grant.

"I am in an abusive relationship."

"I knew that. I could see right through you. You were just afraid to speak because your husband was there."

"He's my ex-husband. He just dominates my life still."

Miss Grant told me she would investigate the situation and keep in touch with me. A week passed, and on Friday, September 12, she called me. She had spoken to the neighbors, and they said, "Yeah, she's been abused." She had spoken to the landlord, and he said, "I've seen Brandon hit her and make her bleed in front of my eyes." They all said that it happened in front of the kids. So it was like I was putting my children in danger.

"Ms. B——," Miss Grant said, "You have to leave Mr. B—— or else we're going to take your kids away from you."

I was crying. "Miss Grant, where will I go? I have no family here. All my family is back in Trinidad." She said, "I'm going to give you the number of a domestic violence shelter. You just call and do what they say. You have until Monday."

Monday morning, Matt texted me, "Are you going to go?" I wrote back, "No, I'm not leaving." He said, "They're going to take the kids away from you." I took my younger son to school and went upstairs to the PTA room, and the president and the treasurer were there. They had an idea of the problem I was having in my home. I sat there and I spoke to the two of them that morning. They told me, "You want your kids, you love your kids, you're a good mother. Go. They'll help you. There is help for you. Go. You may not like where you go, but it's going to be okay, Cindy."

After that, Miss Grant called me. "Did you make up your mind?"

"No."

"I'm going to come to take the kids today if you don't leave."

That's when I decided. "Miss Grant. I'm ready. I'm going to go. What do I have to do?"

She gave me the shelter number, and I called and they told me I had one hour to get my things together and leave. The lady I spoke to on the phone, I'll never forget her—her name was Glenda. She said, "We'll call your older boy at school. You take the younger boy, take your baby, just pack essentials." She told me what documents to bring. All this time I didn't know where I was going. All I knew was I had to go home and pack. The two ladies from the PTA came and helped me, and I'm grateful for that. Glenda called again. "Leave whatever isn't packed and get into the cab. Then call me back." I got a cab in front of the elementary school so that Brandon wouldn't see if he came by the house. I only had fifty dollars in my pocket.

First we got my older son from junior high school. I guess the hotline people spoke to his guidance counselor, because she brought him down and hugged me. "Good luck," she said. Then I called Glenda back. She said, "You tell the cab driver you are going to 116 and Lexington." I had no idea where that was. I'd never been in that part of town. I'd never heard of that before. I had the baby in one of those carriers, and I was holding my boys' hands. "Things are going to be all right, I'm going to take care of you all," I told them. The cab driver overheard the situation. "Ma'am, you're doing the best thing," he said. He dropped me off exactly where Glenda told me, in front of a Burger King. The trip was forty-five dollars, so I was left with five dollars in my pocket. Five dollars for three kids—no food, no nothing. I called Glenda again, and she said, "We'll be there shortly." It was Spanish Harlem, so I was seeing a different culture now. My God, where was I with my kids, my older son still in his school uniform, and all these bags, three suitcases?

Then I saw two men and a lady walking up to me. She said, "Ms. B——? I'm Glenda." And I started to cry. "Don't cry. I had to come see you. You were so strong on the phone." The men took my bags, and we started walking.

"Did anyone in your building see you leave? Anybody besides the cab driver know where you were dropped off?"

I told her no.

"Okay, we are going to take you somewhere now, we are going to take you home."

In my head I was like, "Home? What is home? I just left home."

After a few blocks, we walked into the homeless shelter. And it was one of the most beautiful places I have ever seen. It was so clean—the people were so loving. They made me sign some papers, and then they took me up to the apartment. Everything was well prepared. The living room was huge. The kitchen was magnificent. The apartment was so clean you could drop your food on the floor and eat from it. I had my own room, my own apartment. So I went and sat down with the kids and said, "Listen, we're going to make it work. I left and I'm not going back. We are going to see what can be done. I'm gonna be here for you guys as long as I'm alive. I'm never gonna leave you all." And I hugged them.

In the evening, a young lady came upstairs with a stack of papers and said, "I'm going to do your intake. Are the children citizens?" I told her the boys had green cards with their father and "the baby is a citizen." I showed her my daughter's birth certificate and social security card. The lady brought up some pantry foods and canned foods. She told us not to text Brandon or to answer his calls because he could put a track on the phone and know where we were. In a domestic violence shelter, nobody should ever know where you are. My older son understood. He was very smart in this whole getaway. He is really, really intelligent.

In the night, I talked to Matt. He said he had spoken with Danielle, the domestic violence advocate. "She made sure you went somewhere very good. Danielle knows where you are. She told me it's one of the best shelters." It was called a Tier 1 shelter because it was for women in crisis. Later, I found out it was also a disability shelter. I guess I got in there because of my daughter's sickle cell. I said, "Thank you, Matt. Thank you a lot." Matt was like my mentor. I'm very, very grateful for him, for what he did in my life.

That same evening, my sister in Trinidad called: "Where are you?! What happened?" It turns out that when Brandon realized we were gone, he called my family in Trinidad and said that I ran away with a man.

I said, "Brandon used to beat me a lot. I just didn't tell you. But I left and I'm safe." My brother called, and I told him, "I didn't run off with no man. I'm in a shelter."

He was furious. "You leave your home to go to America to be homeless? When we told you to stay, you refused. Now look what you have to do. Look what you have to go through!" I told him I'd be all right. I knew he was hurting.

From that day on, my family in Trinidad called me every day, sometimes twice a day. They kept real close touch with me now. The next day, my family sent me some money through Western Union.

The shelter also helped me open a public assistance case. I was able to get food stamps and cash assistance for the kids. I got a social worker named Jenny G. I still keep in touch with that amazing woman up to this day. I started doing whatever they asked of me at the shelter. Whatever programs, whatever they required of me, I did it all. There was a different essence in life now. I was working to strengthen myself and to gain strength for the kids and do whatever was best for them and their future. I learned so much in that shelter.

My ex-husband and I both filed for custody of the kids. He hired a paid lawyer. My lawyer was from legal aid. But my God, he was fantastic. He had years of experience with domestic violence. The kids had a wonderful, caring law guardian as well. When the case got nasty, my eldest brother sent my youngest brother and his wife to America. They were with me, side by side in the court. Brandon said he should have custody because I was homeless and couldn't take care of the kids, and he was stable. He also lied and said he never beat me. But Miss Grant from ACS came to court, and she said her investigation showed he was abusive. Brandon had opened his own can of worms with ACS. He had called them on *me* and then they found out the truth about *him*. That's karma. I love that word. I got an order of protection, but the custody case went on for a long time, two years. In the end I won and got full custody of all three kids.

At the same time that the custody case was going on and on, I was doing whatever I was supposed to do. I applied for New York City housing, and I was awarded priority N1 because of the domestic violence. In less than a year, I was supposed to get housing. After 120 days in the crisis shelter, I got moved to a second shelter in Manhattan. When I wasn't in court, I was going to women's groups, going to counselling, doing therapy with my clinician and whatever. The shelter had this scholarship competition where they asked you to write your story. I didn't want to do it, but my caseworker insisted. So I sat down and I wrote my story, and she typed it up for me. I won and got $5,000! I used some of the money to get a license as a certified nursing assistant, because with my daughter being sick, I wanted at least to administer care to her. Meanwhile, she and my two sons were doing well. I had therapy for them. They were doing well in school. I was taking them to little children's plays and other parent-child activities. We were interacting and we were really, really active in the second shelter. Things were very smooth, with no problems at all.

In August, the Department of Housing called me to come see an apartment in the same neighborhood as the first shelter. When I went in there, I wanted to cry—and not tears of joy. The apartment was filthy. The walls were broken down, the fridge was dirty, the stove was dirty, you saw dead cockroaches, you saw garbage, you saw the floor black—literally black and the dirt so piled up it was green with filth. I asked the lady who took me to see it, "Are you going to clean the apartment?"

"Yes, but don't expect a bed of roses."

Matt was with me, and he whispered, "Take it or else you will have to wait a long while before you get another one." So I signed the lease. Public assistance helped pay for the security and the first month's rent, but I had to put in a portion because I was undocumented. My brother sent me the money.

A few months later, the repairs were done, and I went to see the apartment. This time I smiled. It was so beautiful! The apartment was well painted, tiles were removed, and new tiles were put down. There was a new fridge and a new stove, and they fixed the cabinets. They fixed the bathroom, the tubs, everything. Everything was fine. It was perfect. With the money left over from my $5,000 scholarship, I paid ten months' rent, bought a printer, a portable air conditioner, and a television set and stand. My brother sent me $7,000 for the rest of the furniture. On October 22, 2010, just a little over a year after we became homeless, my kids and I moved into the new apartment. To this day, I have my apartment, I have my furniture, and that's my home.

In spring 2011, I joined the Living Well Program, which was the first life skills empowerment program for domestic violence survivors. There were seven of us in the class, six other women and me. Living Well empowered me a lot; it strengthened me a lot to move on. I get excited whenever I talk about it now. There were classes on goal setting and money management. We did art therapy and relaxation techniques. Every class began with an inspirational reading. I took every single reading home and wrote it down in a book. I still look at that book sometimes. The program also matched us with mentors, and it was amazing because my mentor was from Trinidad, too.

Being around the other ladies who went through some type of abuse really, really helped me. At first the people in the group were shy with each other. Nobody would speak or communicate anything about the abuse. Even I didn't want anybody to know who I was or what I went through. But the facilitators, Sophia (Worrell) and Kate, and the social work intern, Iana, talked to us and did some little games and role-playing, and everybody started to open up. The ladies ended up becoming so close. At night, after the sessions ended, we would go to McDonald's and continue talking. I used to invite the ladies home with me because I was the only one who had a home we could go to. In the shelters, I was very shy and didn't make any friends with the other domestic violence survivors. Now I had many friends.

Susan, I remember when you came to help us write our life story. The first day you said, "Just write whatever you can remember about your childhood days." My childhood days were beautiful. I was very loved by my parents and my brothers and sisters. I could tell that part of my story with my eyes shut. But when I finished that, I said, "Susan, I can't write about what happened next." And you said, "Just write whatever you can. It doesn't have to make sense. It doesn't have to come in order." But I was very scared to let the story of my abuse out. I was scared that if I wrote something, my ex-husband would somehow find out where I was. Although I already had my own apartment and an order of protection, I was still scared of him.

The facilitators said, "Write it down. It will give you a sense of independence. You're going to get your self-esteem back." And that's what made me start writing about when everything turned from heaven to hell. I had written a little of my story for the shelter scholarship, but I didn't go into great depth. At Living Well, I was encouraged, step by step, by you, Sophia, Kate, Iana—and of course the other ladies—to tell the whole truth about my whole life.

It did help me get my self-esteem back—just writing my story and giving it to someone to see who I was and what I was before I met my abuser. Just looking back and seeing the difference from my mom's home to when I got married, to coming to America, to going into the shelters, something that I never even heard of and never dreamed I would be living in, given the family I came from. It was like, "Wow! Did I really go through all this in the past seven years? And I was still able to take care of myself and not go into drinking or smoking or just running away or leaving my kids and going back home or trying to kill myself!" I felt encouraged to know that I had all that strength. It gave me confidence that I could do anything I want to do. In the shelters, you get services that teach you how to move on, and you learn how to apply for public assistance, and this and that, but it wasn't that encouraging. In Living Well, the facilitators said, "You have power inside yourself, and you can bring that power out."

On Speakers' Night, three of the ladies and I told our stories in front of a whole audience. When it was over, I was introduced to Marc Greenberg, and he invited me to join the Speakers Bureau. Then I met Dennis Barton and started going public with my story in different schools and universities. I went with Dennis to Connecticut, to New Jersey, and to Staten Island. I went to a university over on the west side of Manhattan, and I spoke at the theatre at Symphony Space. Usually we had a big crowd, and at Symphony Space the crowd was huge.

There were times when I cried while telling my story. There were times when I just had to pause and take a breath. After I was done, people often came up and said they were proud of me. They didn't even know me, but they were amazed that I was so brave. Up to this day, I go out and tell my story on behalf of the IAHH. It's my passion to give back as much as I have received.

I was also a co-facilitator for two Living Well programs. It was a big challenge to come back to a new group of domestic violence survivors. Just like with my class, nobody in the new group wanted to say their story. Nobody wanted to speak to each other. So after the first two sessions, I asked the lead facilitator, "Can I share my story? They want to talk, but they're afraid. Me being a survivor, it might break the ice and help them come out with the words that have been bundled up inside them." So I did tell my story, and I said, "I'm no different from you guys. I was abused, and I know how you feel. But the only way to survive this thing and to get through this is to talk about it." There were tears in the ladies' eyes when I finished, and they came up and hugged me. These ladies stayed in the program, they started writing their stories, and they started talking to each other. It was really, really nice.

Since getting my apartment, I have had a few different jobs. First, the people at the shelter called me and asked me if I could come to babysit. In April 2012, I got my work authorization, and in May, I started to work in the shelter as a child care aide. Next I got a Certified Teachers' Association license online, and now I work in a private daycare agency. I am a full-time assistant teacher with kids two to three years of age. I just love working with kids. I think it's because of the family where I came from—I always enjoyed being with my many nieces and nephews and all the grandchildren.

I have applied for my green card, and my lawyer says I should get it in six months' time. Once it comes, I will finally be able to go back home and visit Trinidad. When I get there, I will have a lot to adjust to. Two of my six brothers are dead. I also lost my mom in July 2013. Without my green card, I was unable to ever see her again. Sometimes when I'm talking to my elder sister, it comes to my head to ask, "How's Ma?" and then I say, "Oh, she's gone." So I know I have to go home and deal with all that. In some ways, my mother's life was very different than mine. She was never abused. My mother never got that at all. And I am working. She was always a housewife and mother. But the strength to keep a family together, I have that from my mother. I have the ability to do hard work, just like how I used to see my mother doing hard work around the house. She had so many kids and the house was always clean—grandkids coming in and out, and the house would still be clean. I see my mother in me at all times.

My eldest son is getting his bachelor's degree at Baruch University. I see him as a very responsible, independent, strong-minded person. He takes care of his siblings. He disciplines my daughter, like he puts her in a timeout, or he will send her to her room or turn the TV off. He helps my younger son with his homework and talks privately to him about teenage life and his development. He is the father figure in the home, and I admire that about him.

My youngest son is a more private person. He spends a lot of time by himself. He is very sensitive. He also has a very verbal expression about him that is so educated and proper. I just love to hear how he speaks. Everybody does. He is so fluent and clear, and if he gets in a debate, he will make sure to win. I tell my youngest son, "You have to be a journalist." What I didn't get from my two sons, I'm getting from my daughter. They were calm, but the girl is all business and feistiness and commotion. We have to keep our eyes on her all the time. She doesn't do a lot of mischief, but it's like she's always wanting, wanting, wanting something. She's very fluent in how she speaks. And she understands so much! It's like sometimes I say, "How you know all this already? Where you learn that already?" My daughter has this elegant way about her, where she loves to dress up fancy. I'm totally the opposite. I love wearing sneakers. My only problem with my daughter is that she is going back and forth to the hospital with her sickle cell anemia. She has to be on penicillin and folic acid daily. But other than that, she's as healthy as can be.

I'm proud of my kids and the strength they have gained. And I'm proud of myself for being a survivor. I got away from the abuse, and I kept strong, and I didn't go back to my batterer. Now I walk with my head high up in the air. When I speak to domestic violence victims, I tell them that there is help out there. But they have to keep away from their batterers if they want to change their lives. If, at the end of the day, they go back to their batterers, at least I can say, "You know what? I did my part. I helped. I did what I wanted to do."

Reflection
Reverend Michelle Nickens

Reverend Michelle Nickens was director of adult education at Rauschenbusch Metro Ministries in Manhattan from 2009 to 2016. She served from 2014 to 2016 as coordinator and facilitator of the Living Well life skills empowerment program for women made homeless due to domestic violence. She wrote this reflection during that time.

In 2005, I was a first-year student at New York City's Union Theological Seminary, an institution of liberal theological education with an expressed commitment to social justice. From the moment I stepped through the gates of Union, I fell in love with the program. I loved the challenging classes, the brilliant professors, the impassioned student body. I also treasured the creative daily chapel services, usually planned and led by one of the many student groups that are part of the Union community. I checked the announcement board daily to see what the topic of the day in chapel would be.

I will always remember one particular day in 2006 when I looked at the board and read that the subject of that day's chapel would be domestic violence. And I will always remember my reaction: "Domestic violence? No thanks, I'll pass." No hesitation, no inner conflict, just a firm decision that I would avoid chapel that day. I could not have begun to tell you why I had such a knee-jerk reaction. I only knew that I felt alarm, distaste, and a visceral resistance to aligning myself with "those" women and that cause.

Of course, the holy irony of it all is that just three short years later, in 2009, I would become an outspoken activist and advocate against domestic and family violence. I wrote and performed a one-woman show about sexual abuse for my graduate thesis project, was ordained to the ministry in 2010 by Metro Baptist Church, and began leading workshops and panels on domestic violence and child sexual abuse throughout the New York metropolitan area. And then in 2014, I began leading the Living Well life skills empowerment program for women who have experienced the dual trauma of homelessness and domestic violence. So what happened to me during those three interim years? How did I go from "No thanks, I'll pass" to "Yes, this is my life's work"?

In essence, due to the unwavering encouragement of certain professors and alumni at Union, I found my own voice and began to explore my own story. I came to realize that I, like many women, had allowed myself to be silenced by unhealthy past relationships and by a traumatic childhood in a family ravaged by alcoholism. I'd come to believe that advocating for others was fine but to tell your own truth was whining. I had been conditioned to believe that uncomfortable and inconvenient truths were best left unexplored and that family secrets were best left unchallenged. Breaking the silence could lead to ridicule and ostracism at best, and could be dangerous to one's health, safety, and security at worst. If I tried to speak, my usually strong voice would falter, and a terrible sense of danger and foreboding would set in. It seemed better to suffer in silence, to numb out with food or alcohol, to be invisible.

Ten years later, I now understand that the confusing morass of emotions I felt is all too typical among those who have experienced abuse, particularly if that abuse happened at the hands of loved ones or those on whom we are dependent.

At the beginning of each cycle of the life skills empowerment program, most of the women are overwhelmed by the challenges they face. They are by turns depressed, angry, hurt, defeated, withdrawn, and frustrated. Many have the extra responsibility of providing a safe space for their children. The result, as one participant stated, is that "your spirit gets beaten down so bad, you don't even recognize who you are anymore, because you've been told that who you are is wrong. You look in the mirror, but you don't see any good in yourself."

However, it doesn't take much time to see that, despite all they have endured, the women in the program have tremendous strength and resilience. In addition to physical abuse and homelessness, many have survived substance abuse or incarceration. As children, many witnessed their mothers being abused or came from homes where their caregivers were ill equipped to give them the love, nurture, and safety they needed. As adults, they often live with their own children in domestic violence shelters, the locations of which are secret. While on the one hand, this helps ensure the women's safety, it also reinforces the sense of secrecy and shame that is already so crippling to their self-esteem. The staff support varies greatly from shelter to shelter. Sometimes, the very social and governmental services created to assist these women are insensitive or even abusive.

When asked why they have joined the program, their responses are varied.

> "Because I don't want my children to grow up like I did. This cycle has to stop with me!"

> "I know I need a place where I can talk about what happened to me, because people who haven't been through it just don't understand."

> "I've never known what it feels like to trust a group of women. I think I need that."

Over the course of the fourteen-week program, a healing transformation begins. Twice a week, we gather faithfully to share a meal, to share our joys and fears, and to give each other encouragement and understanding. Through this process, the women begin rediscovering their voices or finding them for the very first time. They begin to make sense of their own stories through talking, writing, art therapy, movement, meditation, mentoring, and sessions with guest speakers.

The women bring their children to the group, where they too are fed and cared for in their own space by our childcare team. The children love coming to the program. They bond with each other on those evenings, coming to think of each other as brothers and sisters. Several of the women say that their children often remind *them* about the meeting, saying, "Mommy, it's Wednesday. Remember, we go to the church this evening!"

Most of the women in the Living Well life skills empowerment program have never known the support of a circle of women. More so than any other aspect of this program, I believe that the *circle* is the source of healing. When we gather around the table, we create a bond. We come to trust the integrity of the circle, knowing that it is strong enough to hold each of us and any pain we might bring with us. In the circle, the women begin to recognize themselves in each other. They identify both their commonalities and their unique gifts, which are affirmed by the other participants. The circle becomes a place where they can dare to laugh, dare to cry, can feel supported and celebrated in their victories.

As I reflect on the impact that the program has had on my own life, I too must acknowledge the power of the circle. Hearing the stories of the women, witnessing their profound resiliency and determination, seeing the developing bonds of mutual support that allow them to unburden and ultimately experience moments of joy and connection—all of these experiences have a profound impact on me. As an abuse survivor, I know that working with these women has helped me heal.

And as a minister, I recognize that work as a deeply spiritual experience. I see God in the faces of the women of the Living Well life skills empowerment program. I feel the Spirit in those startling moments of recognition when we know that we are more alike than we are different. I often think that Jesus's time with his disciples might have resembled a Living Well circle. The disciples were renamed, repurposed, and renewed as they were called to become their best selves, to heal and be healed, to create a new model of community. I journey with the women of Living Well for fourteen short weeks. But each cycle is always also a journey with God.

Life Story
Heidi Nissen

Heidi Nissen was born on January 23, 1961, in New York, New York. She graduated in 2013 from the Life-Skills Training and Empowerment Program (L-STEP), the life skills empowerment program at Xavier Mission.

I was born in Manhattan—I believe it was Mt. Sinai Hospital—on January 23, 1961.

We lived for a short time, maybe six years, on Clinton Street, a little below the Lower East Side. It was what they call a tenement or railroad flat. I think we were on the fourth or the fifth floor. I remember the gigantic bathtub, and I remember the toilet tank was up above the toilet. I remember you walked in this gigantic door and right across was Dad's studio. I have echoes of being in there. The room was dark. It smelled like paint and turpentine. Everything is kind of patchy, but I'm feeling shades of browns and maroons. If I'm not mistaken, my father preferred oil on canvas. But he mostly made his living from carpentry—a little of this and that. I think painting made him happy. Drinking probably made him temporarily happy. I don't know if he was happy sober.

My father was Puerto Rican and Spanish. Dad didn't speak with an accent, so he was probably born in America. Mom was an Iowa girl, the middle girl in the family. They called her the black sheep. Mom went to Iowa Lutheran College and got her RN. She came to New York to be with a guy who moved to New Jersey. And that didn't pan out. But she started working in New York and she met my dad. There's Tracy who's

ten months older than me and Tina who's four years younger than me, and that's my mother and my dad's children.

One of the last memories I have of my father on Clinton Street was a birthday party with a teddy bear cake and candles, and we were all singing. Dad was a real player. Mom was pregnant with Tina. Big Kathy— who became Dad's second wife—was pregnant with little Louie. There was an argument, and Big Kathy hit Dad with a frying pan. There is no sadness attached to the memory, so it must have been commonplace for there to be that kind of an uproar. Dad ended up with a handful of kids. There were two or three that we never got to know.

My mother was always sad, always busy, always distracted. It seemed like she was always dealing with some crisis. I remember Tina falling into the garbage can and cutting her elbow on a broken plate, and Mom was furious because she had to take her to the emergency room. Mom could be scary, yeah. She had a very intimidating way about her. We used to call it "the look," because she would get this look on her face and everybody would shut up. When I look at old pictures of my mother she's got this great smile, and I just want to think, "Okay, she was happy." But how could she possibly have been that happy with so much going on? There's a picture of her in an old-fashioned starched cap when she graduated from nursing school, and it's like looking in the mirror. She looked exactly like me.

When I was four or five—no, I must have been a little older—our building was condemned. That winter Mom was really sick. There was no heat, and I guess the electricity had been cut off. On Christmas morning, she was in bed, and we all cuddled up with her under the blankets. There were no presents. There was nothing. When I think back, I always get a sense of gloom in that apartment. I remember Mom saying we were the last family in the building. That's probably where the sense of desolation came in. Years later, I found out that the mayor and the city had condemned a whole slew of tenements because they wanted to knock them down and build projects or condominiums—I don't know. But our particular block never got built on. To this day, it's just a parking lot for city parking. I always wondered what life would have been like if they hadn't knocked down our building and I'd grown up there.

When I was seven, they moved us into the Robert Fulton Projects on Nineteenth Street between Ninth and Tenth Avenue, which is now Chelsea. I always laugh when I say "Chelsea"; when I was growing up, we weren't even allowed on Eighth Avenue because it was junkie heaven. Oh my God. The nicest buildings in the neighborhood were our projects. They were only a few years old, and they had these great little parks. We were on the twenty-third floor, and the southern view was awesome. You could look straight down the Hudson over into Jersey. You could see the Statue of Liberty. From our bedroom, you could look down on the Maritime Building. We were just glued to the windows all the time.

Soon after we moved in, Dad came and took us kids for a walk. He must have snuck a bottle with him because we went to the piers. These weren't the Chelsea Piers back then. They were beat-up and dangerous with big holes in the floor, no place for kids. Suddenly, Dad jumped in the water and decided to go for a swim. But when he was done, he couldn't find a ladder to climb back up. "One of yous go to the gas station over on the West Side Highway and call the police," he told us. I think I went, because I remember coming back on the pier and there was a police boat helping Daddy out of the water. Later in the patrol car, he had soaking clothes and a bloody face. They must have beaten the hell out of Daddy for taking us on the pier. The firemen who brought us home told my mother, "If you ever let these kids go with him again, we will call Child Services."

Dad had let her down again. I think my mother was sad and disappointed constantly. Circumstances just kept dealing her crappy hands. She had such short periods of actual happiness. Moving into the projects was kind of a shock for her. Where we were before, on Clinton Street, it was Hispanic and Jewish. In the projects, there were a lot of black people. It wasn't that my mother was racist so much as unknowledgeable. From what I understand, there were no black people in the suburban area where she grew up unless they were housekeepers or maids. Mom eventually overcame her prejudices, but for a long time she was afraid of everything. She didn't want us playing downstairs in the park. We couldn't stay in after-school groups. She just didn't feel safe letting us socially interact with other kids. And she ate a lot. Mom didn't have a drinking problem. Instead everything was about food. She was very heavy, and I thought it was normal. I mean, what is normal—especially when you're growing up?

When I was nine or ten, Mom herniated some discs in her back. At that time, they'd put you in traction for an injury like that. So my sisters and I had to go down and stay with Dad and Big Kathy, who were living in Baltimore. I'm guessing my father was sober by then, because I don't think Mom would have sent us down there otherwise. A few years later, I found out that my dad was actually smoking a lot of pot. But I guess my mom trusted him enough. Anyway, she was stuck in the hospital and really didn't have a choice.

Living in Dad and Big Kathy's house was different, that's for damn sure. Dad always seemed to be working. There were seven of us kids there, including my four half-siblings and my two sisters. Whenever Big Kathy wanted peace and quiet to write in her journal or read or get stoned—which was a lot of the time—she'd lock us in the front room. The house was cool, though. The front room had these gigantic windows that led out to the porch roof. Whenever we got tired of being locked up, the oldest of us would go out on the porch roof, climb down a huge pine tree, and leave the little ones in the front room. All of us were always in trouble. Kathy loved to yell and screech, and she had the best screechy voice, oh my God. We used to call her the Wicked Witch of the West.

After Mom got better and we went back to New York, she started dating Omar, a very handsome Egyptian guy. He had been a patient on the floor of her hospital. I don't remember when Mom married him. I think they did a city hall thing.

Sometime after that, my sister Tracy stole some money out of the change jar on my mother's dresser. Omar thought I'd done it. Mom wasn't home from work yet, and he hogtied me with some telephone wire, so I really couldn't move. When my mom came home, I was basically lying on my side on the floor. They got into a rip-roaring fight. I think there were times that Omar hit her, not that I ever saw. Things between them just got weirder and weirder. Still, they had a baby together, my youngest sister, Zadie.

The first time Omar molested me, I was maybe between eleven or twelve. I told Mom, and she didn't believe me. I remember being hysterical about that. She took us to a doctor friend of hers, Dr. R——, and he didn't even physically examine me, just talked to me. He told Mom I was probably lying about Omar because I was jealous of the time that she spent with him. And the horrible thing is that it happened a few times after that—rape, molestation, hands. There were a lot of other things that went on in the house that I'm not going to include. Sometimes I think about these things, and I rip apart with self-examination. It still keeps my head spinning. How do you resolve this kind of crap?

I started failing a bunch of classes even though I was a good student and loved reading. In seventh grade, my English teacher would hand me books, and I'd just suck them down. Maybe it was a way to escape. You read a story, and you get into something else that has nothing to do with your own reality. I love fiction. Even some nonfiction has been incredible for me. As a kid, I could walk down the block and sit on the curb with a book and stay there for hours.

I must have told my teacher or the assistant principal what was happening with Omar, because one day Daddy came all the way from Baltimore to meet me in the school library. But I'm guessing that his hands were tied, because nothing came of it. My father didn't rescue me. I didn't go back to Baltimore with him.

When school ended that year, I tried to run away to my friend's family in Prospect Park. They were going to their summerhouse, and I wanted them to take me. But when I got there, they had already left. I sat down on their steps and started crying. A woman who turned out to be a judge came out from the house next door. I told her everything about Omar, and she called the police.

After that, I stayed with some family friends from our old building until the state took me away and put me in St. Michael's, this gigantic group home on Staten Island. They put my older sister Tracy in there too. What a nightmare St. Michael's was. I remember kids breaking into my locker, stealing all my clothes, and setting fire to my boots. My roommate beat the hell out of me, so they took her out of the room. Around New Year's there was a riot. All the girls and guys started beating each other up. It was like a mob going from one place to another. They had to lock down the cottages where the babies and toddlers were. My old roommate beat me up again because she thought I was stealing her boyfriend, who was this psycho guy on a bike who kept following me around. After the security guard got her away from me, he had to hide me in the office for safety.

A bunch of kids got arrested, but they were back within a couple of days. Where else were they going to go?

Soon after, I packed whatever clothes I had left, climbed down the fire escape right outside my bedroom window, caught a bus to the Staten Island Ferry, and went back to my mom's house. By then, Omar was gone. He had beaten and raped someone else, and Mom finally pressed charges. Nothing ever came of it in court. Meanwhile, Tracy had also run away from St. Michael's, but nobody could find her. Of course Mom was freaked out. Years later, Mom told me she had heard rumors Tracy was in Hell's Kitchen, and she used to ride the bus looking for her. But for four or maybe five years, my older sister just disappeared.

After Omar left, Mom started interacting more socially with the people in the neighborhood. Maybe she had no choice. When Tracy, Tina, and I were growing up, Mom never let us go outside. With Zadie, she went out and got to know the neighbors. People wanted to talk to Mom because she was very understanding and patient—well, with everybody else she was. You knew that when you talked to Mom she was really listening. Mom was like me that way. She also became the neighborhood nurse. When Pat C. was screaming in labor with her seventh child, Rosemarie called Mom, and Mom ran over to the next building, and baby Patrick basically popped out into her hands.

At seventeen, I was sent back to live with my father in Baltimore, and it was like the clash of the titans. Dad thought I was acting out, which I probably was, but I was resentful. I was pissed. By then he was divorced from Big Kathy, and I spent more time at her house than his. There were times I didn't feel loved by my mom—it's hard for me to say that—but I always felt loved by Big Kathy. Even though she had fallen off the wagon and was in the middle of a meltdown, I knew Big Kathy loved me. She wanted me to be whole. She felt like I needed to reassert my independence, and she was right. It was Big Kathy's idea to get me a place in a women's residence run by nuns. Dad was so mad about that, he tried to get me put in jail for running away, but pretty soon he dropped the charges.

Anyway, I didn't stay at that residence long. By summer I had hitchhiked to Virginia, where I ended up living in a Christian halfway house for about eight months. I met Larry in church. He had red hair and was so adorable and seemed so smart that I ended up moving in with him. But Larry was possessive and a control freak and an alcoholic. He smoked a lot of weed, and I smoked with him and occasionally drank too much. He punched me around a little—broke my nose. At one point we had sex and I didn't want to. It's interesting because I couldn't even in my own head call it rape, even though it really was. I was eighteen years old. He was twenty-seven. Within literally weeks of leaving Larry, I moved in with another guy. This one was a mental abuser. He belittled me and belittled my decisions, and for the longest time, I thought he was right.

Shortly after my nineteenth birthday, I threw a bunch of my clothes in a bag, stole some of my boyfriend's weed so I could sell it to pay for my trip home, and moved back into the projects with Mom. By now, my oldest sister Tracy had shown up with a daughter. Tina and Zadie were there too, and Mom was taking care of all of us. She wasn't in bad shape at the time. I got a job at Gristedes and got my foot caught in a conveyor belt because I was riding on top of it like a horse's ass. I was sober, but I had nothing better to do. The belt sucked the sneaker and ripped open my foot. I lost a lot of the ball of my foot. I'm lucky I have my toes. In the emergency room, Mom came and made some phone calls and found out who the best orthopedic surgeon was and demanded him. When I was on disability, I took my GED and passed.

That summer, Mom took us all on a vacation to Toms River, near the Jersey Shore, and I met Stefan in a bar on the boardwalk. I fell head over heels, I guess. Stefan was very soft-spoken and never argued. I went from abusive boyfriends to somebody that wasn't going to raise his hand to me, wasn't going to try and control me. We got an apartment, and I got pregnant. I was twenty-two and very happy. We didn't have a pot to piss in—I worked as a waitress in a Denny's, and he was a landscaper and got unemployment in the off-season—but I was in love with love.

My son Craig was born in Ocean County Memorial Hospital in Toms River. I remember when they put my baby on my belly. He was just this little, precious thing that was mine and that I could love and would love me. I knew I was going to have a boy, because I knew God wouldn't give me girls and make me go through what my mother went through. Nobody was ever, ever going to hurt my son. Nobody was ever going to lay a hand on him. I could barely let him go into his father's arms. I still can't believe he's a thirty-one-year-old adult now and takes care of himself.

Stefan and I got married, and after a few months, we came back to New York City and lived with my mom. I had quit drinking and smoking weed because I was breastfeeding my son and I wasn't going to do any damage to him. Stefan got a job through a friend working for a furniture mover. My mother, of course, gave us extras. We never had to worry about running out of groceries or running out of diapers, because if the budget ran too tight that week she would throw a few dollars our way.

Heidi and her son, summer 1984

We'd only been living with Mom about a month when I realized Stefan was hiding some of the money from his paycheck. "I'm tired of budgeting," he told me. "I want some party money."

We got into this huge argument. I said, "You know how tough it is living here with my mom? Yes, I love her, but there's always an argument." I was shouting at him now, and I pushed him. Stefan reached up—really just to defend himself—and he pushed me back. I jumped up, and I flipped out and hit him—just clocked him because at this point nobody was going to push me. Stefan had never raised his hand to me in his life, but I was so furious, I threw him out of the house.

The marriage wasn't working anyway. I was just trying to live out some kind of fantasy. We were barely in love and both unhappy, and Stefan expressed it by hiding money and using it to party. We had gotten married for the stupidest reasons and decided to end it. But Stefan loved his son. He sent child support and visited Craig on weekends.

As for my mother, Craig was her sunshine. She definitely favored my son over Tracy's daughter. Craig was the boy she didn't get to raise because she raised all girls and she grew up with all girls. My son loved my mother very much. In fact, he called her "Mom" because everybody in the house called her "Mom." He never called her "Grandma." I was "Heidi." And she was "Mom." It probably should have bothered me, but it didn't. I knew I was Craig's mommy. He was a very precocious and smart kid. When I realized he was talking circles around his first-grade teacher in public school, I decided to stick him in Catholic school because the nuns would sit on him a bit better. Like me, my son always had a book in his face.

Though I had lots of different jobs (school-crossing guard, bookkeeper, waitress—my favorite job was in a pet store), Mom still handled the bills and bought everybody extras. Then her back problems returned, and she had to have more surgery. The doctors went in and removed her damaged disks, and then they shaved the bone and fused it. But Mom was still in constant pain and stopped being able to work. She was getting welfare, but welfare is a joke. Tina and I had to start supporting everybody. Mom owed money, and we were floating a thousand-dollar rent. Zadie was in Notre Dame High School, and tuition was a killer. Plus there was Craig's tuition and Tina's part-time classes at Borough of Manhattan Community College.

The stress for my mother was unbelievable. She had survived her first failed marriage and survived the nightmare of Omar. And now, her bad back and the pain kept her from working. She had to trust her daughters to take care of things, and she wasn't sure we could handle it. Mom was angry and afraid, and the emotional upheaval gave her a ministroke. I can't remember whether the stroke came before or after Mom's back surgery. It sounds weird, but I'm confused about time.

We were always arguing. I wasn't raising Craig to my mother's standards, and she was always bitching about why I couldn't do this or that. I remember one particular morning, I was late coming home. My boyfriend at the time—a terrific guy from New Zealand—had picked me up after a double shift. The plan was to have some quality time and some sex, then run back to wake up Craig and get to my waitressing job by 11:00 a.m. But by accident, I fell asleep, and when I finally got home, my mother was shaking and furious. She called me a whore right in front of my son. I was late for work and trying to take a shower. Mom was crying and yelling and screaming at me, and all I could say was, "I'm sorry, Ma. I gotta go to work." I couldn't even yell back at her because I knew she was just scared. She had been through a lot.

When she was angry, my mother had a mouth. She could cut your heart out and hand it back to you before you even knew what had happened. Maybe she was mentally abusive sometimes. I don't know, because other times she could be so generous and so giving. I know I'm always excusing other people's bad behavior, but it's hard not to excuse my mother's behavior, because she was a wreck.

When I was twenty-eight, my father found out he had leukemia and lung, pancreatic, and liver cancer. I can't remember who contacted who, but my father wanted to see us and meet his grandson. Craig and I went to Baltimore for about a week. Five or six months later, I went back with my sisters to say goodbye. It was like Dad was waiting for all his children to come see him before he died. He even got on the phone and told my mother he'd always loved her. His only boy, little Louie, was the last to arrive, and Dad passed soon after.

I couldn't stay for the memorial service—either I had to get back to work, or I just didn't want to be there, I can't remember—but he had a huge turnout. After Daddy got sober, he did all these good things for other people: he was an active member of AA, he sponsored several people, and he became an alcoholic counselor. I was little resentful, though, because when you're a member of AA, you're supposed to make amends to the people that you've messed up. But Dad never made amends to my sisters and me and my mother. I'm pretty sure he didn't make amends to Big Kathy. Maybe what he did for other people was a form of atonement, but for a long time that bothered me. It sounds needy, but you need your father. You need your parents.

For many years, nothing in particular happened. Mom kept getting more depressed and more reclusive. She put on another fifty pounds, and she was already a heavy woman. Food is a great crutch. It's easy to turn to, because you figure, well, at least it's not drugs or alcohol. I myself would be as big as a house if I didn't make myself move.

Then, in August 2002, Mom had a pain in her arm and thought she was having a heart attack. When we took her to St. Vincent's Hospital, they ran all kinds of tests. After the CT scan, a doctor approached her and said, "You have glioblastoma multiforme." Not a heart attack. Brain cancer. "If we don't operate and take some of it out, you're going to be dead in a couple of weeks."

My mother started to cry. As an RN, she knew exactly what she was dealing with and exactly what would happen. She wanted the surgeon to talk to her straight from the hip. "There's no way I can get the whole tumor out," he told her. He said that it would come back and kill her no matter what.

The very day after my mother's surgery, I was riding my bike down Eighth Avenue, and this cabbie turned and hit my face with his side view mirror. I took an ambulance to St. Vincent's, where my mother was recovering in the ICU. When my sister Tina came downstairs and saw me, she started laughing hysterically—Tina is one of those people who laughs whenever she gets scared. "How bad is it, Tina?" I asked. My sister handed me the cab's side view mirror, which had somehow ended up in my purse—talk about a memento! It looked like I had been beaten with a bat. WHAM! My eye was swollen shut, and there was massive skin trauma. The bruising was hideous. It didn't bleed away or heal for months. People thought I'd been abused, and I hated that. Just the idea of being beaten up hit me really hard. But the worst part was that when Mom revived from the surgery, she kept asking, "What happened to your face? What happened to your face?" I can't remember how many times I had to tell her about the accident.

About two weeks after my mother's surgery, one of the nurses told me, "You can't take her home; you can't do it." At this point, my mother weighed 350 pounds and just getting her out of the bed was overwhelming. Mom had to go to Calvary Hospital in the Bronx, a place she used to call the Tombstone when she was a nurse.

I visited almost every day. I would just sit there and talk and read to her and myself. They were giving her antipsychotics because the tumor was growing again. Mom barely recognized anybody, and my sisters didn't visit much. Shit was hard for her. She was talking to people that weren't there, and she kept swearing there was a man in the corner. She called out for my son a lot. Mom died on January 24, 2003, the day after my birthday. Tina and I were there, and it was very peaceful. It was such a relief to watch her stressed, angry face just completely relax. She was sixty-eight years old.

Her memorial service was really incredible. So many people showed up from the neighborhood. The funeral home gave us this big room, and we welcomed people to stand up and talk about their experience with Mom. The service was only supposed to last from five until eight thirty, but we ended up being in that room until eleven o'clock. Everyone wanted to say something about my mother. She was the neighborhood nurse, and they loved her. Even when she became homebound, people would come just to sit and talk with her. She helped make them feel better.

Not having Mom at home was really hard for me to accept. The apartment felt dead, like a ghost house. I was alone most of the time. My sisters had moved out. Craig had a steady girlfriend and didn't need me anymore. For years, Mom had needed me. It was just like being a parent. Now she was gone, and it really set me adrift. It was so lonely. I was doing pet care at the time, and I don't know why, but I found myself giving up my clients, just handing them off to other people.

I also left my deli job because of my arthritic knee. The cartilage was so severely damaged that there was very little left. For several years, I'd taken opiates—OxyContin, Vicodin, Codeine—all legal prescriptions in the beginning. But after Mom passed, I started taking way too much. When I ran out, I would buy my friend's whole prescription bottle outright. I realized what I was doing, but I didn't even think about it. The whole thing was kind of a blur. There was just a lot of numbness—the numbness of the opiates and the numbness in my head. At the same time, I stopped eating. I lost like sixty-five pounds. I'd been heavy for most of my life, but now I weighed 135. I looked awful—it wasn't a healthy loss, if you know what I mean.

I didn't want to see the people in my neighborhood and hear them say, "How are you? Oh, I'm sorry about your mom. Do you miss her?" I really didn't want that. I mean, I would always say hi to the neighbors and smile, because it's easier to smile. I'm sure some of them knew about my drug habit, but nobody ever said anything. As for my son, he had no idea it was a problem. Wait—now that I think about it, he was aware. He told one of my sisters, "Mom likes her pills."

In early 2006, I got involved with a sweet man named Joe, but he was broken like I was. He was addicted to coke and alcohol. I did my opiates and drank with him. Joe stayed in my apartment a lot, but he wasn't really living there—he lived with his mother and sisters nearby.

I became a problem payer with the rent. I was supposed to be on welfare. But every once in a while, I would stop doing the paperwork and let welfare lapse. When 2007 came, the building wouldn't let me renew the lease. My family had been in that apartment since 1968. I probably could have fought the eviction, could have stopped it. But the more I thought about it, the more I said, "You know what? Let them take the apartment. I can't stand being here anymore." It wasn't my home. It was my mother's home. Even though I had gotten rid of her furniture and redecorated, it was always going to have echoes of Mom. I just couldn't deal with that.

I can't remember if the eviction notice on the door was pink or green. The one they mailed to me was pink. I'm sure of that. My sisters came and took the photo albums and things like that. I found foster homes for my three cats. Other stuff I gave to the neighbors. The only belongings I tried to pack up and keep were my books—I had over a thousand of them. The sheriff was supposed to put them in storage, and if I could pay the storage bill, I'd get them back. That never happened. I have always hoped that somebody either donated my books to a library or at least didn't throw them out. When the marshals came, all I took was a duffle bag of clothes and two or three boxes of personal belongings I couldn't live without, like Craig's schoolwork and different projects I'd saved since he was a kid. It was February 3, 2007.

Craig wanted me to stay with him and his roommate in Queens, but I didn't want to inflict myself on my son. I didn't want to be a burden. For about a week, I slept on a fold-out cot in the basement of Rozzo Fish Market, where Joe worked. I didn't mind the smell. Believe it or not, fresh-cut fish actually smells good, like watermelon or cucumber. From February to June, I squatted in an unfinished apartment that Joe's friend was working on. I could take a shower and bath, but there were no appliances, there was no electricity. It was cold. I slept on a mattress on the floor with a sleeping bag.

Sometimes Joe would pick me up, and I'd ride around with him in the van. He said he was going to borrow money from this one or that one, and we were going to get a room. I kept expecting Joe to help me save myself, and he couldn't. He was never going to save himself either. I think we just stayed together to have somebody to hold, you know what I mean? That was all we ever got out of it from each other.

Throughout this whole mess, the only people I maintained a relationship with were Joe and my son. When I finally decided to go into the shelter system, my son wasn't thrilled. But I explained to him, "Look, they'll help me get an apartment. They'll help me get my life back on track." That was my reason for going into the shelter—to go through the system and get an apartment at the end.

First they sent me to the assessment center in Brooklyn. It was surreal. I had a pair of my mother's surgical scissors and a Swiss Army knife I'd kept with me ever since I lost the apartment, because I was by myself a lot of the time and you never knew what was going to happen. They wouldn't let me bring those things into the shelter. I remember being really distressed and asking if they could hold them so I could take them to somebody the next day, but they didn't do that kind of thing. So I took my mother's scissors and the knife and went outside and threw them in the corner garbage can. I had to wait for a bed on very uncomfortable chairs. I finally got a bed after midnight. It was in a huge room with about fifteen other women, and we each had a locker.

The next day, I met with a very nice lady. She wanted to get me into a medical shelter, because I needed knee replacements. I was using a cane at this point, and I really needed a walker. She contacted two medical shelters—one in Manhattan and the other one in Brooklyn—and basically they were waiting for a bed. But two weeks later, the nice lady went on vacation, and her supervisor said, "It's time for you to go; we're sending you to X—— Women's Shelter."

"Is that a medical shelter?" I asked.

"No," she said.

"But we were waiting for a bed in a medical shelter."

"Well, we don't have one right now, so you're gonna have to go to the first available one that has an elevator—which is X——."

They bused me over to the place, but when I got there, they didn't even have a bed for me.

The intake person said, "You have to wait for the bus, and they'll take you somewhere else. This is your permanent shelter, though. You'll come back tomorrow, and if there's a bed—"

"You're not making any sense here. Why, if this is my permanent shelter, are you sending me away?"

The people were not very kind about explaining it, at least not that night. I got to Tillary Street Women's Shelter at four o'clock in the morning and had about two or three hours sleep.

The next night, I went back over to X—— Women's Shelter. I was sitting in this tiny waiting room, and someone started screaming, "She stabbed somebody, she stabbed somebody!" Security ran upstairs, and everybody else had to step into this huge courtyard. From the windows, you could see this woman fighting and security kind of backing her down the stairs. Her shirt was all bloody because she had attacked someone and smashed the mirrors in the bathroom. While the woman screamed incoherently, the police cars started showing up. They had to take her out in cuffs and put her in an ambulance. Turns out this was normal for X—— Shelter. The cops were there two or three times a week.

Within those first few weeks, I quit taking the opiates—just on my own. It was not easy, but I didn't have the money for it. I wasn't seeing a doctor at this point, and I couldn't get it through Medicaid. I was in terrible pain both emotionally and physically. I started drinking more often— like trading one drug for another—and stuffing my face with shelter food, which was a heavy carb diet at this place. After three or four months in the shelter, I put back on all the weight I had lost—sixty-five pounds.

I went to their on-site psychiatrist, and they put me on a serotonin thing—I can't remember the name of it. They also gave me something to help me sleep, and whoa, I started taking half of that because it turned me into a zombie. I got all my paperwork together to apply for an apartment, and my caseworker supposedly submitted it to the Department of Homeless Services. For several months, I waited for a response and didn't get one. My caseworker got fired in the interim. Turned out she'd been selling crack to some of the clients and was smoking it herself. I got this from a security guard who wanted to get in my pants.

Anyway, I got assigned a new caseworker, Miss Hernandez—a really sweet woman. She told me we had to reapply for housing because the old caseworker had never submitted my packet. I was hysterical. "You're kidding, right? We have to do this all over again? All of this paperwork and all of this nonsense?" Within two weeks of submitting the new packet, we got a response that I was eligible for what they called level I and level II housing. Miss Hernandez also helped me get my Supplemental Security Income.

Meanwhile, I stayed in X—— Women's Shelter maybe ten, eleven months. During the day, I read or watched movies. I hung out in the courtyard and played spades with the girls. One was named Mo. She was a transgender female trying to become a male. She was a sweet kid—just lost, like a lot of folks. But Mo could not tolerate stupid people. And unfortunately, people behave stupidly in the shelter system. She was about six foot two, and she had a big mouth, and she was always drinking. For some reason, she thought I was the bee's knees. Mo just couldn't believe that this fat little white lady could play spades and laugh at somebody cursing her out.

I was very lucky. I could have gotten my butt beat so many times in the shelters, and I didn't. I did have a couple of close calls, though. Once a woman grabbed my cane and smacked me in the leg with it. I grabbed it back and was about to hit her with it when two other residents came and pulled her away. One woman was yelling at the woman who hit me, "Don't you touch her, don't you touch her!" These women knew me. They knew I couldn't abide any physical abuse. Nobody grabs me—nobody hits me anymore!

Another time, this new woman got on the elevator, and I didn't realize she was mentally ill. "Good morning," I said cheerfully.

The woman got in, walked behind me, and whispered, "White trash."

I turned around and looked at her. "Excuse me?"

"That's right. White trailer park trash!"

Luckily, this struck me as hilarious, because my sister had just moved into a trailer park in New Mexico. I burst out laughing, and it totally defused what this woman wanted. She wanted an argument and she wanted a fight—it didn't matter if it was with me or somebody else. But I didn't give it to her. When I stepped off the elevator, she had this look of confusion on her face, like I'd disarmed her. All the antagonism and anger she was going to throw at me were gone.

Still, I always felt threatened in X—— Women's Shelter. There were constant fights. The police were always called. It got to a point where I started to "curfew violate" a lot—we called it CV. You're supposed to lose your bed and get shipped out to another shelter if you do that. For a long time, they held my bed because I had been there a while, and they knew I was just trying to get away from the craziness. Until finally, I CV'd one too many times.

First I got transferred back to Tillary. Then I got transferred to Y—— Shelter in Manhattan. That place was like being back at X—— Women's Shelter. Security was very lax, the women were whacked out of their minds, and the fighting was endless. The housing specialist was popping Xanax. During our first meeting, she kept nodding off to sleep. "Oh man," I thought to myself. "This can't be happening again." A week later, she had her pants on inside out. I should have called the Department of Homeless Services, but I didn't want to rock the boat.

Y—— Shelter was so bad that I kept CV'ing just to get shipped out of there. I spent one or two nights with Joe on his mother's couch, maybe overnight with a friend. I slept on a train maybe two or three times. That was scary. The last time I did that, somebody stole my cane while I was sleeping.

I got transferred to Casa Esperanza in the Bronx. But I decided to CV from there because I was trying to make doctors' appointments in Manhattan, which was two buses and a train ride away. So I ended up in Z—— Shelter, back in Brooklyn, near the J line. My housing specialist, Miss P——, took me to see a couple of terrible apartments. One was in the basement, and the ceilings were only six feet tall. There were overhead pipes everywhere, the bathroom was so small you could barely sit on the toilet, and there was no back entrance, which meant there was no fire exit.

"So what do you think?" Miss P—— said.

"You're joking, right?" I said. "You mean to tell me that you don't know that apartment is illegal?"

Miss P—— looked at me, surprised. "No. Really?" And I knew she was lying.

After that, I think Miss P—— was afraid of me. She probably thought I was going to call the housing department about her. Two weeks later, I got an interview for a terrific SRO in level II supportive housing. The apartment was in Crown Heights, between St. Marks and Prospect. It was small but brand-new, with two big windows, plenty of light, and my own bathtub and shower. A really nice lady interviewed me. A week later, Miss P—— came and said, "The apartment is yours." I moved in on September 24, 2011.

The following May, I had my first knee replacement at the Hospital for Special Surgery; in October 2012 I had my second. When the doctors first put me back on opiates, I was horrified. I wanted to make sure

I wouldn't go overboard again. But supportive housing monitored my meds, and by December I was weaned off the painkillers. Within several months of my second knee replacement, I was ready to move on from supportive housing to scattered-site housing. Now I have a big, one-bedroom apartment with a decent-sized kitchen on the edge of Crown Heights. It has a southern exposure, so my plants love it, and my two new cats sleep in the window.

In 2014, a friend of mine from one of the shelters referred me to the life skills empowerment program. Technically, I wasn't homeless anymore, but the facilitators thought I could benefit from the program. And I really did. Different people came to talk to us—a motivational speaker, a lawyer from legal aid, a person who taught us how to meditate. That was awesome! All of it was empowering and encouraging. There was so much positive reinforcement, and the participants were really motivated to better themselves. My mentor was this sweet lady. I'm pretty sure they picked her for me because I wasn't a tough case. In the program, you were expected to create goals for yourself, realistic goals. I wanted to develop real relationships with my sisters—that happened with one of them. I also needed to lose weight. It was a hard goal, and I still have more to lose, but my health has improved dramatically. I gained confidence talking to participants who had been through some of the same things as me.

Meanwhile, I was still hooking up with Joe every now and then, even though I knew he couldn't help me. Then one night, about two weeks into the life skills empowerment program, Joe came to my apartment, just to say hi and get a hug. Two women from the program were there with me; we were working on something—I can't even remember what it was. Joe went into my bathroom, did some blow and came out drinking a beer. His nose started to bleed.

I looked at him and started to cry. "I can't watch you die," I said. "I can't. I can't help you. I can only help myself. You need to leave, Joe. I'm so sorry, but you have to go." It was very quiet. My friends were stunned into silence. Joe got up and left. Just like that. I've talked to him once or twice since then, but I never saw him again after that.

At the program graduation, I told my life story. That was really tough. There was a church full of people. My son was there, and my sister Zadie came, which was astounding. It felt like I was talking to everybody all at once. That made it very real and scary as hell, and I was partly ashamed. But when I told my story outright and out loud, it was like, Wow! That was me then, and this is me now, and I'm okay. I'm good. I'm great. And I wasn't ashamed anymore.

I was stunned by how many people were affected by my story. When I finished, I was swamped. "You've done so well. You should be so proud of yourself," people said. There were so many hugs and pats on the back. I could barely see because I was too busy crying. My son gave me a big hug and was crying too.

Now that I've graduated, I try to go to the alumni meetings every month. I also told my story to a group of young people in Xavier High School. It was really intense. Afterward, a student came over to me and said, "When I was a baby, my mother went through the system with me and my older brother. And now she won't talk about it."

"I can understand why she might not want to," I told him. "When I was in the shelters, I stopped telling my son what was happening, because it upset him so much. It must have been really hard for your mother."

I've also volunteered for a Health Home program run by CAMBA, the organization that helped get me my first apartment. I gave away condoms and talked to people about safe sex. I enjoy helping people. I like to see people do better for themselves. In a way, I feel like I'm a good example of this. I can say, "You know what? I did this. You can too."

I think of my ability to communicate with people as a gift. At the shelter, I got along with certain women that other people were horribly afraid of, that everyone else would shun. It's probably because I don't see people in shades of black, Hispanic, or Asian, or poor, wealthy, or middle class. People are just people, and I like people. I even have hope for some of the losers of the world. Maybe I get this from growing up in the projects, where you're dealing with everybody. It was just a big mix of races and incomes. It's interesting, because I never thought of my family as poor. I didn't realize what "living in the projects" meant until I got older. I've never been embarrassed about where I'm from or what I've had to do or the way life has happened.

I used to think I was just like my mom. And I'm strong like my mom. And I can take a lot. I mean, my mother really was a spectacular lady. I know this interview may give the impression that she wasn't cool, but Mom was cool. It's just that she was so unhappy and so miserable in the last years of her life. And I know that had to do with guilt about her decisions. I know she sometimes felt like we were big disappointments, but she blamed herself for the way her daughters' lives worked out. And I think that her unhappiness and her way of thinking is what kind of did her in. Mom was sixty-eight when she passed, but she was ready to be done.

That's my biggest fear—that I'll end up like that. But I don't think I will, because I'm cheerful by nature. Once in a while, you look at someone smiling, and you wonder if that's just a disguise. But I think I am generally a happy person. Despite all the bullshit, I've managed to get through a lot of insanity. Even when I didn't realize I was coping, I was. The fact that I didn't become a walking vegetable after the Omar thing, or being abandoned by my dad, or being poor—I guess I have an inner strength and resilience. I definitely gained strength from the situations in my life. Of course, there were times when I was hysterical or crying. Sometimes it still hurts. But as far as I can remember, very little has barreled me over.

I have to tell you, it's astounding. I'm like a Weeble toy. Remember how they used to say, "Weebles wobble, but they don't fall down." That's like me. I don't fall down, or if I do fall down, I get right back up. That's what it is. My mom gave up on life, and I'm not ready to give up. Yeah, I wobble, but I just keep moving.

Making a Difference
Marc Greenberg

Marc Greenberg is cofounder and executive director of the Interfaith Assembly on Homelessness and Housing (IAHH) and co-developer, with New York Catholic Charities, of the life skills empowerment program model for homeless adults. Marc has also helped establish life skills empowerment programs for formerly incarcerated individuals, domestic violence survivors, homeless veterans, and other homeless adults.

Recently, after nearly eight years without contact, I received a Facebook message from Charles, a graduate of a life skills empowerment program founded by the IAHH. He informed me that he was now securely housed and retired after a decade of doing administrative work with Madison Square Garden and that he wanted to drop by the office with a donation for us. When Charles arrived a few days later with a one-hundred-dollar money order, he said, "Marc, I'd like to help. The IAHH helped me find my way at a crucial moment in my life, and I'd like to give back." As it turned out, the IAHH had recently joined a broad campaign called Bring It Home: Better Funding for Better Care, which was advocating for the state to ensure sufficient funding for its existing 40,000 supportive housing units for people with psychiatric disabilities and special needs, many of whom would otherwise be homeless. Our organization had been tasked with identifying, contacting, and encouraging faith leaders to sign a letter to the governor endorsing the campaign. With his administrative background and personal history, Charles was the perfect person to assist in this effort. For me, getting the call from Charles was another affirmation that my thirty-plus years of work with the IAHH has been right on track.

I have always believed that all people are connected in a deeply spiritual sense, but it was an experience I'd had as a young man at the famous concert at Woodstock that first taught me the value and inspiring power of collective action. A hippie community based in New Mexico called the Hog Farm had been asked to help keep the concert peaceful and had decided that the best way to do so was to give free food to the crowd. Having found my way to the banquet because I was hungry, I decided to stay and help feed others. There were five stations: one where the food was being produced and four where the food was being served, each covered by a tarp. All at once, a torrential rain hit the area. Everyone ran underneath the station tarps for shelter. At the same time, the thought came to me—and certainly to other people there—that the station with the stoves and all the electrical equipment was in danger of shorting out. Suddenly, as if by an unspoken signal, each group ran out from underneath its tarp and detached it, then brought the tarp over to the food production station to make a wall against the water. It was as if everyone had experienced what I like to call a group mind: an idea that seemed to emerge from me but that was also a part of the common understanding of everyone around me and that resulted in collective action. At Woodstock, I realized that if people can agree on a thought and a vision, we can make it real.

A little more than a decade later, I attended a very inspiring interfaith event on ecology, spirituality, and community at the Cathedral of St. John the Divine. At the time, I was working with my father to help establish a medium-sized, relatively successful family business but was finding it increasingly stressful to work with him. That night, as the event at St. John drew to a close, I stood up and said, "There are about 300 people here and at least half of us live in New York City. Can't we continue this conversation?" A few days later, James Parks Morton, dean of St. John, called me and said he wanted me to help him bring the conference participants together. Soon after, he invited me—"a nice Jewish boy from Long Island"—to begin volunteering at St. John the Divine, the world's largest gothic cathedral. This led to my coordinating a number of social justice projects and ultimately to my work addressing homelessness.

Dean Morton seemed to know every important public figure at the time—including Mother Teresa, Jackie Onassis, Reverend Jesse Jackson, and the Dalai Lama—and he invited many of them to speak at St. John the Divine. It was at the cathedral where I first heard the great Rabbi Marshall

Meyer preaching from the pulpit, which led me to join the rabbi's synagogue, Congregation B'nai Jeshurun. At St. John, I met many of the most socially active faith leaders in New York City and beyond. Thanks to Dean Morton's expansive vision, I got to know people who expressed their passion for justice through a religious medium. I was exposed to a wide range of wonderful communities built on love that believed in working together to build a better society.

By the early 1980s, there was a glaring need for such social improvement in New York City. Though America was in the midst of the greatest prosperity in decades, a crisis in homelessness had gripped the city, joblessness in poor neighborhoods was staggeringly high, and new legislative initiatives threatened the most vulnerable Americans with the loss of basic supports. In 1982, I helped organize an event that we called the Thanksgiving Food Forum, at which we held a panel discussion about hunger and provided 1,100 Thanksgiving meals. The cathedral's Sunday Soup Kitchen, which has been serving more than 300 meals every Sunday ever since, grew out of this event.

Soon after the Thanksgiving event, I had the good fortune to meet Robert Hayes, the founder of the Coalition for the Homeless. At his suggestion, we organized a press conference on homelessness on Christmas Eve, at which the Episcopal Bishop of New York, Paul Moore, and nearly a dozen other prominent leaders of different faiths called on Mayor Koch to build more affordable housing for homeless people. This resulted in nine months of extensive conversations between faith leaders and New York City officials; the faith leaders pressed the city to respond to the homelessness crisis, and the city pledged to move forward but refused to go public about our dialogue. Bishop Moore organized a sermon series during Lent that included Robert Hayes, Mitch Snyder (a Washington, D.C., advocate for the homeless who founded a large shelter there), two homeless men who called themselves "I Africa" and "I John," and Reverend Jesse Jackson. Ultimately, this effort, along with others, led Mayor Koch to make a $4.4 billion commitment to affordable housing.

In 1983, Lillian Zerwick (who, years earlier, had been declared Woman of the Year by Mayor John Lindsey for creating the first supportive housing model) offered to be a full-time volunteer if the cathedral would dedicate itself to establishing housing as a legal entitlement. In 1984, we joined with many of New York's faith leaders, elected officials, and social service providers to form the Right to Housing Project, which was dedicated to the belief that "decent and affordable housing is a basic human right." During this period, I received guidance and support from faith leaders around the city, including (in addition to Dean Morton) Canon Lloyd S. Casson, then sub-dean of the Cathedral of St. John the Divine; Reverend N. J. L'Heureux Jr., executive director of the Queens Federation of Churches; Charles H. Straut, district superintendent of the United Methodist Church; Rabbi Gary Bretton-Granatoor, associate director of the New York Federation of Reform Synagogues; and Father Donald Sakano, director of Neighborhood Housing for New York Catholic Charities.

In 1986, the IAHH was officially founded on the belief that decent and affordable housing is a basic human right—and that in a civilized society all people have a right to live with dignity and respect, which is virtually impossible without a home. I became executive director; Lloyd Casson gave the organization its name; and we established a board of directors, which soon began to include formerly homeless people (today about a third of the people on our board were once homeless). Our mission was to go to places where homelessness was visible—like soup kitchens, shelters, welfare hotels, and drop-in centers—and ask, "Is this what we are called on to be as a society?"

The IAHH also established an annual June vigil to precede the finalization of New York City Council's budget hearings. The vigil began with a worship service in a church or a synagogue at 7:00 p.m., followed by a march to City Hall Park. There, a few dozen people—both those who were homeless and those who were not—would stay overnight, sharing stories, songs and prayers; waking at 4:30 a.m. to the noise of garbage trucks; finding privacy and washing up in the rest room of the local hospital or coffee shop; gathering in the morning for prayer circle and reflection; and then departing. For those of us who were housed, the event offered a profound experience of solidarity with those who had no place to sleep other than the streets or the shelters.

On June 1, 1988, our convocation was addressed by council member Ruth Messinger (later a Manhattan borough president) and Reverend Floyd Flake (then a US congressman). Close to 400 people attended. When the service concluded, it began to drizzle as we marched to City Hall Park. Before entering, we marched around the park, pausing for a few moments at each of the four sides (north, south, east, and west) to symbolically tear down the walls of injustice, insensitivity, inequity, and discrimination, as in the story of the walls of Jericho. At each stop, we were led by prayers and holy sounds, including a Tibetan bell and a Jewish shofar, sounded by Rabbi Rolando Matalon of Congregation B'nai Jeshurun. Approximately 120 people entered the park, some of us prepared to spend the night. Then the drizzle turned into rain.

Over the next few hours, that rain became a strong shower and then a torrential storm, much like the one I remembered from Woodstock. Most of the crowd dispersed. The few of us who remained used the park benches (which in those days were not bolted in place) to construct rain shelters and made fires in metal garbage cans to keep warm against the unusually cold night wind. By the time the sun rose and the rain finally stopped, twelve of us remained—half of us were homeless.

That morning, we met with seven of the most progressive members of the city council, including Ruth Messinger, who described the city council budget items that we might have an impact on. More importantly, the council members stated that they were at the meeting because they cared about homelessness and told us, "You need to speak with the other members of the council who did not come to this meeting." In response, the homeless members of our group decided to do just that, even if it meant staying in the park for the full month of budget hearings. "We were just told we could make a difference!" they said. And thus began Homeward Bound Community Services, an organization initiated and governed entirely by homeless people (the press dubbed them "Kochville"). From June 1 to Christmas Day, the homeless members of the vigil, joined by other homeless people from around the city, maintained a daily presence in City Hall Park, extending their stay well beyond the month of budget hearings. They received almost daily visits by the city hall press corps and took part in voter registration drives, with help from then Manhattan borough president David Dinkins and the Reverend Jesse Jackson. Every morning when Mayor Ed Koch arrived at city hall, the group greeted him by shouting out, "Good morning!"

Even as the weather got colder, approximately twenty hardcore members of Homeward Bound Community Services maintained their presence in the park. Along with the IAHH and an inspired network of volunteers, other organizations, and the host of a listener-sponsored radio show, Homeward Bound Community Services helped spearhead a series of citywide actions. A December undertaking turned out to be Homeward Bound's final effort. It began with fifty tables giving out donated food and literature about homelessness, followed by a march of an estimated 10,000 people that culminated in a rally. There, Larry Locke, the homeless, charismatic leader of Homeward Bound, was scheduled to speak along with Bishop Moore and Jesse Jackson. Unfortunately, Larry was nowhere to be found. Fortunately, Nelson Prime (another Homeward Bound leader and a contributor to *Sacred Shelter*) was willing to take his place. Nelson's speech was a powerful thing.

The final and 200th day of the City Hall Park vigil was Christmas Eve. The people in the park celebrated by decorating a city hall Christmas tree and eating a happy 200-day birthday cake. Thereafter, they stayed at St. Augustine's Episcopal Church, which was nearby and had offered them shelter. At the church, the guests held regular meetings to discuss housekeeping issues and to explore areas of personal growth and development as well as to air grievances and discuss ongoing plans involving city hall.

Meanwhile, a handful of the advocates and representatives of the faith community who had been supporting the people in the park began discussing ways we could help Homeward Bound's remaining members as well as develop a partnership with them to assist in our advocacy efforts. In addition to me, these discussions included George Horton, Joan Minieri, Sister Ann Murray (all of New York Catholic Charities), and Sister Agnes O'Grady (from the Sisters of Mercy and an economics professor at Mercy College). Our initial objective was simply to help Homeward Bound members share their stories in public as a means of humanizing and putting a face on the homelessness crisis.

Our discussions led to two related developments. One was the commencement of the Education Outreach Program (EOP), the life skills empowerment program model for homeless and formerly homeless people on which *Sacred Shelter* is based. The other was the establishment of the IAHH's Speakers Bureau, through which the IAHH arranged for homeless and formerly homeless program graduates to tell their life stories in religious congregations and other venues throughout the New York metropolitan area. In the early to mid-1990s, the Speakers Bureau averaged about 100 presentations a year, and since its founding, the Speakers Bureau has arranged for more than 1,200 presentations. For twenty years, the IAHH also ran bi-weekly planning and support meetings for the presenters.

Over the years, the IAHH has helped launch several replicate programs, beginning with Project Success (for homeless mothers, which ran from 1994 to 1996), Panim el Panim (founded in 2008), Coming Home (founded in 2010, with the Brooklyn DA's office, for formerly incarcerated individuals), Living Well (founded in 2011 for women who are homeless as a result of domestic violence), and Homecoming (founded in 2012 for military veterans). All of the IAHH's collaborative programs include at least one formerly homeless person as a facilitator, and our office has long been staffed by homeless and formerly homeless people.

Beyond running the Speakers Bureau and helping to found new life skills empowerment programs, much of my attention at the IAHH has been devoted to advocating for public policies that will help build a more compassionate and equitable New York City. Our objective is to identify and join the coalitions and campaigns that are supporting homeless people and housing justice and to find ways that the faith community can make a difference in their success. Each of the great faith traditions calls for people to stand in solidarity with our most vulnerable neighbors. Many New Yorkers of every faith are committed to justice but not fully aware of their counterparts in other faith communities and, even more importantly, not familiar with the details of housing and homeless advocacy and the rich network of organizations working to end homelessness. The IAHH's mission—and my personal role—is to help connect these people to each other.

Recently, for instance, the IAHH was a member of a coalition called Campaign 4 NY/NY Housing, whose goal was to gain a commitment from the mayor and the governor to produce 35,000 new supportive housing units over the next fifteen years. I like to call the Campaign 4 NY/NY Housing a marathon relay—it took three years and three months to begin achieving our goals and required many stages of research, meetings, publicity, and public education. One early event, a forum at the New York Society for Ethical Culture, brought together 750 people. The speakers included elected officials, homeless people and advocates, and fifteen religious leaders. As the campaign proceeded, the IAHH and our allies arranged for 283 faith leaders to sign a letter to the mayor and the governor supporting the campaign and delivered thousands of individual letters to the governor's Albany office.

In November 2016, Mayor Bill de Blasio pledged to produce 15,000 units of new supportive housing over fifteen years, and a few months later he released the funds for half of these units. In January 2016, Governor Andrew Cuomo pledged to produce 20,000 additional units over fifteen years. In April, the New York State budget included $1 billion in funding for the first 6,000 of the 20,000 pledged units. Due to a technicality, however, only $150 million of the $1 billion was made available. With the critical shortage of housing for those with mental disabilities growing worse every day, the Campaign 4 NY/NY Housing was not willing to stand by while $850 million dollars waited on another round of political horse trading in Albany. And so began the final leg of the Campaign 4 NY/NY Housing marathon. We organized a weekly rally, each sponsored by one or more of the over 100 campaign members, in front of the governor's New York City office every Wednesday (the day the governor is supposed to be there), calling for the release of the promised funding. At the rallies, we gathered, offered personal testimony, and walked in a circle holding signs and chanting, "Governor Cuomo, hear our cries. Supportive housing saves lives."

The IAHH was assigned to lead the event on October 12, 2016. When I realized this was the day of Yom Kippur, I decided to conduct that week's rally as a kind of High Holiday service. I bought a shofar and learned how to sound it, and I composed a Yom Kippur service. That morning, about forty people gathered in front of the governor's city office—homeless people, faith leaders, advocates, and concerned citizens. Wearing my tallit and yarmulke, I talked about how Yom Kippur is traditionally seen as the day God finalizes who will get written into next year's book of life. "The gates of Heaven are closing," I called out to Governor Cuomo. "How do you want to be remembered in the book of life?"

In April 2017, thirty-five weekly rallies later and nearly fifteen months after the governor's original pledge, New York State finally passed a $2.5 billion budget to combat homelessness and address affordable housing, including $1 billion immediately available for 6,000 new supportive housing units as the first installment of the governor's 20,000-unit pledge. As I wrote in an email bulletin to IAHH members, "We have much more work to do, but for the moment, it's time to recognize the largest budgetary commitment for supportive housing in US history."

In 1988, after they met with members of the city council, the homeless founders of Homeward Bound Community Services decided to take up residence in City Hall Park because, as they put it, "We were just told we could make a difference!" After more than thirty years of this work, I still identify with that sentiment. I believe I can continue to make a difference in addressing the crisis of homelessness in New York City by inviting people of many faiths to join together to find solutions. I am humbled by my work with the IAHH. I feel deeply grateful for it and blessed by the opportunity to stand in solidarity with those who have been homeless so that I can be the person God intended me to be.

Crossing Boundaries and Listening for Conversion
George B. Horton

George B. Horton is one of the founders of the Education Outreach Program (EOP), the original and longest-running life skills empowerment program, sponsored by New York Catholic Charities. George has facilitated this program since 1989 and is currently director of the Department of Social and Community Development for New York Catholic Charities.

This is a personal reflection that I hope expresses the sense of thanksgiving, deep admiration, and solidarity I feel for the people I have encountered and come to know through listening to more than 500 of their life stories since the life skills empowerment program began at New York Catholic Charities almost 30 years ago. Their life stories and the deep reservoir of faith, suffering, recovery, and courage they have shared have had a profound impact on me. Through them, I have experienced conversion, the grace of turning back to what is the heart of my faith.

In this reflection, I would like to explore the role of religious faith in guiding these life stories of survival and recovery, in urging me to cross boundaries to meet people whose experiences are vastly different from my own, and in strengthening the relationships and community that have developed among us. I am grateful for my Roman Catholic faith, which has enabled me to cross boundaries of class, race, ethnicity, economic status, and gender. And I am grateful for the participants' faith-filled stories of empowerment and healing that have inspired my own, still incomplete, faith journey.

Although I focus on my own experience as a Roman Catholic, it is important to mention that Protestant, Jewish, and other religious faiths have developed replications of the life skills empowerment program within their own congregations. Sometimes the expression of religious beliefs can be divisive and harmful, adding to so much that already segregates us. I tell this story in the hope that other believing people, both religious and nonreligious, will come to better understand and see within their own traditions the command to encounter and "welcome the stranger" and will find the gifts of conversion, healing, justice, and community that await us when we do. In the process we may uncover our own wounds and reservoirs of compassion.

I acknowledge that my life has been one of privilege. Pope Francis urges those of us who have been given so much to go out to the "peripheries" where our poorest brothers and sisters live. He speaks of a responsibility of "accompaniment," of meeting and then walking together, with people on the economic, social, and political margins. By doing this we can overcome the scourge of indifference and uncover new and more fruitful ways of structuring our relationships and communities. Not the least of the fruits of accompanying our most vulnerable sisters and brothers is the opportunity to share in the depth of faith that has guided their survival. The experience will transform us. Once there together, we will fully experience the forgiveness and mercy of God. I cannot think of a better antidote to the current political, social, and economic divisions in America, which threaten to fracture both our religious and national institutions.

Let me begin my story with some background. I grew up in a tough working-class Irish Catholic neighborhood called Morningside, in St. Mary the Morning Star Parish in Pittsfield, Massachusetts. When I walked out my door in the morning, across the street I could see the convent, the rectory, the grammar school that I attended, and just beyond, the brick bell tower of the parish church. From my street, I could see the towering smoke stacks of the GE power transformer plant just over the hill, where almost all of my family worked. (We timed our lives according to both the St. Mary's Church bells and the sharp blare of the GE whistle that blew every working day, morning, noon and evening.) The school playground was across the street, and the Brown Street ball field where we played baseball and football was just two streets away. With my sisters, Janie and Chris, I attended the parish grammar school and later the local Catholic high school, both run by the Sisters of St. Joseph of Springfield. My Irish Catholic mother was a registered nurse, and my Protestant Methodist father was a union member. Early in our education, we learned of Pope

Leo XIII's seminal document on the rights of workers, *Rerum Novarum,* and were vaguely aware that our parish pastor had acted to support workers by helping to settle a lengthy strike at the GE plant. On the national scene, Catholics were nearing the centers of power, which culminated in the election of US president John F. Kennedy in 1960, but we still shared a history and experience of being outsiders who had once lived on the margins ourselves.

My Catholic upbringing and education stressed the achievement of success and excellence in American life, being holy and moral, and practicing the Catholic faith. We also were taught a concern for others, and, even if not always socially and politically explicit (or practiced), an awareness of those who were left behind or were left out of the wealth and power structure. Both my mother and father reinforced these teachings. We learned that God loves each person and that there is a God-given dignity, a light (however easily darkened by sin!) in each one of us. Whatever we chose in life, it would not finally be about ourselves. To be Christ-like was the ideal. I was captivated by this Catholic world, attending daily morning Mass and serving as an altar boy. I was chosen by the priests to become one of them, and this became the compelling goal of my life. I could not imagine life without it. For a bright male child like me, there was much promise, much that was beautiful and good. All seemed pointed in the right direction. Mine was a privileged existence.

In fact, as we have learned over these past many years, the reality of American Catholic life was not a perfect picture. The problems of alcoholism, marital unfaithfulness and strife, and mental illness were hidden and never discussed. We lived in an Irish Catholic ghetto that not only precluded knowledge of African Americans and Jews but also made second-class citizens of French, Polish, and Italian Catholics who lived in the parish and wished to worship there. You could not serve as an altar boy (we only had altar *boys*) unless you were Irish. The harsh Irish Catholic teachings about sin, especially in sexual matters, and the guilt and anxiety associated with that were drilled into us.

There was clerical sexual abuse in our parish, of which I am a survivor. I was eight years old. Like many of the survivors whose stories I have heard in the life skills empowerment program, the experience rocked me to the bottom of my being, and I share with them the legacy of loss, confusion, and anger and the psychic hole and physical numbness that ensued. I had no idea then how pervasive the injury of this sexual abuse, and the loss that accompanied it, was and would be to me, the "tough Irish kid." Like many program participants, I experienced denial, self-recriminations, and broken relationships. I know what participants mean when they describe using substances as an escape mechanism to "stuff their feelings." Although I did not realize it at the time, my dream of becoming a Catholic priest was over. For many years later, I struggled with my relationship with the church.

After graduating from Holy Cross College, serving in the US Army, and then graduating from the University of Pennsylvania Law School in 1973, I lived my own version of the 1960s dropout culture. Over the next few years, I parked cars at the Tanglewood Music Festival; worked as a volunteer with Volunteers in Service to America (VISTA) in a college program for inmates at the Berkshire County House of Correction in Pittsfield; and then, intermittently for about four years, worked for the State of New York, taking care of developmentally disabled persons. During the late 1970s, I attended a doctoral program in philosophy at Fordham University and taught Greek philosophy to undergraduates on a teaching fellowship. In 1978, I suffered the loss of a relationship and the death of my mother, losses that shook me to my core. (In the life skills empowerment program, the grief of losing a parent, child, friend, or other family member is invariably central to our participants' stories.)

Sometime after my mother died, I ran across an advertisement in a church bulletin promoting a series of workshops in Scarsdale on the social teachings of the church. I was living in the Bronx at the time, and each Saturday for six weeks, I rode the train to Westchester for these morning seminars, where we discussed the social documents of the church, including Leo XIII's *Rerum Novarum*, John XXIII's *Pacem in Terris* and *Mater et Magistra*, Paul VI's *Populorum Progressio*, and the Second Vatican Council's *Gaudium et Spes*.

As we read and discussed these documents, I marveled at their radical demands for more just economic and social structures. Most striking to me was the assertion that the social teachings flowed out of the heart of the Gospel and its call for discipleship. To be Catholic was to live these social teachings. They emphasized the sacred God-given life and dignity of every human person; the realization of that dignity in our relationship with God, each other, and the world; the requirement for justice in all our relationships (personal, interpersonal, and global); our responsibility to work for peace and justice; and most significantly, our solidarity, especially with people who were poor and marginalized everywhere. The teachings emphasized that all must be part of the community and each had a right and a responsibility to participate in social and economic structures. A "preferential option for the poor" indicated that our overriding concern must always be for the "least among us." The opening lines of the 1965 *Gaudium et Spes, The Pastoral Constitution on the Church in the Modern World* still reverberate for me today: "The joys and the hopes, the griefs and the anxieties of the men of this age, especially those who are poor or in any way afflicted, these are the joys and hopes, the griefs and anxieties of the followers of Christ. Indeed, nothing genuinely human fails to raise an echo in their hearts." These teachings were like hearing the "good news" again, and they began to recrystallize for me what had been lost from the core of my faith. As I pondered what, at the time, seemed Catholicism's best-kept secret, I kept asking myself: "Does my church believe this?"

During the 1960s and '70s, following Vatican II, a liberation theology movement arose in Latin America in response to the vast poverty, disparities of wealth, and oppression of poor and indigenous peoples. Liberation theology emerged out of a pastoral process in which the poor found their voices and articulated their experience of poverty, disenfranchisement, and oppression and then reflected together on that experience through the lens of the Word of God in scripture. People formed small base communities for solidarity and communion. There was trust and confidence that by coming together, poor and oppressed people would gather the strength to act for justice and to help realize the reign of God, a reign that would extend to all of us. A special role for the poor and oppressed in the establishment of God's kingdom was recognized.

In 1981, I went to work for New York Catholic Charities in the foster care office. Beginning in 1986, I became the director of New York Catholic Charities' Ministry to the Homeless and Hungry, an office that was established to support the profusion of church shelters, emergency food programs, and agencies that had mushroomed in New York City to respond to the growing crisis of homelessness. Along with homeless people and various advocacy groups and leaders (including Marc Greenberg of the IAHH), New York Catholic Charities worked for reform and to enact public policies for housing, homelessness prevention, drug treatment, and mental health services. New York Catholic Charities also supported homeless service and empowerment efforts by organizations like Part of the Solution (POTS) in the Bronx, founded by Father Ned Murphy, Society of Jesus; the Emmaus Community in Harlem, founded by Father David Kirk; and the Life Experience and Faith Sharing Associates (LEFSA), founded by two Catholic sisters, Sister Dorothy Gallant and Sister Teresa Skehan (discussed in more detail below).

It was in partnership with the IAHH and with support from those organizations that the first life skills empowerment program, the Education

Outreach Program (EOP), was formed at New York Catholic Charities. The initial concept was quite simple: to elicit the voice of people who had experienced homelessness; to forge a path to personal and communal restoration; to raise public consciousness about their lives; to restore their place in the community; and to reform public policies that were harmful to them.

Although not always explicitly, we relied on the principles of Catholic social teaching and liberation theology to guide the life skills empowerment program. The overarching goal was to offer the participants a program that would belong to them and be a source of solidarity for them. The storytelling curriculum was based on the idea that each person had a God-given dignity and right to be heard when decisions were being made about their lives. The voices and histories of people who had been silenced were heard, and their infinite value and right to a place at the table were recognized. We hoped the participants would gain self-esteem and begin to heal by writing their life stories and that sharing these stories with larger audiences would change stereotypes about homelessness, help reform harmful public policies, and contribute to restoring the right order of society.

During the past thirty years, I have had the privilege of sitting with more than 500 of our program participants, listening to their life stories, and helping them prepare for their presentations to their classmates. Only one principle has guided me, a gift of my faith and Catholic social teaching: an absolute trust in each one of them as created in the image and likeness of God and in their capacity to shine the God-given light within them. Their stories in turn are faith stories. The presence of God or a higher power in their lives, although not always explicit, is almost universally acknowledged. Certainly, participants' exposure to 12-step programs and their participation in church communities (mostly Protestant) have helped form the faith that they bring. However, at bottom (often the turning point in their lives is when they "hit bottom"), they truly and deeply believe they have been saved. Many, many times I have heard in their memories of complete despair—often when in the midst of uncontrollable addiction, complete loss of self, breakdown, and utter loneliness—an allusion to the psalmist pleas: "Out of the depths I cry to you, O Lord!; O Lord, make haste to help me."[1] This is the moment of conversion for the participants, the moment of turning in their lives. Although theologies may differ, the conviction of this fundamental experience cannot but move others who hear these stories and awaken to a dimension of the presence of the divine, often unthinkingly discarded in today's society.

In our New York Catholic Charities' life skills empowerment program, these stories are first told within the presence of our program participants and staff. This is an amazing moment when participants recognize similarities and connections in their stories and realize they are no longer alone with their pain but can help each other make it through. A swell of compassion emerges, often accompanied by tears. The shame and denial that have prevented participants from speaking dissipates as they understand that the traumas they experienced in childhood were not their fault. The participants end up ministering to each other. You can see the soft candlelight of self-esteem begin to flicker as the speakers come to recognize their own self-worth and uniqueness. Participants often observe that they would not be who they are without their pasts and that they are in a unique position to do outreach and help others who are still alone, "sick and suffering" on the streets.

Near the end of the program, participants tell their stories in public, often at the Fordham University Lincoln Center Campus Chapel, to past graduates, friends, family, and mentors. They stand there recounting their emergence from a life of eating out of garbage cans, shooting up in drug dens, experiencing sexual abuse and domestic violence, and living on the roofs of abandoned buildings. Their courage, resiliency, and faith inspire a palpable sense of pride and gratitude among the audience. It is a moment of conversion for the speakers, for their listeners, and for me. *Deo gratias* can be the only refrain.

In our EOP life skills empowerment program (and in religious congregations and drug and alcohol programs), many participants begin to find a sense of family, community, and home. Another organization called LEFSA (Life Experience and Faith Sharing Associates) further deepens this experience. As described in the Introduction, LEFSA, now a sponsored ministry of the Sisters of Charity, was founded more than thirty years ago by Sister Dorothy Gallant (Sisters of Charity) and Sister Teresa Skehan (Sisters of Mercy), who felt a call to come to New York City to work with people who were homeless and living in the shelter system. From the beginning, LEFSA focused on the empowerment of homeless people, and the nuns incorporated principles from liberation theology, including reflection on life experience through the light of scripture, to change oppressive conditions of society.

Thirty years later, LEFSA's emphasis on the significance and empowerment of the person who has undergone suffering and oppression has resulted in a leadership composed primarily of formerly homeless people, including my friends James Addison and Deborah Canty, whose stories are recounted in this book. James is the program director and Deborah is a LEFSA team member. This group of formerly homeless people conducts weekly prayer, reflection, and scripture sessions in New York City shelters; monthly gatherings for study and leadership; monthly men's and women's support groups; and a weekly street ministry to homeless people living in and near New York City's Port Authority Bus Terminal. LEFSA also supports public policy efforts, including housing, prison reform, and anti-racism advocacy. LEFSA provides a stable and lasting family for its members.

I myself am one of them. I attend the LEFSA men's group and when I can, the Saturday Leadership study days. There I find prayer, faith sharing, study, welcome, and absolute acceptance for all. Barriers that create isolation and separation are removed. Transformation becomes a possibility for everyone. It is this gift of community that I most treasure, where I am most spiritually at home, and where my journey of conversion is most alive. I cannot say enough about the impact that Sister Dorothy, Sister Teresa, Deborah Canty, James Addison, and the men and women members of LEFSA have had on my life.

Once restored to faith, compassion, and community, our EOP life skills empowerment program participants and friends almost always want to give back to the community. More than one has chosen some form of church ministry, including LEFSA. Our graduates also work in nonprofit organizations, drug and alcohol programs, and domestic violence shelters; they volunteer in food pantries, soup kitchens, and 12-step programs. They help people find housing and participate in public policy advocacy. One of our graduates always prepares a poem for LEFSA celebratory events, and many of our graduates have returned as keynote speakers for our life skills empowerment program graduations. The light, once rekindled in them, becomes a light for others as well. The old adage that to teach a person to fish is better than to give a person a fish results in a better outcome when we teach a person to fish for others. In this way, acts of outreach to others who are still lost expand and multiply, like ripples in water.

Not all of our participants stay. Some disappear, while others return after a time away. Many have died. The trauma these women and men have suffered in their lives—childhood sexual, physical, and mental abuse; the loss of parents and siblings at early ages; imprisonment, drug addiction, and other social ills including poverty, discrimination, and disenfranchisement—make the Christian symbol of the cross, redemption and resurrection, a hopeful sign that can be sustaining as they follow the difficult road of recovery. Though many may no longer be physically present, they remain in the living memory of our life skills empowerment program and LEFSA communities.

Dorothy Day, a founder of the Catholic Worker movement (and whose cause for Catholic sainthood is now underway), lived out the conviction that every person we encounter has the "light of Christ" in them and deserves infinite respect and love. She was also fond of saying "all is grace." I am grateful for all the grace that has been given to me: my faith, our program mentors and teachers, and my coworkers at New York Catholic Charities—especially Sister Ann Murray, a Holy Child sister, now retired, who began the life skills empowerment program with me; Alison Hughes-Kelsick, who has faithfully directed our program for the past twenty years; and Monsignor Kevin Sullivan, executive director of New York Catholic Charities, for his participation as a program presenter and for his support and friendship over all these years.

Above all, I am grateful for the participants in our life skills empowerment program, who have taught me about faith and have helped me cross boundaries to find the gifts of conversion and community, the "sacred shelter" waiting on the other side.

Acknowledgments

Like the life skills empowerment program for homeless and formerly homeless individuals that *Sacred Shelter* represents, the composition of this book has involved an entire community. The book began in 2013 when George Horton told me he had long dreamed of its existence. Along with James Addison, Dennis Barton, Marc Greenberg, and Michelle Riddle, we formed an advisory board that collaborated in planning the book's goals and details. Throughout the many years required to complete the project, the people on the board have guided me and "had my back," as Michelle Riddle was apt to put it. I am deeply indebted to each one of them.

There is no adequate way to thank the thirteen people who relate their life stories in *Sacred Shelter*. What they did was courageous and intense. It required hours of interviews, searching self-consciousness, and brutal honesty. People told me about their deepest beliefs, their greatest joys, and their most painful memories—these last were often overwhelming and numerous. Why were they willing to expose themselves this way? Without fail, all the memoirists in *Sacred Shelter* said they opened up their lives to be of service. Their history of overcoming homelessness and other traumas, they hoped, would inspire and help others. They did it to be generous. That I was entrusted with their words is one of the greatest honors of my life. I cannot pretend to have been worthy of it.

Thanks are also due to the other contributors who wrote short reflections about running or volunteering for a life skills empowerment program. Their words speak to the caring community the program both

305

depends on and helps foster. I am particularly indebted to my rabbi, Jeremy Kalmanofsky, for bringing the life skills empowerment program to Congregation Ansche Chesed, where I first learned about it.

I am grateful to Fordham University for the 2014–15 Faculty Fellowship that helped me launch this book and for subsequent support provided by Faculty Research Grants, a Book Publication Award, a Dean's Internal Funding Award, and several grants from the English Department's Faculty Research Expense Program. My friend, colleague, and department chair par excellence Glenn Hendler oversaw and supported many of my efforts to get funding. I thank everyone at Fordham University Press, and especially Fredric Nachbaur, for shepherding *Sacred Shelter* through the publication process and turning it from an idea into an object. The two anonymous reviewers for the press helped me make it a better book. Bruce Gilbert produced the beautiful portrait photography.

When I first began *Sacred Shelter*, I had no idea of the logistical complications and manuscript challenges that awaited me. Today, I am indebted to many people for having managed them. Amy Starecheski, co-director of the Columbia University Oral History Master of Arts Program, responded to countless emails about recording equipment and transcription help. Through her, I met Samuel Robson, an oral history program graduate, who—after teaching me how to use the equipment (not an easy task)—lovingly and painstakingly transcribed all the interviews and then put most of them in chronological order. Beth Adelman, humanities grants officer at Fordham, generously proofread and commented on an earlier version of the manuscript. At a pivotal juncture, Anita Lightburn, director of Fordham's Beck Institute for Religion and Poverty, offered excellent suggestions about how to structure it. Samantha Sabalis, both before and after receiving her PhD from Fordham's English Department, was my trusted and encouraging assistant. She researched and helped shape the bibliographical information in the Introduction, repeatedly proofread the manuscript, secured photographs, and corresponded with the contributors. After Samantha's assistantship ended, Julia Cosacchi, a current doctoral candidate, masterfully continued the project. When my final deadline loomed large, a mountain of new questions arose, and I was at my wit's end. Thanks to Lynn Bayard, Carolyn Casselman, Lewis Clayton, and Katherine Zinser, I received the quick and invaluable help I needed. I truly appreciate their hard work and goodness.

Thanks also to the OpEd Project, which influenced this book in so many ways, and especially to the organization's indefatigable founder, Katie Orenstein, and to the wise and generous Catherine O'Neill Grace.

From nearly the beginning and certainly to the end of this project, Karen Pittleman has been my organizer, my advisor, my anchor, and my friend. Her great good sense and unfailing encouragement gave me stamina and hope (as did her readiness to laugh at my jokes and to text me photos of guinea pigs wearing hats). *Sacred Shelter* exists because of her help.

I am blessed with many dear friends who buoy me. Here I name only those who have been of particular assistance with this book: Julia Barclay-Morton, Robin Bower, Lenny Cassuto, Laura Dukess, Diva Goodfriend-Koven, Eve Keller, James Krasner, Jules Law, Melanie Rubin, Laura Tanner, and Wendy Wall. I am especially indebted to Allyson Booth, Frank Boyle, and Elizabeth Kolbert, who read and commented on portions of the manuscript. Frank Boyle also lent me his office, in which I conducted several interviews.

My family has been a constant source of support. Thank you to my brothers Mark Greenfield and Ben Greenfield; to my brother- and sisters-in-law Laura Barnett, Abby Greenfield, John Rinehimer, and Barrie Weissman (with a special shout out to Laura, whose expertise in oral history informed this book); to my mother-in-law Thelma Weissman; and to my beanstalk of a nephew Jack Allen Greenfield.

My beloved parents, Judy and Jay Greenfield, have been keenly interested in this book and helpful at every stage. They are also my role models. Growing up in my parents' home, I learned that it was my obligation to oppose social injustice and to help build a more tolerant and inclusive community. In their own ways, large and small, my mother and father did this all the time—and still do. I am guided by their generosity and kindness.

Though they are all grown up, my children, Anna Weissman and Lenny Weissman, remain my pride and joy. Both of them amaze and inspire me.

Matthew Weissman championed this book from the start. As always, his love and humor have sustained me. He is my comfort and my home.

Susan Celia Greenfield
July 2018

Notes

Introduction

1. The definition of *homeless* is complex and contested. The McKinney-Vento Homeless Assistance Act, passed by Congress in 1987, describes a homeless individual as one "who lacks a fixed, regular, and adequate nighttime residence" or whose residence is a temporary shelter or institution or a "public or private place not designed for . . . regular sleeping accommodation for human beings." Quoted in Neil Larry Shumsky, *Homelessness: A Documentary and Reference Guide* (Santa Barbara, Calif.: Greenwood, 2012), 234. Christopher Jencks argues that this definition obscures the fluid ways many homeless people move between conventional housing, shelters, and the street on a regular, even weekly basis. *The Homeless* (Cambridge, Mass.: Harvard Univ. Press, 1994), 6. The Congressional definition also ignores the "hidden homeless population" who double up with friends or relatives, though the definition of homeless children and youths in the McKinney-Vento Act was expanded in 2001 to include those sharing others' housing. Barratt A. Lee, Kimberly A. Tyler, and James D. Wright, "The New Homelessness Revisited," *Annual Review of Sociology* 36 (2010), 503; Roy Grant et al., "Twenty-Five Years of Child and Family Homelessness: Where Are We Now?" *American Journal of Public Health* 103, no. S2 (2013), e3. According to Craig Willse, the very term *homeless* is ideologically suspect because "it directs attention to an individual, as if living without housing is a personal experience rather than a social phenomenon" with structural roots. As an alternative, Willse advocates using the term *housing deprivation*, which "expresses that living without housing is systemically produced and must be understood as the active taking away of shelter." *The Value of Homelessness: Managing Surplus Life in the United States* (Minneapolis: Univ. of Minnesota Press, 2015), 2.

Joel Blau discusses different definitions of *homelessness* and their ramifications for policy in *The Visible Poor: Homelessness in the United States* (New York: Oxford Univ. Press, 1992), 8–9.

2. As Blau explains, "More than any other single phenomenon, it is the interaction between the relative decline of income and the relative increase in housing costs that explains the growth of the homeless population" (*The Visible Poor*, 75). "Simply put, the number of housing units affordable and available to the lowest income Americans is far less than the number required." Alex F. Schwartz, *Housing Policy in the United States: An Introduction* (New York: Rout-ledge, 2006), 34. Lee, Tyler, and Wright describe the "emerging consensus in the sociological research community that homelessness is, fundamentally, a structural problem rooted in the larger political economy: too many poor people compet-ing for too few low-income housing units" ("The New Homelessness Revis-ited," 514). Also see the National Coalition for the Homeless fact sheet, "Why Are People Homeless?" July 2009, http://www.nationalhomeless.org/factsheets /why.html.

3. For a brief summary of the policy changes that diminished affordable housing, see Deborah K. Padgett, Benjamin F. Henwood, and Sam J. Tsemberis, *Housing First: Ending Homelessness, Transforming Systems, and Changing Lives* (New York: Oxford Univ. Press, 2016), 19, and Schwartz, *Housing Policy*, 36–37. For a longer summary, see Blau, *The Visible Poor*, 60–76. On Reagan's 70 percent reduction of HUD's budget authority, see Schwartz, *Housing Policy*, 40. On the notorious HUD scandal during the Reagan years, see Blau, *The Visible Poor*, 72–73. Though Reagan's reductions were particularly severe, cuts to HUD are not unique to Republican administrations; in 2011, President Obama reduced HUD funding by 5 percent. Melissa J. Doak, "The Housing Problem," in *Social Welfare: Fighting Poverty and Homelessness*, 2011 ed. (Detroit: Gale, 2011), "Rea-sons for the Lack of Low-Income Housing," http://link.galegroup.com/apps /doc/EJ1529200106/OVIC?u=nysl_me_fordham&sid=OVIC&xid=4536166a. On the loss of SROs, see Blau, *The Visible Poor*, 75; Jason Adam Wasserman and Jeffrey Michael Clair, *At Home on the Street: People, Poverty, and a Hidden Culture of Homelessness* (Boulder, Colo.: Lynne Rienner Publishers, 2010), 9; and Coalition for the Homeless, "Why Are So Many People Homeless?," accessed July 22, 2016, http://www.coalitionforthehomeless.org/the-catastrophe-of -homelessness/why-are-so-many-people-homeless. In a biting critique of the neoliberal capitalist motives underpinning current approaches to homelessness, Willse argues that "what to do with the homeless, rather than what do about housing" or about "poverty alleviation" has "become the obsession of govern-ment policy, social service practice, and social scientific inquiry" (*The Value of Homelessness*, 54).

4. Blau, *The Visible Poor*, 33–59, and Padgett, Henwood, and Tsemberis, *Housing First*, 16. For a good summary of the effects of welfare and employment changes in New York City, see Anthony Marcus, *Where Have All the Homeless*

Gone? The Making and Unmaking of a Crisis (New York: Berghahn Books, 2006), 37–38. For an explanation of the transition from the Keynesian welfare state to the current neoliberalist model and the resulting lowering of wages and cuts to social programs, see Jan Rehmann, "Root Causes of Poverty—Neoliberalism, High-Tech Capitalism, and Economic Crisis," in *Pedagogy of the Poor: Building the Movement to End Poverty*, ed. Willie Baptist and Jan Rehmann (New York: Teachers College Press, 2011), 53–66. Reaganomics is generally blamed for the economic conditions that created modern homelessness, but Democratic administrations have perpetuated the problem; the devastation resulting from President Clinton's 1996 Welfare Reform Bill is especially notorious. David Wagner and Jennifer Barton Gilman, *Confronting Homelessness: Poverty, Politics, and the Failure of Social Policy* (Boulder, Colo.: Lynne Rienner Publishers, 2012), 142, 150–3, 166; also see Rehmann, "Root Causes of Poverty," 61–62. For good summaries of the overall relationship between the loss of affordable housing and the rise of poverty and income inequality, see Desiree Hellegers, *No Room of Her Own: Women's Stories of Homelessness, Life, Death, and Resistance* (New York: Palgrave McMillan, 2011), 5–11; Talmadge Wright, *Out of Place: Homeless Mobilizations, Subcities, and Contested Landscapes* (Albany: State Univ. of New York Press, 1992), 13–14; and Wagner and Gilman, *Confronting Homelessness*, 23–26. For a detailed explanation of the more recent crisis in housing affordability and availability for the poor, see Alex F. Schwartz, *Housing Policy*, 11–43.

5. After 1975, African Americans were far more likely to be homeless than during the previous skid-row period (when the average homeless person was a middle-aged white man). For a good summary of the socioeconomic and historical sources of this racial change, see Kenneth L. Kusmer, *Down and Out, On the Road: The Homeless in American History* (New York: Oxford Univ. Press, 2002), 241–3, and Wagner and Gilman, *Confronting Homelessness*, 143–4. On the greater proportion of homeless people of color and especially homeless African Americans since the 1970s, see Lee, Tyler, and Wright, "The New Homelessness Revisited," 505; Padgett, Henwood, and Tsemberis, *Housing First*, 17; Willse, *The Value of Homelessness*, 173–4; and National Coalition for the Homeless, "Who Is Homeless?" Aug. 2007, http://www.nationalhomeless.org/publications/facts/Whois.pdf.

6. *Sacred Shelter* does not focus on homeless families, but it is important to recognize their unprecedented growth beginning in the 1980s and the dire effect this has had on children. According to Roy Grant et. al., "It is clear that the size of the homeless family population consistently increased during the 1980s and thereafter. There were about twice as many homeless families in 1987 as there were in 1984. By 1993, 43% of the nation's homeless were families with children, and 30% of all homeless people in the United States were children" ("Twenty-Five Years of Child and Family Homelessness," e3). The trend has continued. In November 2016, New York City homeless shelters

housed 15,899 families every night, with family members making up "more than three-quarters of the 62,840 people in homeless shelters." Giselle Routhier, *Family Homelessness in NYC: City and State Must Meet Unprecedented Scale of Crisis with Proven Solutions* (New York: Coalition for the Homeless, Jan. 2017), 4, http://www.coalitionforthehomeless.org/wp-content/uploads/2017/01/Family-Homelessness-1-2017_FINAL.pdf. For a series of articles focusing on a homeless New York City child and her family, see Andrea Elliott's "Invisible Child" series, *New York Times*, Dec. 9, 2013, http://www.nytimes.com/projects/2013/invisible-child/#/?chapt=1.

7. "Our History," Interfaith Assembly on Homelessness and Housing, accessed July 22, 2016, http://www.iahh.org/about/our-history. On New York Catholic Charities' early involvement, see J. L. Lauria, "Vigil for Housing," *Catholic New York*, June 16, 1988.

8. John Jiler, *Sleeping with the Mayor: A True Story* (Saint Paul, Minn.: Hungry Mind Press, 1997), 22. See Marc Greenberg's reflection in this volume for a different perspective on this event.

9. Though many "advocates for 'the homeless' argue that unhoused people are incapable of organizing on their own, archival and contemporary evidence belies the assumption. . . . The historical record is rich with evidence that impoverished people can and do organize." Daniel R. Kerr, *Derelict Paradise: Homelessness and Urban Development in Cleveland, Ohio* (Amherst: Univ. of Massachusetts Press, 2011), 249. The members of Homeward Bound Community Services are proof in point. See also the actions of the Rosewater 2000 coalition in Cleveland in the early 2000s, which organized a series of camps as an alternative to inhumane conditions in the shelter system (Kerr, *Derelict Paradise*, 239–41). For successful alliances between homeless-led organizations and outside community and university groups in Chicago and San Jose, see Wright, *Out of Place*, 225–51. For more on homeless people's history of advocacy, resistance, and protest, as well as a discussion of the personal and "individual benefits" homeless activists sometimes experience, see Lee, Tyler and Wright, "The New Homelessness," 512.

10. For a media reference to the group's desire for an abandoned building, see Mark Mooney and Carl J. Pelleck, "Koch Benches Park Curfew Plan," *New York Post*, Sept. 2, 1988, and Jiler, *Sleeping with the Mayor*, 118–19, 126, 205–16, and 258.

11. Lauria, "Vigil for Housing."

12. An ongoing study of the program by the Beck Institute on Religion and Poverty (described later in the Introduction) reports, "Participants consistently acknowledged sharing their life story with program staff and mentors as a transformative experience, offering liberation, healing, growth, and self-acceptance." Anita Lightburn and Amanda Sisselman, "Developing an Evidence-Based Model for Faith-Based Community Programs for People in Transition: Report to the New York Community Trust" (New York: Beck Institute for Religion and Poverty, 2014), 6–7.

13. The Beck study is still in progress. Some initial data and information is recorded in Lightburn and Sisselman, "Developing an Evidence-Based Model." Also see the following newsletters from the Beck Institute on Religion and Poverty: *Coming Home 2017: Rye Presbyterian Church*, https://www.fordham.edu/download/downloads/id/9719/rye_coming_home_2017_newsletter.pdf and *Coming Home 2017: The Unitarian Universalist Fellowship of Poughkeepsie*, https://www.fordham.edu/download/downloads/id/9720/poughkeepsie_coming_home_2017_newsletter.pdf.

14. Wasserman and Clair, *At Home on the Street*, 2.

15. For more on StoryCorps, go to https://storycorps.org/.

16. There is a significant body of literature by homeless and formerly homeless people. See, for instance, Lee Stringer, *Grand Central Winter: Stories from the Street* (New York: Seven Stories Press, 2010) and Cadillac Man, *Land of the Lost Souls: My Life on the Streets* (New York: Bloomsbury, 2009). There is also a range of publications and creative writing programs that include homeless authors. See *The Pilgrim* magazine in Boston, the *Denver VOICE,* and Street Lit, a creative writing program run out of the Austin Resource Center for the Homeless. Zachary Jason, "Inside the Literary Magazine Helping Homeless Writers Be Heard," *Boston Globe,* May 19, 2016, https://www.bostonglobe.com/magazine/2016/05/19/inside-literary-magazine-helping-homeless-writers-heard/58FQxrMl1N4143rP5kSkBI/story.html; Laura Bond, "Deepening Literary Lives: Homeless Writers Share Their Stories," *Confluence Denver,* Nov. 18, 2015, http://www.confluence-denver.com/features/homelessness_writing_111815.aspx; and "Street Lit: Sharing Literature and Creativity with Austin's Homeless," accessed Jan. 13, 2018, http://streetlit.org.

17. Beck recorded demographic information from the program cycles that took place in fall 2012 and spring 2013: "The majority (70%) of participants were single. More than half of participants had children, with 30% recording two or three children. The majority of participants identified as African American (59%)." Lightburn and Sisselman, "Developing an Evidence-Based Model," 2.

18. Coalition for the Homeless, "Basic Facts About Homelessness: New York City," accessed Jan. 12, 2018, http://www.coalitionforthehomeless.org/basic-facts-about-homelessness-new-york-city/.

19. Alessandro Portelli, "What Makes Oral History Different," in *The Oral History Reader*, 3rd ed., ed. Robert Perks and Alistair Thomson (New York: Routledge, 2006), 39. There are a number of valuable books about homeless people that include more traditional oral histories. For a selection, see Desiree Hellegers, *No Room of Her Own*; Marjorie Bard, *Shadow Women: Homeless Women's Survival Stories* (Kansas City, Mo.: Sheed and Ward, 1990); Barbara Seyda, *Nomads of a Desert City: Personal Stories from Citizens of the Street* (Tucson: Univ. of Arizona Press, 2001); Elliot Liebow, *Tell Them Who I Am: The Lives of Homeless Women* (New York: Free Press, 1993); and Steven Vanderstaay, *Street*

Lives: An Oral History of Homeless Americans (Philadelphia, PA: New Society Publishers, 1992).

20. Michael Frisch, *A Shared Authority: Essays on the Craft and Meaning of Oral and Public History* (Albany: State Univ. of New York Press, 1990), 61.

21. Portelli, "What Makes Oral History Different," 39.

22. I did a few chronologies myself; Samuel Robson did the majority of them.

23. Of the seven graduates interviewed at StoryCorps in spring 2010, four tell their stories in *Sacred Shelter*: Rodney Allen, Edna Humphrey, Lisa Sperber, and Akira. In addition, Cindy (pseudonym) was interviewed at length by Shelia Gilliam, who was a student in the master of arts program in oral history at Columbia University. Aspects of both the StoryCorps interviews and the Columbia University interview have been interwoven into the stories that appear in *Sacred Shelter*.

24. Portelli notes that "when, as is often the case, [interviews] are arranged for publication omitting entirely the interviewer's voice, a subtle distortion takes place: the texts give the answers without the questions, giving the impression that a given narrator will always say the same thing, no matter what the circumstances—in other words, the impression that a speaking person is as stable and repetitive as a written document. When the researcher's voice is cut out, the narrator's voice is distorted" ("What Makes Oral History Different," 39).

25. Frisch, *A Shared Authority*, 83–84.

26. As Desiree Hellegers puts it in her excellent collection of oral histories by homeless women, had the speakers "themselves worked directly with the transcripts of the interviews, they would undoubtedly have made different editorial decisions than I have done here" (*No Room of Her Own*, 26).

27. Frisch, *A Shared Authority*, 84.

28. Portelli, "What Makes Oral History Different," 36–38.

29. Isabel Wilkerson, *The Warmth of Other Suns: The Epic Story of America's Great Migration* (New York: Vintage Books, 2010), 418, 270–1.

30. Richard Rothstein, *The Color of Law: A Forgotten History of How Our Government Segregated America* (New York: Liveright Publishing, 2017), xii.

31. Rothstein, *The Color of Law*, 20–21, 43–54, 63–67, and Richard Rothstein, "Historian Says Don't 'Sanitize' How Our Government Created Ghettos," interview by Terry Gross, *Fresh Air*, National Public Radio, Philadelphia, PA, May 14, 2015.

32. Joshua Freeman, *Working-Class New York: Life and Labor Since World War II* (New York: New Press, 2000), 185.

33. For an explanation on why deindustrialization had a particularly dire effect on African Americans, see Kusmer, *Down and Out, On the Road*, 242.

34. See Kevin Baker, "'Welcome to Fear City'—The Inside Story of New York's Civil War, 40 Years On," *The Guardian*, May 18, 2015, https://www.theguardian.com/cities/2015/may/18/welcome-to-fear-city-the-inside-story-of-new-yorks-civil-war-40-years-on; Freeman, *Working-Class New York*, 275–6; Elizabeth Hinton, *From the War on Poverty to the War on Crime:*

The Making of Mass Incarceration in America (Cambridge, Mass.: Harvard Univ. Press, 2016), 184, 299–300; Marcus, *Where Have All the Homeless Gone?*, 38; and J.A. Stoloff, "A Brief History of Public Housing" (paper presented at the American Sociological Association Annual Meeting, San Francisco, Calif., August 14 2004), 11, 14, 18.

35. Sean Gardiner, "Heroin: From the Civil War to the 70s, and Beyond," *City Limits,* July 5, 2009, http://citylimits.org/2009/07/05/heroin-from-the-civil-war-to-the-70s-and-beyond; see also Thomas A. Johnson, "Police Clear 'Drug Supermarket' Off Block," *New York Times,* Sept. 19, 1979, http://www.nytimes.com/1979/09/19/archives/police-clear-drug-supermarket-off-block-cautious-optimism-found.html.

36. The explicit racism underlying Nixon's policies and war on crime has now been widely recognized. Many commentators quote H. R. Haldeman, Nixon's chief of staff, who says that in 1969 Nixon told him, "You have to face the fact that the whole problem is really the blacks." Quoted in Hinton, *From the War on Poverty,* 142, and Ta-Nehisi Coates, "The Black Family in the Age of Mass Incarceration," *The Atlantic,* Oct. 2015, chap. 5, http://www.theatlantic.com/magazine/archive/2015/10/the-black-family-in-the-age-of-mass-incarceration. John Ehrlichman, another Nixon aide, wrote that in 1972, the Nixon election strategy was aimed at attracting "the racists. . . . That subliminal appeal to the antiblack voter was always in Nixon's statements and speeches on schools and housing" (quoted in Coates, "The Black Family," chap. 5). Ehrlichman later told the reporter Dan Baum, "The Nixon campaign in 1968, and the Nixon White House after that, had two enemies: the antiwar left and black people. . . . We knew we couldn't make it illegal to be either against the war or black, but by getting the public to associate the hippies with marijuana and blacks with heroin, and then criminalizing both heavily, we could disrupt those communities. We could arrest their leaders, raid their homes, break up their meetings, and vilify them night after night on the evening news. Did we know we were lying about the drugs? Of course we did." Quoted in Dan Baum, "Legalize It All: How to Win the War on Drugs," *Harper's Magazine,* Apr. 2016, http://harpers.org/archive/2016/04/legalize-it-all.

37. Coates, "The Black Family," chap. 2.

38. Hinton, *From the War on Poverty,* 315–6, and Michelle Alexander, *The New Jim Crow: Mass Incarceration in the Age of Colorblindness* (New York: New Press, 2010), 50–51.

39. Alexander, *The New Jim Crow,* 53; also see 98. Pager quoted in Coates, "The Black Family," chap. 5.

40. Alexander, *The New Jim Crow,* 99–100; Coates, "The Black Family," chap. 5.

41. Ekow N. Yankah, "When Addiction Has a White Face," *New York Times,* Feb. 9, 2016, https://www.nytimes.com/2016/02/09/opinion/when-addiction-has-a-white-face.html; Crenshaw quoted in Katharine Q. Seelye, "In Heroin

Crisis, White Families Seek Gentler War on Drugs," *New York Times*, Oct. 30, 2015, http://www.nytimes.com/2015/10/31/us/heroin-war-on-drugs-parents.html.

42. Ta-Nehisi Coates, "We Should Have Seen Dallas Coming," interview by Brian Lehrer, *The Brian Lehrer Show*, WNYC, New York, July 12, 2016.

43. Routhier, *Family Homelessness in NYC*, 6. Domestic violence was presented as a reason for homelessness by 30 percent of families with children entering temporary housing in the 2016 fiscal year, while 25 percent named eviction and 17 percent named overcrowding.

44. For an overview of the relationship between intimate partner violence and housing instability, see Gilroy et al., "Homelessness, Housing Instability, Intimate Partner Violence, Mental Health, and Functioning: A Multi-Year Cohort Study of IPV Survivors and Their Children," *Journal of Social Distress and the Homeless* 25, no. 2 (2016), 86–87. Studies have shown the significant numbers of homeless women who have experienced domestic violence. For instance, in a sample of 162 homeless adults from five emergency homeless shelters in Central Florida, 66 percent of single women and 59 percent of women with children had experienced domestic violence. Carole Zugazaga, "Stressful Life Event Experiences of Homeless Adults: A Comparison of Single Men, Single Women, and Women with Children," *Journal of Community Psychology* 32, no. 6 (2004), 647. A larger study of 737 homeless women in four Florida cities found that 63 percent had been physically assaulted by an intimate partner in their lifetime. Jasinski et al., *The Experience of Violence in the Lives of Homeless Women: A Research Report* (Washington, D.C.: US Department of Justice, 2005), 23.

45. See Lisa A. Goodman, Katya Fels, and Catherine Glenn, "No Safe Place: Sexual Assault in the Lives of Homeless Women," *VAWnet Applied Research Forum* (Sept. 2006), 3–4; Daniel B. Herman et al., "Adverse Childhood Experiences: Are They Risk Factors for Adult Homelessness?" *American Journal of Public Health* 87, no. 2 (1997), 252; Lee, Tyler, and Wright, "The New Homelessness Revisited," 509; Zugazaga, "Stressful Life Event Experiences of Homeless Adults," 643–54.

46. Quoted in "In Memoriam: Sister Dorothy Gallant, SC," Sisters of Charity New York, accessed Dec. 16, 2016, http://www.scny.org/in-memoriam-sister-dorothy-gallant-sc.

47. "Community Ministries," All Angels' Church, accessed Dec. 16, 2016, http://www.allangelschurch.com/#/ministries/community-ministries.

48. The Dalai Lama and Arthur C. Brooks, "Behind Our Anxiety, the Fear of Being Unneeded," *New York Times,* Nov. 4, 2016, http://www.nytimes.com/2016/11/04/opinion/dalai-lama-behind-our-anxiety-the-fear-of-being-unneeded.html.

49. Brian Lehrer, "Remembering Elie Wiesel," *The Brian Lehrer Show*, WNYC, New York, July 5, 2016, http://www.wnyc.org/story/remembering-elie-wiesel-obit/.

50. Pema Chödrön, *Coming Closer to Ourselves: Making Everything the Path of Awakening*, read by the author, Sounds True, 2012, 5 compact discs.

51. Coalition for the Homeless, "State of the Homeless 2018—Fate of a Generation: How the City and State Can Tackle Homelessness by Bringing Housing Investment to Scale," 1, http://www.coalitionforthehomeless.org /wp-content/uploads/2018/03/CFHStateoftheHomeless2018.pdf. Across the United States, HUD estimates a homeless population of 553,742 for 2017. US Department of Housing and Urban Development, "The 2017 Annual Homeless Assessment Report (AHAR) to Congress," Dec. 2017: 1, https://www .hudexchange.info/resources/documents/2017-AHAR-Part-1.pdf. In general, "The struggle against homelessness in the past three decades has shown a lack of real progress in addressing the basic social and structural causes of deep poverty that are embedded in the problem of homelessness" (Wagner and Gilman, *Confronting Homelessness*, 174). The cost and availability of housing continues to be a leading cause for homelessness. See "State of the Homeless 2018," 13, and New York Housing Authority, "NYCHA 2017 Fact Sheet," Apr. 13, 2017: 3, https://www1.nyc.gov/assets/nycha/downloads/pdf/factsheet.pdf. For current initiatives to alleviate homelessness in New York, see Coalition for the Homeless, "State of the Homeless 2018," 23–24. For the potential impact on national homelessness of President Donald Trump's proposed budget for 2018, see Douglas Rice, "Trump Budget Would Increase Homelessness and Hardship in Every State, End Federal Role in Community Development," *Center on Budget and Policy Priorities*, May 23, 2017, https://www.cbpp.org/blog/trump-budget -would-increase-homelessness-and-hardship-in-every-state-end-federal-role-in.

Life Story: James Arthur Addison

1. Romans 7:15 (English Standard Version).
2. John 21:20–22 (English Standard Version).

Reflection: Rabbi Jeremy Kalmanofsky

1. Genesis 32:23–33:10, *JPS Hebrew-English Tanakh* (Philadelphia: Jewish Publication Society, 2003).

Reflection: Reverend Alistair Drummond

1. Mark 3:3–5 (New Revised Standard Version).

Crossing Boundaries and Listening for Conversion: George B. Horton

1. Psalm 130:1; Psalm 70:1 (English Standard Version).

ESE SELECT TITLES FROM EMPIRE STATE EDITIONS

Allen Jones with Mark Naison, *The Rat That Got Away: A Bronx Memoir*

Salvatore Basile, *Fifth Avenue Famous: The Extraordinary Story of Music at St. Patrick's Cathedral.* Foreword by Most Reverend Timothy M. Dolan, Archbishop of New York

Edward Rohs and Judith Estrine, *Raised by the Church: Growing up in New York City's Catholic Orphanages*

Janet Grossbach Mayer, *As Bad as They Say? Three Decades of Teaching in the Bronx*

William Seraile, *Angels of Mercy: White Women and the History of New York's Colored Orphan Asylum*

Andrew J. Sparberg, *From a Nickel to a Token: The Journey from Board of Transportation to MTA*

Anthony D. Andreassi, C.O., *Teach Me to Be Generous: The First Century of Regis High School in New York City.* Foreword by Timothy Michael Cardinal Dolan, Archbishop of New York

Daniel Campo, *The Accidental Playground: Brooklyn Waterfront Narratives of the Undesigned and Unplanned*

Gerard R. Wolfe, *The Synagogues of New York's Lower East Side: A Retrospective and Contemporary View, Second Edition.* Photographs by Jo Renée Fine and Norman Borden, Foreword by Joseph Berger

Howard Eugene Johnson with Wendy Johnson, *A Dancer in the Revolution: Stretch Johnson, Harlem Communist at the Cotton Club.* Foreword by Mark D. Naison

Joseph B. Raskin, *The Routes Not Taken: A Trip Through New York City's Unbuilt Subway System*

Phillip Deery, *Red Apple: Communism and McCarthyism in Cold War New York*

North Brother Island: The Last Unknown Place in New York City. Photographs by Christopher Payne, A History by Randall Mason, Essay by Robert Sullivan

Stephen Miller, *Walking New York: Reflections of American Writers from Walt Whitman to Teju Cole*

Tom Glynn, *Reading Publics: New York City's Public Libraries, 1754–1911*

Greg Donaldson, *The Ville: Cops and Kids in Urban America, Updated Edition.* With a new epilogue by the author, Foreword by Mark D. Naison

David Borkowski, *A Shot Story: From Juvie to Ph.D.*

R. Scott Hanson, *City of Gods: Religious Freedom, Immigration, and Pluralism in Flushing, Queens*. Foreword by Martin E. Marty

Dorothy Day and the Catholic Worker: The Miracle of Our Continuance. Edited, with an Introduction and Additional Text by Kate Hennessy, Photographs by Vivian Cherry, Text by Dorothy Day

Pamela Lewis, *Teaching While Black: A New Voice on Race and Education in New York City*

Mark Naison and Bob Gumbs, *Before the Fires: An Oral History of African American Life in the Bronx from the 1930s to the 1960s*

Robert Weldon Whalen, *Murder, Inc., and the Moral Life: Gangsters and Gangbusters in La Guardia's New York*

Joanne Witty and Henrik Krogius, *Brooklyn Bridge Park: A Dying Waterfront Transformed*

Sharon Egretta Sutton, *When Ivory Towers Were Black: A Story about Race in America's Cities and Universities*

Pamela Hanlon, *A Wordly Affair: New York, the United Nations, and the Story Behind Their Unlikely Bond*

Britt Haas, *Fighting Authoritarianism: American Youth Activism in the 1930s*

David J. Goodwin, *Left Bank of the Hudson: Jersey City and the Artists of 111 1st Street*. Foreword by DW Gibson

Nandini Bagchee, *Counter Institution: Activist Estates of the Lower East Side*

Carol Lamberg, *Neighborhood Success Stories: Creating and Sustaining Affordable Housing in New York*

Elizabeth Macaulay Lewis and Matthew M. McGowan (eds.), *Classical New York: Discovering Greece and Rome in Gotham*

Susan Opotow and Zachary Baron Shemtob (eds.), *New York After 9/11*

Andrew Feffer, *Bad Faith: Teachers, Liberalism, and the Origins of McCarthyism*

For a complete list, visit www.empirestateeditions.com.